NEW GCSE SCIENCE

Additional Science A

For Specification Modules B4–B6, C4–C6 and P4–P6

OCR

**Twenty First
Century Science**

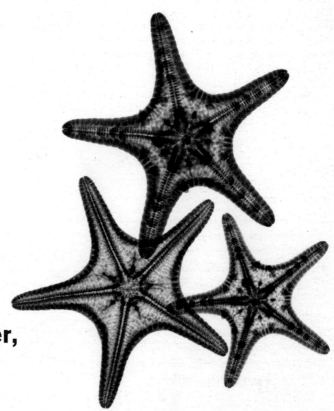

Series Editor: Ed Walsh

**Authors: Alison Alexander,
Peter Ellis, Sarah Jinks,
Dave Kelly, Gareth Price,
Shaista Shirazi**

Student Book

William Collins' dream of knowledge for all began with the publication of his first book in 1819. A self-educated mill worker, he not only enriched millions of lives, but also founded a flourishing publishing house. Today, staying true to this spirit, Collins books are packed with inspiration, innovation and practical expertise. They place you at the centre of a world of possibility and give you exactly what you need to explore it.

Collins. Freedom to teach

Published by Collins
An imprint of HarperCollinsPublishers
77–85 Fulham Palace Road
Hammersmith
London
W6 8JB

Browse the complete Collins catalogue at:
www.collinseducation.com

10 9 8 7 6 5 4 3 2 1

ISBN-13 978 0 00 741522 9

British Library Cataloguing in Publication Data
A Catalogue record for this publication is available from the British Library

Commissioned by Letitia Luff
Project managed by Jane Roth
Contributing authors: Ed Walsh; John Beeby; 'Bad Science' pages based on the work of Ben Goldacre
Typesetting, design, layout and illustrations by Ken Vail Graphic Design
Design manager: Emily Hooton
Edited by Anne Trevillion and Anna Clark
Proofread by Anna Clark and Anne Trevillion
Photos researched by Caroline Green
Production by Kerry Howie
Cover design by Julie Martin

Printed and bound by L.E.G.O. S.p.A. Italy

Acknowledgements can be found at the back of the book

Contents

How to use this book

Welcome to Collins New GCSE Additional Science for OCR 21st Century

The main content

Each two-page lesson has three sections:

The **first section** outlines a basic scientific idea

The **second section** builds on the basics and develops the concept

The **third section** extends the concept or challenges you to apply it in a new way.

The third section can also provide extra information that is only relevant to the Higher tier (indicated with 'Higher tier only').

Each section contains a set of questions that allow you to check and apply your knowledge.

Look for:

> 'Did you know?' boxes

> internet search terms (at the bottom of every page)

> 'Watch out!' hints on avoiding common errors

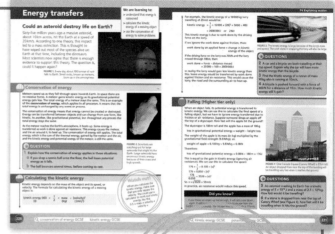

Watch out!

ALL the content of the book, except that marked 'Higher tier only', will be assessed at both Foundation and Higher tier.

Module Introduction

Each Module has a two-page introduction.

Link the science you will learn in the coming Module with your existing scientific knowledge.

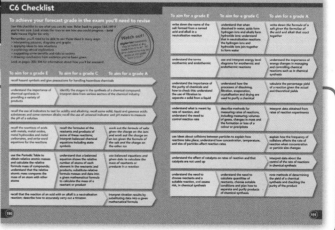

Module Checklists

At the end of each Module is a graded Checklist.

Summarise the key ideas that you have learnt so far and check your progress. If there are any topics you find tricky, you can always recap them!

Exam-style questions

Every Module contains practice exam-style questions for Foundation and Higher tier. There is a range of types of question and each is labelled with the Assessment Objective that it addresses.

Familiarise yourself with all the types of question that you might be asked.

Worked examples

Detailed worked examples with examiner comments show you how you can raise your grade. Here you will find tips on how to use accurate scientific vocabulary, avoid common exam errors and improve your Quality of Written Communication (QWC), and more.

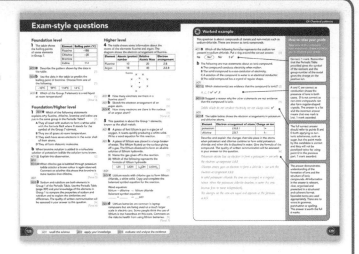

Preparing for assessment

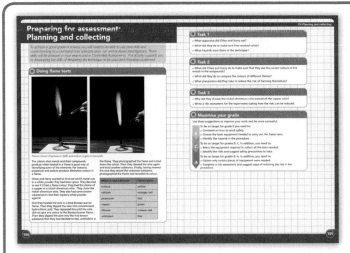

Each Module contains a Preparing for Assessment activity. These will give you practice in tackling the essential skills that you will need to succeed in your Controlled Assessment tasks, as well as in your exam.

There are two types of Preparing for Assessment activity.

> Planning and collecting: build skills in formulating a hypothesis, designing techniques and choosing equipment

> Analysing, evaluating and reviewing: build skills in analysing data, evaluating procedures and reviewing your confidence in the hypothesis.

Practical work and exam skills

A section at the end of the book guides you through your practical work, your Controlled Assessment tasks and your exam, with advice on: planning, carrying out and evaluating an experiment; using maths to analyse data; what to expect in your Controlled Assessment; the language used in exam questions; and how best to approach your written exam.

Bad Science for Schools

Based on Bad Science by Ben Goldacre, these activities give you the chance to be a 'science detective' and evaluate the scientific claims that you hear every day in the media.

Glossary

Check on the meaning of scientific vocabulary that you come across.

B4 The processes of life

What you should already know...

All living things are built up of cells

Your body is made of cells that are too small to see with the naked eye.

Cells can be specialised to do a particular job, but they all share similar structures.

Cells have a nucleus and cytoplasm held within a membrane.

 Which part of the cell controls how it functions?

Photosynthesis in green plants makes sugar

Photosynthesis needs light, carbon dioxide and water, making sugar and oxygen.

Only plants can carry out photosynthesis.

Plants often store energy captured by photosynthesis for use later, for example for producing seeds and fruits.

Many animals depend on plants to produce food that they can eat. Other animals eat these animals. All depend on photosynthesis.

 Why is a potato tuber more useful as a food than the leaves?

Respiration provides energy for living things

All living things need a supply of energy to allow them to keep essential processes running in their cells.

Humans need food and oxygen, which are taken to the cells in the body by the blood. These are used in respiration to produce energy.

 Why does your heart rate go up when you start to exercise?

Increased activity needs more energy from respiration. The heart pumps more blood to the muscles so that they have enough food and oxygen for the increase in the rate of respiration and to take away the extra carbon dioxide produced.

In B4 you will find out about...

> how photosynthesis captures energy in sunlight to produce food for the whole world

> what happens to the chemicals made by photosynthesis in green plants

> how plant roots take up water by osmosis

> how plants take up minerals from soils by active transport

> how photosynthesis is affected by light and carbon dioxide levels

> how materials move into and out of plants to maximise photosynthesis

> environmental factors that control where plants can grow

> ways to measure the success of plants in an area

> how plants store the products of photosynthesis

> respiration which makes energy in glucose available to reactions in the cells

> building up and breaking down of complex molecules in living organisms

> the structures in cells that organise the reactions that happen in them

> the chemicals produced by anaerobic respiration in microbes and how these are useful to us in brewing, baking and for making biofuels

Photosynthesis

We are learning to:
> describe the process of photosynthesis
> understand the importance of photosynthesis
> understand that plants convert the glucose they produce by photosynthesis into many different chemicals

What happens on the Dragon's Back?

This village in China is embedded in the paddy fields that supply the people with rice. The landscape is known as the Dragon's Back because the fields give the hills a serrated edge, like the spines on a dragon's back.

China is the world's largest producer of rice. In rice-growing regions, the whole of the landscape has been cut into narrow paddy fields to make sure that every inch of space is used. Even the rain that falls is collected and used to flood the fields, to increase the rice crop. So, what do the plants do with sunshine and all that water?

FIGURE 1: The Dragon's Back.

Food from fields

All our food comes ultimately from **photosynthesis**. Only green plants are able to convert energy in sunlight into energy in chemicals. Photosynthesis produces **glucose** (a simple sugar). Light energy is needed to drive photosynthesis, so it is often included in the equation.

$$\text{carbon dioxide} + \text{water} \xrightarrow{\text{light energy}} \text{glucose} + \text{oxygen}$$

Oxygen is a waste product in the reaction.

Plants can convert the glucose into a range of other chemicals, such as starch, cellulose and proteins. Starch and proteins are food molecules that provide energy to animals through food chains. For humans, the food part of rice is the grain. We can eat the grains because most of the grain is protein or starch. Humans can digest protein and starch. The leaves are mainly cellulose, which we cannot digest.

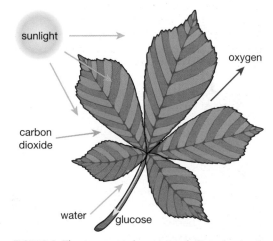

FIGURE 2: The inputs and outputs of photosynthesis.

QUESTION

1 **a** List the chemicals used for photosynthesis.

b What else is needed for photosynthesis?

c List the chemicals produced by photosynthesis.

Did you know?

Rice is so important to Chinese culture that their word for rice and food is the same: 'fan'. Instead of asking, 'How are you?', a Chinese speaker will often ask, 'Have you eaten rice today?'.

The reactions of photosynthesis

Photosynthesis is actually a series of chemical reactions. It is usually summarised as a single simple equation.

A chemical in the plant called **chlorophyll** absorbs the light energy needed for photosynthesis. Chlorophyll is green, and this is what gives plants their green colour. The energy from the light is used to drive several reactions, which eventually build molecules of glucose. The plant can then use the glucose to make other chemicals – see Figure 3.

Chlorophyll is only present in the parts of the plant that are in the light. It is found in small structures in the cells called **chloroplasts**.

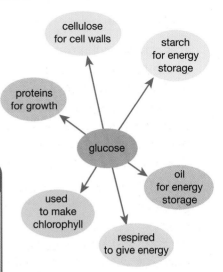

FIGURE 3: Possible fates of glucose made by photosynthesis.

QUESTIONS

2 a What is the name of the chemical that absorbs light energy for photosynthesis?

b Where in the plant is this chemical found?

3 A carbon atom that enters a rice plant in carbon dioxide through the leaf might end up in a starch molecule in the bowl of fried rice in a farmer's hut. Describe the route it takes to get there.

Other photosynthesisers

Not all plants that carry out photosynthesis are easy to see. The oceans are full of microscopic algae called phytoplankton. These single-celled plants are too small to see individually, but large populations of them can sometimes be seen from Earth orbit as a green smudge in the water. They produce about 60% of the oxygen in our atmosphere and provide food for krill, a small prawn-like animal, which in turn is food for baleen whales.

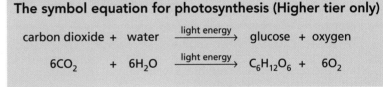

The symbol equation for photosynthesis (Higher tier only)

$$\text{carbon dioxide} + \text{water} \xrightarrow{\text{light energy}} \text{glucose} + \text{oxygen}$$

$$6CO_2 + 6H_2O \xrightarrow{\text{light energy}} C_6H_{12}O_6 + 6O_2$$

QUESTIONS

4 a The Earth's atmosphere contains 10^{15} tonnes of oxygen. How many tonnes of this was produced by phytoplankton?

b An average human requires 0.26 tonnes of oxygen per year. There are roughly seven billion people alive today on the planet. If all the phytoplankton died out tomorrow, how many years' supply of oxygen is left in the atmosphere?

5 How many molecules of carbon dioxide are needed to make one molecule of glucose?

FIGURE 4: The largest creature on the planet, the baleen whale, depends on photosynthesis by some of the smallest organisms – the phytoplankton.

oxygen phytoplankton

11

Diffusion

Jungle revenge?

This is one of the temples in the Angkor Wat complex in Cambodia. Over 1000 years old, it was abandoned just over 500 years ago. After that the jungle took over, splitting rocks and growing through stone courtyards. How do the plants have the strength to do this?

FIGURE 1: Safe for tourists to walk around now, but only a few years ago getting to these temples was impossible. The walls were falling down and the pathways were blocked by stones and huge jungle plants.

Water and living things

Water is essential in all living things for:

> keeping chemicals in solution

> taking part in important reactions

> keeping cells the correct shape

> acting as a heat store.

The human body is more than 50% water. It takes a lot of energy to warm water up and, once heated, water takes a long time to cool down. This helps to prevent the body from suffering from sudden changes in temperature. This is important because the chemical reactions in our cells go much faster when temperatures rise and slow down too much when they get low.

What happens when you dry up? Have a look at the table.

Did you know?

A Bactrian camel can drink 120 litres of water in under five minutes. That is like a human being drinking over 400 mugs of coffee in the same time.

Percentage of normal water level (%)	How do you feel?
100	Healthy and happy!
99	Thirsty
98	Very thirsty
97	Tired, moody and you may be sick
95	Pale and ill; very irritable and aggressive
90	You don't have enough water to sweat so your body temperature starts to rise
85	Dangerously ill – you may start seeing things; doctors are worried
80	You're dead

QUESTIONS

1 List three reasons why the body needs water.

2 What percentage of their body's water can someone lose but still survive?

3 An average human adult male weighs 70 kg and is roughly 57% water. What is the mass of water in his body?

Q diffusion GCSE

Diffusion

Toast burning in the kitchen can soon be smelled on the other side of the house. This is because the molecules of smoke in the air move by **diffusion** around the whole house.

Diffusion happens because molecules are constantly and randomly bouncing around. This movement makes them spread out, so eventually they are evenly spread over the space available. This means that overall, molecules spread from an area where their concentration is higher to where their concentration is lower.

The rate at which molecules spread depends on:

> the temperature (particles bounce around more quickly as it gets hotter)

> any walls or barriers to their movement

> the difference in concentration in the two areas (the bigger the difference in concentration, the faster they spread).

Diffusion does not need any energy input – it happens because of the movement of molecules. Water diffuses between cells in living organisms without any need for the organism to do anything.

The gases carbon dioxide and oxygen move in and out of the leaves of plants by diffusion.

QUESTIONS

4 Why doesn't water diffuse through the walls of a glass?

5 Why don't plants leaves fill up with carbon dioxide if it keeps diffusing in during the day?

Osmosis

Osmosis is a special kind of water movement. Water moves by diffusion from areas of high concentration of water to areas of low concentration of water.

A solution with a high concentration of water is called a 'dilute solution', and one with less water is called a 'concentrated solution'. So osmosis is the overall movement of water from a dilute to a more concentrated solution by diffusion.

Cells contain chemicals as well as water, so the solution inside is not as dilute as pure water. Each cell is surrounded by a membrane that lets small molecules through, but not large ones. This is called a **partially permeable membrane**. Water molecules are very small and can pass into and out of cells by osmosis.

If a cell is placed in pure water, the water molecules move from outside (the more dilute solution) to inside (the more concentrated solution). This makes the cell swell with the extra water and the membrane gets stretched like the skin of a balloon. If red blood cells are placed in pure water, they take in so much water they burst.

If a cell is placed in a solution that is very concentrated, water leaves the cell by osmosis and the cell wrinkles up – a bit like a dried prune.

Water moves into plant root cells by osmosis. In a plant the forces produced by water moving into a cell can be very large. Look again at the picture of the temple (Figure 1). Rocks there have been split apart as roots swell with water to crack the whole stone.

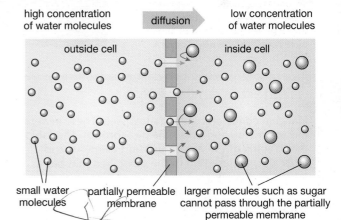

high concentration of water molecules   diffusion   low concentration of water molecules

outside cell   inside cell

small water molecules   partially permeable membrane   larger molecules such as sugar cannot pass through the partially permeable membrane

FIGURE 2: Water molecules are small enough to pass through pores in the partially permeable membrane.

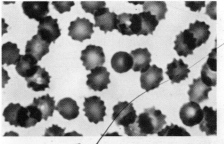

FIGURE 3: These cells have lost water by osmosis. They are shrivelled like prunes.

QUESTION

6 Why is the cell membrane called 'partially permeable'?

Minerals in the soil

We are learning to:

> understand the importance of minerals to plants

> (Higher) understand how active transport moves substances through cells

Metal miracle or mining madness?

Metals are strong, easy to form into useful shapes and last a long time. We live in a world dominated by metals – but digging them out of the ground can produce toxic wastelands. How can we repair the damage done by our technology?

FIGURE 1: Mining waste often contains toxic metals. In some areas of the United States whole towns have had to move because metals in mining waste, such as lead and zinc, have poisoned the environment.

Minerals and metals

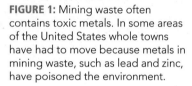

Plants need mineral salts to grow well. These minerals include metals and other chemical groups. The table shows some of the most important elements and what they are used for in the plant. Soil that has a low level of minerals is not fertile.

Element	What is it used for?
potassium	Building proteins, cell growth, fruit development and resistance to diseases.
nitrogen	Increases rapid growth, essential for photosynthesis and all proteins.
phosphorus	Essential part of photosynthesis, encourages rapid growth, especially in the root.
magnesium	Essential part of **chlorophyll** used in photosynthesis (chlorophyll is the green chemical in plants that absorbs light energy). Magnesium is also an essential part of many other chemicals in cells.

Chemicals and plants.

FIGURE 2: It may not look or smell very nice, but this horse manure contains valuable minerals for the plants on this allotment.

🔍 mineral nutrition plants GCSE

The elements listed in the table on page 14 are all taken up as parts of other chemicals. Nitrogen is taken up as nitrates. Plants use energy from respiration to react nitrates with the sugar glucose to make **amino acids**. These can then be built up into large protein molecules. This building up of larger molecules is called **synthesis**.

The elements listed in the table on page 14

QUESTIONS

1 Which of the elements listed in the table are metals?

2 Manure is a rich source of nitrogen. What would you expect to see in the plants if you treated a field with manure prior to planting?

Hyperaccumulators

Minerals in the soil are useful to plants. Some of these mineral nutrients contain metals. All plants will take these up from the ground to grow. Some plants can also take up toxic metals and lock them away in their cells to stop them causing damage. Plants growing on spoil heaps from lead mines can do this. Some plants end up with higher levels of a toxic metal in their cells than exists in the soil.

Some plants are so good at taking up metals that they are called 'hyperaccumulators'. They accumulate very high levels of metal. We are now planting these species in areas where other plants will not grow. The metal-tolerant plants take up the metals from the soil. The plants can then be harvested and the metal disposed of safely. Over years the level of dangerous metals in the soil goes down and it becomes safe for other species.

QUESTIONS

3 Plant waste can be made into compost, which is spread on the soil to improve it. Why are the plants harvested from mining spoil heaps not composted?

4 Describe how a researcher could find plants that were tolerant of lead in the soil and how they could test how much lead the plants could tolerate.

Active transport (Higher tier only)

Water goes into plant roots by osmosis because there is usually more water in the soil than in the plant. Water moves from a dilute to a more concentrated solution. This needs no energy input from the plant.

Minerals such as nitrates are usually more concentrated in plant cells than in the soil. To take these up, the plant has to use energy. Proteins in the cell membranes of root cells pump chemicals from the outside to the inside of the cell. This is called **active transport**. Active transport is movement of chemicals into or out of a cell, using energy from respiration. The cell controls the direction in which the chemicals move, not the difference in concentration.

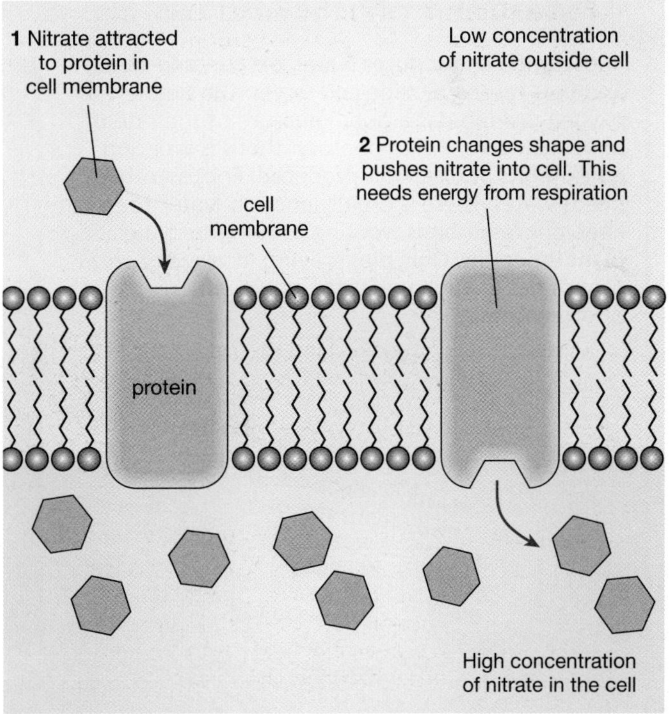

1 Nitrate attracted to protein in cell membrane

Low concentration of nitrate outside cell

2 Protein changes shape and pushes nitrate into cell. This needs energy from respiration

cell membrane

protein

High concentration of nitrate in the cell

FIGURE 3: Active transport.

QUESTION

5 Osmotic uptake of water is hardly affected by temperature. However, active uptake of mineral salts is significantly reduced at low temperatures. Suggest why this may happen.

active transport GCSE

Speeding up photosynthesis

How many plants would you need to get to Mars?

Humans take in food and oxygen, and give out carbon dioxide and other wastes. Green plants take in carbon dioxide and water, and make food and oxygen. Could this be the perfect system for a trip to Mars? It will take up to five years to get there and back. If astronauts could travel with their own micro-farm, maybe they would have enough food and oxygen to keep them alive.

FIGURE 1: A bioreactor similar to this experimental one could produce algae to make food and oxygen in space.

Measuring photosynthesis

Photosynthesis produces water, oxygen and sugar, and uses carbon dioxide and water. The amount of oxygen produced is a good measure of the rate of photosynthesis. When photosynthesis is working quickly, lots of oxygen is produced. Photosynthesis needs water. There is usually enough water to keep photosynthesis working at full rate if the plant is healthy. Only plants living in very dry areas cannot get enough water for maximum photosynthesis.

Watch out!

It is almost impossible to measure the rate of photosynthesis directly. Scientists measure the changes in other chemicals and use these to work out how the rate of photosynthesis is changing.

FIGURE 2: Many commercial growers increase the levels of carbon dioxide in their greenhouses to help the plants grow more quickly.

Q rate of photosynthesis GCSE

Photosynthesis also needs carbon dioxide. Carbon dioxide is rare. Only about 0.4% of the air is carbon dioxide. This is not usually enough to keep photosynthesis at full speed. The table shows the yield from greenhouse plants at different levels of carbon dioxide.

Greenhouse conditions	Mass of 10 lettuce heads (kg)	Mass of saleable tomatoes (kg)
no carbon dioxide added	0.9	4.4
carbon dioxide added	1.1	6.4

QUESTIONS

1 Look at the data in the table.

  a What is the percentage increase in mass for each of the crops when carbon dioxide is added?

  b Which crop shows the greater percentage increase?

2 Only saleable crops were measured. How might this have affected the results?

Light and carbon dioxide

An increase in carbon dioxide levels increases the rate of photosynthesis – but only up to a point. The level part of the graph shows that the lack of something else is stopping the reaction going faster. This is called the **limiting factor** because it is limiting the rate.

With extra light this limiting factor does not have an effect until much higher levels of carbon dioxide. But eventually, even with extra light, the rate of reaction stops increasing and the graph levels off.

FIGURE 3: How the rate of photosynthesis depends on carbon dioxide concentration. The green trace shows what happens at normal light levels. The blue trace shows what happens at high light levels.

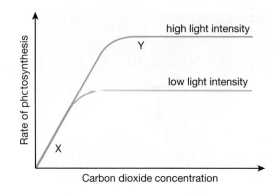

Did you know?

Cannabis growers use artificial lights to speed up growth so that they can harvest the drug more quickly. Police look for houses with surprisingly high electricity bills because they might be using it to power lights for an illegal cannabis crop.

QUESTIONS

3 Explain the term 'limiting factor'.

4 In Figure 3, what is acting as the limiting factor at: a X? b Y?

Photosynthesis and temperature

The graph in Figure 4 shows how the rate of oxygen production changes as temperature rises. It shows results for two light levels. The rate of oxygen production is taken as a measure of photosynthesis.

QUESTIONS

5 a Describe what happens to the rate of photosynthesis at high light intensities.

  b Suggest a reason why the rate of photosynthesis seems to drop at temperatures above about 35 °C.

6 Oxygen is also involved in respiration. How will this affect the measured rate of photosynthesis?

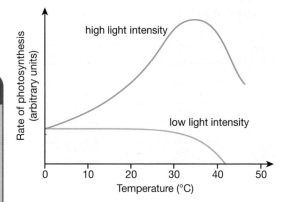

FIGURE 4: How the rate of photosynthesis at two light levels depends on temperature.

Preparing for assessment: Analysing, evaluating and reviewing

To achieve a good grade in science you will need to be able to use your skills and understanding to understand how scientists plan, run and evaluate investigations. These skills will be assessed in your exams and in Controlled Assessments. This activity supports you in developing the skills of analysing data and evaluating an investigation.

✳ Cabomba! – investigating photosynthesis in water plants

People who keep fish often include a few strands of *Cabomba* in their fishtanks. The weed gives out oxygen in the light. A GCSE class was looking at samples of *Cabomba* bought from different aquarium suppliers in the local area to see which was the most active weed. The experimenter wanted to see if the different sources of weed produced different levels of oxygenation in the aquarium.

Each weed sample was placed in a beaker of hydrogen-carbonate solution (1% weight per volume) and arranged so that the bubbles coming off could be seen easily. A student watched for 20 minutes counting the bubbles that were released every minute. The table below shows the data from three samples.

Bubbles of gas given off in one minute intervals

Time from start (mins)	FishCo	FishWeed	Jones Aquatic Suppliers
0	5	2	1
1	7	1	2
2	7	2	0
3	8	4	0
4	7	4	0
5	8	6	0
6	9	6	0
7	9	7	0
8	6	8	0
9	8	8	0
10	8	9	0
11	8	6	0
12	7	8	0
13	9	6	0
14	7	8	0
15	6	5	0
16	5	7	0
17	3	11	0
18	2	3	0
19	2	2	0
20	3	2	0

Task 1

> Summarise the data in a way that makes the answer of the original question possible.

> Explain why you chose to summarise the data in this way.

> List the factors that the students would need to keep the same so that the investigation was a fair test.

 # Task 2

> Identify any data points that are outliers. Explain how you have chosen these.

> How good do you think this experiment is at producing accurate data?

 # Task 3

> Has the experiment provided data that is relevant and useful for answering the original question?

> Suggest how the experiment could be modified to improve the quality of the data gathered.

 # Task 4

> Look at any significant issues revealed by the data, accounting for any surprise results.

> What does this say about the repeatability of the data?

> Comment on the usefulness of the readings to answer your original question.

 # Maximise your grade

Use these suggestions to improve your work and be more successful.

E

To be on target for grade E you need to:

> Comment on how the data was collected and its accuracy or repeatability.

> Comment on the limitations to accuracy or range of data.

> Identify individual results which are outliers, or justify a claim that there are no outliers.

> Identify the factors that need to be controlled to produce results that can be used for a fair comparison.

C

To be on target for grades D, C, in addition, you need to:

> Suggest improvements to the apparatus or techniques, or alternative ways to collect data.

> Use the general pattern of the results as a basis for assessing accuracy and repeatability.

A

To be on target for grades B, A, in addition, you need to:

> Describe and justify improvements to the apparatus or techniques, or alternative ways to collect the data.

> Consider critically the repeatability of the evidence, accounting for any outliers.

Measuring plant distribution

What makes the rhododendron a botanical bully?

Why are conservation workers so keen to cut down rhododendrons, burn them and generally hurt them any way they can? What's so bad about these plants?

The trouble with rhododendrons is that they tend to crowd out all other species, and that's bad for wildlife.

FIGURE 1: Conservationists burn off rhododendron plants to stop them taking over an area of countryside.

Measuring plant distribution

It is easy to tell the difference between a lush rainforest and a dry desert. How can we tell if an area in this country has a good amount of healthy plants? Ecologists need to:

> identify the plants they find

> measure how common the plants are in an area.

An **identification key** is a way to find the scientific name for an organism by answering yes/no questions. By examining a specimen carefully, it is possible to identify it and so find its correct scientific name. This name will be recognised by scientists all over the world – even if they do not speak the same language. So, a Malaysian researcher in the rainforests of Borneo may not recognise the name 'stinging nettle', but knows what is meant by *Urtica dioica*.

QUESTIONS

1 What two factors does an ecologist need to record when describing plants present in an area?

2 State one advantage of using common names and one advantage of using scientific names for a plant species.

Q1. Is the fruit roughly spherical? Yes – go to Q2 Q2.
No – go to Q3 Q3.

FIGURE 2: Part of an identification key.

Measuring abundance

Abundance is a measure of how common a species is in an area. An abundant species is common; one that is less abundant will be rare.

The easiest way to measure abundance is to count the plants. It is not possible to count all of the plants in an area, so you need to take a sample. A **quadrat** is a frame, usually square, of wood or metal, that ecologists put on the ground. They can then count the number of plants inside the frame. Once they have counted the plants in a number of quadrats, they can produce an average figure.

FIGURE 3: In this area bluebells are abundant but primroses are very rare.

Q plant distribution GCSE

An ecologist studying bluebells noticed that they tended to grow better nearer the edge of the woodland. To gather data to test this idea, a sequence of quadrats was taken in a straight line from the centre of the woods out into the field beside it. A line of quadrats is called a **transect**. Sometimes transects are so long that researchers pick one sample every five metres rather than having the quadrats touching each other in a line. The position of each quadrat in the transect is recorded carefully, so the researcher knows what was present in each quadrat sample and where it was taken.

FIGURE 1: Sampling life on a rocky beach. By using a quadrat these students can make sure that a representative area is sampled. They can then use the data to draw charts showing what grows where.

> ### ⦿ QUESTIONS
>
> **3 a** What is the scientific meaning of the word 'abundance'?
>
> **b** A quadrat usually covers an area of 0.25 m². If a field measured 12 m by 5 m and a team of ecologists took 80 quadrat samples, what percentage of the total field did they sample?
>
> **4** Give two advantages of using a transect to study plant distribution in an area.

Back to the rhododendrons

Nothing seems to grow under a rhododendron bush. Why is this? There could be two reasons:

1 The rhododendrons might block out the light.

2 The rhododendrons might use up all the minerals in the soil.

How could you investigate these possibilities? Here, quadrats are useful because they organise the data collection and make it easy to record where in the area each sample was collected. Results near a bush and under a bush can be compared. The table shows some data collected in a valley in Snowdonia, Wales.

> ### ⦿ QUESTIONS
>
> **5** Give one piece of evidence from the table that shows that rhododendrons reduce biodiversity in an area.
>
> **6 a** Suggest two factors that might affect how well plants grow in the shade of a rhododendron bush.
>
> **b** Describe a practical investigation you could do to see which of these factors was the most important.

Quadrat results near and under a rhododendron bush in Snowdonia.

Factor	Quadrat				
	1	2	3	4	5
distance from centre of bush (m)	0	1	2	3	5
light level (measured using a light meter)	12	27	76	88	100
moisture content	67	73	86	93	100
nitrogen content	52	54	73	89	100
species A (rhododendron)	100	63	0	0	0
species B (grass)	0	24	56	64	100
species C (moss)	0	56	66	93	100
species D (fern)	5	67	43	45	100

All factors except distance are expressed as a percentage of their maximum value.

Respiration

Do I look big in this?

Obesity has been linked to 80% of type 2 diabetes, three-quarters of all heart problems and nearly half of colon and breast cancers. The proportion of UK citizens who are obese has doubled since 1985. What has caused this?

FIGURE 1: Oliver Hardy was the lovable fat clown, but his obesity almost certainly led to a series of heart attacks and the stroke that killed him in 1957.

We all need energy from food

Moving your arm to open this book requires a sequence of reactions in your eyes to see it, your brain to interpret what you see, nerve cells to carry impulses to your muscles and another set of reactions to contract the muscle fibres. All of these reactions need energy.

Respiration is the chemical reaction used by all living organisms to produce the energy they need to make other reactions in their cells happen.

These reactions may lead to:

> movement (in muscles)

> building (synthesising) complex chemicals for growth and repair.

Respiration using oxygen is called **aerobic respiration**. This type of respiration takes place in both animal and plant cells, and in some microorganisms.

glucose + oxygen → carbon dioxide + water (+ energy released)

Glucose is a type of simple sugar. The food we take in is converted to glucose to enable respiration to occur. Any energy left over is used to build fat, which stores energy for when we cannot get enough food.

FIGURE 2: The average British teenager gets through the equivalent of 36 bags of sugar every year. Sugar supplies about 16% of their energy intake!

 QUESTIONS

1 Why does the body need energy even while you are asleep?

2 Write down the equation for photosynthesis (you can find this on page 10). What do you notice about this and the equation for respiration?

Building up

Growth and repair of an organism need protein. Plants can make amino acids from nitrate ions absorbed through the roots (sees pages 14–15) and reacted with glucose produced by photosynthesis. Microorganisms can also synthesise amino acids in a similar way.

nitrates + glucose → amino acids → proteins

No animals can do this, so they need to get their protein from other living things. Digestion breaks down the protein in food to amino acids, and the body then joins these together to make the type of protein needed for muscle building or tissue repair. Respiration provides the energy needed to drive these reactions.

Q energy and weight loss

Plant polymers

When photosynthesis is fast, more sugar is produced than is needed. The plant uses energy from respiration to synthesise **polymers** like starch from the excess glucose, which then act as a store of energy. These storage molecules depend on the exact species, but all of our food crops were chosen because they store energy as chemicals that we can digest.

Another important polymer made by joining glucose molecules together is cellulose. This is a tough chemical that gives plant cell walls their strength. Humans cannot digest cellulose because we do not have the enzymes needed to break the bonds between the glucose units.

Plant species	Main storage chemicals	Main storage site
sugar cane	sugar	in stem
potato	starch	underground tubers
soya beans	protein	seeds
cocoa	fat	seeds

Energy storage chemicals in plants.

Plants break down their energy stores when they need to. A potato tuber is a food store that gives up its energy when it starts to 'chit'. Chitting is when small shoots start to grow to become new potato plants.

FIGURE 3: Gardeners often chit their seed potatoes before they plant them in the spring. This increases the chances of getting a good crop.

QUESTIONS

3 a Why does a potato tuber need a store of energy?

b What is the starch in the tuber converted into before it is used for respiration?

4 Why is cocoa, the source of chocolate, a bad plant for dieters?

Watch out!

Don't forget that plants carry out respiration as well as photosynthesis. It is just that during daylight photosynthesis goes much faster, so the plant does not give out carbon dioxide.

The respiration reaction

Respiration is a series of chemical reactions that release a small amount of energy with each step. The aerobic respiration equation describes the overall change from the series of reactions.

> **Symbol equation for aerobic respiration (Higher tier only)**
>
> glucose + oxygen → carbon dioxide + water (+ energy released)
>
> $C_6H_{12}O_6 + 6O_2 \rightarrow 6CO_2 + 6H_2O$ (+ energy released)

Respiration provides the energy to move chemicals into and out of cells by active transport (see page 15). The nitrates a plant needs to make amino acids are taken up from the soil by active transport.

QUESTION

5 A drug company has produced a pill that they claim increases the rate of respiration reactions in our cells. They claim it will be useful for athletes and other people who need a lot of energy. Describe an experiment you could do to test the claim that it increases the rate of respiration.

FIGURE 4: This photograph shows burning sugar cane. Carbon dioxide and water vapour are produced, but the overall effect of the reaction is very different from respiration. Why?

Anaerobic respiration

Could you be an Ironman?

Ironman races are for the seriously fit. Participants have to swim 2.4 miles, cycle 122 miles and then run 26.2 miles. To beat the 2010 world champion, you would need to do that in under 8 hours 10 minutes! How do these 'ultra athletes' train and what is happening in their bodies as they push themselves to the limit and beyond?

FIGURE 1

 ## Energy crisis

The athletes in endurance races make huge demands on the energy reserves of their bodies. They will use up over 40 kJ in 8 hours. That is about four times the amount an average British teenager uses in a day.

This energy comes from respiration. Respiration requires oxygen, so the athletes will be breathing deeply and pumping blood around their bodies very rapidly to supply the hard-working muscles. Sometimes this is not quite enough.

glucose + oxygen → carbon dioxide + water (+ energy released)
16 kJ energy per gram of glucose

If the athlete needs more energy but cannot get any more oxygen to the muscles, the body has a back-up plan – respiration that does not need oxygen. The reaction is slightly different:

glucose → lactic acid (+ energy released)
2 kJ per gram of glucose

The back-up creates two problems:

> it does not give out as much energy

> it produces lactic acid, which is poisonous.

Aerobic respiration (pages 22–23) is always the body's first choice. Respiration that does not need oxygen is called **anaerobic respiration**.

QUESTIONS

1 Give two differences between aerobic and anaerobic respiration.

2 Why is anaerobic respiration only used by the body in extreme cases?

Q aerobic respiration athletes

What happens to the lactic acid?

Lactic acid is poisonous. Your muscles can cope with a small amount of it, but if the level rises too high they start hurting and eventually stop working. After the race is over, the athlete's body clears away the lactic acid in this reaction:

lactic acid + oxygen → water + carbon dioxide

The amount of oxygen needed to clear out all the lactic acid is called the **oxygen debt**. Runners breathe very deeply even after the race has finished to get in extra oxygen to clear the lactic acid. A good measure of fitness is how quickly you recover from exercise – the faster you recover, the fitter you are.

FIGURE 2: Athletes recovering after the hill race at the highland games in Pitlochry.

QUESTIONS

3 What is an oxygen debt? How is it paid back?

4 A runner in the London marathon used to take a few puffs of oxygen from a gas cylinder as well as a drink of water when he stopped to rest around the course. Is this fair? Give reasons for your answer.

Other anaerobic reactions

Some bacteria live in areas with low oxygen levels and have to use anaerobic respiration to get energy. Bacteria living in rivers or ponds polluted by sewage need to do this. Lactic acid is only one of the waste products they produce – you will notice some of the others with your nose!

Rice plants in paddy fields have their roots submerged in water. There is very little oxygen available, so the roots carry out anaerobic respiration.

Tetanus is a disease caused by an anaerobic bacterium that is common in soils and manure. In the UK the disease is rare, but it kills nearly 400 000 people every year across the world. Tetanus bacteria are inhibited by oxygen and can only get into the body through a puncture wound – perhaps from stepping on a dirty nail. The wound is a low-oxygen environment so the bacteria reproduce and release a poison that causes muscles to twitch, and finally to tense up completely.

QUESTIONS

5 Why is anaerobic respiration unsuitable as the only energy source for an active animal?

6 About 40% of people who get tetanus die. How many people in the world catch tetanus every year?

FIGURE 3: The roots of the rice plants are covered in water, which provides anaerobic conditions

FIGURE 4: This rubbish is ugly and can spread tetanus if a child playing barefoot on the beach steps on a rusty nail or torn metal can.

Q anaerobic respiration

Organising the cell

Doctor, am I normal?

Every day technicians in hospitals look through microscopes at cells taken from a patient. What these technicians see can save lives. Sometimes one of the first signs of illness is a change in the structure of a cell. But what does a 'normal' cell look like?

FIGURE 1

Cells and microscopes

Through an early light microscope, an animal cell looked a bit like a blob of grainy jelly. As microscopes became more powerful and scientists learned how to stain things in the cells, they were able to notice some structures in the jelly. These structures help to organise the reactions in the cell in the same way that a home is organised with different rooms for different jobs.

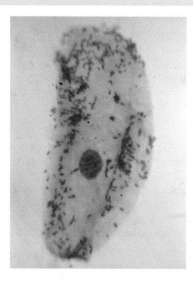

FIGURE 2: A cell seen through a light microscope.

QUESTIONS

1 List the features of the cell you can see in the photograph.

2 Give one advantage of staining a cell with a dye that only colours DNA.

Did you know?

At roughly 0.1 mm in diameter, the human egg cell is just about big enough to see without a microscope. It is the largest cell in the human body.

Cell similarities and differences

Similarities

The diagrams on the next page show the structures for four typical cell types: animal, plant, bacterium and yeast. They all have **cytoplasm** and a **cell membrane**.

Cytoplasm is where most of the chemical reactions take place. This is what looked like the grainy jelly to early scientists. The outside of the cytoplasm is covered by the cell membrane, but this is far too thin to see using light microscopes. The cell membrane controls what enters and leaves the cell. Gases and water can pass in and out of the cell freely but the membrane is a barrier to other chemicals.

All the cells shown use DNA to store their genetic code. The genetic code carries information that the cells use to make enzymes and other proteins. In plant and animal cells, the genetic code is normally held in the **nucleus**. The nucleus is an area of the cytoplasm separated off by membrane.

Plant and animal cells have **mitochondria** embedded in the cytoplasm. Respiration takes place in the mitochondria. This process converts the energy in glucose into a form the cell can use. Anaerobic respiration uses enzymes present in the cytoplasm.

🔍 cell nucleus   cell ultrastructure   cell sizes

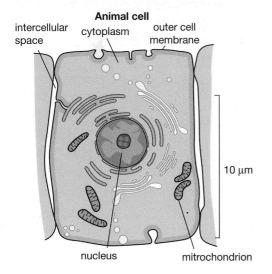

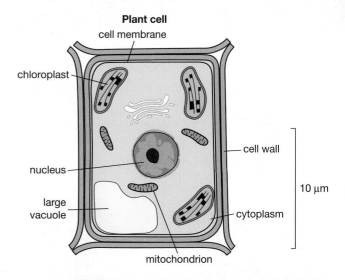

FIGURE 3: The structures of typical animal and plant cells.

Differences

Plant cells usually have a cell wall made of **cellulose** that is big enough to see with a light microscope. It lets water and other chemicals pass through easily. Some yeasts and bacteria also have cell walls, but these are not usually made of cellulose. Animal cells do not have a cell wall.

Cells of green plants have **chloroplasts** embedded in the cytoplasm. These contain **chlorophyll** and carry out photosynthesis.

QUESTIONS

3 List two structures found in cells from green plants but not found in animal cells.

4 What is the function of:

a the nucleus?

b mitochondria?

c chloroplasts?

Bacterial and yeast cells

A yeast cell, like an animal and a plant cell, has its DNA in a nucleus, and it has enzymes for respiration in mitochondria. A bacterial cell has no nucleus or mitochondria. The DNA for the genes and the enzymes for respiration float around free in the cytoplasm. This is less efficient than in animal and plant cells, where the important chemicals are held inside membrane-bound structures.

QUESTIONS

5 How many times longer is a typical plant cell compared with a typical bacterium?

6 How does a bacterial cell store its genetic code if it does not have a nucleus?

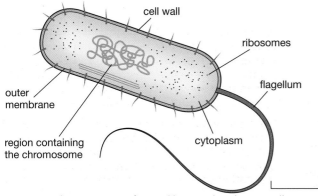

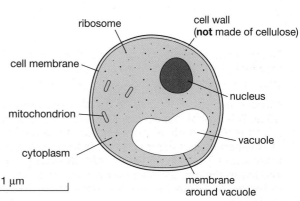

FIGURE 4: The structures of typical bacterial and yeast cells.

Enzyme reactions

How do enzymes help the pack get clean?

It's never easy cleaning the blood and mud off rugby shirts and shorts! In the past these cotton clothes would have been boiled to remove the stains, but nowadays they can be washed in temperatures as low as 30 °C and the amount of soap needed has reduced! So what's happened?

FIGURE 1

 Enzymes and washing

Enzymes are proteins, found in living things, that speed up reactions. Enzymes in biological washing powder speed up the breakdown of fat and protein. Many stains are protein (e.g. blood, egg) or dirt held on to the fabric by fat (grease). The enzymes break down the blood or dissolve the fat and let the mud drift away in the water. Enzymes work much better than soap for this – and at lower temperatures.

 QUESTIONS

1 How does an enzyme affect the speed of a reaction?

2 The enzyme in washing powder that dissolves fat cannot dissolve mud. How does it help to clean muddy stains from rugby players' socks?

FIGURE 2: Grains of biological washing powder contain enzymes.

🔍 active site enzymes   lock and key hypothesis

How do enzymes work?

Enzymes are made in cells from a long chain of amino acids joined together. The correct order for the amino acids is coded by the genes. The chain is twisted around on itself to give a complicated three-dimensional shape. This shape is very important for how the enzyme works.

The lock and key model explains how an enzyme speeds up a reaction. The chemicals the enzymes work on are called the **substrates** and the chemicals they produce are called the **products**. A part of the enzyme, called the **active site**, is a special shape that allows the substrate to fit neatly into it – like a key in a lock. When the substrate is locked in, the enzyme brings about a change and the substrate is broken into two parts. These product molecules are then released from the enzyme because they do not fit. The enzyme can then be used again to break down more substrate molecules.

Some enzymes join chemicals together. Again, the molecules fit into active sites on the enzyme, but now the enzyme shape brings the important parts of the substrate molecules close together so that they can react. Once they react they do not fit and are released. Sometimes the cell uses energy from respiration to help this reaction work.

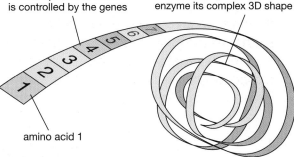

amino acid chain – the sequence of acids is controlled by the genes

tightly coiled chain of amino acids gives the enzyme its complex 3D shape

amino acid 1

FIGURE 3: The structure of proteins depends on the sequence of amino acids in the chain.

QUESTION

3 Use the lock and key model to explain:

a why each enzyme can only work with one reaction

b how the products are released from the active site.

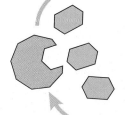

2 Substrate molecule fits in active site in enzyme.

3 Reaction occurs and products made; the enzyme speeds up this reaction.

1 Substrate molecules move towards active site in enzyme.

4 Product molecules do not fit in the active site so are released. The enzyme can then be used again with new substrate molecules.

FIGURE 4: The lock and key model shows how enzymes speed up reactions.

Enzyme pathways

Sugar burns at over 1000 °C to give out light and heat. Respiration in a cell is the same reaction but at a much lower temperature and with no energy wasted as light. Respiration is a series of mini-reactions linked together in an **enzyme pathway**. Some of the energy in the glucose is taken out with each small reaction. Since an enzyme only works in one particular reaction, each step needs its own enzyme. This stops the reaction running out of control and damaging the cell.

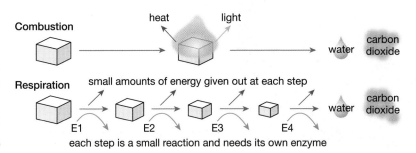

Combustion

heat   light

water   carbon dioxide

Respiration   small amounts of energy given out at each step

E1   E2   E3   E4

water   carbon dioxide

each step is a small reaction and needs its own enzyme

QUESTIONS

4 Give two similarities and two differences between combustion and respiration.

5 There are over 20 small reactions in aerobic respiration. What does this tell you about the number of enzymes in the pathway?

FIGURE 5: An enzyme pathway splits a large reaction into a series of smaller steps.

Enzymes

We are learning to:

> understand the factors that affect the rate of enzyme reactions

> explain how temperature affects the rate of enzyme reactions

> explain how pH affects the rate of enzyme reactions

Why do apples go brown?

A bump on an apple will produce a bruise, which converts a sweet, crisp apple into an inedible brown mush. One apple may be nothing to worry about, but every year almost a quarter of the entire world's harvest is lost to spoilage reactions like this. What causes it and how can we prevent it?

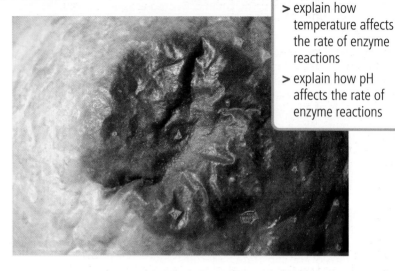

FIGURE 1

Enzyme breakdown

Apples contain enzymes that react with oxygen in the air to turn the flesh into that mushy brown goo. The speed at which this enzyme works is affected by both temperature and pH. An increase in temperature tends to increase the rate of decay, as shown in the graph. When the enzyme is working as quickly as possible, the enzyme is at its **optimum** temperature. When the temperature goes above a certain level the enzyme is damaged and stops working altogether.

FIGURE 2: Rate of decay of apple against temperature.

QUESTIONS

1 What does the word 'optimum' mean?

2 What is the optimum temperature for the enzymes that turn apples brown?

Did you know?

Your packet of crisps is filled not with air, but with nitrogen. This prolongs the shelf life of the crisps because there is no oxygen to react with chemicals in the crisps.

Lemon juice to the rescue

A good fruit salad stays bright and colourful even after it has been exposed to the air. How does this happen? A squeeze of lemon juice, or even lemonade, does the trick. The acid in the lemon juice slows down the reaction of the enzyme that makes the apple go brown.

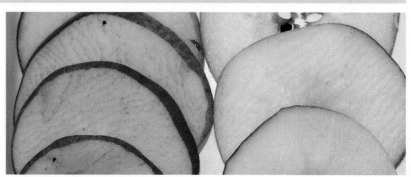

FIGURE 3: Which of the apple slices here have been treated with lemon juice?

Q enzyme reactions

A graph of decay rate against pH shows the same pattern as the temperature graph, Figure 2. There is a particular pH that provides the optimum conditions for the enzyme to work. The table shows the activity for the enzyme pepsin found in the stomach.

pH	Percentage of protein digested in 5 minutes (%)
1	95
2	97
3	53
4	26
5	2

Have you ever wondered why human cannibals could eat a piece of human flesh but their own stomach does not digest itself? Cells lining the stomach secrete small amounts of alkaline mucus, which coats the stomach wall. If a pepsin molecule gets near the wall the pH is too high for it to work, so the stomach is unaffected. When you die these cells stop working so the pepsin starts to digest the stomach wall. That is one of the reasons why dead bodies tend to rot from the inside out.

QUESTIONS

3 Draw a suitable graph to show how the rate of reaction of pepsin is affected by pH.

4 What is the optimum pH for pepsin?

Explaining the results (Higher tier only)

How does temperature affect the rate of enzyme reactions? Enzymes depend on the shape of their active site to work properly. As the temperature rises, the enzyme molecules are literally shaken apart. The active site is destroyed. Often the whole protein molecule is disrupted. You can see this when you boil an egg. The protein is disrupted so much that it forms a solid lump. This is called **denaturing** the enzyme.

But a rise in temperature *increases* the rate of a reaction. In enzyme reactions there is a balance between these two effects:

> damage to the enzyme by over-heating slows the reaction

> a rise in temperature increases the rate of reaction.

The graph in Figure 2 shows how these effects balance out to produce a curve like a camel's hump.

Preserving food

Many of the ways we preserve food depend on preventing enzymes in the food, or in microorganisms that land on it, from working. For example:

> drying – removes water from the food, making the enzymes come out of solution

> pickling in vinegar – affects the pH, so damaging the enzymes

> freezing – slows down the spoilage reactions

> canning (sealing in an air-tight container) food that has been boiled – the boiling denatures the enzymes and the sealing stops microorganisms with new enzymes getting into the food.

Proteins and pH

Protein molecules are held together by bonds that bend the chain into the correct shape. These bonds, called hydrogen bonds, are damaged by changes in pH. This changes the shape of the active site the substrates need to link to for the enzyme to work.

Watch out!

Do not use words like 'killing' the enzyme. Enzymes are not alive so cannot be killed. Use 'denatured' instead.

QUESTIONS

5 Use the lock and key model to explain how pH affects enzyme activity.

6 Use the lock and key model to explain how each of the following preserves food from enzyme spoilage:

a pickling with vinegar

b freezing

c sealing foods in tin cans.

Fermentation

We are learning to:
> recognise fermentation as a form of anaerobic respiration
> understand the industrial importance of fermentation
> explain how fermentation can make animal waste into valuable gas

Why is fermentation our favourite reaction?

The Egyptians were brewing beer about 6000 years ago – before the pyramids were built. The Chinese have been making soya beans easier to digest by making tofu for thousands of years. Today, biodigesters are converting waste into useful fuel gases.

FIGURE 1

What is fermentation?

Animals carry out aerobic and anaerobic respiration. Anaerobic respiration produces toxic chemicals and releases very little energy (see pages 24–25). Microorganisms have a more useful type of anaerobic respiration called **fermentation**. Fermentation is much more varied than aerobic respiration and different microbes produce a wide range of waste products. The table shows the products of different fermentation reactions.

Fermentation products and the uses of the fermentation reaction by humans.

Microorganism	Fermentation product	Use of fermentation reaction by humans
yeast	ethanol	brewing alcoholic drinks
yeast	carbon dioxide	raising bread and other baked foods
lactobacillus	lactic acid	converting milk to yoghurt and cheese
acetobacter	ethanoic acid	converting wine to vinegar

QUESTIONS

1 Give one difference between anaerobic respiration in animals and fermentation in microorganisms.

2 Bacteria deep in the soil can often carry out anaerobic respiration. Why is this an advantage for these bacteria?

Bread and wine

Yeast is an essential part of bread-making. The dough is mixed with a small amount of yeast in sugar and water and is then left to rise in a warm place for up to an hour. During this time the yeast breaks down sugar in the mixture to make carbon dioxide and alcohol. The word equation below summarises this reaction.

glucose → ethanol + carbon dioxide (+ energy released)

The carbon dioxide bubbles are trapped in the dough and make it light and fluffy. When the bread is cooked, the protein in the dough goes solid to give a network of tiny protein-coated bubbles. You can see these when you slice a loaf of bread.

Q fermentation GCSE   anaerobic respiration

In China, a boiled mixture of grains is mixed with rice infected with a type of fungus. The fungus breaks down the starch to a sugary liquor that contains lactic acid. Yeast is added and fermentation begins. This can take several months, but some of the most expensive wines may be left for decades. At the end the liquid is sold as a yellow liquor. Sometimes this powerful liquid is distilled to produce a drink called white liquor, or *bai jiu*.

FIGURE 2: Chinese rice wine – as strong as vodka but cheaper than a cup of coffee in Beijing!

QUESTIONS

3 a Why is the bread dough left for a short while before cooking?

b Why doesn't bread continue to rise after it has been cooked?

4 a What happens to the carbon dioxide produced during fermentation of rice wine?

b Why is the fungus added after the mixture has been boiled, not before?

Biogas digesters

In India, manure from cows is held in an air-tight steel container so that the microbes in the manure have to use anaerobic respiration. Anaerobic respiration by these microbes produces methane rather than carbon dioxide. The mixture warms up and methane bubbles up to be collected in the space in the container. The gas is drawn off at regular intervals and sold. It is used for cooking and heating. After a few weeks the microbes have used up the available foods and respiration slows down. The manure in the digester can be used for fertiliser on the fields.

Did you know?

A cow produces enough methane from its gut to fill nearly 20 large gas cylinders every year.

FIGURE 3: The gas collects under the metal hood of the digester and is drawn off at regular intervals.

QUESTIONS

5 What gas collects in the biogas container?

6 What gas is produced when the biogas burns?

7 Why is biogas production particularly useful on farms in India and some parts of Africa?

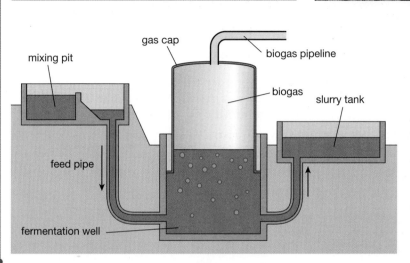

FIGURE 4: Inside a biogas digester.

B4 Checklist

To achieve your forecast grade in the exam you'll need to revise

Use this checklist to see what you can do now. Refer back to pages 10–33 if you're not sure. Look across the rows to see how you could progress – **_bold italic_** means Higher tier only.

Remember you'll need to be able to use these ideas in many ways:
> interpreting pictures, diagrams and graphs
> applying ideas to new situations
> explaining ethical implications
> suggesting some benefits and risks to society
> drawing conclusions from evidence you've been given.

Look at pages 300–306 for information about how you'll be assessed.

Watch out!

Higher tier statements may be tested at any grade from D to A*. All other statements may be tested at any grade from G to A*.

To aim for a grade E	To aim for a grade C	To aim for a grade A
understand that all food comes from energy captured from sunlight by photosynthesis; understand that food energy passes through the living world along food chains	understand that plant and animal bodies have energy locked up in them and that some sorts of chemicals are easier to build up and break down than others	describe photosynthesis as a series of chemical reactions which produce glucose which, in turn, drives the manufacture of other complex chemicals
understand that plants need water, carbon dioxide and light to make food through photosynthesis; recall the products of photosynthesis and use the word equation	recall the symbol equation for photosynthesis	
describe the factors that affect the rate of photosynthesis and how these may affect the distribution of plants in an area		understand how different factors can be limiting at different times in the photosynthetic reaction
understand that diffusion is the movement of molecules from places of high concentration to places of lower concentration; understand that osmosis is the movement of water molecules from a dilute to a less dilute solution through a partially permeable membrane	understand that osmosis is a special case of diffusion; understand the importance of diffusion and osmosis to plants, in the transport of oxygen, carbon dioxide and water; **_understand that active transport is transport against a concentration gradient and requires energy from respiration_**	

To aim for a grade E	To aim for a grade C	To aim for a grade A
understand that energy produced by respiration in living things is used for movement and to drive other important processes in the cell	understand that energy from respiration is used for the synthesis of large molecules (polymers, amino acids and proteins) *and for active transport (for example for the absorption of nitrates by plant roots)*	
recall that aerobic respiration requires oxygen, and that anaerobic respiration takes place in conditions of low oxygen; recall the reactants and products of aerobic respiration and use the word equation	understand the energy production by aerobic and anaerobic respiration systems is very different and that this has implications for the cell; *recall the symbol equation for aerobic respiration*	recall the reactants and products of anaerobic respiration in a) animal cells and in b) plant cells/yeast, and use the word equations
recall the common structures in plant, animal and microbial cells: nucleus, cell membrane, cytoplasm, mitochondria (plant, animal and yeast cells), cell wall (plant, yeast and bacterial cells), circular DNA (bacterial cells), chloroplasts and vacuole (plant cells)	describe these cell structures and their functions, and understand how these help to organise the chemical reactions within the cell to make the cell more efficient	
understand what an enzyme is and what it does to the speed of chemical reactions; understand that enzymes work best in particular, optimum conditions of temperature and pH	understand that particular reactions need their own enzyme (the lock and key model); *explain how temperature and pH can change the efficiency of an enzyme*	
understand that fermentation is an example of anaerobic respiration in microorganisms and give examples of ways this reaction has been used by humans to produce useful products		understand where anaerobic respiration is most likely to occur and use word equations to describe the reaction

Exam-style questions

Foundation level

AO1 **1** The following statements are about respiration. Choose the term to correctly complete each sentence.

a Respiration *always / sometimes / never* requires oxygen. [1]

b Respiration takes place in the *lungs / brain / all over the body*. [1]

c Plants respire *only in the light / only in the dark / at all times*. [1]

[Total 3]

2 A gardener explored the effect of watering on the yield of tomato plants. The data collected is shown in the table.

Average yield per tomato plant, given different amounts of water.

Watering regime	Eventual yield of fruit / kg
Never allowed to wilt	2.04
Allowed to wilt once before fruit formed	1.83
Allowed to wilt once after fruit formed	1.75
Allowed to wilt often	1.48

AO2 **a** The gardener had eight plants in the greenhouse. What would be the total extra mass of useful fruit if he never allowed them to wilt, compared with if he allowed them to wilt often? [3]

AO1 **b** Give three ways besides regular watering the gardener could increase the yield of tomatoes. [3]

[Total 6]

Foundation/Higher level

AO2 **3** **a** A gardener near the coast used seawater to water his garden. Almost all of the plants died. Explain why this happened. [3]

b When a hospital patient is connected to a drip a solution of salts and sugar in water passes directly into the bloodstream. Explain what would happen if the drip contained pure water not a solution. [3]

4 Plaintain wine is a popular drink in the Cameroon. Plantains, which look like green bananas, are peeled, sliced and boiled for 10 minutes. The liquid is filtered and sugar added. After it has cooled down yeast is added and the mixture left for a week. The wine can then be filtered off and drunk straightaway or bottled for later.

AO2 **a** Using your scientific ideas about fermentation explain why the makers of the wine:
   i   boiled the fruit,
   ii filtered the liquid,
   iii let it cool and
   iv added yeast. [4]

AO3 **b** Bottled plantain wine is always very fizzy when it is opened but fresh plantain wine is 'still'. Explain the reason for this difference. [3]

[Total 7]

AO2 **5** Biogas is produced by fermentation of manure. Explain why biogas is described as a 'carbon neutral' fuel even though it releases carbon dioxide when it is burnt. The quality of written communication will be assessed in your response. [6]

[Total 6]

AO2 **6** Use your scientific knowledge to explain why:

a a teaspoon of sugar added to the water for cut flowers keeps them fresh for longer. [2]

b a tablespoon of salt makes them wilt. [2]

[Total 4]

Higher

AO3 **7** The uptake of nitrates from the soil by plants is much higher in summer than in winter. Give two reasons for this. [2]

[Total 2]

AO1 **8** Using the idea of a lock and key model for enzyme action, explain the following.

a Enzymes can make reactions go much more quickly even though the enzyme is not used up by the reaction. [4]

b Over-heating (not boiling) an enzyme stops it from working permanently. [2]

c Cooling an enzyme slows down the rate of reaction but it can speed up again when the mixture is re-warmed. [2]

[Total 8]

AO1 recall the science   AO2 apply your knowledge   AO3 evaluate and analyse the evidence

✴ Worked example

1 The graph below shows the oxygen input/output for a sample of *Elodea* pondweed as the light intensity changes.

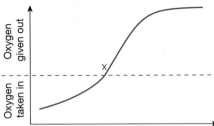

a Where on the graph is the rate of photosynthesis at its highest? [1]

At the top of the graph where the trace levels out.

b A student said that photosynthesis was not occurring at point X on the graph. Is this correct? Give a reason for your answer. [3]

No, it is not correct ✔ because no oxygen is being taken in ✔.

c If extra carbon dioxide was added to the flask would the position of X change? Explain your answer. [3]

No ✔ because at X light is the limiting factor and an increase in carbon dioxide concentration would have no effect. ✔

d Suggest a plan for an investigation to see if the wavelength (colour) of the light has any effect on the rate of photosynthesis. [4]

Set up a flask with Elodea in it and illuminate it with white light for a given period of time.

Measure the volume of oxygen bubbling off from the weed. ✔

Repeat the experiment but place a filter between the lamp and the plant so that the light that falls on the plant is a particular wavelength, e.g. red light. ✔

Measure the volume of oxygen produced in the same time period, as a measure of the rate of photosynthesis. ✔

Repeat the experiment with a range of other filters keeping all other factors constant. ✔

How to raise your grade

Take note of the comments from examiners – these will help you to improve your grade.

> Correct: 1 mark.

> Two correct points, but to get the third mark it's necessary to explain your thinking. It is not enough just to state the answer. The explanation is that photosynthesis must be occurring to provide the oxygen needed for the plant for respiration.

> This also gains 2 marks out of a possible 3. The answer correctly mentions that light is a 'limiting factor'. A full-mark answer needs to explain that light intensity is the limiting factor because an increase in the light level gives an increase in the rate of photosynthesis at the same carbon dioxide concentration.

> This is an excellent answer and gains full marks. Explain what you would do, why you are doing it in this way and how you would collect and interpret the results. Avoid phrases like 'measure the rate of photosynthesis' because this does not describe what you would measure. A better answer, as here, is to state that you would measure the volume of oxygen produced to give you a measure of the rate of photosynthesis.

B5 Growth and development

What you should already know...

Cells that have specific functions are said to be specialised

The specific function of the red blood cell is to carry oxygen. It has special features that allow it to carry out this job.

The white blood cell is part of the body's immune system and can produce antibodies.

Muscle cells can contract and hence move parts of the body.

 Name two other specialised cells.

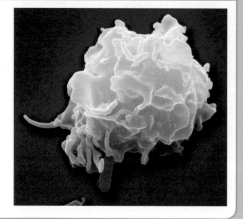

Genes are instructions found in the nuclei of cells

Genes are instructions for a cell that describe how to make proteins. They are sections of very long DNA molecules that make up chromosomes in the nuclei of cells.

Some characteristics are determined by genes, some are determined by environmental factors, and some are determined by a combination of genes and the environment.

 Name examples of characteristics determined by genes, by the environment, by both.

Stem cells are unspecialised cells that can develop into specialised cells

Adult stem cells are unspecialised cells that can develop into many, but not all, types of cells.

Embryonic stem cells are unspecialised cells that can develop into any type of cell.

Both types of stem cells offer the potential to treat some illnesses.

 Name an illness that can be treated by stem cell therapy.

In B5 you will find out about...

> how animals and plants develop specialised cells to form different organs

> the ability of plant meristems to regenerate whole plants

> how the environment affects the growth and development of plants

> the effect of plant hormones on the development of plants

> how an organism produces new cells

> how genes control the growth and development of a cell

> the processes of cell growth and mitosis in the cell cycle

> the difference between meiosis and mitosis

> the importance of the number of chromosomes in gametes

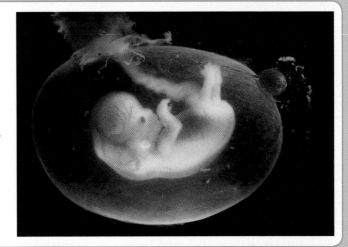

> the stage at which most embryonic cells become specialised and form different types of tissue

> stem cells that remain unspecialised and what happens to them at a later stage

> the structure of the genetic code in DNA and the mechanism for protein production

> how the 'switching on' of genes in specialised cells allows them to carry out their specific function

> the ethical decisions that need to be taken when using embryonic stem cells and how this work is regulated

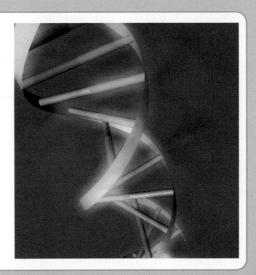

How do organisms develop?

How do these cells end up looking like a person?

This bundle of cells is an embryo at the eight-cell stage. At this stage all the cells are identical and their nuclei carry the same information. Yet some of these cells develop into kidney cells or skin cells or muscle cells. How does the cell know what it is supposed to grow up to be?

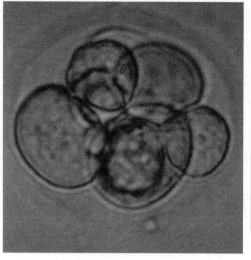

FIGURE 1: Embryonic cells.

 Cell adaptations

Some living organisms are made up of just one cell. These are called **unicellular** organisms. All seven life processes can take place inside the one cell. Most organisms are **multicellular** – they are made up of many cells. The different cells share the work of the whole organism. Each cell has its own particular job to do, and is **specialised** to do that job. The cells have different shapes and sizes (**adaptations**) to help them carry out their specific function.

Cells doing the same job are often grouped together. A group of cells like this is called a **tissue**. For example, muscle tissue is made up of identical muscle cells. Muscle tissue contracts (gets shorter) to move other parts of the body. Epithelial cells (skin cells) work together as epithelial tissue to provide coverings for various parts of the body.

An **organ** is made up of different tissues that work together to do a particular job. For example, muscle tissues and epithelial tissues work together as the organ called the heart. Organs often work together in **organ systems**. Different organ systems carry out different jobs and work to make up the whole organism.

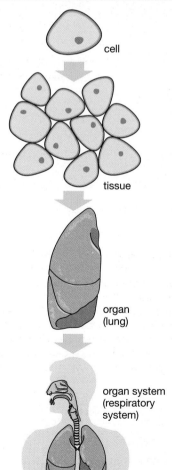

cell

tissue

organ (lung)

organ system (respiratory system)

FIGURE 2: Cells work together as tissue. Many tissues together form an organ. Organs make up an organ system, and all the organ systems form a complete organism.

QUESTIONS

1 Put these in order of size (smallest to largest).

cells   organs   whole body   tissue   organ systems

2 Why do cells have different shapes?

3 Name an organ and write down which organ system it belongs to.

🔍 cell specialisation

Cell specialisation

All organisms start life as a **zygote** (a fertilised egg cell). A zygote grows by dividing itself (cell division) and making new cells in a process called **mitosis**. A zygote divides to produce two daughter cells. Each daughter cell is identical to the cell they came from and to each other. The daughter cells divide again to produce two daughter cells each, and so on. This group of cells is called an **embryo**. As the embryo develops, one cell may change its shape and structure to become adapted to do a particular job. In other words, it becomes **differentiated** to carry out a particular function and the cell is then specialised.

Two specialised cells in the blood are red blood cells and white blood cells. Each one has its own particular shape and structure to help carry out its function. Red blood cells carry oxygen to all the cells in the body. The shape of a red blood cell is adapted to help its function. It has a large surface area, allowing efficient absorption of oxygen.

White blood cells are an important part of the immune response. When a pathogen enters the body, white blood cells act in specific ways to kill the pathogen. For example, they may change shape to engulf the pathogen and kill it or they may produce antibodies that kill or disable the pathogen. To do this, they need to have lots of energy and be able to produce chemicals.

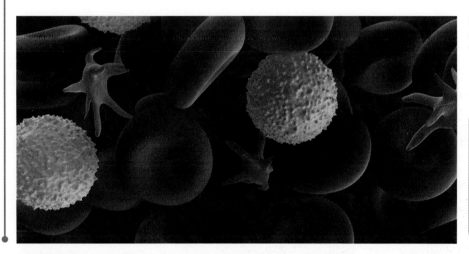

FIGURE 3: Red and white blood cells are specialised cells with very different functions.

QUESTIONS

4 How does a zygote grow?

5 What is a specialised cell? Explain with an example.

How cells differentiate

A specialised cell will start to carry out its particular function when it has the size, shape or chemicals that allow it to work. The size, shape and chemicals of a cell are determined by genes in the DNA of the nucleus. All body cells contain the same genes in their DNA. They undergo differentiation because of the turning on and off of genes in their DNA. Genes that are turned off will no longer instruct the cell what to do. The genes that are turned on (**active**) control how the cell behaves and looks. Cells that are not specialised are able to carry on dividing and growing to form more identical cells.

Watch out!

Do not confuse specialisation with cell division. Cell division is how cells divide. Cell specialisation is how a cell carries out its job.

QUESTIONS

6 Why does a cell in the muscle tissue become a muscle cell instead of a kidney cell?

7 What kind of genes will be switched on in a white blood cell?

Did you know?

Bone is also a tissue.

Stem cells

We are learning to:
> recall that in a human embryo up to the eight-cell stage, all the cells are identical

> understand that after the eight-cell stage, most of the embryo cells become specialised and form different types of tissue

> understand that some cells remain unspecialised until a later stage

How can stem cells help Lassie?

Stem cell therapy is being used to treat arthritis in dogs, but humans will have to wait many years for the same treatment to be available. This is because using stem cells from human tissues raises a lot of ethical and moral questions. The stem cells for the treatment of dogs come from their body fat and it causes no lasting damage to the dog when they are harvested. What are the ethical issues involved in using stem cells from humans?

FIGURE 1

Fertilisation

In most species, sexual reproduction involves the joining of **sex cells** from two parents. In male animals, the sex cells are called **sperm**. In female animals, the sex cells are called **eggs**. During sexual reproduction, the sperm cell and the egg cell join together. This is called **fertilisation**. The fertilised egg cell is called a **zygote**. The zygote will divide many times to become an **embryo**. Eventually the embryo will develop into an individual organism.

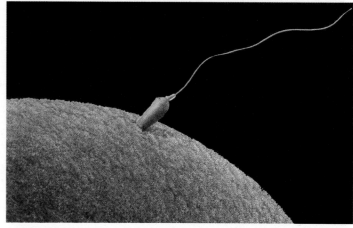

FIGURE 2: The joining of the sperm nucleus and the egg nucleus is called fertilisation.

> **QUESTIONS**
>
> **1** What is the joining of a male sex cell and a female sex cell called?
>
> **2** What is a fertilised egg cell called?

What are stem cells?

When the embryo is at the eight-cell stage (see Figure 1 on page 40), all the cells are identical to each other and have the ability to become any type of cell. These cells are called **embryonic stem cells**. When a stem cell divides, each new cell has the potential either to remain a stem cell or become differentiated to become another type of cell with a more specialised function, such as a muscle cell, a red blood cell, or a nerve cell.

As the embryo develops, its differentiated cells form tissues and organs. Sometimes undifferentiated cells can be found among differentiated cells in a tissue or organ. These are called **adult stem cells** and they can later differentiate to become one of the specialised cells of that tissue or organ. For example, adult stem cells found in bone marrow can divide and differentiate to become any type of blood cell, such as a red blood cell or any of the different types of white blood cells.

🔍 fertilisation

Adult stem cells usually differentiate into the types of cells found in the tissue where they are located. Thus, a liver stem cell is only able to differentiate into a liver cell type but not into a nerve cell.

Watch out!

'Adult' stem cells come not only from adults, but from newborns and children as well.

QUESTIONS

3 What is the difference between an adult stem cell and an embryonic stem cell?

4 Can adult stem cells found in the bone marrow differentiate to become kidney cells?

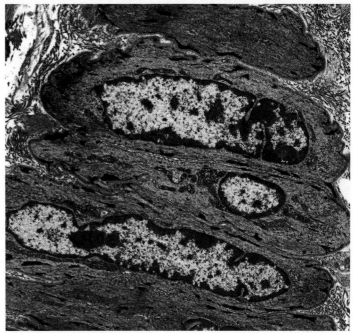

FIGURE 3: These muscle cells are specialised cells that started off as stem cells.

The importance of stem cells

Stem cells are important for living organisms for many reasons. In the embryo, stem cells give rise to the entire body of the organism, including all of the many specialised cell types and organs such as the heart, lung, skin, sperm, eggs and other tissues. In some adult tissues, such as bone marrow, adult stem cells replace cells that are lost through normal wear and tear, injury, or disease.

The ability to reproduce themselves by cell division and to become differentiated to any type of cell also makes stem cells extremely interesting to scientists. They offer potential new treatments to replace cells lost to diseases and injuries. Stem cell research may help develop alternatives to organ transplantation as well as look at the effects of new drugs and help us to understand the causes of birth defects.

QUESTIONS

5 Why are stem cells important?

6 Suggest a way that stem cells may help reduce the need for organ transplantation in the future.

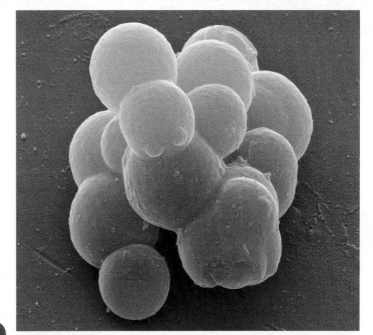

FIGURE 4: These stem cells have the potential to become almost any cell in the body. They are taken from umbilical cord blood.

Did you know?

Stem cell therapies are not new. Doctors have been performing bone marrow stem cell transplants for decades.

Q embryonic stem cells   adult stem cells

Stem cells in plants

How are plants and animals similar?

There are many ways in which animals are obviously different from plants. Can you think of all the different ways there are? Even in reproduction, plants produce young in a different way from animals. Plants have a very different structure from animals, but they do have cells, tissues and organs. They even have stem cells.

We are learning to:

> understand the different types of tissue within organs of a plant

> understand that in plants, only cells within special regions can divide

> understand that plants also have stem cells

FIGURE 1: There are many ways that animals and plants are different from each other. How many ways can you think of in which they are similar to each other?

Plant cells

Plant cells, like animal cells, have specialised features for different functions. Some of the specialised cells found in plants are described below.

> **Palisade cells** are found near the top of leaves so they get a lot of light from the Sun. They are rectangular and full of chloroplasts. Lots of palisade cells make up palisade tissue.

> **Xylem cells** are adapted to carry water and mineral salts to where they are needed in the plant. Dead xylem cells join together to form long tubes known as xylem tissue.

> **Phloem cells** carry dissolved substances such as sugars and amino acids to every part of the plant. They are adapted to carry out this function by joining other phloem cells to make long thin tubes.

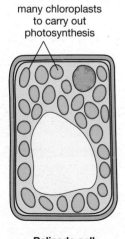

many chloroplasts to carry out photosynthesis

Palisade cell

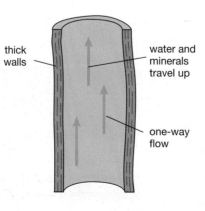

thick walls

water and minerals travel up

one-way flow

Xylem cell

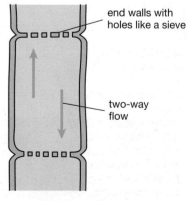

end walls with holes like a sieve

two-way flow

Phloem cell

FIGURE 2: How are palisade, xylem and phloem cells different?

🔍 palisade cells   xylem   phloem

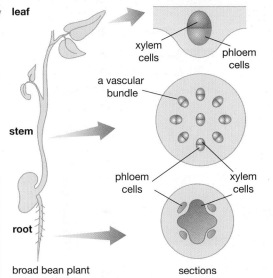

leaf

xylem
cells

phloem
cells

a vascular
bundle

stem

phloem
cells

xylem
cells

root

broad bean plant

sections

FIGURE 3: Different plant cells make up different tissues, and these work together to form organs of a plant, such as the leaf, stem and root.

QUESTIONS

1 How are palisade cells adapted to their function?

2 How is the structure of a phloem cell adapted to its function?

Did you know?

Xylem cells are dead cells joined together like long straws.

Watch out!

Phloem cells, xylem cells and palisade cells form phloem tissue, xylem tissue and palisade tissue, respectively. These tissues work together to form plant organs.

Cell division in plants

Just like animal cells, plants cells that have already been differentiated are no longer able to divide. Only the cells in special regions called **meristems** are able to divide. The function of cells in the meristem is similar to that of stem cells found in animals. These are cells that remain unspecialised and are able to divide to form identical unspecialised cells. Some of the cells resulting from this division remain in the meristem and continue to produce more cells, while others differentiate and are incorporated into tissues and organs of the growing plant.

A cell in the meristem divides by mitosis to become two identical daughter cells. The two daughter cells are separated by a cell plate that later becomes a cell wall for each cell. The daughter cells may either divide further or they may differentiate into specialised cells.

QUESTIONS

3 Which cells in a plant are able to divide?

4 Would a differentiated plant cell be able to divide?

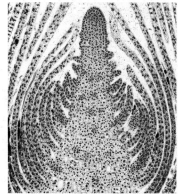

FIGURE 4: The meristem region in the shoot of a plant, magnified fifty times.

Cell specialisation in plants

Meristems are found in the tips of shoots and roots as well as in buds and flowering parts of the plant. Unlike animals, which stop growing when they become adult, plants grow throughout their life. The cells of the meristem divide to increase height and girth of the plant and the length of the roots, as well as developing into the leaves, flowers and branches of the plant. During their life, plants can regrow whole organs such as leaves and roots if they are damaged.

Did you know?

Plant cells are able to expand their cell walls to allow for cell growth.

QUESTIONS

5 Compare all the ways that animals and plants are different using the information on pages 42–45.

6 Name some target cells that are affected by auxin.

🔍 meristem

Plant clones

Is regeneration only science fiction?

Imagine cutting your nails and watching each piece grow and develop into an exact copy of you. Plants have an amazing ability to regenerate damaged parts. It is also possible to chop up some plants into many pieces and get a whole plant from each piece. What is the secret of this ability?

FIGURE 1

Plants from cuttings

It is possible to produce new individuals from certain plants by putting the cut end of a shoot into water or moist earth. Roots grow from the base of the stem into the soil while the shoot continues to grow and produce leaves. The ability of plants to reproduce this way is how most of our fruit plants and houseplants are grown.

Gardeners often dip cuttings into rooting powder that contains a chemical which promotes the production of roots from the stem. Given the right conditions, the cutting can grow into a whole plant. This new plant is an exact copy, or **clone**, of the parent plant that provided the cutting. Busy Lizzies and geraniums are commonly grown from cuttings.

FIGURE 2: Taking cuttings is a technique used by gardeners to produce plants like these geraniums.

QUESTIONS

1 How can you grow a plant from cuttings?

2 What is rooting powder?

Tissue culture

Growing plant cuttings is a lengthy and expensive business. Cuttings can only be taken in particular seasons, otherwise they fail to grow. Plant cuttings can take many months to root and grow into full plants. To save time and money, horticulturalists use another method of cloning plants called **tissue culture**.

Tissue culture involves taking small pieces of plant tissue from a root or stem and treating it with enzymes to separate the cells. The cells are then placed individually on nutrient jelly containing plant hormones that promote the growth of roots, stems and leaves. This gives a large number of plants in a short time. These new plantlets will eventually become big enough to be grown in compost.

tissue culture

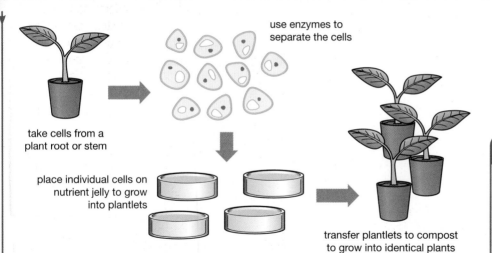

use enzymes to separate the cells

take cells from a plant root or stem

place individual cells on nutrient jelly to grow into plantlets

transfer plantlets to compost to grow into identical plants

FIGURE 3: The steps in tissue culture.

Tissue culture using meristem cells

Tissue culture involves the use of almost any tissue of a plant and gives rise to a large number of plants that are clones of the parent plant. However, sometimes irregularities may take place that cause the plants to become variants – genetically different to the parent plant.

If the plant to be cloned is valuable, novel or has desirable features, it can be cloned using meristem cells. This method of propagation is used to produce multiple copies of clones of the parent plant. The cells of the meristem are dividing rapidly and have the ability to develop into any cell in plant tissue. These cells are all exact clones of the parent plant, so each individual plant produced from these cells is genetically identical.

Auxins (Higher tier only)

Examples of plant hormones that promote growth are **auxins**. Hormones are chemical messages that are produced in one part of an organism and transported in very small quantities to another part to help co-ordinate and control the growth of other cells. Unlike animal hormones, which target specific cells, plant hormones seem to affect every cell in the plant. Auxins affect cells by causing changes in cell division and elongation of the cell.

FIGURE 4: These plantlets are all genetically identical to each other.

Watch out!

In tissue culture, the exact conditions required by plant cells are different for each plant species.

Preparing for assessment: Planning and collecting

To achieve a good grade in science you will need to be able to use your skills and understanding to understand how scientists plan, run and evaluate investigations. These skills will be assessed in exams and in Controlled Assessments. This activity supports you in developing the skills of planning a safe and reliable investigation.

✳ Clone your cauliflower! – micropropagation

Chloe's group is finding out about micropropagation – how whole plants can be regenerated from small pieces of plant material. Unlike animal cells, many plant cells are totipotent, meaning that each cell has the capacity to regenerate the entire plant. This fact lies at the foundation of all tissue culture work.

They swabbed their working area with ethanol and Chloe divided a piece of the white part of the cauliflower, the curd, into pieces. She sterilised the surface tissue of these cauliflower 'explants' using Milton solution. Aseptic conditions were important to prevent contamination.

Chloe rinsed the explants in sterile distilled water. Her partner took the tube of growth medium, flamed the neck, and used sterilised forceps to pick up an explant and quickly drop it into the tube. She flamed the neck of the tube once more, and replaced the plug.

They kept the tubes in a warm, light place. Their teacher told them that growth should be visible within 10 days, along with any contamination.

Task 1

> What do you think they expected to see after 10 days?

> What equipment did they need to use?

 ## Task 2

> Explain why they used the techniques that they did.

> What hazards would they have to manage, and how might they have done this?

 ## Task 3

> What do you think their prediction was?

> What scientific ideas should they have made use of in predicting an outcome?

Task 4

> Suggest a testable hypothesis based on this procedure.

> How would their techniques enable them to gather reliable evidence?

> Write a suitable risk assessment for the investigation.

Maximise your grade

Use these suggestions to improve your work and be more successful.

E

To be on target for grade E you need to:

> Offer a testable prediction for the students and justify it, using relevant scientific terms.

> Identify equipment the students could use to collect data.

> Identify and comment on hazards they encountered.

C

To be on target for grades D, C, in addition, you need to:

> Identify major factors and scientific knowledge the students should use to make a testable hypothesis.

> Suggest techniques and equipment the students should use which are appropriate for the range of data required.

> Identify any significant risks for the students and suggest some precautions.

A

To be on target for grades B, A, in addition, you need to:

> Suggest what the students could investigate and propose a testable hypothesis.

> Suggest equipment and techniques the students should use to achieve precise and reliable data.

> Produce a full and appropriate risk assessment.

Plant development

We are learning to:
> understand how growth and development of plants is affected by the environment
> understand how phototropism increases the plant's chance of survival

How do plants know which way to grow?

Have you ever wondered why the plant that fills an empty spot in the hallway always seems to have its leaves facing away from the room and towards the window? And no matter how often the plant is rotated to display the leaves inside the room, before too long the plant is back with the stem showing and leaves facing towards the window again. Why do you think this happens? What is causing the plant to move this way?

FIGURE 1

How light affects plants

A plant needs light, carbon dioxide and water to be able to make food (**photosynthesise**). Light helps a plant shoot tip to develop the green coloured chemical called chlorophyll. The chlorophyll absorbs the light energy used for photosynthesis, so without chlorophyll, a plant cannot photosynthesise. Without photosynthesis, a plant would not be able to grow.

A plant growing in plenty of light will grow straight. If light falls on only one side of the plant, the plant will grow towards the light.

Watch out!

Plants do not 'bend' towards light, they grow towards it.

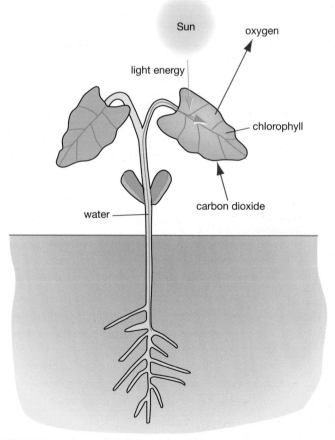

FIGURE 2: A plant needs light, carbon dioxide and water to make food.

QUESTIONS

1 What are the important factors needed for photosynthesis?

2 Why is photosynthesis important?

🔍 photosynthesis GCSE

Phototropism

When a seedling starts to grow, its shoots always grow towards light. This growth response to light is called **phototropism**. Shoots growing towards light are said to be **positively phototropic**. By growing towards the source of light, a shoot brings its leaves into the best situation for photosynthesis. Similarly, flowers are brought into the best situation where they can be seen and pollinated by insects.

Did you know?

In 1880, Charles Darwin and his son Francis were the first scientists to investigate why shoots grow towards light.

QUESTIONS

3 What does positively phototropic mean?

4 What are the advantages of phototropism?

FIGURE 3: Some flowers need insects to help their pollination.

Auxin and phototropism (Higher tier only)

The explanation for phototropism required creative hypotheses, observation and testing. This scientific process led to the discovery of auxin, a plant growth hormone, and its action in light.

Auxin is naturally found in the tips of shoots and roots. In the shoots, auxin causes growth of cells in the shoot tip. In the roots, auxin has the *opposite effect*. The auxin slows down growth in the growing root.

The phototropic response in plants is due to the effects of auxin. When a shoot gets light from one side, most auxin is found in the shaded part of the shoot tip. Auxin seems to enable the cells walls to be stretched more easily by the pressures developed in the vacuoles. This makes the cells on the shaded side expand and elongate. The shoot then curves towards light.

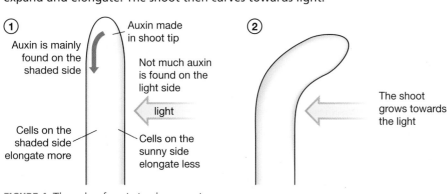

FIGURE 4: The role of auxin in phototropism.

Did you know?

Some vine shoot tips exhibit negative phototropism, which allows them to grow towards dark, solid objects and climb them.

Watch out!

Shoots and roots do not only respond to light. They can respond to gravity and moisture too.

QUESTIONS

5 Where is most auxin found in a plant where light falls from one side?

6 Explain how auxin makes a shoot grow towards light.

🔍 positive phototropism   negative phototropism

Mitosis

We are learning to:
> recall that cell division by mitosis produces two new cells that are genetically identical
> describe the cell cycle

How old are you really?

Some cells in your body do not live nearly as long as you do. For example, skin cells and cells lining the intestine are constantly being shed and your red blood cells live for just over 100 days. What happens when these cells die? How are they replaced?

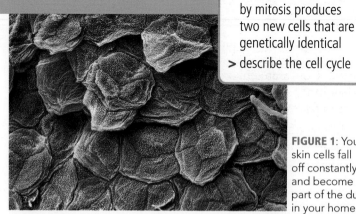

FIGURE 1: Your skin cells fall off constantly and become part of the dust in your home.

Mitosis

There are a fixed number of chromosomes in each species. Human body cells each contain 46 chromosomes (or 23 pairs). This means there are 46 chromosomes in each of your kidney cells, in every skin cell, nerve cell and so on.

New cells are needed for the organism to grow. They are also needed to replace cells that are worn out or damaged. The new cells must be the same as the original cells so that they can do the same job. The cell division that takes place in the normal body cells and produces identical daughter cells is called **mitosis**. In mitosis, a cell divides by splitting into two new **daughter** cells. These daughter cells are identical to each other and the cell they came from. This means that they each have the same number of chromosomes as each other and the parent cell.

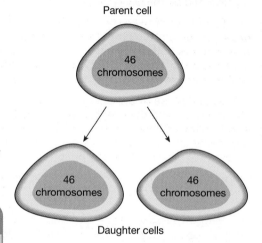

FIGURE 2: In mitosis the daughter cells have 46 chromosomes each, the same as the parent cell. How does this happen?

QUESTIONS

1 What is mitosis?
2 How many chromosomes are there in a human liver cell?

Stages in mitosis

Before a cell can divide in mitosis it must make a copy of its chromosomes to give to the daughter cell. Figure 3 shows what happens to pairs of chromosomes during mitosis.

This shows four of the cell's chromosomes in two pairs

Each chromosome makes an identical copy of itself.

The cell divides in two. Half of the chromosomes go into each daughter cell

Each daughter cell is an exact copy of the original cell

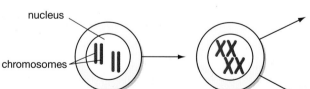

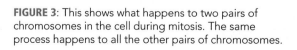

FIGURE 3: This shows what happens to two pairs of chromosomes in the cell during mitosis. The same process happens to all the other pairs of chromosomes.

Q mitosis

QUESTIONS

3 What would happen if the cell split into two before making a copy of its chromosomes? (Hint: How many chromosomes would the daughter cells have if the cell could not copy chromosomes?)

4 Draw a labelled diagram of the stages of mitosis with just one pair of chromosomes.

Watch out!

There are 46 chromosomes in the nucleus of your cells (except your sex cells). They are arranged in 23 pairs. One chromosome in each pair is inherited from your father and one from your mother.

The cell cycle

The term 'cell division' is misleading since it implies that the cell must halve to produce two daughter cells. In reality, there is a phase of cell growth before the cell can divide. These two phases of the cell are represented by the cell cycle.

The first phase of the cell cycle is cell growth. During this phase, the cell grows, accumulates nutrients for the second phase of the cell cycle and makes copies of its chromosomes. At the end of this phase, there is an increase in the number of organelles (the specialised structures within the cell) that are going to take part in the process of mitosis.

The second phase of the cell cycle is mitosis. During this phase, the original chromosomes and their copies are divided into identical sets in two nuclei. This is followed immediately by a process in which the nuclei, cytoplasm, organelles and cell membrane are divided into two cells containing equal amounts of each of these components.

Once the parent cell has completely divided, each daughter cell enters the first phase of the cell cycle.

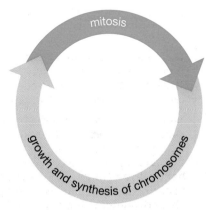

FIGURE 4: The cell cycle has two phases. The number of chromosomes is doubled at the end of the growth and synthesis phase.

QUESTIONS

5 How many chromosomes are there in a human cell at the end of the first phase of the cell cycle?

6 How many chromosomes are there in a human cell at the end of the second phase of the cell cycle?

Did you know?

There is a limit to how many times cells undergo mitosis. However, cancer cells undergo mitosis indefinitely.

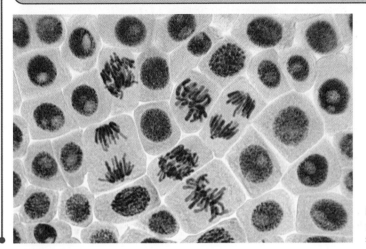

Watch out!

Chromosomes are copied and the number of organelles increases during cell growth.

FIGURE 5: Different stages of mitosis in hyacinth root cells. Notice how the nucleus has increased in size in the cells that are about to divide.

Meiosis

Do human cells always have 46 chromosomes?

We already know that each cell in the body of a human has 46 chromosomes in its nucleus. A human embryo results from the joining of the sperm nucleus and the egg nucleus. Can a human embryo have more or less than 46 chromosomes?

FIGURE 1: An aquatic rat has 92 chromosomes in each nucleus.

Meiosis

We have seen that mitosis is the type of cell division that takes place during the growth of an organism or when replacing dead or old cells.

There is another type of cell division, called **meiosis**. Meiosis takes place in the testes of a male and in the ovaries of a female. Meiosis is a cell division that results in the formation of sex cells (**gametes**). The gametes of a male animal are called sperm cells. The gametes of a female are called ova – which mature later to become egg cells. Gametes are different from body cells as they contain only half the number of chromosomes in a body cell. An egg and a sperm cell are shown on page 42.

Did you know?

Meiosis in human females begins before birth but stops before it is complete. The process does not resume until after puberty.

⊙ QUESTIONS

1 Where does meiosis take place in females?

2 How are gametes different from body cells?

Stages of meiosis

Figure 2 shows what happens to the pairs of chromosomes during meiosis.

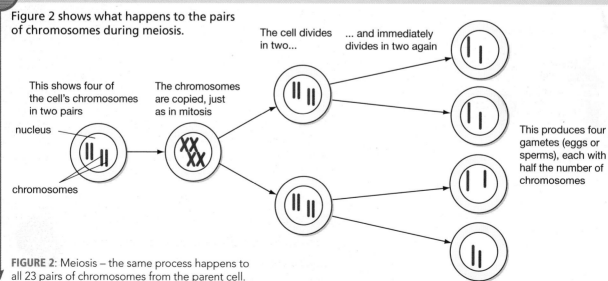

This shows four of the cell's chromosomes in two pairs

The chromosomes are copied, just as in mitosis

The cell divides in two...

... and immediately divides in two again

nucleus

chromosomes

This produces four gametes (eggs or sperms), each with half the number of chromosomes

FIGURE 2: Meiosis – the same process happens to all 23 pairs of chromosomes from the parent cell.

🔍 gametes   meiosis

Did you know?

In most species, the females give birth to the offspring. In seahorses, the males give birth. The female seahorse places egg cells in the male's pouch. He adds sperm cells that fertilise the egg cells. Each fertilised egg cell develops into a baby seahorse.

● QUESTIONS

3 How many chromosomes are there in a human cell just before cell division?

4 Why are the daughter cells not identical to the parent cell?

Watch out!

In meiosis, the number of chromosomes halves. Make sure you apply this to all examples, however many chromosome there are.

The importance of meiosis

Sperm cells and egg cells join in fertilisation to become a zygote. In a human zygote, there are 46 chromosomes in total. Half of these (23) come from the mother and the other 23 come from the father.

If human sex cells had 46 chromosomes each, then a zygote would end up with 92 chromosomes. All humans have 46 chromosomes in their body cells; therefore a zygote with 92 chromosomes would not work.

As a result of meiosis, gametes contain only half the full chromosome number. So when human gametes join together at fertilisation, the zygote formed contains the right number of 46 chromosomes.

Watch out!

Make sure you know the difference between mitosis and meiosis. Mitosis results in two cells with the same number of chromosomes as the parent cell; meiosis results in four gametes with half the number of chromosomes as the parent cell.

FIGURE 3: A cabbage has nine chromosomes in each gamete. How many chromosomes are there in the body cells of a cabbage?

● QUESTIONS

5 Where do you think meiosis occurs in a plant?

6 Explain why meiosis is called a 'reduction division'.

 reduction division

Chromosomes, genes and DNA

What can DNA tell us about our posh food?

Caviar, one of the most expensive food delicacies in the world, is a mass of eggs from a fish species called sturgeon. Caviar is strictly regulated to make sure that sturgeon does not become extinct. Samples of caviar are monitored by DNA testing to ensure that they are legally farmed and not taken from protected species of fish. How can the DNA of fish eggs show where they have come from?

We are learning to:

> recall that DNA has a double helix structure
> recall that both strands of the DNA molecule are made up of four different bases that always pair up in the same way: A with T, and C with G
> understand that the order of bases in a gene is the genetic code

FIGURE 1: Caviar.

Chromosomes and DNA

Inside nearly all cells there is a nucleus, which contains long thread-like structures called **chromosomes**. Chromosomes occur in pairs. There are different numbers of pairs for different species of living organism. Humans have 23 pairs of chromosomes in their cell nuclei, kangaroos have six pairs and apples have 17 pairs.

Chromosomes are made up of a long molecule called **DNA**. A DNA molecule is made of thousands of single DNA 'units'.

QUESTIONS

1 What do chromosomes look like?
2 Where is DNA found?

Did you know?

Broccoli, cauliflower and Brussels sprouts are the same species. All have the same nine pairs of chromosomes.

FIGURE 2: Fruit fly chromosomes.

Structure of DNA

A single unit of DNA is made up of three molecules:

> a phosphate

> a sugar

> a **base**.

The sugar and phosphate molecules join up and form the 'backbone' of the DNA strand. The bases are attached to the sugar molecules.

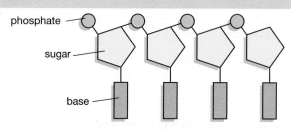

FIGURE 3: The units that make up DNA.

Q chromosomes   genes   DNA

A DNA molecule is actually two strands of molecules facing each other in such a way that it looks like a ladder. The sugars and phosphates are the uprights of the ladder and the bases are like the rungs. The strands of the DNA molecule are twisted around each other to form a **double helix** – like a spiral staircase.

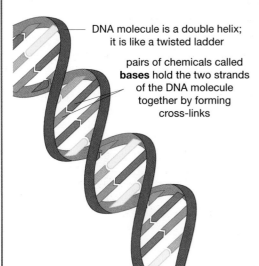

DNA molecule is a double helix; it is like a twisted ladder

pairs of chemicals called **bases** hold the two strands of the DNA molecule together by forming cross-links

Watch out!

Four different bases are used to produce DNA.

FIGURE 4: The DNA double helix.

◉ QUESTIONS

3 Draw a diagram of a single unit of DNA.

4 What is meant by a double helix?

Genes and base pairs

A DNA unit has one of four different bases, referred to as A, T, C and G. Each unit is called a **nucleotide**. A molecule of DNA is made of two strands joined together by the bases of a unit on each side of the strand. Each base is held together in a **base pair** and the bases always pair up in the same way:

A pairs with T

C pairs with G

Proteins determine what a cell will look like and what it will do. These proteins are determined by genes.

Genes are sections of a DNA molecule. A DNA molecule is made up of thousands of genes arranged like beads on a necklace. The sequence of bases in each gene contains a particular set of instructions, usually coding for a specific protein. This sequence of bases on DNA that codes for a protein is called the **genetic code**.

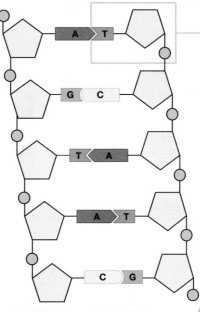

one of four different nucleotides that make up DNA

FIGURE 5: Base pairs in DNA.

Watch out!

The order going from largest to smallest is chromosome – gene – single DNA unit. A chromosome is a long chain of DNA. A gene is a section of DNA. A DNA molecule is made up of single units called **nucleotides**.

◉ QUESTIONS

5 Are genes made of protein? Explain your answer.

6 Explain what the genetic code is.

Making proteins

We are learning to:

> recall that the genetic code is in the cell nucleus
> understand that proteins are produced in the cell cytoplasm
> understand that genes do not leave the nucleus

How is DNA like an architect's plan?

An architect's plan contains all the information necessary for building a house. The complete set of instructions may be contained on a few sheets of paper. To build the house, these instructions must be interpreted and put into action by a builder. With nothing more than building materials and the few sheet of instructions, the builder has to construct the house exactly as the architect intended. In the same way, the coded information in DNA must be interpreted to build proteins in the cell.

FIGURE 1

Proteins are made in the cytoplasm

DNA is only found inside the nucleus of a cell, but the cell structures that make protein are found outside the nucleus in the **cytoplasm** of the cell. The proteins produced in a cell determine what the cell will look like and what its job will be. Since DNA controls the making of protein, there needs to be a way to get information from the nucleus to the structures that make the protein.

QUESTIONS

1 Where is DNA found?

2 What happens in the cytoplasm?

Watch out!

DNA codes for protein but stays *inside* the nucleus. The proteins are made in the cytoplasm.

cell **membrane** controls the movement of substances in and out of the cell

nucleus carries genetic information

cytoplasm where many chemical reactions happen

genetic information is carried on **chromosomes**

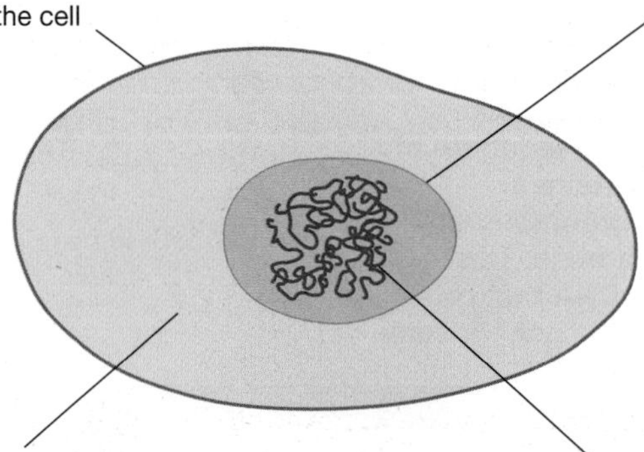

FIGURE 2: Each cell in the body makes proteins. DNA controls the making of protein but the actual assembly of the protein is carried out in the cytoplasm.

cell cytoplasm

Getting the message across

DNA cannot leave the nucleus, so another molecule has to carry the instructions from the DNA to small structures in the cytoplasm, called **ribosomes**, that make proteins. This 'messenger' molecule copies instructions found on the DNA and carries it out of the nucleus to the ribosomes.

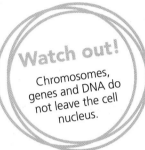

Watch out!

Chromosomes, genes and DNA do not leave the cell nucleus.

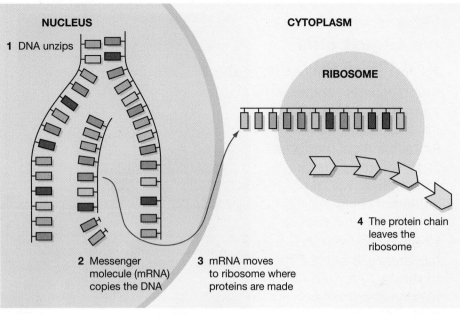

NUCLEUS

1 DNA unzips

CYTOPLASM

RIBOSOME

4 The protein chain leaves the ribosome

2 Messenger molecule (mRNA) copies the DNA

3 mRNA moves to ribosome where proteins are made

FIGURE 3: DNA makes a copy of itself called mRNA. The mRNA moves out of the nucleus into the cytoplasm to the ribosome.

QUESTIONS

3 What are ribosomes?

4 Where are ribosomes found?

Making proteins (Higher tier only)

To make a protein, lots of **amino acids** have to join together. The type and sequence of the amino acids determines what the protein will be. A set of three bases in a DNA strand carries the code for one amino acid. This means the sequence of bases in DNA determines the order in which amino acids are arranged to make a protein. Each gene codes for a particular combination of amino acids, which makes a specific protein.

By determining which proteins are produced in a cell, the genetic code of the genes also determines the structure and function of the cell. This sequence is decided by the genetic code of the sections of DNA (genes). The molecule called **messenger RNA** (**mRNA** for short) copies the base sequence on the DNA and carries it out of the nucleus to the ribosomes. The mRNA attracts another molecule (tRNA) which gives up the amino acid that it carries. The amino acids then bond together to form a long chain – the protein.

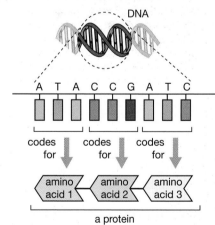

DNA

A T A C C G A T C

codes for   codes for   codes for

amino acid 1   amino acid 2   amino acid 3

a protein

FIGURE 4: DNA codes for specific amino acids that join together to form a protein.

QUESTIONS

5 What determines what the cell looks like?

6 Do you think that the protein that digests sugars in milk is identical to the protein that digests sugars in fruit? Explain your answer.

Did you know?

The size of a gene is measured in base pairs. The longest gene in the human cell is one that codes for a muscle protein. It is 2 400 000 base pairs long.

Cell specialisation and gene activity

Why doesn't my ear digest a fly that lands on it?

Chromosomes contain thousands of genes, each of which codes for a protein. If a cell produced all the proteins that are coded, there would be a flood of chemicals in the cell. A cell in the ear would be able to produce the chemicals needed for digestion. This does not happen because some of the codes are switched off.

FIGURE 1

We are learning to:

> understand that many genes in a particular body cell are not active

> understand that in stem cells genes can be switched on

> understand stem cells have the potential to produce cells needed to replace damaged tissues

> discuss the ethical arguments around the use of embryonic stem cells

How do cells know which proteins to make?

All body cells in a human contain 46 chromosomes. These chromosomes have thousands of genes that are able to code for many different proteins. If all these codes were active, the cell would not be able to carry out any function normally and it would be wasteful in terms of space, energy and materials. This is why many genes in body cells are not active: they are said to be **switched off**. This way, the cell only produces the proteins it needs to function. Specialised cells make only those proteins that allow them to carry out the functions they are adapted to perform.

FIGURE 2: If you were sitting in one room, would you leave the lights on in all the other rooms? That would be a waste of energy. Similarly, genes that are not needed are switched off.

QUESTIONS

1 Where are genes found?

2 Why are only some genes active?

Watch out!
Only some genes are active in a cell.

Specialisation of embryonic stem cells

Up to the eight-cell stage (page 40), when the cells of an embryo divide by mitosis, two identical daughter cells are produced. Beyond this stage, after each cell division there are two paths that each daughter cell may follow.

> The cell may divide again by mitosis to form identical daughter cells. The daughter cells from this division can then divide by mitosis or undergo differentiation.

> The cell may undergo differentiation to become a specialised cell. It will then start making specific proteins and will undergo a dramatic change in size and shape.

Watch out!
Once a cell is specialised, some of its genes are no longer active.

Q active genes

Specialised cells produce specific proteins because the genes coding for these proteins are **active** or **switched on**. Embryonic stem cells are able to differentiate into any cell type. This is because any of the genes in their chromosomes are able to be switched on. In specialised cells, only the genes needed for that particular cell are switched on. For example, muscle cells make specific proteins that allow the cell to contract.

The ability of embryonic stem cells to differentiate into any type of cell makes them important in scientific research looking at replacing damaged or diseased tissue.

 QUESTIONS

3 Why are specialised cells able to produce specific proteins?

4 How does the number of genes switched on in cells of an eight-cell embryo compare with the number of genes switched on in a 16-cell embryo?

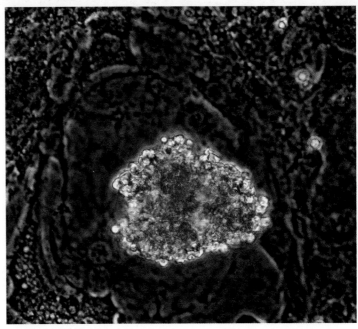

FIGURE 3: A light micrograph of a red blood cell developing from a cultured stem cell. This is a technique being developed to produce red blood cells from human stem cells. Stem cells are cells that have the potential to develop into any type of specialised cell.

Stem cell therapy

Currently, if a brain cell or nerve cell dies, there is a very rare possibility of it being replaced by another normally functioning cell. With a few exceptions such as liver and skin cells, the human body cannot replace cells that have become damaged or died. Stem cells have given scientists the key to developing brain and nervous tissue to replace damaged or diseased tissue. This may further develop into the potential to grow whole organs to replace damaged or diseased hearts, lungs, kidneys or any other organs.

Did you know?

Several animals can replace cells damaged in the heart, but humans cannot. Damaged heart cells in humans cause scarring and lead to heart attacks.

 QUESTIONS

5 What are the benefits of stem cell therapy?

6 Why would an organ developed from the patient's own stem cells be better than a transplanted organ from a donor?

FIGURE 4: With stem cell therapy, the need for organs from donors could be eliminated.

Stem cell cloning

We are learning to:
> understand ethical decisions involved when using embryonic stem cells
> understand that it is possible to switch on inactive genes in the nucleus of a body cell to form cells of all tissue types

Who owns your body parts?

The film 'Never Let Me Go' is based on a book about cloned children who have been brought into the world for the sole purpose of providing organs to other normal people. The outer world wants these children because of the benefits of having organs when needed, but they do not want to know about the consequences of allowing this to happen. This raises ethical questions such as who has a right to say whether you should donate an organ or tissue.

FIGURE 1: Who should have the right to donate this baby's organs or tissues?

Stem cells in research

Embryonic stem cells come from embryos at the eight-cell stage. They have the ability to become any type of cell in the body. They are used in research to help scientists develop new cells to replace damaged or diseased cells. Scientists use stem cell research to develop these cells to become whole organs. Using stem cells in such a way to replace injured or diseased organs will help reduce the need for organ transplants from other donors.

Adult stem cells come from bone marrow and umbilical cords of newborns. These cells can also be differentiated to some kinds of cells, but these types of cells are limited. For example, stem cells from the bone marrow can only differentiate to become blood cells. Scientists are developing ways to use these cells to become all types of cells.

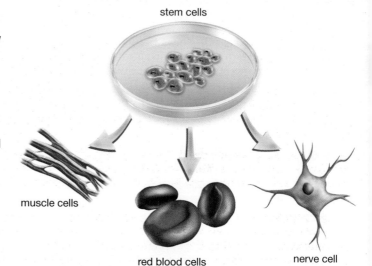

FIGURE 2: Stem cells can grow into muscle, blood and nerve cells, among others.

QUESTIONS

1 Why are embryonic stem cells important for research?

2 Why is it useful to be able to develop whole organs?

Did you know?

Stem cells from umbilical cords are particularly beneficial in treating spinal injuries.

🔍 stem cell research

Ethical issues in stem cell research

There is a huge ethical debate surrounding the use of stem cells in research. Using embryonic stem cells means that the embryo is not able to develop into a fetus. Many people, including scientists, treat this as a destruction of life and raise moral questions about whether this is right.

To replace the use of embryonic stem cells that specialise into specific cells, scientists have developed a procedure called **therapeutic cloning** in which they remove a nucleus from an egg cell and replace it with a nucleus from a body cell. This has the advantage that the cells produced will have identical genes. For example, new brain cells can be developed by using the nucleus of the patient's normal brain cells.

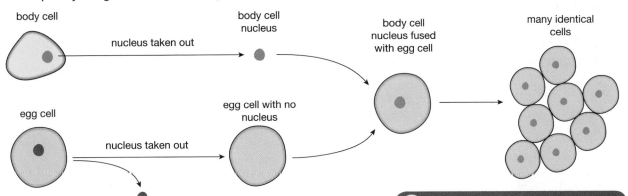

FIGURE 3: How therapeutic cloning works.

However, there are some ethical issues raised by therapeutic cloning too. Not all countries allow their scientists to use this procedure. The UK is one of a handful of countries in Europe that has been allowed use of therapeutic cloning techniques to develop stem cell research by the European Union. One of the biggest ethical issues is about who donates the eggs for this procedure.

QUESTIONS

3 What are the arguments for and against use of embryonic stem cells?

4 Why are scientists interested in developing therapeutic cloning?

Reactivating inactive genes in cloned cells (Higher tier only)

Once a cell differentiates, only those genes needed by that particular cell remain active, the other genes become inactive. For a differentiated cell to revert back to stem cell, the genes that become inactive have to be reactivated again. Under normal conditions, specialised cells cannot become stem cells again.

In 2006, Japanese scientists managed to transform cloned mouse skin cells to look and behave like embryonic stem cells. In other words, they were able to take a cell that had differentiated back to its original state as a stem cell. This stem cell had the potential to differentiate again and become any kind of cell.

Armed with this ability, scientists are now exploring new ways to use these stem cells. However, there are ethical considerations involved too, as these cells have the potential to develop into a human embryo, producing a clone of the donor. Many nations are already prepared for this by having legislation in place that bans human cloning.

Watch out!

There are different types of cloning. Although there are some common features, each has its own scientific basis and it own particular ethical issues.

QUESTIONS

5 How can a differentiated cell become a stem cell?

6 Why is the ability to make specialised cells behave like embryonic stem cells so important?

🔍 therapeutic cloning   gene activation

B5 Checklist

To achieve your forecast grade in the exam you'll need to revise

Use this checklist to see what you can do now. Refer back to pages 40–63 if you're not sure. Look across the rows to see how you could progress – *bold italic* means Higher tier only.

Remember you'll need to be able to use these ideas in many ways:
> interpreting pictures, diagrams and graphs
> applying ideas to new situations
> explaining ethical implications
> suggesting some benefits and risks to society
> drawing conclusions from evidence you've been given.

Look at pages 300–306 for information about how you'll be assessed.

To aim for a grade E	To aim for a grade C	To aim for a grade A
recall that a fertilised egg cell (zygote) divides by mitosis to form an embryo; recall that up to the eight-cell stage the cells of an embryo are unspecialised and identical (embryonic stem cells)		
understand that after the eight-cell stage most embryo cells become specialised and form different types of tissue; understand that that some cells (adult stem cells) remain unspecialised	understand that adult stem cells can become specialised at a later stage to become many, but not all, types of cell required by the organism; explain the characteristics of specialised and unspecialised cells	
understand that in plants only cells in special regions can divide	understand that the new cells produced from plant meristems are unspecialised and can develop into any kind of plant cell	
understand that the growth and development of plants is affected by the environment, for example in phototropism; recall that phototropism increases the plant's chance of survival	explain how phototropism increases the plant's chance of survival; *explain phototropism in terms of the effect of light on the distribution of auxin in a shoot tip*	
describe the main processes of the cell cycle; explain the characteristics of parent and daughter cells; understand why, in meiosis, it is important that the cells produced only contain half the chromosome number of the parent cell		

To aim for a grade E	To aim for a grade C	To aim for a grade A
describe the structure of DNA; recall that genes code for the production of proteins	understand that the order of bases in a gene is the genetic code for the production of a particular protein	*explain how the order of bases in a gene is the code for building up amino acids in the correct order to make a particular protein*
understand that the genetic code is in the cell nucleus of animal and plant cells, but proteins are produced in the cell cytoplasm	understand that genes do not leave the nucleus, but a copy of the gene (messenger RNA) is produced to carry the genetic code to the cytoplasm	explain how messenger RNA is used to carry the genetic code to the cytoplasm
understand that adult stem cells and embryonic stem cells have the potential to produce cells needed to replace damaged tissues		*understand that in carefully controlled conditions of mammalian cloning it is possible to reactivate inactive genes in the nucleus of a body cell*
understand that although all body cells in an organism contain the same genes, many genes in a particular cell are not active (are switched off) because the cell produces only the specific proteins it needs		understand that in specialised cells only the genes needed for the cell can be switched on, whereas in embryonic stem cells any gene can be switched on during development to produce any type of specialised cell

Exam-style questions

Foundation level

AO1 1 Copy and complete the sentences about DNA:

DNA is made from _____ different bases. The strands of DNA are held together by the bases to form a _____ helix. [2]

[Total 2]

AO2 2 Which part of the bean seedling below, A, B or C, does *not* contain a meristem?

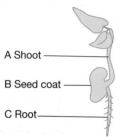

A Shoot

B Seed coat

C Root [1]

[Total 1]

Foundation/Higher level

AO2 3 a A zygote grows to form an embryo. Scientists can take individual cells from an embryo and make identical copies of the embryo. This is not successful after a certain stage of embryo development. Why is this? [1]

AO2 b An embryo grows into a female cow. Every cell in the cow contains the same genes. Only some of the cells in the cow produce milk. Explain, using ideas about genes and protein production, why this is so. [2]

AO1 c Say whether each statement is true or false.
A All animal cells remain unspecialised in the adult.
B All plant cells become specialised in the fully grown plant.
C Nuclei from plant and animal cells can be used to form clones.
D Many cells in plants and animals have some inactive genes. [2]

[Total 5]

AO1 4 Describe what happens to cells when growth and development occurs in an organism. [4]

[Total 4]

AO2 5 During pregnancy, an umbilical cord and a placenta join the embryo to the mother. At birth the umbilical cord is cut. Stem cells can be obtained from the umbilical cord. Many people think that the stem cells for treating human conditions should be obtained from umbilical cords rather than human embryos. Suggest one reason why they might think this. [1]

[Total 1]

Higher level

6 Genes in a nucleus have a unique sequence of the bases A, T, C and G. The bases operate in triplets, with each triplet coding for an amino acid. The order of the amino acids determines which protein is produced. This means that genes code for the production of proteins. The diagrams show how this works.

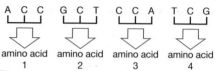

AO2 a What would be the order of amino acids in a protein if the sequence of bases in a DNA molecule was as shown in the diagram below? (The direction of reading is from left to right.) The first amino acid has been done for you. [2]

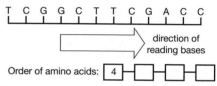

AO2 b Write down the amino acid order if the bases of the original DNA molecule were read in the opposite direction (from right to left). [2]

AO2 c Mutations can occur in the genetic code. For example, a mutation could cause another base G to be inserted into the original DNA molecule between bases G and G, as shown in the diagram below.

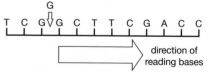

How many of the amino acids will *not* be affected by this mutation? [1]

[Total 5]

AO3 7 Four people try to explain the link between meiosis and fertilisation.

Jo: 'Fertilisation causes the zygote to have the full chromosome number.'

Lee: 'Fertilisation avoids the chromosomes mixing together inside the zygote nucleus.'

Ray: 'Meiosis produces gametes with 23 chromosomes each.'

Sue: 'Since the number of chromosomes in gametes is halved, twice as many gametes can be produced.'

Which two people's ideas, when put together, give the best explanation of the link between meiosis and fertilisation? Give justifications for your responses. [4]

[Total 4]

AO1 recall the science   AO2 apply your knowledge   AO3 evaluate and analyse the evidence

✳ Worked example

AO1 **1** What is phototropism and why is it important for plants? [3]

The bending of a plant towards light is called phototropism.
Plants need light for photosynthesis and can make more food
if they bend towards light. ✔

AO3 **2** Some friends were discussing what happens when cells become specialised. Here's what they thought:

1

'All genes are switched on and become active.'

2

'Some genes are lost from cells as they become specialised.'

3

'Some genes are added so that cells become specialised.'

4

'Some of the inactive genes are activated.'

5

'Some of the active genes are switched off.'

Which two statements are correct? Give justifications for your responses. [4]

Statements 4 and 5. ✔

How to raise your grade

Take note of the comments from examiners – these will help you to improve your grade.

A plant 'bending' towards the light is an inadequate explanation; there should be a reference to growth. 'The plant grows towards light' is a better response that would have gained a mark.

The statement that plants need light for photosynthesis is correct and one mark is gained for this. However 'making food' is the same marking point as 'carrying out photosynthesis' and so this does not gain an extra mark.

The third mark would be gained by stating that plants that grow towards light have a competitive advantage over plants that don't grow towards light and, therefore, their chances of survival increase.

The answers are correct but gain only 1 mark because no justifications are given. A possible response to get full marks would be:

When a cell is specialised, only the genes necessary for the cell to carry out its job are switched on. The other genes are switched off.

Statement 1 is not correct because the cell would not work if all genes were active.

Statements 2 and 3 are not correct because genes cannot leave or be added to the cell.

B6 Brain and mind

What you should already know...

Organ systems are made out of organs, tissues and cells working together

Cells can specialise for different functions. Many cells with similar structures and functions working together are called a tissue.

An organ contains different tissues working together to carry out a particular role, for example the heart pumps blood around the body.

Different organs can work together to form organ systems.

 Give an example of a human organ system and the organs that make it up.

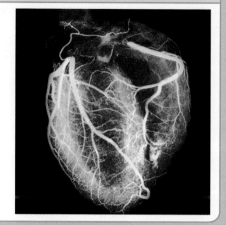

Behaviour is influenced by internal and external factors

Instincts don't need learning. Birds instinctively build nests and some insects hide under stones.

Imprinting happens in newborn birds when they hatch. They fix on the first moving thing they see and then follow it around, assuming it is their mother who will keep them safe.

Conditioning is a learned behaviour involving a response to a stimulus.

Imitation helps animals learn useful behaviour and skills from others.

 Give an example of an instinct and why it is useful.

Behaviour can be investigated and measured

Behaviour can be investigated by observation in laboratories or in the organism's environment.

Animals that migrate can be tagged with tracking devices to study their behaviour and migration patterns.

In the laboratory scientists can control conditions to test ideas about how organisms respond to different environments.

 Why is it helpful to tag whales when trying to study them?

In B6 you will find out about...

> how animals detect changes in the environment

> the different ways animals can respond to the environment

> reflex responses and how they lead to simple behaviours that help survival

> the differences between hormonal and nervous responses

> the structure of the nervous system and neurons

> how different parts of the nervous system link up to form reflex arcs

> how neurons connect with other neurons and cells with synapses

> the structure of the brain and how scientists study the brain

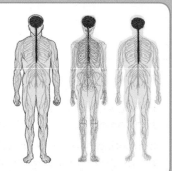

> how reflex responses can be learned through conditioning

> the scientist Pavlov and his investigation into conditioning in dogs

> how conditioned responses can help animals to survive

> how evolution of a larger brain gives humans a better chance of survival

> how the brain changes when we learn new things

> what makes learning easier for our brain

> how our memory works and the models scientists use to explain memory

Sending messages

We are learning to:

> describe the structure of the nervous system

> understand the roles of different kinds of neurons

> describe the differences between the messages sent by neurons and hormones

In what way is electricity like testosterone?

The body uses both electricity and testosterone to send messages. If you pick up something that is too hot, neurons (nerve cells) carry electrical signals to tell you to let go. The body also uses hormones, such as testosterone, to send messages. Hormones can tell you to grow, to store sugar and can even influence whether you like someone or not.

FIGURE 1: For long-term responses the body uses hormones to respond to the environment. Testosterone helps build muscles in response to weight training.

How does the body send messages?

Organisms with many cells need to be able to send messages between cells in parts of their body that are far apart. As **multicellular** organisms evolved, so did their communication systems – the **nervous system** and the hormonal communication system. These two systems carry different types of messages.

The nervous system sends messages using cells called **neurons** and specialised organs called the brain and the spinal cord. Neurons are used for fast responses when a change needs to happen quickly, for example dropping something hot. But neuron messages do not last very long.

The hormonal communication system produces **hormones** for longer-lasting messages. Hormones are chemicals. Their effect is much slower than neurons, but the long-lasting response is useful, for example when a teenager goes through puberty.

> **Watch out!**
>
> 'Neuron' is the scientific word for a single nerve cell. Try to use scientific language in your answers.

QUESTIONS

1 If your body needed to send a response after stepping on a pin, which would be used – neurons or hormones?

2 Body responses can be fast or long-lasting. Give examples of your own of one fast response and one long-lasting response.

Neurons – the fast response

Neurons are special cells that can conduct electricity. Neurons are some of the longest cells in the body, reaching from the bottom of the spine to the soles of the feet. There are different types of neurons:

> **Sensory neurons** connect **receptors** that detect changes in the environment (such as heat or pressure) with the brain and the spinal cord.

> **Motor neurons** connect the brain and the spinal cord to **effector** cells such as muscles, which contract and produce a **response** such as movement.

> **Did you know?**
>
> If all the neurons in a human body were laid out end to end, they would stretch for 100 km.

Q hormones GCSE   neurons GCSE

The whole nervous system can be thought of as two parts. The **central nervous system (CNS)** is made up of the brain and the spinal cord and 'makes decisions' for the rest of the body. The **peripheral nervous system (PNS)** is made up of sensory and motor neurons. The CNS is connected to all parts of the body via the PNS.

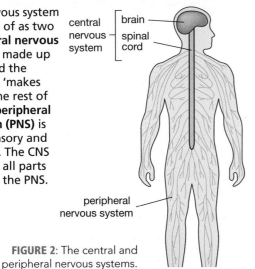

FIGURE 2: The central and peripheral nervous systems.

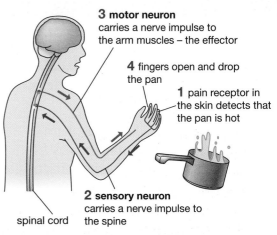

3 motor neuron carries a nerve impulse to the arm muscles – the effector

4 fingers open and drop the pan

1 pain receptor in the skin detects that the pan is hot

2 sensory neuron carries a nerve impulse to the spine

FIGURE 3: How a message travels from receptor to effector.

QUESTIONS

3 Your CNS detects information from sense organs. How many different kinds of senses can your body detect?

4 Explain why the tongue could be considered to be both a receptor and an effector organ.

Hormones – the long-lasting response

Hormones are chemical messengers produced in **glands** all over the body. They travel through the blood to their target cells and have many different roles in the body.

Insulin is a hormone made in the pancreas. It targets the liver and muscles to store sugar as glycogen. If someone's body stops producing insulin, they develop type 1 diabetes. Other important examples of hormones include the sex hormones. Oestrogen is made in the ovaries and testosterone is made in the testes. These hormones cause the changes that occur at puberty and help regulate sperm and egg production.

thyroid gland
This makes a hormone called **thyroxin**. This controls the rate of chemical reactions in the body

adrenal gland
These make **adrenaline**. This gets the body ready for action in the 'fight or flight' response

testes
These make **testosterone**. This controls the development of male characteristics in puberty

pituitary gland
This is sometimes called the master gland because it makes hormones that control other endocrine glands. It also makes **growth hormone**

pancreas
This makes hormones called **insulin** and **glucagon**. These control the amount of sugar in the body

ovaries
These make the female hormones called **oestrogen** and **progesterone**. These cause the development of female characteristics during puberty and control the menstrual cycle

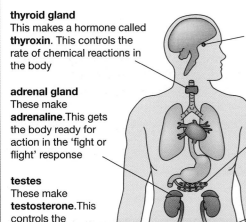

FIGURE 4: The glands of the hormone messaging system.

QUESTIONS

5 Three hormones are mentioned in the paragraph above. Other hormones are mentioned in Figure 4. Choose one of these, state where it is made, and find out more about what it does.

6 Adrenalin is sometimes called the 'fight or flight' hormone. Some evidence suggests that excess adrenaline can lead to anxiety. When is adrenaline helpful and when is it unhelpful?

Q nervous system GCSE   endocrine system GCSE

The structure of a neuron

Our neurons conduct electricity, so why don't we get electric shocks?

Neurons are covered with a layer of fat, which acts like an insulator. It protects the surrounding cells from the electricity and makes sure the signal travels in the right direction.

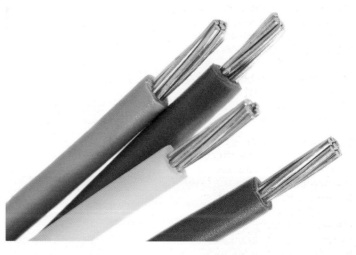

FIGURE 1: Neurons are a bit like wires – both have insulation and can conduct electricity.

Structure of a neuron

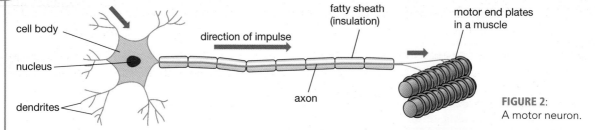

cell body

nucleus

dendrites

direction of impulse

fatty sheath (insulation)

motor end plates in a muscle

axon

FIGURE 2: A motor neuron.

Neurons are highly **specialised** cells and look very different from other types of cells. They have three main parts:

> the **cell body** – this contains the cell's nucleus, which controls what is going on in the cell, and **dendrites**, which detect changes in the environment called **stimuli** that start the electrical signal in the cell

> the **axon** – a long extension of the cell that carries the electrical signal or **impulse**. It is surrounded by a fatty insulating sheath (cover)

> motor end plates – these connect to another cell, which could be another neuron or another cell that produces a response, called an **effector**. Effectors can be muscle cells, which cause movement responses, or **glands**, which release chemicals made by the body, for example saliva in the mouth.

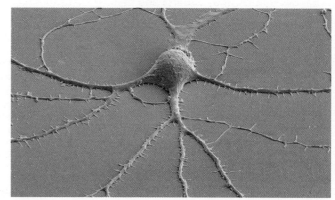

FIGURE 3: This photo of a neuron, taken using a scanning electron microscope, shows the cell body and dendrites.

QUESTIONS

1 What are the similarities and differences between a wire and a neuron?

2 Why does the cell body need so many dendrites branching from it?

Q neurons GCSE   axon nerve cell

The axon

Even though it looks as if it is made from different sections, the whole of a neuron is *one* cell with *one* cell membrane. The axon is made of an extension of the membrane, which forms a long thin tube filled with **cytoplasm**. The axon of some neurons has to be long enough to reach from the bottom of the spine to the soles of the feet, which makes neurons the longest cells in the body.

The role of the axon is to send electrical impulses to effectors or to the central nervous system. Surrounding the axon is a fatty sheath made of **myelin**. The myelin sheath has two roles: it makes the impulse travel much faster, and it acts as an insulator, protecting surrounding cells from the electrical impulse.

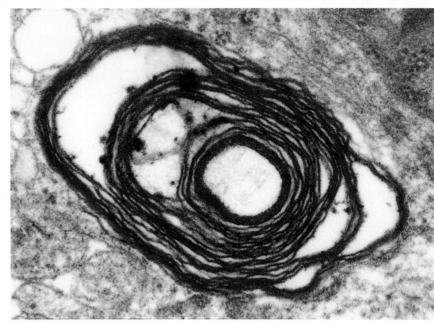

FIGURE 4: The fatty sheath (red) wraps around the axon (centre) and acts as an insulator.

Did you know?

Giant squid have some of the largest axons, which can be up to 1 mm in diameter. Scientists find them useful for studying the electrical impulses that travel through the axon.

QUESTIONS

3 Why is fat a good material for the sheath of the axon?

4 Multiple sclerosis is a disease in which the fatty sheath is damaged. Research some symptoms associated with this disease.

Functions of neurons

A bunch of neurons can be grouped into a **nerve**. Nerves can be easily seen by the eye and are white and stringy, whereas as individual neurons can only be seen using a microscope. You can think of a nerve as being like a thick rope made of lots of lengths of string (neurons). Rope is much stronger than string, and the same is true for nerves and neurons.

Neurons have to transmit impulses rapidly so the body can respond to stimuli as quickly as possible. The speed of the impulse is affected by three factors:

> Temperature – the higher the temperature, the faster the impulse. In general, warm-blooded animals can respond to a stimulus more quickly than cold-blooded animals.

> Axon diameter – the larger the axon diameter, the faster the impulse. Some animals that live in cold conditions, such as the squid, have evolved very thick axons to speed up their responses.

> Fatty myelin sheath – neurons with a fatty sheath can transmit impulses up to 100 m/s whereas neurons without a fatty sheath can only manage 1 m/s.

QUESTIONS

5 Which types of animals would you expect to have the fastest nerve impulses, and which the slowest?

6 Why is it an adaptation to group neurons together to form a nerve?

multiple sclerosis

Synapses

We are learning to:
> locate where synapses are found
> explain the function of synapses

How do nerve impulses jump across gaps?

Neurons do not connect directly to other neurons – there is always a small gap. Outside the body, electricity can jump across gaps by sparking, but this does not happen inside the body. To transmit a signal across a gap, neurons change the signal from an electrical one to a chemical signal.

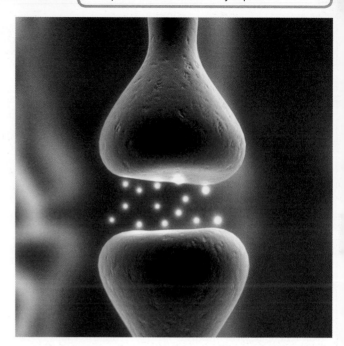

FIGURE 1: Chemicals transmit messages across the gap.

 ## What is a synapse?

Neurons send information around the body, passing on their messages to specific cells. Some neurons (motor neurons) send messages to effector cells in muscles or glands, which do not conduct electricity. Some neurons send messages to other neurons, but the electrical impulse cannot jump across the gap between adjacent neurons. To transmit the message from one cell to the next, the electrical impulse of the neuron is changed briefly into a chemical signal.

Synapses are the special junctions (joining points) between a neuron and another cell where electrical impulses are changed into chemical signals. Synapses are specialised structures and messages can only travel across them in one direction.

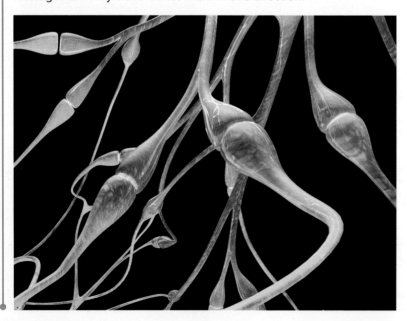

FIGURE 2: The many possible synapses between two neurons (one red, one blue).

QUESTIONS

1 Why does the message at a synapse need to change from electrical to chemical?

2 Why do we need synapses?

Q synapse GCSE

Where do we find synapses?

Synapses are found at junctions between a neuron and the cell next to it. Sometimes one neuron will have many synapses connecting it to many other cells. This allows different neurons to share information, and means that neurons in the central nervous system can collect information from different types of stimuli. For example, in deciding whether food is good to eat, neurons in the brain can get information from taste and smell receptors, as well as from the receptors in the eyes. Synapses are very important in the brain, where the connections between neurons help us to learn and remember.

Did you know?

A typical neuron can link to between 1000 and 10000 other cells via synapses.

QUESTIONS

3 Which types of neurons will have the most synapses?

4 Why do neurons need to connect to more than one cell?

What do synapses do? (Higher tier only)

The message carried by a neuron is passed across a synapse by chemicals called **transmitter substances** that are released when the impulse reaches the end of the neuron. The transmitter substances diffuse across the gap and bind to **receptor molecules** on the membrane of the next cell. These initiate an impulse in the next cell. If this cell is another neuron, the new impulse will also be electrical. If it is a muscle cell, the impulse will be chemical and may initiate contraction of the muscle.

The chemical transmitters are specific to where the synapse is, for example serotonin is a chemical transmitter substance that is found in the brain.

QUESTIONS

5 Make a flow chart showing the passage of a neuron impulse to a muscle cell.

6 Many drugs and poisons act on synapses. Cocaine works by stopping dopamine, a transmitter substance, from being released from the receptor molecules on the synapse. Find two more drugs or poisons that act on synapses.

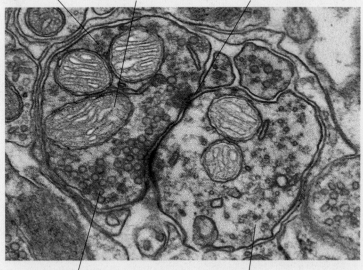

mitochondria – these make the energy needed to release and re-absorb the chemical transmitter substance

neuron sending the electrical signal

gap between the two cells where the chemical transmitter substance has been released

vesicles storing chemical transmitter substances

cell that the signal is going to

FIGURE 4: Electron micrograph of a synapse. The blue circles are vesicles that store chemical transmitters. Some of the transmitter substance has been released into the synapse gap.

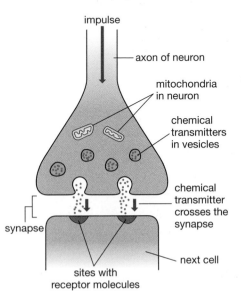

impulse

axon of neuron

mitochondria in neuron

chemical transmitters in vesicles

chemical transmitter crosses the synapse

synapse

next cell

sites with receptor molecules

FIGURE 3: How a nerve impulse passes across the synapse to the next cell.

Linking nerves together

We are learning to:
> describe how the nervous system responds to the environment
> understand the connection between stimuli and receptors
> understand the connection between effectors and responses

Why do we get goose bumps when we're scared?

Goose bumps are an evolutionary response to fear from when humans had much more hair. If the effector muscles surrounding the hair contract, the hair stands on end. This make us look bigger and scarier to the threat that scared us.

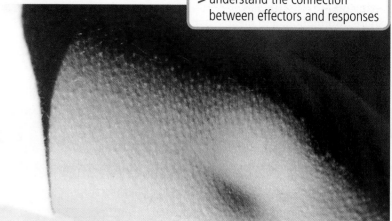

FIGURE 1

Stimuli and receptors

The nervous system responds to changes in the environment called stimuli. Many different kinds of change can be detected, including temperature, pressure, light and sound. The stimuli are detected by special cells called **receptors**.

For each kind of stimulus there is a specific type of receptor, such as light receptors and temperature receptors. Sometimes the receptors are part of complex organs whose major role is to detect stimuli, for example:

> eyes detect changes in light using light receptors in the retina

> ears detect changes in sound using sound receptors in the eardrum.

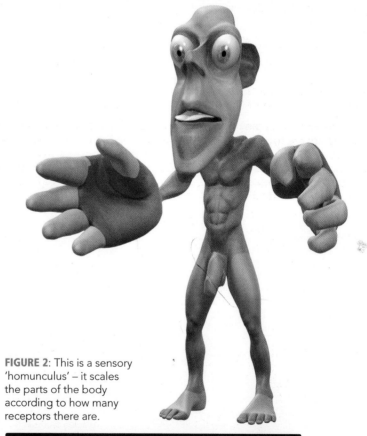

FIGURE 2: This is a sensory 'homunculus' – it scales the parts of the body according to how many receptors there are.

QUESTIONS

1 We commonly talk about having five senses: sight, smell, sound, taste and touch. What other stimuli can our bodies detect?

2 The skin can detect many kinds of stimuli. List as many different kinds of receptors as you can that the skin might have.

Did you know?

Butterflies have taste receptors on their feet.

Q types of receptors

Effectors and responses

Once the central nervous system has made a decision about what to do about a specific stimulus, a response must be made. Responses are co-ordinated by effectors. The most common effectors are muscles and glands.

Glands make essential chemicals such as enzymes and hormones. Responses often control the release of these chemicals, for example the hormone insulin only needs to be released after we eat sugar.

Muscles are used for movement and muscle contraction can help the body to move away from dangerous stimuli. They also make the heart beat and ensure food passes though the digestive system. Tiny muscles are needed for the eyes to work. Like receptors, effectors can also be part of complex organs, for example muscle cells are part of complex organs like the heart.

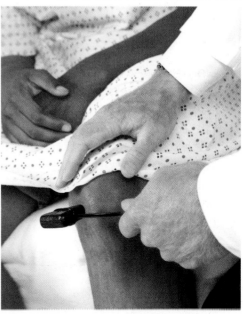

FIGURE 3: A doctor checking the 'knee jerk' response. The muscles around the knee contract and the leg straightens.

QUESTIONS

3 What responses would you have to a sudden loud noise? Which effectors would be needed for the response?

4 The heart can act as an effector, when would it be useful for the heart to beat faster?

Nervous co-ordination

Relay neurons in the central nervous system connect sensory neurons to motor neurons and so co-ordinate the body's responses to stimuli. **Involuntary** responses are called **reflexes**.

An example of a simple reflex might be a pupil contracting in response to light shining in the eye. The light is the stimulus. Light receptors in the retina detect the change in light and send an impulse to the central nervous system using sensory neurons. The relay neurons in the central nervous system make a decision to make the pupil smaller and send an impulse to the effector muscles around the iris. The response is for the iris to contract, which makes the pupil smaller so that it lets less light into the eye.

| Stimulus bright light | Receptor light receptors in the retina | Sensory neurons | Brain | Motor neurons | Effectors circular and radial muscles in the iris | Response pupil contracts |

FIGURE 4: An example of a reflex pathway.

FIGURE 5: This shows the 'pupillary response' to bright light. Use a ruler to see how much smaller the pupil is in bright light.

QUESTIONS

5 Make a flow chart similar to Figure 4, explaining the reflex that makes people cough when they get food stuck in their throat.

6 As people get older the small hairs in the ears that detect sound waves become more brittle and can break. What effect would this have on someone's hearing?

The reflex arc

We are learning to:
> describe the parts of a reflex arc
> give examples of reflex arcs
> understand why reflex arcs need to be automatic

Why do we jump when a fly lands on us?

We detect the movement of the fly on our skin using touch receptors, which sends a message to the central nervous system. The response is to contract the muscles in our skin that are near to the fly, which knocks the fly off our skin.

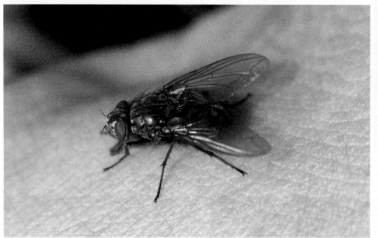

FIGURE 1: When a fly lands on someone, reflex arcs co-ordinate the 'jump' response.

What is a reflex arc?

A reflex is a simple response to a stimulus. The journey of the impulse from receptor to effector is called a **reflex arc**. A spinal reflex arc has a fixed pathway:

1   A change in the environment, called a stimulus, is detected by special cells called receptors.

2   Receptors start an electrical impulse in sensory neurons.

3   The impulse travels through the sensory neurons into the spinal cord.

4   Relay neurons in the spinal cord co-ordinate a response to the stimulus and send another electrical impulse to motor neurons.

5   Motor neurons carry the message to effectors (muscles and glands).

6   The response to the original stimulus occurs. This is either a muscle contraction or a release of chemicals from glands.

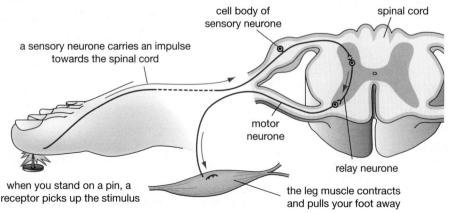

a sensory neurone carries an impulse towards the spinal cord

cell body of sensory neurone

spinal cord

motor neurone

when you stand on a pin, a receptor picks up the stimulus

relay neurone

the leg muscle contracts and pulls your foot away

FIGURE 2: The parts of the nervous system involved in a reflex arc.

Q reflexes GCSE   reflex arc GCSE

An example of a reflex is putting your hand over a flame. The change in temperature is the stimulus, detected by temperature receptors in your skin. The response is to move your hand away. The effectors are the muscles in your arms.

QUESTIONS

1 When you step on a pin, what is the receptor and what is the effector in the reflex arc?

2 List all the parts of the reflex arc that are involved in sneezing.

When do we use reflex arcs?

Simple reflexes are automatic, require no learning and happen from birth. We use reflex arcs to respond quickly to stimuli that could harm us. Simple reflexes include choking when we have food stuck in our throat, blinking when something comes towards our eyes, and sneezing when we have something stuck in our nose.

Did you know?

The world record for the fastest sneeze is over 50 m/s.

QUESTIONS

3 Most reflex responses are co-ordinated by the relay neurons in the spinal cord. When would the reflex arc use the relay neurons in the brain?

4 Why is it important for some responses like choking to be unlearned reflexes instead of learned behaviour?

When do we override reflex arcs? (Higher tier only)

Reflex arcs are made of fixed pathways. Responses are rapid and automatic because the central nervous system does not need to process the information. If the stimulus comes from below the neck, the impulse bypasses the brain completely and the spinal cord co-ordinates the response. This makes the response much faster.

However, sometimes it is important for the brain to be able to override reflex arcs. One important reflex response is breathing when we need oxygen. Breathing has to happen when we are asleep, and so must be an unconscious reflex response. However, if we are underwater it is essential that we do not breathe in, as we would fill our lungs with water and drown. In this situation the brain overrides the reflex response by modifying the response to the motor neuron so it stops our muscles from contracting and breathing in. Overriding reflex arcs can be just as important to survival as the original reflexes.

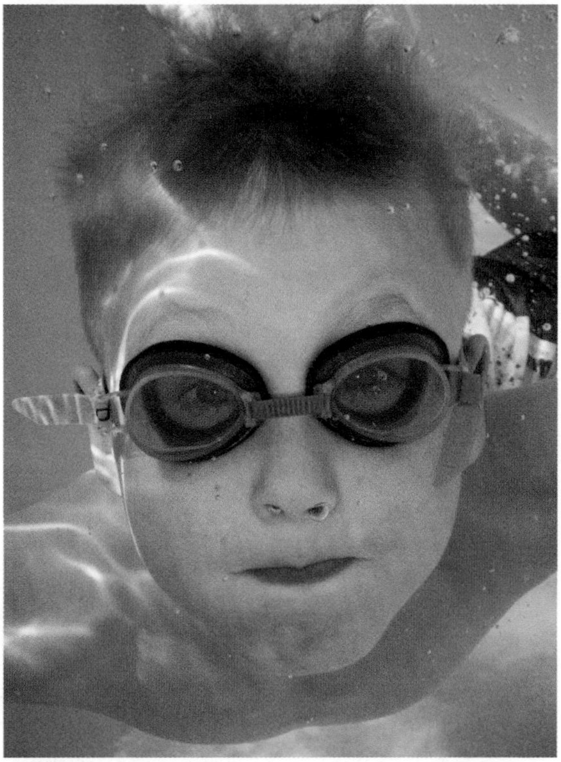

QUESTIONS

5 Another reflex arc we can override is holding onto something hot. Why is this useful?

6 Training can help people to override some reflex responses. If you wanted to stop the blinking reflex when something came close to your eye, how could you do it?

FIGURE 3: This boy is holding his breath, overriding his reflex response to breathe.

Reflexes and behaviour

Why do hedgehogs curl up into a ball?

Curling up into a ball is a defence behaviour. It is a reflex response by the hedgehog to dangers such as other animals.

FIGURE 1

Simple behaviour

All animals have certain **behaviour** that helps them to survive changes in their environment. Behaviour can be **learned** or **instinctive**. Instinctive behaviour comes from reflex responses. Reflex responses don't need to be learned and help all animals to survive.

For example, if you lift up a rock, any woodlice hiding underneath it will move away from the light to another dark place. This is the woodlouse's reflex response to light. The behaviour of the woodlouse helps it to survive. By moving to a dark place, woodlice stay hidden from predators and are less likely to dry out.

All animals have instinctive behaviours controlled by reflex responses, for example all animals will move away from fire. However, simple animals have a simple nervous system, which means that they cannot learn behaviours. These animals need reflex responses to survive changes in their environments.

FIGURE 2: Woodlice can be used to show how reflex responses lead to behaviour. How could you design an experiment to show this?

QUESTIONS

1 Woodlice like to live in dark, damp places and have a reflex response to light. Can you describe the responses woodlice might have to other stimuli?

2 Why is it useful for some responses to be instinctive?

instinctive animal behaviour

Aiding survival

Most reflex responses have evolved to aid survival, for example searching for food and escaping from predators. Simple behaviours such as hiding or running away from larger animals are simple reflexes, but they lead to more complex behaviour such as an animal being able to escape from predators.

To help them find food, animals are born liking sweet tastes and disliking bitter tastes. Human tongues can detect sugar at 1 in 200 molecules, and bitter tastes at 1 in 2 000 000 molecules, which means we are much more likely to identify bitter tastes than sweet tastes.

FIGURE 3: A toad hides itself from predators by burying under the soil.

QUESTIONS

3 What other reflex responses allow animals to find food?

4 Why is it more important for survival to detect bitter tastes than sweet tastes?

Human reflexes

Even though we are complex animals, humans also have involuntary responses that lead to behaviour. Adult reflexes include dropping hot objects and the contraction of the pupil of the eye in bright light. Doctors can check reflexes by tapping the lower leg just beneath the kneecap (see page 77), which will make the knee jerk upwards. This shows that the nerves and muscles are working correctly. These responses, and others such as blinking when objects come close to our eyes and breathing, remain with us for life. Other responses only occur in newborn babies.

Newborn babies have a number of reflexes that help them to survive when they are very young, but stop working as they get older. Important newborn reflexes are grasping, stepping and suckling. Newborn babies will grasp anything that touches the palm of their hand. This has evolved to help them to cling onto their parents when they are being carried. The suckling response is also a reflex. Babies will suck anything that is placed near their mouth, which helps babies to breastfeed or feed from a bottle. The suckling reflex stops working when babies are around 2 months old and is replaced by voluntary suckling. Another reflex, which is not fully understood, is the stepping reflex. When babies are placed with the soles of their feet on a flat surface their legs move up and down in a 'stepping' motion. This could help babies practise movements for when they begin to walk.

FIGURE 4: Our eyelids will close involuntarily when an object is placed near them.

FIGURE 5: Very young babies will grasp anything that touches their palm.

Did you know?

Under the age of 4–6 months babies will hold their breath and move their arms and legs if their faces are put into water. This gives a carer more time to rescue them if they are at risk from drowning.

QUESTIONS

5 If a patient is unconscious doctors use light, sound and pain reflexes to test for levels of consciousness. Which of those reflexes – light, sound and pain – would be the first to come back to an unconscious patient? Explain your answer.

6 Why do you think newborn reflexes stop as a baby grows older?

🔍 newborn reflex

Preparing for assessment: Planning and collecting

To achieve a good grade in science you will be able to use your skills and understanding to understand how scientists plan, run and evaluate investigations. These skills will be assessed in your exams and in Controlled Assessments. This activity supports you in developing the skills of formulating a hypothesis and making decisions about data collection.

✳ Pumped up : measuring reaction times

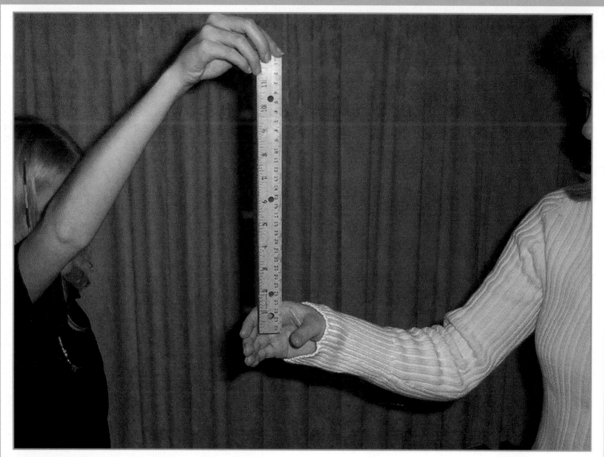

We can measure reaction times using the ruler test.

It is important for scientists to understand the factors that affect people's reaction times. This could be vital, for example, when judging the time it takes for people to respond to danger such as a traffic accident on motorways.

Sadim ran a test by asking some of the people in his class to catch a ruler as it was dropped. He then gathered data about reaction times. Once data was collected for an individual he could then see whether certain factors affected their reaction times. One investigation he wanted to try was to investigate the effect on reaction times of stimulants such as energy drinks containing caffeine.

Task 1

> Make a list of variables that might affect people's reaction times.

> For each variable suggest whether you could control it and, if so, how.

 Task 2

> Make a prediction about what you think will happen to people's reaction times if they drink a stimulant such as 'Red Bull' energy drink.

> Write a hypothesis by explaining the prediction using scientific ideas.

 Task 3

> How should Salim select people to take part in the investigation?

> How many repeats should he do of each reaction time?

> How many people does he need to make sure the results are representative?

> How can he control the other variables to make sure the investigation is fair?

> Suggest how preliminary data would indicate to Salim the number of measurements that need to be collected.

 Task 4

> What calculations could he do with the data to compare reaction times before and after the stimulant?

> How could he judge the reliability of the data by looking at the outliers?

Maximise your grade

Use these suggestions to improve your work and be more successful.

E

To be on target for grade E you need to:

> Be able to produce a testable prediction.

> Decide how much data needs to be collected.

C

To be on target for grades D, C, in addition, you need to:

> Be able to justify a prediction.

> Suggest how data should be collected in order to be reliable.

> Suggest how outliers can be used.

A

To be on target for grades B, A, in addition, you need to:

> Use specialist scientific vocabulary in a prediction.

> Suggest how preliminary data can indicate the number of measurements that need to be collected.

Conditioning

We are learning to:
> describe what conditioning is
> explain some examples of conditioning
> understand some of the ethical implications of scientific research into conditioning

How do you make a child scared of Santa Claus?

A response to a stimulus can be altered by conditioning. If someone is shown a non-scary 'secondary stimulus', such as Santa Claus, together with a scary primary stimulus, such as a loud noise, eventually the secondary stimulus on its own is enough to make the person scared. This was done on a little boy called Albert in 1920.

FIGURE 1

What is conditioning?

The scientist John B. Watson wanted to test whether humans could learn to associate two previously unlinked stimuli. He designed an experiment where he showed an 8-month-old boy named Albert a white rat, which Albert liked and tried to touch. He then showed Albert the rat again, but at the same time crept up behind him and made a loud noise. The noise made Albert jump and start to cry.

Watson repeated this several times, always making the loud noise when Albert was looking at the rat. He then showed Albert the rat without the noise. Albert showed signs of distress, even though there was no loud noise – Albert had been **conditioned** to associate two unlinked stimuli together. Later Albert began to show signs of fear when he was shown any white furry object, including a fur coat and a Santa Claus mask with a white beard.

A conditioned response is a **learned response**. It occurs when animals link a response to two or more stimuli that are not connected. In the case of Little Albert:

> the loud noise was the primary stimulus – there should be a reflex response to it, because it might be a sign of something harmful

> the white rat was the secondary stimulus – it should not have a reflex response associated with it.

Baby Albert liked the white rat	→	Albert heard a sudden loud noise every time he saw the rat

Albert became scared of the rat and of anything white and furry

FIGURE 2: How Albert became conditioned.

QUESTIONS

1 Explain why Albert was scared of fur coats.

2 Do you think an experiment like this would be done today? Suggest some ethical issues.

Pavlov and his dogs

Ivan Pavlov was the first scientist to carry out experiments into conditioning. He won a Nobel Prize for his research in 1904. He worked with dogs and measured the amount they salivated (produced saliva). He noticed that dogs began to salivate before they were given food. He started to ring a bell (secondary stimulus) every time they were given food (primary stimulus). After a while the dogs salivated when he rang the bell, even if they were not given food. The stimulus of the bell sound, normally unconnected to feeding, had become linked to the stimuli of the smell and taste of food – a conditioned reflex had been formed.

conditioning   Pavlov   Little Albert

FIGURE 3: A preserved dog from the Pavlov Museum showing how Pavlov collected saliva.

Conditioning and survival (Higher tier only)

Conditioned responses are like reflex responses, as they have evolved to help us to survive. A conditioned response is often called a **conditioned reflex**. Sometimes it is useful for two stimuli that are unrelated in time to be linked by the same response. An example of this is when we eat something and later we are sick. Even though the response occurs much later than the original stimulus, our brain links the food we ate earlier to the sickness we feel later and we are less likely to eat the same thing again.

Animals have also evolved conditioned reflexes that help survival. Many poisonous animals and plants are bright red or yellow (a secondary stimulus). If an animal eats a poisonous animal or plant (primary stimulus) it will later be sick (final response). Animals quickly learn the conditioned response that links brightly coloured animals and plants with feeling sick. In the conditioned reflex behaviour, the learned behaviour of avoiding brightly coloured food does not have a direct link to the final response of being sick (see Figure 5). This is advantageous for brightly coloured plants and animals that are not poisonous, as some animals will avoid eating them.

FIGURE 4: A poisonous frog.

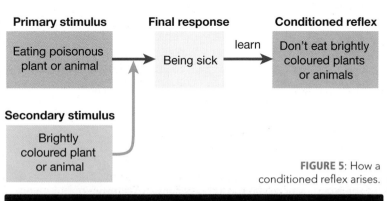

Primary stimulus

Eating poisonous plant or animal

Final response

Being sick

learn

Conditioned reflex

Don't eat brightly coloured plants or animals

Secondary stimulus

Brightly coloured plant or animal

FIGURE 5: How a conditioned reflex arises.

Did you know?

The secondary stimulus does not give rise to a conditioned response until it has been linked in our brains to the primary stimulus.

Brain structure

We are learning to:
> describe some parts of the brain
> understand how scientists discover what different parts of the brain do
> understand why we have evolved a bigger brain

Do we really use only 10% of our brain?

It is a popular myth that we only use 10% of our brains and that geniuses like Albert Einstein used more. In reality we use all of our brain, and most of the brain is active all the time. However, when we are resting we may only be using 10%.

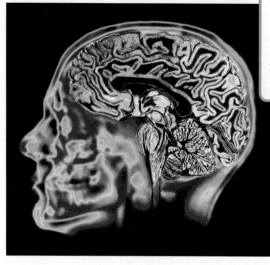

FIGURE 1: An MRI scan showing the brain structure.

The brain's cerebral cortex

The brain is the **co-ordinator** of the body. It is made of billions of neurons all working together to respond to stimuli and to remember our experiences. The **cerebral cortex** is the outer layer of the brain. It is made of a very large sheet of tissue folded to fit into the skull. The folds give the characteristic groove shapes on the outside of the brain.

The cerebral cortex is much bigger in humans than in other animals. This part of the brain is concerned with traits that make us human, such as:

> intelligence – how we think and solve problems

> memory – how we remember experiences

> language – how we communicate verbally and non-verbally

Did you know?

The brain is 3% of the body's weight but uses 20% of the body's energy.

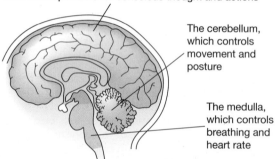

The cerebral cortex (the wrinkled surface layer of the brain), which is responsible for conscious thought and actions

The cerebellum, which controls movement and posture

The medulla, which controls breathing and heart rate

FIGURE 2: The main areas of the human brain.

QUESTIONS

1 Why is the cerebral cortex folded?

2 Why is the cerebral cortex bigger in humans than in chimpanzees?

Studying the brain

Scientists who study the nervous system are called **neuroscientists**. Neuroscientists have discovered how the brain works in two main ways.

The first way is to stimulate various parts of the brain using electrical impulses and look at the responses that are caused. This technique was first used in the 19th century but is now used by neurosurgeons whilst they are performing brain surgery. The technique requires the brain to be exposed by removing part of the skull. Electrodes are then used to stimulate different parts of the brain. When conscious and alert patients have different parts of their brain stimulated they can report memories and sensations and help to map the functions of different parts of the brain.

Q brain structure   cerebral cortex GCSE

A non-invasive way of looking at the brain is to make images with special scanners such as magnetic resonance imaging (MRI) machines. Brain images are useful for two main reasons:

1 We can compare healthy people's brains with brains from people who have diseases like Alzheimer's, or with people who have brain damage.

2 We can look at the activity of different parts of the brain when it is stimulated in different ways, like listening to music and being asked to speak a foreign language.

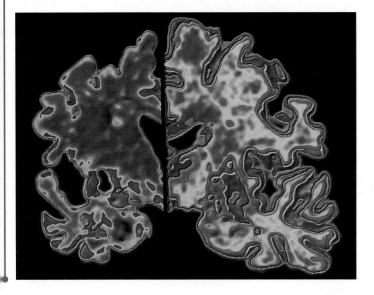

QUESTIONS

3 Why is it better to use imaging techniques to map the brain than to use electrical stimulation?

4 Carry out research to find out what kind of information can be revealed from an MRI scan of the brain.

FIGURE 3: An MRI scan comparing the shrunken brain of someone who has Alzheimer's (left) with a healthy brain (right).

The evolution of the brain

As humans have evolved, our brains have become bigger in comparison to our body size. *Homo erectus* lived 1.7 million years ago. They were a similar size to humans now, but their brains were only half the size of ours.

An important adaptation is not just the size of the brain, but the number of folds in the cerebral cortex. More intelligent mammals, such as dolphins and chimpanzees, have many more folds in their cerebral cortex than the smoother brains of less intelligent mammals, such as mice. As humans evolved our brains have become larger with an increased number of folds in the cerebral cortex. As our brains have developed we have become better at adapting to new situations, which means individuals are more likely to survive.

QUESTIONS

5 The evolution of bigger brains has led to more difficult childbirths. In terms of evolution why is this a price worth paying?

6 Neanderthals lived alongside early *Homo sapiens*. Find out what was interesting about their brain size.

FIGURE 4: Skulls belonging to some ancestors and relatives of modern humans.

Learning

Why does making your brain denser make you cleverer?

As you learn you build new connections between neurons. The more connections you have, the quicker you can adapt to new situations and the cleverer you are.

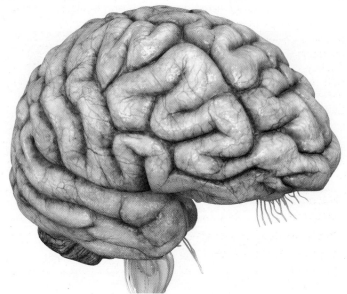

FIGURE 1: New neuron pathways are formed in the brain when we learn new things.

Learning and the brain

The brain is a complex organ made of billions of neurons. The brain is involved in both **instinctive** and **learned** responses. It can *respond* to stimuli using reflexes and it can *learn* from experiences, which allows us to have more complex responses.

Learning happens when certain pathways in the brain become more likely to transmit impulses. Transmitting impulses between neurons forms links between neurons called a **neuron pathway**. The more the same pathway is used, the stronger that pathway becomes. This means that the more times we repeat a task, the better our brain becomes at knowing how to complete the task. The neuron pathway also becomes stronger when there is a strong stimulus associated with it such as colour, light, smell or sound, which is why many babies' toys are in bright colours or make noises.

FIGURE 2: As children play they learn by building new neuron pathways in the brain.

QUESTIONS

1 Why does repeating actions help us learn?

2 Why does mimicking their parents help children to learn?

Q learning by repetition

Learning strategies

To improve at a skill we need to have strong neuron pathways. The best way to do this is to repeat the action, because every repetition strengthens the neuron pathway. This is why we get better at certain skills when we practise. Research shows you need to spend around 10000 hours to completely master a skill like playing the piano or hockey, or becoming fluent in a language. It gets harder to learn new things as we get older, as children and teenagers make new neuron pathways more easily.

FIGURE 3: Aimi Kobayashi was a child prodigy who started playing the piano at three and was giving full concerts with orchestra by the age of seven.

QUESTIONS

3 Think about your experience of learning – what things help you learn faster?

4 Other than age, what other factors might prevent people from learning new skills?

Development and learning (Higher tier only)

With the billions of neurons in our brains, the potential number of neuron pathways is huge. This means we can adapt to new situations and learn how to respond to new stimuli. However, if a child is isolated during development and is not presented with new situations, then that child may not progress in their learning.

Children who have been isolated during development are called 'feral'. Over history there have been many anecdotal instances and some instances that are well documented from the last 50 years. 'Genie' was a feral child discovered in California. She had been kept imprisoned by her parents for the first 13 years of her life. When she was rescued she could not talk, and even with extensive therapy she mostly communicated non-verbally with occasional one-word answers. Incidences like Genie have supported the theory that children can only learn some skills at certain ages, and if they miss learning them it is almost impossible to learn the skills at a later date.

Did you know?

Children who learn two languages before the age of five have a different brain structure from that of children who learn only one language.

QUESTIONS

5 Research another instance of a rescued feral child, for example Alex the 'Dog Boy' or Danielle Crockett. What similarities are there in their behaviour and their ability to communicate? What does this imply about when children learn how to communicate using verbal language?

6 The brain is made of billions of neurons, and there is a vast amount of potential pathways. Is there a limit to the range of new situations we can adapt to, or the amount that we can learn?

Q feral children language   learning by repetition

Memory

We are learning to:
> describe what memory is
> explain how we use models to describe memory
> consider the limitations of memory models

How can you remember a list of words?

How can you make this list of words easy to remember?

| elephant | blue | bucket | Sun | ball of string | three |

The best way to try to remember unlinked objects is to try and link them. You could make a story about a blue elephant holding three buckets tied together with a ball of string standing in the sunshine.

What is memory?

Memory is the storage and retrieval (bringing back, or remembering) of information. It is not enough to store memories – we also need access to them when we need them. There are two types of memory:

> **short-term memory** – this is information from our most recent experiences, which is only stored for a brief period of time

> **long-term memory** – information from our earliest memories onwards is stored for a long period of time.

Remembering information is essential if we want to learn from our experiences. Some things help us to remember information more easily:

> patterns – our brains remember information in patterns more easily than random information, for example123456 is easier to remember than 572943.

> repetition – repetition of information makes the neuron pathways in our brain stronger making it easier to retrieve the information

> strong stimulus – strong colours, bright light, strong smells or loud sounds are all stimuli that can help us to remember information.

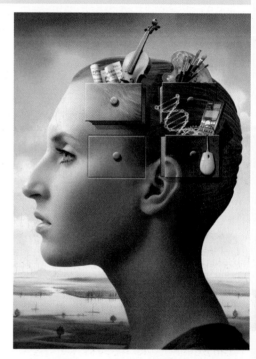

FIGURE 1: Memory is how we store and retrieve our experiences.

Did you know?

In London taxi drivers, the part of the brain that is involved with spatial awareness (the hippocampus) is much larger than average. The hippocampus is largest in drivers who have been on the job longest. This suggests that as taxi drivers memorise more spatial information, their hippocampus continues to grow.

FIGURE 2: Taxi drivers in big cities like London need to remember a huge number of roads and directions.

Q memory GSCE

QUESTIONS

1 Think about a recent memory. Describe how you retrieve the information. Do you remember the information in words or pictures?

2 Why do we need memories?

Using models – why they are useful?

Understanding how memories are made is a complex area of research. Scientists use models to help explain how we remember and retrieve information. One of the most famous models is the **multi-store model**, which was proposed in 1968. The model splits memory into three different type of storage, called **stores**:

> sensory memory – holds information for 1–2 seconds. Each type of sense (taste, sight, smell) has its own store

> short-term memory – this has a *limited* capacity and can only store information for a few seconds

> long-term memory – this has an *unlimited* capacity and information can be stored for a long time.

Information is transferred between the stores by **control processes**. Paying attention to sensations allows information to pass from the sensory memory into the short-term memory. Once in the short-term memory repetition or 'rehearsal' of the information means it can pass into the long-term memory. At each store memories can be lost if not enough attention is paid to the sensation or if it is not rehearsed or retrieved.

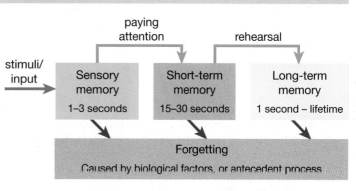

FIGURE 3: The multi-store memory model.

QUESTIONS

3 Compare the three different memory stores. What are their similarities and differences?

4 Why might forgetting some information be an adaptation for survival?

Using models – why they are limited?

Unfortunately, the way our brain stores memories is more complicated than most models can explain. Other models have been proposed since the multi-store model, but none provides an exact explanation as to how memory works. The multi-store model has been criticised for being too linear and not allowing for subdivision of the short-term and long-term memory stores. The model also does not differentiate between the different types of stimulus and how they are stored, or individual differences in performance.

QUESTIONS

5 Why is it important to evaluate memory models?

6 The multi-store model is not the only memory model. Research either the working memory model or the levels of processing model. Compare the model you have chosen with the multi-store model.

Drugs and the nervous system

Why do some drugs change the way we act?

Many drugs, both legal and illegal, change the way synapses work in the brain. This affects the way the brain works and changes our behaviour and our responses to the environment.

We are learning to:
> explain what some drugs do to the nervous system
> understand the long-term consequences of taking Ecstasy

FIGURE 1: Some drugs change the way we respond to the environment.

Substances that affect the nervous system

Many drugs and toxins affect the way our nervous system works. They affect the transmission of impulses across synapses (see page 74). Sometimes they stop the transmission altogether. Sometimes they change the speed of transmission, or make the impulse stronger or weaker.

Prozac is a prescribed **antidepressant** that makes synapses in the brain more sensitive to a particular chemical **transmitter substance**. Transmitters substances carry the chemical impulses across the synapse and Prozac helps makes the impulse stronger. Over time this makes people feel less depressed. However, when people stop taking Prozac the synapses often go back to the way they worked before, so other treatments for depression are often given alongside Prozac.

Many toxins (poisons) also block synapses and stop impulses from being transmitted. For example, if a toxin blocks a transmission that was intended to make a muscle contract, it can cause muscle paralysis and even stop the heart from beating.

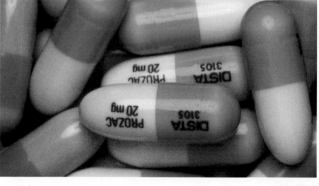

FIGURE 2

QUESTIONS

1 How do some drugs affect the nervous system?

2 Why might a short course of antidepressants not be helpful in the long term?

Other drugs that target the synapses

Beta blockers are prescribed drugs. They work in the opposite way to Prozac, as they block adrenaline receptors in synapses and stop the transmission of impulses. Beta blockers stop the hormone adrenaline from making the heart beat faster, and so stops people from feeling anxious.

The illegal drug **Ecstasy** affects the working of the same chemical transmitter substance as Prozac, effectively increasing its impact in the brain. Like antidepressants, Ecstasy only works short term. But Ecstasy use can have long-term consequences – there can be very severe side-effects.

FIGURE 3: Ecstasy is an illegal drug that affects the way brain synapses work.

QUESTION

3 What are the similarities and differences between Prozac and Ecstasy?

Did you know?

Some people have taken Ecstasy occasionally without serious long-term side-effects, but Leah Betts and other teenagers have died after using Ecstasy just once.

How Ecstasy works (Higher tier only)

Ecstasy, or 3,4-methylenedioxymethamphetamine (**MDMA**), prevents re-absorption (removal) of a transmitter substance called **serotonin** at synapses in the brain. It blocks the receptors on the synapse where serotonin is re-absorbed (see Figure 4). This causes more serotonin than usual to be released into the gap, which means the neuron response is much greater and gives users a feeling of wellbeing and happiness.

The increase in serotonin associated with Ecstasy use leads to a feeling of wellbeing and self-acceptance. However, the brain only has a limited amount of serotonin, so when the drug wears off there is a 'come down' during which users feel tired and irritable. Users have also reported physical effects of attention loss, anxiety and paranoia, and physiological effects of insomnia, teeth grinding and dizziness. Long-term repeated users of Ecstasy have increased rates of depression and 70–80% have impaired memory and learning difficulties. In a study on looking at the effect of Ecstasy on monkey brains, researchers found that neuron axons became shorter and axon terminals grew abnormally.

Without Ecstasy   **With Ecstasy**

serotonin that has been re-absorbed
serotonin transporter
Ecstasy
serotonin
synapse
serotonin receptor
neuron impulse

FIGURE 4: How Ecstasy stops serotonin from being re-absorbed back into the synapse. More is released, so the neuron response is much longer.

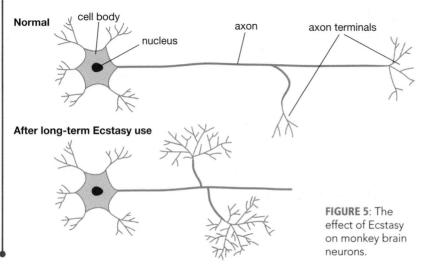

Normal

cell body
nucleus
axon
axon terminals

After long-term Ecstasy use

FIGURE 5: The effect of Ecstasy on monkey brain neurons.

QUESTIONS

4 How does Ecstasy change the way synapses work?

5 What are the short-term and long-term effects of taking Ecstasy on the nervous system?

B6 Checklist

To achieve your forecast grade in the exam you'll need to revise

Use this checklist to see what you can do now. Refer back to pages 70–93 if you're not sure. Look across the rows to see how you could progress – **bold italic** means Higher tier only.

Remember you'll need to be able to use these ideas in many ways:
> interpreting pictures, diagrams and graphs
> applying ideas to new situations
> explaining ethical implications
> suggesting some benefits and risks to society
> drawing conclusions from evidence you've been given.

Look at pages 300–306 for information about how you'll be assessed.

Watch out!

Higher tier statements may be tested at any grade from D to A*. All other statements may be tested at any grade from G to A*.

To aim for a grade E	To aim for a grade C	To aim for a grade A
describe how the body sends messages using the nervous system and using hormones	understand that hormones are made in glands and send long-lived but slow chemical messages through the blood, and understand that neurons send fast but short-lived electrical impulses	understand that the evolution of multicellular organisms has allowed the development of complex body systems such as the nervous system and hormonal system
recall that the nervous system is made up of the brain, spinal cord (central nervous system) and neurons (peripheral nervous system); describe the parts of a neuron	understand how the structure of a neuron is related to the function of transmitting electrical impulses	
understand that synapses are gaps between a neuron and another cell, which allow impulses to be transmitted from the neuron to the next cell	*understand that specific chemical transmitters send the information across synapses, which start another impulse in the next cell*	
understand that the body contains different types of receptors that detect specific stimuli such as light and pressure	understand that receptors can make up complex organs such as the skin or the retina in the eye	
understand that responses are usually a muscle contracting or the gland releasing enzymes or hormones	understand that effectors can make up complex organs such as the cardiac muscle in the heart	

To aim for a grade E	To aim for a grade C	To aim for a grade A
recall that a reflex arc involves an impulse travelling from a receptor through sensory neurons to the relay neurons in the central nervous system, and then back to an effector through motor neurons; understand that reflex responses are involuntary and aid in our survival and can lead to behaviour in simple animals		*understand that the fixed paths of neurons allow responses to be automatic and rapid; understand that in some cases our brain can override a reflex response if it aids our survival*
recall two examples of conditioning including Pavlov's dogs	understand that in a conditioned response the brain links a secondary stimulus (no reflex response) to a primary stimulus (reflex response); *understand that conditioned responses are a form of learning that can help us survive*	*understand that in a conditioned response the final response has no connection to the secondary (neutral) stimulus*
recall that the brain is made of billions of neurons that can learn from experience	recall that the cerebral cortex is the part of the brain concerned with intelligence, memory, language and consciousness	understand that the evolution of a larger brain has given humans a better chance of survival
understand that skills can be learnt with repetition	understand that learning happens when pathways in the brain become stronger and that this happens when we repeat actions; *understand that some skills can only be learnt at certain development stages, such as language*	
understand that memory involves storing and retrieving information and can be split into short-term and long-term memory	understand that information is easier to memorise if it has a pattern, a strong stimulus or there is repetition; understand that we can use models to show how memory works	understand that memory models are limited in explaining how memory works
understand that drugs such as Prozac, Ecstasy and beta blockers affect the transmission of chemical impulses across synapses of the nervous system		*understand that Ecstasy blocks the receptor sites where the transmitter serotonin is removed, so that serotonin stays in the synapse for much longer, and this affects the nervous system*

Exam-style questions

Foundation level

AO1 **1** Once completed, the flow chart below will show the reflex arc that happens when someone steps on a pin. Complete the reflex arc sequence by placing the letter corresponding to the correct step in each box:

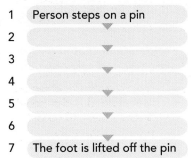

1 Person steps on a pin
2
3
4
5
6
7 The foot is lifted off the pin

A The impulse travels through relay neurons
B Pain and pressure receptors in the foot detect the pin
C The muscles in the leg contract
D The impulse travels through sensory neurons
E The impulse travels through motor neurons   [3]

[Total 3]

Foundation/Higher Level

2 This graph shows the correlation between height and brain size of today's humans (*Homo sapiens*) and extinct hominid species.

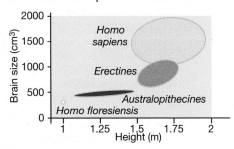

AO2 **a** From the graph state:
(i)   the name of the hominid with the largest brain.[1]
(ii) which hominid ancestor had the smallest brain. [1]
(ii) which human ancestor had the smallest range of heights.   [1]

AO2 **b** (i) What is the relationship between height and brain size?   [2]
(ii) To what extent do all of the species follow this trend?   [2]

AO3 **c** Which of the human ancestors do you think would be the most intelligent and why?   [2]

[Total 9]

3 When Alice was little, her brother put a plastic spider on her hand and then made a loud noise behind her, which made her jump. Even now she is older, she is still scared of spiders. She has formed a conditioned response.

AO2 **a** Which is the neutral stimulus and which is the significant stimulus?   [2]

AO2 **b** Draw a flow diagram to show the original reflex response to the significant stimulus and how the brain has linked the neutral stimulus to it.   [3]

AO2 **c** Suggest which of the following organisms you think Alice would be most scared of and why.   [2]

dog snake spider plant worm woodlouse frog

[Total 7]

AO1 **4** Explain the way our brain learns new things and what things make it easier for the brain to learn. The quality of your written communication will be assessed in your answer to this question.   [6]

[Total 6]

Higher level

3 Groups of people were tested for the ability to memorise faces. One group had never taken drugs, a second group were regular uses of ecstasy and a third were regular users of cannabis. The graph shows the percentage of correctly matched faces in a face-recognition test.

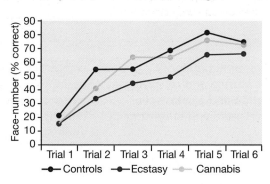

(From: Learning and memory deficits in ecstasy users and their neural correlates during a face-learning task, Roberts, Gloria M. P.; Nestor, Liam; Garavan, Hugh. Brain Research, Oct. 2009, Vol.1292, pp71–81)

AO2 **a** What are the similarities and differences between the three groups over the six trials?   [2]

AO3 **b** What could be causing the improvement over the six trials?   [1]

AO2 **c** Describe the way ecstasy effects synapses.   [2]

[Total 5]

AO1 recall the science   AO2 apply your knowledge   AO3 evaluate and analyse the evidence

Worked example

1a The diagram shows a model of how memory works. Jack is trying to learn a set of French words for a vocabulary test. He reads them over and over again from a page in a text book.

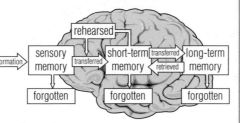

AO2 **(i)** By repeatedly reading through the words, which process in the diagram is he doing? [1]

Rehearsal. ✔

AO1 **(ii)** This is a model of memory called the multi-store model. Explain why this model is limited. [2]

It doesn't show how information moves between stores, it just focuses on where memory is stored. ✔

b To help learn about the brain and memory, scientists compare healthy brains with those of patients with brain diseases. This diagram shows cross-sections of brains.

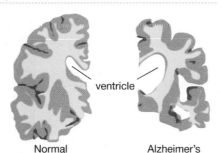

ventricle

Normal   Alzheimer's

AO2 **(i)** Note two differences in the diagram between a healthy brain and a brain with Alzheimer's. [2]

The brain with Alzheimer's is smaller and the ventricle is bigger. ✔ ✔

AO1
AO3 **(ii)** Other than comparing the brains of healthy and diseased patients, how can scientists map regions of the cerebral cortex? Which method would you choose for observing brain development in children, and why? [3]

They can use an MRI machine ✔ *or electrocute the brain.*

The scan is better because it is less invasive.

AO1 c Suggest three things that make it easier for humans to remember information. [3]

People memorise information in different ways and what works for some people doesn't work for others. It is easier to learn information if it has a pattern, ✔ *or if there is a strong stimulus linked to it. Repeating the information over a long period of time makes it easier for the information to pass from the short-term memory to the long-term memory.* ✔

How to raise your grade

Take note of the comments from examiners – these will help you to improve your grade.

This has been correctly identified from the model: 1 mark.

This gains just 1 mark. A second mark would require the answer that the model is too simple and doesn't show that there are different types of short- and long-term memory.

These are both correct; other points could have included bigger gaps in the language and memory centres.

The second point uses incorrect terminology – electrodes are placed inside the brain and stimulate different parts. The MRI scan is less invasive but the mark isn't given as a reason is needed for why this is better; in children you don't want to risk of damaging important parts of the brain by using electrodes.

The first sentence is unnecessary and wouldn't gain any marks. The mention of pattern gains a mark. To gain a mark for the mention of a strong stimulus an example such as bright light or loud sound should be added. The final point about repetition is thorough with good use of terminology and use of the model at the beginning of the question; therefore, it would gain a second mark.

C4 Chemical patterns

What you should already know...

Elements can be classified

The atoms of an element can be represented by a symbol. The symbols of all the elements are shown in the Periodic Table.

Metals are generally solids, shiny, malleable and are good conductors of heat and electricity. Non-metals may be solids, liquids or gases and are poor conductors of heat and electricity.

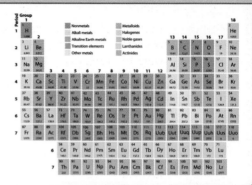

 Which elements have the symbols C, O, Na, Mg?

Compounds are formed when elements join together

Water is a compound of hydrogen and oxygen.

Metals and non-metals combine to form compounds, some of which are called salts.

Oxygen reacts with most other elements to form compounds called oxides.

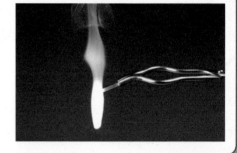

 What is the name of the compound formed when magnesium burns in oxygen?

Changing state involves energy

The particles in a solid are held together by a force. Energy must be supplied to make the particles move to change the solid into a liquid. More energy is needed to make particles spread out as a gas. The stronger the forces between the particles, the greater the energy needed to change the state.

 Why does salt have a higher melting point than water?

Atoms contain particles that have a charge

Particles can have a positive or negative electric charge. Particles with opposite charges attract but if they have the same charges they repel. When charged particles are moving they form an electric current.

 Two balloons suspended by strings both have a positive charge. What will happen to the balloons when held close together?

In C4 you will find out about...

> the first attempts to put the elements in order

> methods of discovering new elements, such as using the flame colours of elements

> how Mendeleev designed his Periodic Table and why scientists came to accept it

> how atoms of elements are built up from protons, neutrons and electrons

> how elements are arranged in the Periodic Table by the order of the number of protons in their atoms

> how electrons are arranged in atoms and how this explains the arrangement of the rows and columns of the Periodic Table

> the similarities and trends of the alkali metals, Group 1 of the Periodic Table, their properties and reactions with oxygen, water and the halogens

> the similarities and trends of the halogens, Group 7 of the Periodic Table, their properties and reactions with alkali metals, iron and compounds of other members of the group

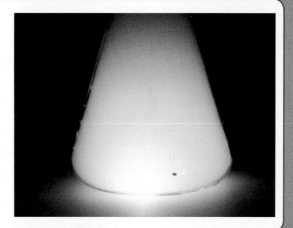

> why compounds of metals and non-metals conduct electricity when they are molten

> how the atoms of metals and non-metals form ions when they react together

> the arrangement of ions in crystals

> how to work out the formula of compounds of metals and non-metals

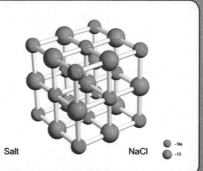

Salt   NaCl

- Na
- Cl

Looking for patterns

We are learning to:

> understand that scientists used creative ideas in looking for patterns in elements

> explain how other scientists learned about and reacted to the new ideas

> understand that explanations are unlikely to be accepted if they cannot account for new evidence

How many elements do we know about?

Two thousand years ago, Greek philosophers said there were just four elements, although 10 substances that we now call elements were known. Most elements have been discovered since the end of the 18th century. The 112th element to be discovered was named Copernicium in 2010.

FIGURE 1: The Ancient Greeks believed that there were just four basic elements: fire, air, earth and water. Most scientists believed this until the 16th century.

Elements and atoms

In the 17th century the chemist Robert Boyle wrote the modern definition of an element. This states that an **element** is a substance that cannot be broken down into anything simpler.

Antoine Lavoisier used this definition to explain how elements burn together in oxygen to form compounds. He published this new idea in a book in 1789 and most chemists were soon using it.

The chemist John Dalton proposed that all elements were made up of tiny particles called atoms. Atoms could not be broken up and were identical in the same element. In 1802 he produced the first list of the **relative atomic mass** of 20 elements. The relative atomic mass was the mass of an atom of the element compared to the mass of hydrogen, the lightest element.

FIGURE 2: Dalton's symbols for atoms of the elements.

Watch out!

Atomic masses are now compared with carbon, which is given an atomic mass of 12.

QUESTIONS

1 How did scientists in the 1790s learn about Lavoisier's ideas?

2 Dalton thought that an oxygen atom was seven times heavier than a hydrogen atom. What relative atomic mass would Dalton have given for oxygen?

 elements discovery timeline

Triads and spirals

By 1817, a total of 49 elements had been discovered. The chemist Johann Döbereiner noticed that in groups of three similar elements (triads), the average of the masses of the lightest and the heaviest atoms was very close to the atomic mass of the middle element. Lithium (7), sodium (23) and potassium (39) are, for example, similar reactive metals. The average of the atomic masses of lithium and potassium is 23, which is the atomic mass of sodium. Döbereiner did not publish his idea in a scientific journal until 1829 and not much notice was taken of it. Most scientists thought it was silly to look for patterns because each element was an individual with its own 'personality'.

Other scientists found numerical patterns. The Frenchman de Chancourtois was the first to list all the known elements in order of their atomic mass. He arranged the elements in a spiral and found that similar elements, such as lithium, sodium and potassium, appeared in a vertical line. Unfortunately Chancourtois' illustration was left out of his publication of 1862, so readers couldn't understand the idea and ignored it.

FIGURE 3: Johann Döbereiner.

Did you know?

New apparatus and methods resulted in discoveries of new elements. The invention of the battery and development of electrolysis resulted in the discovery of many new elements in the early 19th century.

QUESTIONS

3 Döbereiner thought that chlorine, bromine and iodine formed another of his triads. He used atomic masses of 35.5 for chlorine and 127 for iodine to predict the atomic mass of bromine. Was he correct?

4 Why do you think few scientists thought there was a pattern in the elements?

Musical elements

Discoveries of elements slowed in the mid-1800s, and most chemists still thought there was little point in looking for patterns. John Newlands however thought he could see a pattern in which every eighth element seemed to be similar, like the notes in a musical scale or 'octave'. He published his Law of Octaves with a table of all the elements in 1866. At a meeting of the Chemical Society of London most members thought the idea was nonsense because, although it showed some patterns, he had also grouped elements which were very different together. A new burst of element discoveries was also taking place, making Newlands even more of a laughing stock.

FIGURE 4: John Newlands.

H	1	F	8	Cl	15
Li	2	Na	9	K	16
G	3	Mg	10	Ca	17
Bo	4	Al	11	Cr	19
C	5	Si	12	Ti	18
N	6	P	13	Mn	20
O	7	S	14	Fe	21

FIGURE 5: Part of Newlands' table. Note the numbers are simply the order of the elements and some have different symbols from those we use today.

QUESTIONS

5 Look at Newlands' table. Suggest evidence to support his idea that there is a pattern, and evidence that disproves it.

6 Why was the discovery of new elements a disaster for Newlands?

Q Döbereiner   Chancourtois   Newlands

Finding new elements

We are learning to:
> recall that some elements produce distinctive flame colours
> explain how flame colours led to the discovery of new elements
> understand that Mendeleev's Periodic Table was accepted because it made successful predictions

Why is the discovery of new elements important?

In 1860 a new era of element discovery was about to start. This was an important test of the chemical theories of Mendeleev. Even today, the discovery of new heavy elements provides evidence that may support or disprove theories about the matter that makes up the Universe.

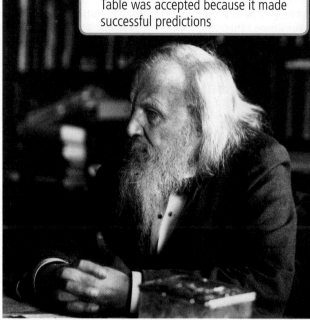

FIGURE 1: Dmitri Mendeleev.

 ## Colourful flames

The many colours in fireworks come from salts of different elements mixed with gunpowder. In 1859 Robert Bunsen and Gustav Kirchhoff used a special gas burner with a colourless flame to identify the exact colours of flames produced by each element. Within two years they found two new elements, caesium and rubidium. Other chemists used their method and soon more new elements were being found.

The Russian chemist Dmitri Mendeleev was convinced that there was a pattern to the elements. He wrote everything he knew about each element on a separate card and arranged the cards in columns and rows. He found that if he left some gaps he could produce a repeating pattern in seven columns of elements. He published his **Periodic Table** of the elements in 1871. He also published predictions for the properties and atomic masses of elements that would fill the gaps.

QUESTIONS

1 Why did Bunsen have to use a burner with a colourless flame?

2 What did Mendeleev have to do to produce repeating patterns in the seven columns of elements?

FIGURE 2: Each colour in the firework is produced by the salt of a different element. Lithium salts produce a red colour.

Q Bunsen Kirchhoff spectra

Lines of discovery

New practical techniques produced a rush of new elements. In the 18th century it was apparatus for handling gases, then it was electrolysis, and in the 1860s it was Bunsen and Kirchhoff's flame colour apparatus. The light produced by an element in Bunsen's burner was passed through a prism, which split the light into a spectrum. Each element produced a different set of coloured lines – a **line spectrum**. New elements had patterns of lines that were different from the known elements. Bunsen and Kirchhoff's spectroscopic method worked with very small samples of compounds so rare elements could be discovered.

In 1875 the first of Mendeleev's predicted elements was discovered using spectroscopy. In 1879 and 1886 two more followed. Chemists began to agree that Mendeleev's table represented a real pattern in the elements.

FIGURE 3: The line spectrum of sodium is two single yellow lines, so close together they look like one.

QUESTIONS

3 Explain why the development of new apparatus was important in chemistry.

4 How was Bunsen and Kirchhoff's invention of use to Mendeleev?

Mendeleev's success

Mendeleev constructed his Periodic Table according to two rules.

> *Put the elements in order of their relative atomic mass.*

Sometimes he swapped elements around to give a better pattern and said the data was wrong.

> *Put elements that are chemically similar in the same column.*

Properties included the formula of the oxides of the elements. The formulae of lithium oxide, Li_2O, sodium oxide, Na_2O, and potassium oxide, K_2O, show that lithium, sodium and potassium should be in the same column.

Following these rules produced gaps, for example below aluminium. Gallium, a new element discovered in 1875, fitted this gap perfectly. The success of Mendeleev's predictions convinced scientists that the Periodic Table revealed a true pattern of relationships between elements and was a useful guide to the properties of elements.

Reihen	Gruppo I. — R²O	Gruppo II. — RO	Gruppo III. — R²O³	Gruppo IV. RH⁴ RO²	Gruppo V. RH³ R²O⁵	Gruppo VI. RH² RO³	Gruppo VII. RH R²O⁷	Gruppo VIII. — RO⁴
1	H=1							
2	Li=7	Be=9,4	B=11	C=12	N=14	O=16	F=19	
3	Na=23	Mg=24	Al=27,3	Si=28	P=31	S=32	Cl=35,5	
4	K=39	Ca=40	—=44	Ti=48	V=51	Cr=52	Mn=55	Fe=56, Co=59, Ni=59, Cu=63.
5	(Cu=63)	Zn=65	—=68	—=72	As=75	So=78	Br=80	
6	Rb=85	Sr=87	?Yt=88	Zr=90	Nb=94	Mo=96	—=100	Ru=104, Rh=104, Pd=106, Ag=108.
7	(Ag=108)	Cd=112	In=113	Sn=118	Sb=122	Te=125	J=127	
8	Cs=133	Ba=137	?Di=138	?Ce=140	—	—	—	— — —
9	(—)	—	—	—	—	—	—	
10	—	—	?Er=178	?La=180	Ta=182	W=184	—	Os=195, Ir=197, Pt=198, Au=199.
11	(Au=199)	Hg=200	Tl=204	Pb=207	Bi=208	—	—	
12	—	—	—	Th=231	—	U=240	—	— — —

FIGURE 4: The version of the Periodic Table that Mendeleev published in 1871.

Watch out!

Mendeleev's Periodic Table is not the same as the modern table but showed that there is a relationship between the elements.

QUESTIONS

5 Why did Mendeleev put zinc, cadmium and mercury in the same column as magnesium, calcium and strontium?

6 Look at a modern Periodic Table. Find two elements in the wrong order according to Mendeleev's first rule.

Did you know?

Mendeleev did not predict the existence of the Group 0 gases. When they were discovered in the 1890s chemists found that they formed an entirely new column in Mendeleev's table – yet another success for his idea.

Q Mendeleev Periodic Table

Preparing for assessment: Planning and collecting

To achieve a good grade in science you will need to be able to use your skills and understanding to understand how scientists plan, run and evaluate investigations. These skills will be assessed in your exams and in Controlled Assessments. This activity supports you in developing the skills of designing the technique to be used and choosing equipment.

✳ Doing flame tests

Flame colours of potassium (left) and sodium (right) compounds.

The colours that metals and their compounds produce when heated in a flame is good way of identifying some of the elements. For instance, potassium and sodium produce distinctive colours in a flame.

Chloe and Harry wanted to find out which metal was in a white powder they had been given. They decided to see if it had a flame colour. They had the choice of a copper or a nickel–chromium wire. They chose the nickel–chromium wire. They also had some known substances to test their mystery white powder against.

First they heated the wire in a blue Bunsen burner flame. Then they dipped the wire into concentrated hydrochloric acid. They repeated this until the wire did not give any colour to the Bunsen burner flame. Then they dipped the wire into the first known substance that they had decided to test, and held it in

the flame. They photographed the flame and noted down the colour. Then they cleaned the wire again and tried another substance. Finally, having cleaned the wire they tested the unknown substance, photographed the flame and recorded its colour.

Metal in test substance	Flame colour
sodium	yellow
calcium	orangey red
potassium	lilac
copper	green
lithium	crimson red
unknown	lilac

Task 1

> What apparatus did Chloe and Harry use?

> What did they do to make sure they worked safely?

> What hazards were there in the technique?

 Task 2

> What did Chloe and Harry do to make sure that they see the correct colours of the metals in the compounds?

> What did they do to compare the colours of different flames?

> What precautions did they take to reduce the risk of harming themselves?

Task 3

> Why did they choose the nickel–chromium wire instead of the copper wire?

> Write a risk assessment for the experiment stating how the risks can be reduced.

Maximise your grade

Use these suggestions to improve your work and be more successful.

E

To be on target for grade E you need to:

> Comment on how to work safely.

> Choose the basic equipment needed to carry out the flame tests.

> Identify the hazards in the procedure.

C

To be on target for grades D, C, in addition, you need to:

> Select the equipment required to collect all the data needed.

> Identify the risks and suggest safety precautions to take.

A

To be on target for grades B, A, in addition, you need to:

> Explain why certain pieces of equipment were needed.

> Complete a risk assessment and suggest ways of reducing the risk in the procedure.

Building atoms

How do we know what's in an atom?

In the 1890s many experimental results showed that atoms could not simply be 'tiny hard balls'. They had to contain smaller particles and also contain space. Further experiments revealed the particles that made up the atoms. Scientists developed a new model of atomic structure. This model explained the patterns that Mendeleev had found in the properties of elements.

FIGURE 1: A diagram of an atom showing the electrons orbiting round the nucleus, which is made up of protons and neutrons (the nucleus is not to scale).

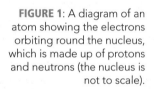

Inside the atom

No-one can see inside atoms. They are so small that a million atoms can line up across a hair. Experiments show that atoms are made up of even smaller particles. There are **electrons** with a negative electric charge and almost no mass. Then there are **protons** – positively charged particles that have the same mass as a hydrogen atom. Lastly, there are **neutrons** with no charge but the same mass as the proton.

Protons and neutrons are found in a bundle at the centre of each atom called the **nucleus**. The diameter of the nucleus is about one-thousandth of the whole atom but contains almost all the mass of the atom. The electrons whizz around the nucleus in **orbits** or **shells**.

Particle	Charge	Mass	Position in atom
proton	+1	Same as hydrogen atom	In nucleus at centre of atom
electron	−1	Almost zero	In shells around nucleus
neutron	0	Same as hydrogen atom	In nucleus at centre of atom

The particles that make up atoms.

QUESTION

1 Which particle in an atom:

a has a positive charge?

b is not found in the nucleus?

c has the same mass as the neutron?

electrons protons neutrons

Counting particles

An atom does not have an electric charge overall because the positive and negative charges cancel out. The number of electrons and protons must be the same. The number of protons in an atom is called the **proton number**. The number of electrons in an atom is the same as the proton number.

The electrons in an atom are responsible for its chemical properties. All the atoms of an element behave in the same way, so they must have the same number of electrons and therefore the same number of protons. Each element has its own proton number which makes it different from every other element.

The modern Periodic Table lists the elements in the order of their proton number.

relative atomic mass	3	4	5	6	7	0
symbol						4 **He** helium 2
name	11 **B** boron 5	12 **C** carbon 6	14 **N** nitrogen 7	16 **O** oxygen 8	19 **F** fluorine 9	20 **Ne** neon 10
proton number	27 **Al** aluminium 13	28 **Si** silicon 14	31 **P** phosphorus 15	32 **S** sulfur 16	35.5 **Cl** chlorine 17	40 **Ar** argon 18
64 **Cu** copper 29	65 **Zn** zinc 30	70 **Ga** gallium 31	73 **Ge** germanium 32	75 **As** arsenic 33	79 **Se** selenium 34	80 **Br** bromine 35	84 **Kr** krypton 36

FIGURE 2: Part of the modern Periodic Table.

Did you know?

Mendeleev's order of elements was the same as in the modern Periodic Table, although he did not know about proton number. His guess that tellurium should come before iodine was correct even though its relative atomic mass is higher than iodine's.

QUESTIONS

2 a Carbon has a proton number of 6. How many protons and electrons are there in every carbon atom?

b Nitrogen is the next element in the Periodic Table after carbon. What is the proton number of nitrogen?

3 Look at a Periodic Table (see page 309). What is the name, symbol and relative atomic mass of the element with proton number 11?

Using the Periodic Table (Higher tier only)

The Periodic Table is a useful guide to the particles in atoms. Once you find the element in the table you can give its proton number and the number of protons and electrons. The sum of the protons and neutrons in the nucleus of the atom gives the relative mass of the atom.

For example, aluminium is element number 13 in the Periodic Table and has a relative atomic mass of 27. This means its proton number is 13 so it has 13 protons in the nucleus and 13 electrons in shells around it. The number of neutrons in the nucleus can be worked out:

number of protons + number of neutrons = **relative atomic mass**

13 + number of neutrons = 27

So, the number of neutrons = 27 − 13 = 14

Watch out!
The number of neutrons is *not* the same as the number of protons and electrons except in some of the lighter elements in the Periodic Table.

QUESTION

4 Use a Periodic Table to find the number of protons, electrons and neutrons in an atom of: **a** helium (He), **b** sulfur (S), **c** potassium (K), **d** iron (Fe).

Arranging electrons

We are learning to:
> describe how electrons are arranged in shells around the nucleus of an atom
> explain how the electron arrangement of elements is related to the Periodic Table

Why do atoms exist?

Positive charges attract negative charges. The physicist Ernest Rutherford, who did many experiments to find out about atoms, suggested that negatively charged electrons orbited around the positively charged nucleus of atoms. Scientists wanted to know what stopped the electrons from falling into the nucleus. The Danish scientist Niels Bohr developed a theory to explain the structure of atoms.

FIGURE 1: Niels Bohr won the Nobel Prize in 1922 at the age of 37 for his theory of the arrangement of electrons in atoms.

 ## Sorting electrons

Bohr suggested that electrons are arranged in orbits or shells around the nucleus. The first shell, which is closest to the nucleus, can have up to 2 electrons. The next shell can take up to 8 electrons. The **electron arrangement** of an atom can be written down quickly as a set of numbers separated by full stops.

The electron arrangement of an oxygen atom is 2.6. This means there are 2 electrons in the first shell and 6 in the second shell.

The electron arrangement of a chlorine atom is 2.8.7. Chlorine has 2 electrons in the first shell, 8 in the second and 7 in the third shell.

The arrangements can also be shown in diagrams like those in Figure 2.

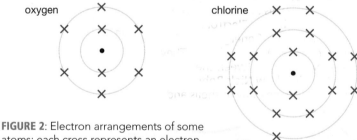

FIGURE 2: Electron arrangements of some atoms: each cross represents an electron.

QUESTIONS

1 The electron arrangement of sodium is 2.8.1.

  a How many electrons are there in the first, second and third shells of a sodium atom?

  b How many electrons are there altogether?

2 The electron arrangement of a carbon atom is 2.4. Draw a diagram to show this arrangement like those shown in Figure 2.

Following the rules

The electron arrangement of an element can be worked out from its proton number. Electrons are put into the first shell first, then the second, then the third. In the first 20 elements the maximum number of electrons in the third shell is 8.

The proton number of potassium is 19. With 2 electrons in the first shell, 8 in the second and 8 in the third, there is one electron left over for the fourth shell. The electron arrangement is 2.8.8.1.

The horizontal rows in the Periodic Table are called **periods**. From left to right across a period, the number of electrons in the outer shell increases from one element to the next. There are only two elements in the first period because the first shell can only have two electrons in it. The second and third period both have eight elements.

1 **H** hydrogen 1							4 **He** helium 2
7 **Li** lithium 3	9 **Be** beryllium 4	11 **B** boron 5	12 **C** carbon 6	14 **N** nitrogen 7	16 **O** oxygen 8	19 **F** fluorine 9	20 **Ne** neon 10
23 **Na** sodium 11	24 **Mg** magnesium 12	27 **Al** aluminium 13	28 **Si** silicon 14	31 **P** phosphorus 15	32 **S** sulfur 16	35.5 **Cl** chlorine 17	40 **Ar** argon 18

FIGURE 3: The first three periods of the Periodic Table.

Watch out!
The dots in the electron arrangement are just to separate the numbers – they are not decimal points.

QUESTIONS

3 Write in figures and sketch a diagram of the electron arrangement of:

a lithium (proton number 3)

b neon (proton number 10)

c magnesium (proton number 12).

4 Look for phosphorus (P) in a Periodic Table (page 309). Write down and sketch its electron arrangement.

Shells and levels

The shell that an electron is in represents the **energy level** of the electron. The closer the electron is to the nucleus, the lower the energy level of the electron. Figure 4 shows the energy levels and the electron arrangement for chlorine. Electrons can only have the amount of energy corresponding to these energy levels. They cannot have an energy between the energy levels. This is how Niels Bohr explained why electrons stay in shells and do not fall into the nucleus.

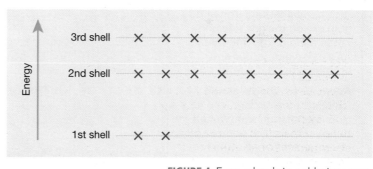

FIGURE 4: Energy levels in a chlorine atom.

QUESTIONS

5 Where in the Periodic Table would you expect to find the element with electron arrangement 2.8.8? Sketch a diagram showing its energy levels and state its proton number.

6 An element has the electron arrangement 2.8.8.2. What is its proton number? Find the element on the Periodic Table. Explain its position and give its name and symbol.

Did you know?

The flame colours of elements are caused by electrons moving between the energy levels in the atom and giving out energy. Each element has its own set of energy levels, and so each element has its own spectrum.

The Periodic Table

How does our night life depend on the Periodic Table?

The first 'neon' signs used the gas neon to produce an orange light. The properties of the gas allow it to be used like this. From the Periodic Table, other gases are predicted to have similar properties to neon. Argon and krypton glow with different colours to make different coloured signs.

FIGURE 1

Finding elements in the Periodic Table

In the modern Periodic Table the elements are in the order of their number of protons, called the **proton number**. Their electron arrangement is then used to put the elements into rows. The rows are called **periods.** This way of arranging the elements means that we can use the position of an element in the table to predict its properties.

In the Periodic Table metals such as magnesium, iron and gold are on the left side and in the middle. The non-metals such as oxygen, sulfur and bromine are on the right side.

As we move along a **period** from left to right the elements change from metals to non-metals. The number of electrons in the outer shell increases from 1 to 8 along a period.

H																	He
Li	Be		metals		non-metals							B	C	N	O	F	Ne
Na	Mg											Al	Si	P	S	Cl	Ar
K	Ca	Sc	Ti	V	Cr	Mn	Fe	Co	Ni	Cu	Zn	Ga	Ge	As	Se	Br	Kr
Rb	Sr	Y	Zr	Nb	Mo	Tc	Ru	Rh	Pd	Ag	Cd	In	Sn	Sb	Te	I	Xe
Cs	Ba	La	Hf	Ta	W	Re	Os	Ir	Pt	Au	Hg	Tl	Pb	Bi	Po	At	Rn
Fr	Ra	Ac	Rf	Db	Sg	Bh	Hs	Mt	Ds	Rg							

FIGURE 2: The Periodic Table showing the areas occupied by metals and non-metals.

QUESTIONS

1 Look at the Periodic Table.

   a Name two elements that are metals.

   b Name two elements that are non-metals.

2 How do we know that the Periodic Table is based on successful theories?

Watch out!

Remember that metals are conductors of electricity and are shiny and malleable. Non-metals do not have these properties.

Q Periodic Table metal non-metal

Properties across a period

Look at the third period of elements from sodium across to argon.

Sodium has a proton number of 11 and electron arrangement 2.8.1. As we move to the right each element has an additional proton and electron until we get to argon, which has the electron arrangement 2.8.8.

The first three elements, sodium, magnesium and aluminium, are metals. The **melting point** of these metals increases from left to right. The last four elements are non-metals. Two of them, phosphorus and sulfur, are solids with low melting points. The last two, chlorine and argon, are gases. The element in the middle, silicon, has a very high melting point and is known as a semi-metal or metalloid.

Argon is an **inert** element. This means that it does not react with any other elements.

These changes in properties across a period are called **trends**. The trends that we see in period 3 also occur in the other periods. It is this repeating or 'periodic' pattern that gives the table its name.

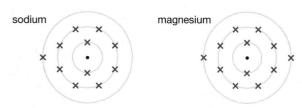

FIGURE 3: Magnesium follows sodium in the Periodic Table and has one extra proton and one extra electron in the third shell.

QUESTIONS

3 Give one way in which sodium, magnesium and aluminium are similar.

4 Describe or sketch a graph showing the change in melting points of the elements across period 3.

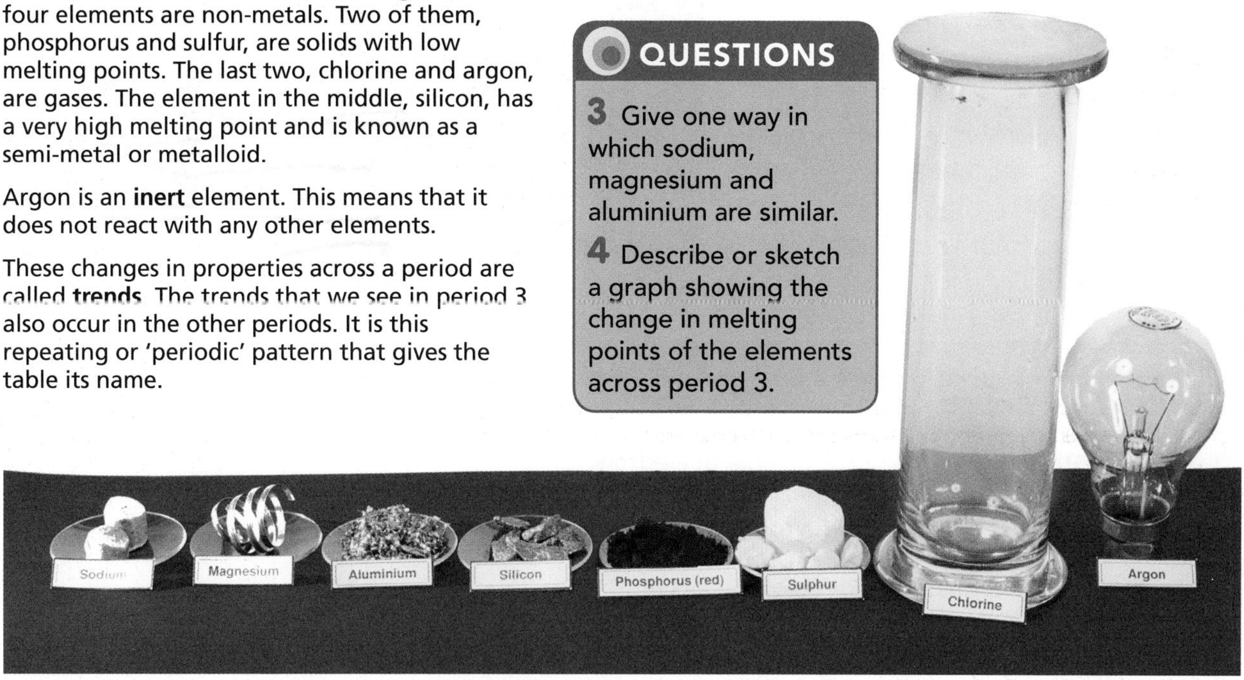

FIGURE 4: The elements of period 3 – sodium, magnesium, aluminium, silicon, phosphorus, sulfur, chlorine and argon.

Electrons and properties (Higher tier only)

The chemical properties of an element are governed by its electron arrangement and in particular by the number of electrons in its outer shell. As we can work out the electron arrangement of an element from its position in the Periodic Table, we can use the table to predict the properties of any element:

> elements with one, two or three electrons in their outer shell are metals

> elements with five, six or seven electrons in their outer shell are non-metals

> elements with eight electrons in their outer shell are the inert gases.

Did you know?

Hydrogen is not a metal but is often put on the left of the Periodic Table because it has only one electron in its outer shell. It has unique properties because it has the simplest atoms with just one proton and one electron.

QUESTIONS

5 Would you expect the element with the electron arrangement 2.8.18.8.1 to be a metal or a non-metal? Explain your answer.

6 Find calcium (Ca) in the Periodic Table (on page 309). State its proton number and electron arrangement, and predict whether it is a metal or non-metal.

Group 1 – the alkali metals

We are learning to:
> explain that groups of elements in the Periodic Table have similar properties
> recall the symbols and properties of the Group 1 metals
> use data and patterns in groups to make predictions about properties of elements

Why do we need to predict element properties?

Francium is on the left of the Periodic Table below caesium. It was one of the last of the elements that Mendeleev predicted and was discovered by the nuclear chemist Marguerite Perey in 1939. It is so rare and decays radioactively so quickly that very little is available to test its chemical properties, but they can be predicted from francium's similarity to other members of Group 1.

FIGURE 1: Marguerite Perey discovered the element francium while studying radioactive decay under Marie Curie.

What are groups?

The columns in the Periodic Table are called **groups** of elements. The group number is the number of electrons in the outer shell of the atom.

Some of the groups have been given names. For example, the first group on the left, Group 1, is known as the **alkali metals**. Group 1 is made up of six elements: lithium, sodium, potassium, rubidium, caesium, francium.

When Mendeleev designed his Periodic Table he put elements that had similar properties in the same group. That is still true with the modern Periodic Table. All the elements in a group have similar physical properties and chemical reactions with other elements and compounds.

Li lithium	Be beryllium	
Na sodium	Mg magnesium	
K potassium	Ca calcium	Sc scandium
Rb rubidium	Sr strontium	Y yttrium
Cs caesium	Ba barium	La lanthanum
Fr francium	Ra radium	Ac actinium

FIGURE 2: Group 1 in the Periodic Table – the alkali metals.

Watch out!
Remember – groups are vertical columns, periods are horizontal rows.

QUESTION

1 a   What are the names and symbols of the top three members of Group 1?

  b   Why are these metals put in Group 1?

The properties of the alkali metals

The alkali metals have one electron in the outer shell of their atoms, which is why they are all in Group 1. They are soft and can be cut easily with a steel knife. As they are metals they conduct electricity and are malleable.

When freshly scratched or cut, the metal surface is shiny and silver in colour. In moist air the surface turns dull rapidly. This is because the metals corrode or **tarnish** by reacting with oxygen in the air. To slow down the reaction the metals are kept in oil and out of contact with the air.

The reaction of the alkali metals with oxygen is speeded up by heating the metal. The metals burn with brightly coloured flames and form the metal oxide, for example:

sodium + oxygen → sodium oxide

If freshly cut samples of lithium, sodium and potassium are left in the air, the potassium tarnishes the quickest, followed by sodium and then lithium. This shows that *the alkali metals get more reactive further down the group.*

Other properties, such as melting point, boiling point and density, also show a gradual change or trend down the group.

FIGURE 3: Freshly cut sample of sodium.

FIGURE 4: Sodium burning in air. Note the colour of the flames.

QUESTIONS

2 Write a word equation for the reaction of lithium with oxygen.

3 Would you expect rubidium to tarnish more slowly or more quickly than potassium? Explain your answer.

4 Look at Figure 5. Describe the trend in melting points in Group 1.

Did you know?

Liquid sodium is used as a coolant in some nuclear reactors. It is never allowed to come into contact with the air as it would ignite spontaneously.

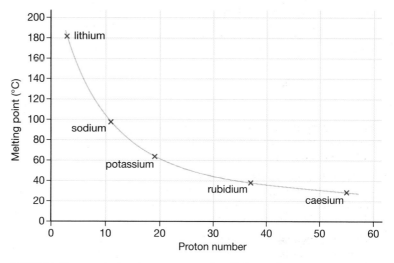

FIGURE 5: The trend of melting points in the alkali metals.

Electron arrangements in Group 1 (Higher tier only)

The fact that all Group 1 metals have one electron in their outer shell explains the similarity in their properties. Going down the group the number of shells increases and the atoms get bigger. The outer electron is further and further away from the nucleus, in a higher and higher energy level.

QUESTIONS

5 In which shell does caesium have one electron?

6 Group 1 metals all react with oxygen. Use the electron arrangement of the atoms in Group 1 to explain the similarities in the reaction of these elements with oxygen.

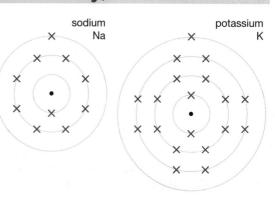

FIGURE 6: The electron arrangements in Group 1 atoms.

Group 1 – reactions with water

Do alkali metals really explode in water?

A television science programme showed what happens when the alkali metals react with water. They used much more metal than is allowed in a school laboratory. When caesium was dropped into a bath of water, it exploded and destroyed the bath. Was this true, or did the programme-makers cheat?

What happens when sodium is put in water?

A small piece of sodium in a bowl of cold water floats on the surface and moves around fizzing. The gas that is given off can be lit by a lighted splint. The piece of sodium eventually disappears and pH indicator added to the water turns blue. These observations show that hydrogen gas is given off and an alkaline solution is formed.

The word equation for the reaction of sodium with water is:

sodium + water → hydrogen + sodium hydroxide

A similar reaction happens with the other Group 1 metals but the reaction can be more violent. Alkali metals *can* explode in water. They are flammable, as is the hydrogen gas given off. The hydroxide formed can be corrosive and harmful. Group 1 metals must be kept away from water for safety.

FIGURE 1: Sodium reacting with cold water.

highly flammable

toxic

corrosive

harmful

explosive

oxidising

FIGURE 2: Take precautions when you see these hazard symbols.

QUESTIONS

1 What evidence is there that sodium hydroxide is an alkali?

2 What is formed when lithium reacts with cold water?

3 What is the word equation for the reaction of potassium with cold water?

Reactions of the alkali metals

The equation for the reaction of sodium with water can be written in symbols:

$2Na(s) + 2H_2O(l) \rightarrow H_2(g) + 2NaOH(aq)$

This **balanced symbol equation** shows that two atoms of solid (s) sodium react with two molecules of liquid (l) water to form one molecule of hydrogen gas (g) and two formula units of sodium hydroxide in 'aqueous' (aq) solution, that is, in water. The letters in brackets are called **state symbols**.

For the reaction of any Group 1 metal with water, the formula of the metal hydroxide formed and the balanced equation are similar. Using M to stand for any of the metals, we can write the general equation:

$2M(s) + 2H_2O(l) \rightarrow H_2(g) + 2MOH(aq)$

 alkali metals water

Down the group the reaction with water get more violent. Lithium fizzes on the surface quite gently; sodium is noticeably faster and may explode if the piece is larger. Potassium always explodes with lilac-coloured flames, and rubidium explodes more violently.

FIGURE 3: Potassium reacting with cold water.

QUESTIONS

4 What are the formulae of lithium hydroxide and potassium hydroxide?

5 Predict what you might observe if rubidium was added to cold water. Name the products of the reaction.

Writing balanced equations (Higher tier only)

To write a balanced equation, first write a word equation for the reaction. Then replace the names of the elements and compounds with the symbols and formulae.

For example, when lithium burns in air it forms lithium oxide:

$$\text{lithium} + \text{oxygen} \rightarrow \text{lithium oxide}$$
$$\text{Li} + \text{O}_2 \rightarrow \text{Li}_2\text{O}$$

Next, count up the number of atoms of each element on each side of the equation. The symbol itself stands for one atom and the little number after the symbol tells you if there is more than one atom of the element.

Element	Left side Number of atoms	Right side Number of atoms
Li	1	2
O	2	1

The number of atoms of each element must be the same on both sides – we cannot make or destroy atoms.

There are two oxygen atoms on the left but only one on the right. To balance the equation, put a large figure 2 in front of the formula for Li_2O.

$$\text{Li} + \text{O}_2 \rightarrow 2\text{Li}_2\text{O}$$

Element	Left side Number of atoms	Right side Number of atoms
Li	1	$2 \times 2 = 4$
O	2	$2 \times 1 = 2$ ✔

The oxygen is now balanced. To balance the lithium we need a 4 in front of the Li on the left.

$$4\text{Li} + \text{O}_2 \rightarrow 2\text{Li}_2\text{O}$$

Element	Left side Number of atoms	Right side Number of atoms
Li	$4 \times 1 = 4$	$2 \times 2 = 4$ ✔
O	2	$2 \times 1 = 2$ ✔

The equation is balanced. Lastly, add the state symbols:

$$4\text{Li(s)} + \text{O}_2\text{(g)} \rightarrow 2\text{Li}_2\text{O(s)}$$

Watch out!

The elements oxygen and hydrogen are found as molecules of two atoms.

QUESTION

6 Write balanced symbol equations with state symbols for the reaction of:

a lithium with cold water   **b** sodium with oxygen gas   **c** rubidium with cold water.

🔍 balancing chemical equations GCSE

Are all salts salty?

Like sodium chloride, the chlorides of the other Group 1 metals are white solids that dissolve in water, but only sodium chloride actually tastes pleasantly salty. Potassium chloride is often used as a substitute for sodium chloride in 'low-sodium salt' but has a more bitter taste and is poisonous in large amounts.

FIGURE 1: 'Lo Salt' contains potassium chloride instead of sodium chloride.

> **We are learning to:**
>
> > describe and explain the reactions of the Group 1 metals with chlorine

 Burning without oxygen

When a piece of sodium is heated until it is burning and then put into a container of chlorine gas, it continues to burn with a yellow flame. A white smoke forms. The sodium continues to burn because it reacts quickly with the chlorine, making sodium chloride.

sodium + chlorine → sodium chloride

Sodium chloride is often called 'salt' but it is in fact one of many different salts and should be known as 'common salt'. The other alkali metals also burn in chlorine gas to make similar salts.

FIGURE 2: Sodium burning in chlorine. Note the yellow glow of the sodium flame and the white smoke.

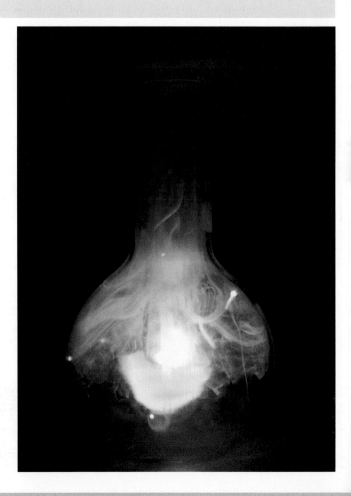

 QUESTIONS

1 Why do we say the sodium 'burns' in chlorine?

2 What is formed when potassium burns in chlorine?

3 What do you think lithium chloride looks like?

🔍 alkali metals chlorine

Formulae and equations

The formula of sodium chloride is NaCl. This shows that every sodium atom combines with a chlorine atom. The balanced chemical equation for the reaction of sodium with chlorine is:

$$2Na(s) + Cl_2(g) \rightarrow 2NaCl(s)$$

The other alkali metals form chlorides with similar appearances and formulae and the balanced chemical equations are the same if the metal's symbol is substituted for sodium.

As in their reactions with oxygen and water, alkali metals further down the group react more violently with chlorine than those at the top. There is thus a pattern in the reactions of all the elements in the group. They all react in a similar way with other elements and compounds but the reactions get more violent as you replace the metal with one further down the group.

Did you know?

Small crystals of sodium chloride are white, but larger crystals are colourless and as clear as glass.

QUESTIONS

4 What are the formulae of lithium chloride and potassium chloride?

5 What would you expect to see if hot rubidium was put in chlorine gas?

6 Look at the equation for the reaction of sodium with chlorine. How many sodium atoms react with each chlorine molecule?

7 What are the similarities and differences in the reactions of the Group 1 metals?

FIGURE 3: This view of the Dead Sea shows evaporation ponds where potassium chloride, in addition to sodium chloride, is extracted from the seawater.

Electrons and reactivity (Higher tier only)

The reactivity of the alkali metals with chlorine illustrates the similarity and the trend of the electron arrangements of these Group 1 elements. They each have one electron in the outer shell but as the atoms get larger down the group, this outer electron is further from the nucleus. The further the single outer electron is from the nucleus, the easier the atom finds it to combine with other elements, such as chlorine and oxygen, to form a stable compound; that is, its reactivity increases.

Watch out!

Do not confuse the properties of the elements with their compounds. Reactive metals form stable compounds.

QUESTIONS

8 Write a balanced chemical equation with state symbols for the reactions of:

a potassium (K) with chlorine

b caesium (Cs) with chlorine.

9 Explain the similarities and differences in the reactions of the Group 1 metals.

Did you know?

Lithium chloride, like potassium chloride, was used as a salt substitute until its medical effects were discovered. It is now used as a drug for the treatment of mentally ill patients suffering from bipolar disorder.

Q Group 1 alkali metals (summary)

Group 7 – the halogens

We are learning to:
> recall the formulae and properties of some elements in Group 7
> use patterns in their behaviour to predict properties of other members of Group 7

How are Group 7 elements similar?

Iodine solution has been used to clean wounds since the early 19th century. Chlorine is added to water to make it fit to drink. Both chlorine and iodine kill microorganisms. If we look carefully at the properties of these and other Group 7 elements, we find other similarities.

FIGURE 1

Which elements are halogens?

The Group 7 elements form a vertical column in the Periodic Table on the right of the table amongst the non-metals. The elements are in the same group because they have similar chemical properties, but they appear to be quite different at normal temperature and pressure.

> Fluorine (F) is a very pale yellow gas.

> Chlorine (Cl) is a pale green gas.

> Bromine (Br) is a dark red-brown liquid that evaporates easily to form a reddish brown gas.

> Iodine (I) is a dark grey solid but on warming becomes a purple gas.

> Astatine (At) is the most rare element on Earth and has never been seen in large enough quantities to describe its appearance.

FIGURE 2: Examples of the some of the halogen elements – chlorine, bromine and iodine.

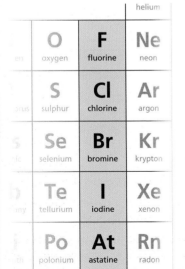

		helium
O oxygen	**F** fluorine	Ne neon
S sulphur	**Cl** chlorine	Ar argon
Se selenium	**Br** bromine	Kr krypton
Te tellurium	**I** iodine	Xe xenon
Po polonium	**At** astatine	Rn radon

FIGURE 3: Group 7 of the Periodic Table, the halogens.

Watch out!

There is no Group 7 element in the first period of the Periodic Table.

Did you know?

Astatine was the last of Mendeleev's predicted elements to be verified. It was produced in atomic bombardment experiments in 1940 but not found naturally for another 3 years. There may only be about 30 g in the entire Earth's crust.

QUESTION

1 Name the member of the halogens group which:

a is a dark grey solid at normal temperatures and pressures

b has the symbol Cl

c evaporates to form a reddish brown gas when warmed

d is extremely rare.

Patterns in Group 7

An important similarity between all the halogens is that, as elements, the atoms are joined together in pairs to form **diatomic molecules**. Diatomic means 'two atoms'. The formulae of the elements show this.

Element	Formula
fluorine	F_2
chlorine	Cl_2
bromine	Br_2
iodine	I_2
astatine	At_2

The formulae of diatomic molecules of halogens.

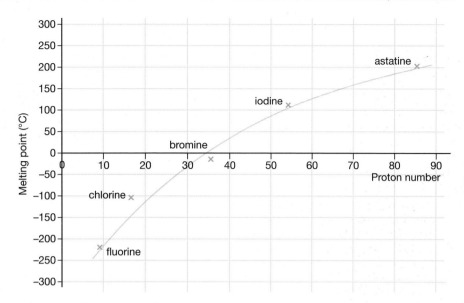

FIGURE 4: The trend of melting points in the halogens.

The formulae of the compounds of the halogens are also similar. They each react with sodium to form a compound where an atom of the halogen combines with each atom of sodium, so the formula of sodium fluoride is NaF, sodium chloride is NaCl, and so on. Note how the name of the element changes in the compound, with the ending becoming -ide instead of -ine. If you see the -ide ending you know that the substance is a compound. In fact the name halogen means 'salt maker'.

Like Group 1, the halogens show a trend or pattern in their properties as you go from the top of the group, fluorine, to the bottom, iodine. There is so little astatine that its properties are uncertain. For example, the melting points of the elements increase in a fairly smooth curve that gets flatter down the group.

QUESTIONS

2 What does the formula Cl_2 tell you?

3 Which halogens would remain a solid at the temperature of boiling water?

4 What pattern would you predict for the boiling points of the halogens?

Electron arrangements of the halogens (Higher tier only)

All the halogens have seven electrons in the outer shells of their atoms. For instance fluorine has the electron arrangement 2.7. The similarity in the electron arrangement is the reason why the halogen elements have similar chemical properties. The patterns in the group can be explained by the increasing number of shells and size of the atoms down the group.

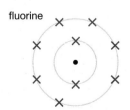

FIGURE 5: The electron arrangement of fluorine.

QUESTIONS

5 What is the electron arrangement of chlorine (proton number 17)?

6 How many electron shells does an iodine atom have?

7 Why is it possible to predict the properties of astatine despite there not being enough atoms to test all its properties?

🔍 Group 7 halogens

Patterns in Group 7

We are learning to:
> explain that the halogens become less reactive down the group
> understand the safety precautions needed for working with halogens

Why can't fluorine be stored in a bottle?

Fluorine is the most reactive non-metallic element. It reacts with nearly every other element, often violently. It even reacts with glass. The only way of storing fluorine for a period of time is in a container lined with a compound of fluorine such as Teflon (polytetrafluoroethene).

FIGURE 1: Henri Moissan holding a test tube of fluorine gas. He succeeded in collecting it in 1886 but could not store it. Many scientists were injured while trying to extract fluorine from its compounds.

Reactive non-metals

All the halogen elements are very reactive. They react with most elements and many compounds. This make the elements and their vapours very hazardous, so they are classed as **corrosive** and **toxic**. Experiments with the elements must be carried out in a fume cupboard by experienced chemists.

All the halogens react violently with alkali metals and other metals such as iron and form compounds known as **halides**. For example:

> sodium + bromine → sodium bromide

> potassium + iodine → potassium iodide

> iron + chlorine → iron chloride

FIGURE 2: Iron reacts vigorously with chlorine producing flames and smoke of iron chloride.

QUESTIONS

1 Write word equations for the reactions of:

   a potassium with chlorine

   b iron with bromine.

2 Why is it important to carry out reactions with halogens in a well-ventilated area?

Q halogens reaction iron

Patterns of reactivity

The halogens become less reactive down the group. Sodium will burn in chlorine but its reaction with iodine is less violent. The same pattern is seen in the reaction of iron with the halogens. Iron will burn when in contact with fluorine but needs to be heated to react with iodine.

The difference in the reactivity of the halogens can be shown in **displacement reactions** where one halogen will take the place of another in its compounds. Chlorine will displace bromine from potassium bromide solution.

chlorine + potassium bromide → potassium chloride + bromine

$Cl_2(g)$ + $2KBr(aq)$ → $2KCl(aq)$ + $Br_2(aq)$

However, bromine will not displace chlorine from its compounds. This shows that chlorine is more reactive than bromine. Similar tests show that the elements further down the group are less reactive.

FIGURE 3: Chlorine water (a solution of chlorine in water) is added to potassium bromide solution and displaces orange-coloured bromine.

QUESTIONS

3 Look at the equation for the reaction of iron with chlorine.
$2Fe(s) + 3Cl_2(g) → 2FeCl_3(s)$

a How many atoms of chlorine combine with each atom of iron?

b How many formula units of iron chloride are formed for each atom of iron in the equation?

4 Predict whether bromine will react with potassium iodide solution. Explain your answer and name any products that may be formed.

Watch out!

In displacement reactions it is the lower of the halogens that is displaced from its compounds as the element.

Explaining reactivity (Higher tier only)

In the case of non-metals, it is the smaller atoms that combine most readily with other elements. Going down the halogen group, the number of shells increases and the outer shell gets further from the nucleus. Therefore the reactivity of the halogens decreases down the group.

The equations show the similarities of the reaction. For example, with the alkali metals the pattern is:

$2M + X_2 → 2MX$

Here M stands for the symbol of any Group 1 element and X for the symbol of any Group 7 element, for example sodium, Na (M), and chlorine, Cl (X):

$2Na + Cl_2 → 2NaCl$

QUESTIONS

5 What is the formula of the compound formed when sodium reacts with iodine?

6 Write a balanced chemical equation for the reaction of:

a iron with bromine

b chlorine with potassium iodide solution.

7 Would you expect astatine to take part in displacement reactions with halides? Explain your answer.

Did you know?

In the 1980s halogens were found to be responsible for the growing hole in the ozone layer above the Antarctic. They broke away from CFC (chlorofluorocarbon) molecules, used in fridges, fire extinguishers and aerosols, when the molecules reached the stratosphere. CFC compounds have now been banned.

halogens displacement

Ionic compounds

We are learning to:
> explain how Group 1 and 7 elements form ions
> explain how the properties of compounds of Group 1 and 7 depend on ions
> explain how ideas are developed to account for the properties of compounds

Why is sodium chloride safe to eat?

Sodium is a flammable metal that reacts with water. Chlorine is a toxic, corrosive green gas. But sodium chloride is a solid that dissolves in water, is unreactive, and safe to touch and taste. When elements combine to form compounds their atoms are changed and so their properties change.

FIGURE 1: Sodium, chlorine and sodium chloride.

Explaining properties

The compounds of the Group 1 metals and Group 7 non-metals, such as sodium chloride, have lots of similarities. They are colourless, crystalline solids. They have high melting points and when they are melted they will conduct an electric current.

When we think of an explanation for the properties of these compounds we have to make sure that all these facts can be accounted for. We can use our imagination to see how our ideas explain the facts.

An electric current is produced when charged particles move through a substance. Electric current flows through molten sodium chloride, so the molten salt must be made up of charged particles. The charged particles are called **ions**. Ions are atoms that have gained a positive or negative charge.

We say that the compounds of Group 1 and Group 7 are **ionic compounds** because they are made up of ions.

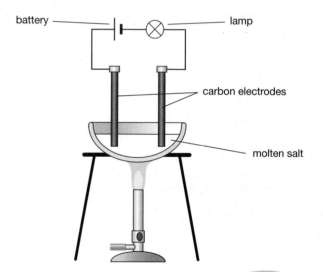

FIGURE 2: When the salt is molten the lamp lights up, showing that a current is passing through it.

Watch out!
Ions are formed from atoms by gaining or losing electrons and have a charge. Atoms do not have an electric charge.

QUESTIONS

1 How do we know that ionic compounds such as sodium chloride are made up of ions?

2 Name another ionic compound.

Positive and negative ions

An ionic compound is made up of positively charged ions and negatively charged ions. The positive ions are atoms that have lost electrons.

In sodium chloride the sodium ion is a sodium atom that has lost one electron, so it has a positive charge. Its symbol becomes Na^+. The chloride ion is a chlorine atom that has gained one electron, so it has a negative charge. Its symbol becomes Cl^-. Overall the sodium chloride has no charge because all the positive sodium ions are balanced by the negative chloride ions.

We can use this explanation to predict that other Group 1 and Group 7 compounds are also made up of positive and negative ions. All the Group 1 metals will form ions with a 1+ charge and all the Group 7 elements will form ions with a 1– charge. Thus lithium iodide is made up of Li^+ and I^- ions.

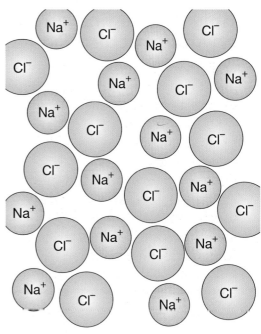

FIGURE 3: Molten sodium chloride consists of positive and negative ions.

QUESTIONS

3 Why do chloride ions have a negative charge? (Hint: Electrons have a negative charge.)

4 What are the symbols and charges of the ions in potassium bromide, KBr?

Forming ions

When a metal atom forms a positive ion, it loses the electrons from its outer shell.

Thus a sodium atom, Na, with the electron arrangement 2.8.1, becomes a sodium ion, Na^+, with the electron arrangement 2.8. Note that this electron arrangement is the same as that of a neon atom.

When a non-metal atom forms a negative ion, it gains electrons in its outer shell.

Thus a chlorine atom, Cl, with the electron arrangement 2.8.7, becomes a chloride ion, Cl^-, with the electron arrangement 2.8.8. Note that this electron arrangement is the same as that of an argon atom.

Together, the sodium and chloride ions form the compound sodium chloride.

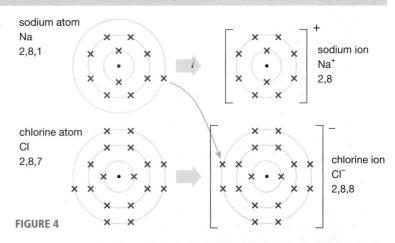

FIGURE 4

Did you know?

A 'complex ion' is two or more atoms joined together with an overall electric charge. For example sodium hydroxide is an ionic compound containing the hydroxide ion $(OH)^-$ in which the O and H atoms are joined together with an extra electron.

QUESTIONS

5 The electron arrangement of lithium (Li) is 2.1 and that of fluorine (F) is 2.7. What are the electron arrangements and charges of the ions in lithium fluoride (LiF)?

6 'Atoms gain or lose electrons to get the same electron arrangement as atoms of the Group 0 gases.' Is this statement true for compounds of Group 1 and 7? Why do you think it may be important?

Understanding ions

We are learning to:

> explain how ionic compounds form crystalline solids

> explain what happens when ionic compounds melt or dissolve in water

> work out the formulae of ionic compounds and the charges on ions

How did we find out about crystal structures?

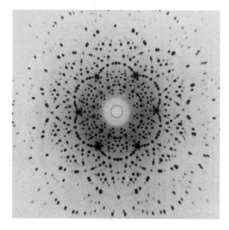

X-ray crystallography is a technique used to analyse crystals. It produces pictures that scientists use to work out the positions of particles in the crystal. Sodium chloride was the first substance to be investigated in this way, by the father and son team of William Henry Bragg and William Lawrence Bragg in 1913.

FIGURE 1: The X-ray pattern produced by the mineral beryl.

 Crystals

Ionic compounds such as sodium chloride and copper sulfate form crystals which have a regular shape. In the crystals the ions pack together in a regular pattern which is repeated over and over again. This pattern is called a **crystal lattice**.

FIGURE 2: Sodium chloride crystals and hydrated copper sulfate crystals.

In the sodium chloride lattice each positively charged sodium ion is surrounded by six negatively charged chloride ions. Each chloride ion is surrounded by six sodium ions. This pattern is repeated and builds up to form the cubic sodium chloride crystals.

QUESTIONS

1 How can we tell that the ions in sodium chloride crystals are arranged in a lattice?

2 Why does the crystal of an ionic compound have a fixed shape?

Did you know?

Sodium chloride crystals are transparent to infrared light. Large crystals can be used as lenses and prisms in infrared spectroscopy machines, which use infrared light to analyse substances.

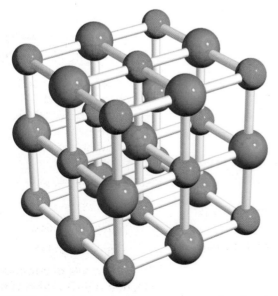

FIGURE 3: A model showing the arrangement of sodium ions (silver) and chloride ions (green) in a sodium chloride crystal.

🔍 ionic crystal lattice

Breaking the lattice

In the solid state the ions are fixed in the lattice. When the ionic substance melts, the ions become free to move.

When an ionic compound dissolves in water the ions leave the lattice. They are separated by water molecules and can move freely.

When an electric current is passed into a liquid ionic compound or a solution, the charged ions move to the electrodes and complete the circuit. This is why an ionic compound conducts electricity when it is liquid or in solution, but not when it is a solid.

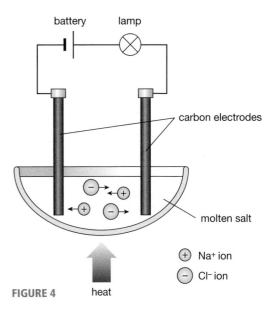

carbon electrodes

molten salt

$+$ Na^+ ion

$-$ Cl^- ion

FIGURE 4   heat

QUESTIONS

3 What happens to the ions in a solid when it melts?

4 A solution of sodium chloride can conduct electricity but a sodium chloride crystal cannot. Why is this?

Formulae and charges (Higher tier only)

The formula of sodium chloride is NaCl. In sodium chloride crystals the charge on the Na^+ ions is balanced out by an equal number of Cl^- ions. When the charges of the ions are equal and opposite there are equal numbers of the positive and negative ions.

In calcium chloride, $CaCl_2$, there are twice as many chloride ions as calcium ions. This is because the calcium ion has a 2+ charge.

A simple way to work out the formula of an ionic compound is to cross over the number of the charge on each ion, as shown in Figure 5.

Magnesium ions have a 2+ charge, bromide ions have a 1– charge. So Mg^{2+} and Br^- form the ionic compound magnesium bromide, $MgBr_2$.

The formula of aluminium oxide, Al_2O_3, can be worked out from the symbols and charges of the ions.

FIGURE 5: The cross-over method for working out the formula of an ionic compound.

You can work back from the formula to find the charge on an ion if you know the charge on the other ion. The sum of the charges of all the ions in the formula must add up to zero.

For example, the formula of potassium sulfide is K_2S. What is the charge on the sulfide ion?

Potassium is in Group 1 so has a charge of +1 on its ions. If z is the charge on the sulfide ion, then:

$$2 \times (+1) + z = 0$$
$$z = -2$$

The sulfide ion has a charge of –2.

Watch out!

The formulae of ionic compounds do not show the charges on the ions.

QUESTIONS

5 Use the symbols and charges of the ions mentioned above to work out the formula of each of the following ionic compounds:

  a sodium bromide

  b magnesium oxide

  c potassium oxide

  d aluminium sulfide.

6 The formula of strontium chloride is $SrCl_2$. What is the charge on the strontium ion?

C4 Checklist

To achieve your forecast grade in the exam you'll need to revise

Use this checklist to see what you can do now. Refer back to pages 100–125 if you're not sure. Look across the rows to see how you could progress – *bold italic* means Higher tier only.

Remember you'll need to be able to use these ideas in many ways:
> interpreting pictures, diagrams and graphs
> applying ideas to new situations
> explaining ethical implications
> suggesting some benefits and risks to society
> drawing conclusions from evidence you've been given.

Look at pages 300–306 for information about how you'll be assessed.

Watch out!

Higher tier statements may be tested at any grade from D to A*. All other statements may be tested at any grade from G to A*.

To aim for a grade E	To aim for a grade C	To aim for a grade A
recall what is meant by the relative atomic mass of an element; understand that elements put in order may show patterns	understand that scientists, such as Dobereiner and Newlands, used the properties and relative atomic masses of elements to find patterns; understand what Newlands' table of elements showed; recall that these ideas were initially dismissed by some other scientists	explain how data accounts for or conflicts with Newlands' table of elements
recall that some elements have distinctive flame colours	understand that each element gives a particular line spectrum of light	
recall that Mendeleev produced a successful ordering of elements in his Periodic Table, allowing elements to be predicted	understand the principles that Mendeleev used to arrange his Periodic Table	understand that the agreement between Mendeleev's predictions and later observations increased confidence in his ideas
recall the relative mass and charge of the proton, neutron and electron and where they are found in atoms	understand that the number of protons and electrons is the same in atoms of an element and that the modern Periodic Table lists elements in the order of their number of protons	*use the information in the Periodic Table to work out the number of protons, neutrons and electrons in an atom*
understand that electrons are arranged in shells, and interpret diagrams showing the arrangements	work out the electron arrangement of an atom given the number of electrons or protons, or the Periodic Table	understand that the shells represent energy levels filled from the bottom upwards
understand that in the rows of the Periodic Table, called periods, the number of outer shell electrons increases from 1 to 8		*understand that the chemical properties of elements depend on the electron arrangement of their atoms and hence their position in the Periodic Table*

To aim for a grade E	To aim for a grade C	To aim for a grade A
understand that groups of elements with similar chemical properties form a column in the Periodic Table; recall the names and symbols of the top three elements in Group 1 (the alkali metals)	understand that the group number is the number of outer shell electrons; use data on the physical properties of Group 1 to identify patterns; *understand that Group 1 metals are reactive because of their single outer electron*	*understand that the electron arrangements of the Group 1 elements explain both their similarities and trends in their properties down the group*

describe the reaction of lithium, sodium and potassium with oxygen, with cold water, and with chlorine; understand that reactions of the alkali metals become more vigorous down the group; recall hazard symbols and explain how to handle alkali metals safely

recall the word equations for the reactions of alkali metals with water, and with chlorine	interpret balanced symbol equations for the reactions, including state symbols	*balance unbalanced equations and write balanced symbol equations for the reactions, including state symbols*
recall the names and appearance of the elements in Group 7 (the halogens) and recognise their symbols	recall that the halogens form diatomic molecules; interpret data on their physical properties to describe patterns in the group	*understand that the electron arrangements of the Group 7 elements explain both their similarities and trends in their properties down the group*

understand that the halogens become less reactive down the group, as shown by their reactions with alkali metals, with iron and by displacement reactions; explain the safety precautions necessary in handling the halogens

recall the word equations for the reactions of halogens with alkali metals and with iron	interpret balanced symbol equations for the reactions, including state symbols	*balance unbalanced equations and write balanced symbol equations for the reactions, including state symbols*
recall the properties of compounds of the alkali metals with the halogens, and understand that they are called ionic compounds because they consist of ions	understand that ions are charged atoms that have lost (+) or gained (−) electrons; understand that ionic compounds can conduct in the molten state because the ions can move	explain the formation of the charges on the ions in compounds formed between the alkali metals and the halogens
understand that ionic compounds are crystalline because the ions form a regular crystal lattice	understand why ionic compounds are non-conductors when solid but become conductors when molten or when dissolved in water	work out the formulas of ionic compounds given the symbols and charges on the ions; work out the charge on one ion given the formula of the compound and the charge on the other ion

Exam-style questions

Foundation level

1 The table shows the boiling points of some elements in Group 7.

Element	Boiling point (°C)
Fluorine	−188
Chlorine	−35
Bromine	
Iodine	114

AO2 **a** Describe the pattern shown by the data in the table. [1]

AO2 **b** Use the data in the table to predict the boiling point of bromine. Choose from one of the following. [1]

−10°C	59°C	114°C	14°C

AO1 **c** Which of the Group 7 elements is a red liquid at room temperature? [1]

[Total 3]

Foundation/Higher level

1 AO2 **a** Which of the following statements explains why fluorine, chlorine, bromine and iodine are put in the same group in the Periodic Table? [2]

    A They all react with sodium to form a white solid with the formula NaX where X stands for the symbol of the Group 7 element.

    B They are all gases at room temperature.

    C They each have seven electrons in the outer shell of their atoms.

    D They all form diatomic molecules.

b When bromine solution is added to a colourless solution of potassium iodide the solution turns brown.

AO1 **(i)** Explain this observation. [2]

AO2

AO3 **(ii)** When chlorine gas is bubbled through potassium iodide solution a brown colour is again observed. Comment on whether this shows that bromine is more reactive than chlorine. [1]

AO1

[Total 5]

AO2 **3** Sodium and rubidium are both elements in Group 1 of the Periodic Table. Use the Periodic Table (page 309) and your knowledge of the elements in Group 1 to compare the properties of sodium and rubidium and to explain the similarities and differences. The quality of written communication will be assessed in your answer to this question. [6]

[Total 6]

Higher level

4 The table shows some information about the atoms of the elements fluorine and argon. The diagram shows the electron arrangement of fluorine.

Element	Atomic (proton) number	Relative Atomic Mass	Electron arrangement
Fluorine	10	20	2.8
Argon	18	40	2.8.8

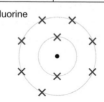

fluorine

AO1 **a** How many electrons are there in a fluorine atom? [1]

AO1 **b** Sketch the electron arrangement of an argon atom. [1]

AO2 **c** How many neutrons are there in the nucleus of an argon atom? [1]

[Total 3]

5 This question is about the Group 1 elements, known as the alkali metals.

AO1 **a** A piece of hot lithium is put in a gas jar of oxygen. It reacts quickly producing a white solid. Write a word equation for this reaction. [1]

AO1 **b** A piece of lithium was placed in a large beaker of water. The lithium floated on the surface giving off a gas. The lithium dissolved to form an alkaline solution of lithium hydroxide.

    (i) Name the gas given off in the reaction. [1]

    (ii) Which of the following represents the formula of lithium hydroxide

LiH	LiOH	Li_2OH	$Li(OH)_2$

AO1 [1]

AO2 **c** Lithium reacts with chlorine gas to form lithium chloride, a white solid. Copy and complete the balanced symbol equation for the reaction.

Word equation:
lithium + chlorine → lithium chloride
Balanced symbol equation:
_____ + _____ → ___LiCl [2]

AO3 **d** Lithium batteries are common in laptop computers but are being used on a much larger scale in electric cars. Some people think the use of lithium is too hazardous on this scale. Comment on the risks to health from using lithium batteries. [2]

[Total 7]

AO1   recall the science   AO2   apply your knowledge   AO3   evaluate and analyse the evidence

Worked example

This question is about compounds of metals and non-metals such as sodium chloride. These are known as ionic compounds.

AO1 **a** Which of the following formulae represents the sodium ion present in sodium chloride. Put a ring around the correct answer. [1]

Na ⟨Na⁺⟩ Na⁻ S ✔

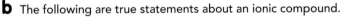

b The following are true statements about an ionic compound.
 A The compound conducts electricity when molten.
 B The solid compound is a non-conductor of electricity.
 C A solution of the compound in water is an electrical conductor.
 D The solid compound has a crystal of regular shape.

AO1
AO2 **(i)** Which statement(s) are evidence that the compound is ionic? [2]

 A, C, D ✔ ✔ ✘

AO3 **(ii)** Suggest a reason why the other statements are not evidence that the compound is ionic. [1]

 Solids which do not conduct electricity are not always ionic. ✔

AO1
AO2 **c** The table below shows the electron arrangements in potassium and chlorine atoms.

Element	Electron arrangement of atoms	Charge on ion
potassium	2.8.8.1	1+
chlorine	2.8.7	1−

Describe and explain the changes that take place in the atoms when potassium and chlorine combine to form solid potassium chloride and when this is dissolved in water. Give the formula of the compound. The quality of written communication will be assessed in your answer to this question. [6]

 Potassium atoms lose an electron to form a potassium 1+ ion with the electron arrangement 2.8.8.

 Chlorine atoms gain an electron to form a chloride 1− ion with the electron arrangement 2.8.8.

 In solid potassium chloride the ions are arranged in a regular lattice. When the potassium chloride dissolves in water the ions become free to move independently.

 The charges on the ions are equal and opposite so the formula is KCl.

How to raise your grade

Take note of the comments from examiners – these will help you to improve your grade.

Correct: 1 mark. Remember that the Periodic Table provided gives the symbol of the element and the group number of the metal gives the charge on the positive ion.

A and C are correct as conduction shows the presence of ions in both cases. D is not correct as non-ionic compounds can also form regular shaped crystals. The answer is a list and the incorrect answer means that one mark is lost. 1 mark awarded.

The full correct answer should refer to points B and D both applying to non-ionic substances, such as sugar, but the point made by the candidate is correct and they will not be penalised twice for using point D in the previous part. 1 mark awarded.

The answer demonstrates understanding of the formation of ions and the structure of ionic compounds. All information in the answer is relevant, clear, organised and presented in a structured and coherent format. Specialist terms are used appropriately. There are no errors in grammar, punctuation or spelling. This answer is worth the full 6 marks.

What you should already know...

There are important differences between elements, compounds and mixtures

Elements cannot be broken down into anything simpler and have distinctive properties.

Compounds have two or more elements chemically joined together. Compounds have different properties from the elements that make them and have formulas which show the number of atoms of each element that are joined together.

Mixtures may contain two or more elements or compounds, not chemically combined, and show the properties of each of the substances present.

 How can you show that air is a mixture containing both oxygen and carbon dioxide?

Elements can be classified as metals and non-metals

Metals are shiny, malleable, conduct heat and electricity and generally have high melting points.

Non-metals may be solids, liquids or gases and are generally poor conductors of heat and electricity.

The Periodic Table shows the name, symbol, proton number and relative atomic mass of all the known elements.

 How could you show that an unidentified material is a metal?

Some substances are soluble in water

A solution consists of a solute, such as common salt, dissolved in a solvent, such as water. Substances that dissolve are said to be soluble, while substances that do not dissolve are insoluble.

How could you show that sodium carbonate is soluble?

There are different types of rock and all rocks undergo changes over a long period of time

Igneous rocks are formed from magma rising up into the Earth's crust from the upper mantle.

Igneous rocks undergo changes into sedimentary and metamorphic rocks that alter their structure and the substances that make them up.

 State one difference between an igneous rock and a sedimentary rock.

In C5 you will find out about...

> the elements and compounds that make up the air, and their percentages in dry air

> the formation of molecules by covalent bonds between pairs or groups of atoms

> the properties of simple molecular substances, including melting and boiling points

> reasons why simple molecular substances do not conduct electricity

> the parts of the Earth that make up the hydrosphere

> substances found in the sea, which include ionic compounds such as sodium chloride

> ionic bonds that holds ions together in ionic compounds

> the properties of ionic compounds and how they are explained

> simple tests on solutions of ionic compounds to identify the ions

> the abundance of elements found in minerals in the Earth's crust

> substances with giant covalent structures

> the properties of diamond, graphite and silicon dioxide

> the parts of the Earth that make up the lithosphere

> extracting metals from ores using oxidation and reduction reactions

> interpreting and writing balanced chemical equations

> comparing and using the relative atomic mass of elements

> using electrolysis to extract metals

> the properties and bonding of metals

> the impact of our use of various metals

Molecules in the air

We are learning to:

> recall the elements and compounds that make up the air

> explain that non-metallic elements and compounds form molecules

> understand that in molecules the atoms are joined by covalent bonds

Why don't we find metals in the air?

If you went prospecting for metals you might look in rocks and the sea, but not in the air. In the air there are only non-metallic elements, such as oxygen, and compounds of non-metals, such as carbon dioxide. To find the reason for this we need to look at the types of bonds that can form between atoms.

FIGURE 1: The Earth's rocks, oceans and air are made up of elements.

Air

Air is a mixture of many different gases including water vapour. **Dry air** is air that has had the water vapour removed. The gases in dry air are the elements nitrogen, oxygen and argon and compounds such as carbon dioxide. The particles that make up these gases are atoms, such as argon atoms, and **molecules**. Molecules are groups of atoms joined together.

Oxygen and nitrogen form molecules containing two atoms of the element. The formulae of the molecules are written as O_2 and N_2. Carbon dioxide is a simple molecular compound. Its molecules are made up of two atoms of oxygen joined to an atom of carbon. The formula is CO_2.

Other non-metallic elements form molecules, such as chlorine, Cl_2. Compounds between non-metallic elements are also molecular, for example water, H_2O.

Substance	Formula	Percentage of dry air (%)
nitrogen	N_2	78
oxygen	O_2	21
argon	Ar	1
carbon dioxide	CO_2	0.04

The four gases that make up most of dry air (the percentages are rounded).

QUESTIONS

1 What is the formula of the molecules of the gas that makes up 21% of dry air?

2 What percentage of dry air is the compound with the formula CO_2?

Molecules and models

Atoms in a molecule are joined together by one or more **covalent bonds**. We cannot see molecules in a gas and we cannot see the bonds between the atoms. Nevertheless we can make models to show the arrangement of atoms in molecules. These models may be 3-D, which you can hold and rotate to examine them, or they may be diagrams representing the molecules.

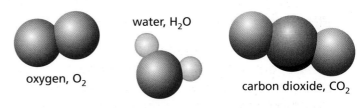

water, H_2O

oxygen, O_2

carbon dioxide, CO_2

FIGURE 2: Models show how atoms are joined together in molecules.

One type of diagram is a 2-D drawing showing the bonds between the atoms as straight lines. Another type of diagram shows the 3-D shape of the molecule. Arrows and dotted lines reveal whether atoms should be above or below the surface of the paper.

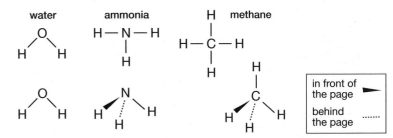

FIGURE 3: 2-D and 3-D diagrams of some simple molecules.

QUESTIONS

3 Draw 2-D diagrams for these molecules:

a chlorine, Cl_2

b methane, CH_4.

4 Explain why 3-D diagrams may be more use than 2-D diagrams.

Did you know?

A temperature over 1000 °C is needed to break the covalent bonds in water molecules to separate the atoms. The strongest simple molecule is carbon monoxide, CO, which needs a temperature over 3000 °C to split it.

Watch out!

2-D diagrams of molecules do not always show the correct shape of the molecule.

Covalent bonds (Higher tier only)

A covalent bond is formed when atoms share a pair of electrons. Usually one electron comes from the outer shell of each atom. The atoms in the molecule have the same electron arrangement as unreactive gas atoms such as argon. This arrangement can be shown by 'dot and cross' diagrams.

A bond is a force holding atoms together. In a covalent bond the force arises because the positively charged nuclei of both atoms are attracted to the negatively charged shared pair of electrons. This force holds the atoms together strongly and rigidly. The atoms in a molecule cannot move freely, which explains why simple molecules have a fixed shape.

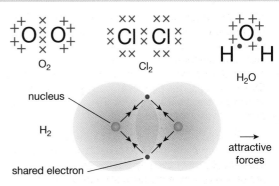

O_2

Cl_2

H_2O

nucleus

H_2

shared electron

attractive forces

FIGURE 4: The covalent bond.

QUESTIONS

5 Look at the dot and cross diagram of the water molecule. Explain why water is less reactive than hydrogen gas or oxygen gas.

6 Explain why the double covalent bond in the oxygen molecules holds the atoms together more strongly than the single covalent bond in chlorine molecules.

Simple molecular substances

Are simple molecular substances always gases?

We are learning to:

> use data about the properties of simple molecular substances

> explain the properties of simple molecular substances

> compare the forces between atoms in molecules and between molecules

Nitrogen (N_2) exists as a simple molecule in the air. But you may have heard of 'liquid nitrogen'. If you pour some liquid nitrogen at room temperature it quickly boils and turns into a gas. Simple molecular substances such as nitrogen have low boiling points.

FIGURE 1: Liquid nitrogen turns to gas at room temperature.

Looking at the data

Some properties of substances, such as melting and boiling points, can be measured. The data can be put as numbers into tables and chart. As these data show quantities we refer to them as **quantitative** data.

We can also compare the qualities of one substance with another, such as saying one is harder than another, or we can describe their behaviour. This is **qualitative** data.

The table shows the melting and boiling points of some molecular elements and compounds with small molecules, such as those in the air. They have very low melting points. From their boiling points, you can see that these are all gases at room temperature (25 °C). Very little energy is needed to allow the molecules to move freely as gases.

Substance	Melting point (°C)	Boiling point (°C)
nitrogen	−210	−196
oxygen	−218	−183
carbon dioxide		−79
chlorine	−101	−25
methane	−182	−164

Pure molecular substances with small molecules have other similar properties. They are poor conductors of electricity. When they are solid (such as iodine) they are brittle and weak.

FIGURE 2: Solid carbon dioxide turns straight into a gas at −79 °C. This is called sublimation.

QUESTIONS

1 Look at the table. Which element has the lowest boiling point?

2 On Mars the air is mainly made up carbon dioxide. What happens to the Martian air when the temperature is below −80 °C?

Forces between molecules

We can use ideas about forces between molecules to explain the properties of simple molecular substances. We can use our imagination to visualise what happens when the molecules of a substance are in the solid, liquid or gaseous states.

The attractive forces between small molecules are very weak. Very little energy is needed for molecules to overcome these forces and move apart, so simple molecular substances have low melting and boiling points. This explains why the substances in the air are gases at room temperature.

Molecules of elements and compounds have no electrical charge, so pure molecular substances cannot conduct electricity.

We can use these ideas to predict that other substances with low melting and boiling points, such as bromine, are also molecular substances.

FIGURE 3: Sulfur hexafluoride is sealed inside this electricity substation to provide insulation.

Did you know?

Sulfur hexafluoride, SF_6, is a simple molecular compound. It is used in electricity substations that change the voltage of electricity supplied to homes because it is a very good insulator. It has a boiling point of −64 °C and is unreactive.

QUESTIONS

3 Explain why methane has very low melting and boiling points (see the table on page 134).

4 Which of the following is likely to be a simple molecular substance – hydrogen chloride (boiling point −85 °C) or barium chloride (boiling point 1560 °C)? Explain your answer.

Intermolecular and intramolecular forces

For small covalent molecules, the forces *between* molecules (known as **intermolecular** forces) are weak, but the forces *within* molecules (known as **intramolecular** forces) are strong. This is because attractions between the nuclei and shared electrons form covalent bonds that hold atoms together inside molecules. These covalent bonds are strong.

Thus when a molecular substance with small molecules is melted, boiled or stretched, the molecules are easily separated from one another but the molecules themselves are not broken up into separate atoms.

Watch out!

The forces between small molecules are weak, but the forces holding the atoms together inside the molecules are strong.

QUESTIONS

5 Covalent bonds involve attraction between negatively and positively charged particles, but molecular substances do not conduct electricity. Explain this statement.

6 When we boil water at 100 °C the steam is made up of water molecules, not separate hydrogen and oxygen atoms. Why is a much higher temperature needed to split up water molecules?

Ionic crystals

We are learning to:

> recall that salts are ionic compounds that are found dissolved in water on the Earth's surface

> understand that the ions in ionic compounds are arranged in a lattice structure held together by ionic bonds

> explain how the properties of ionic compounds depend on the forces between ions and the arrangement of the ions in the crystal lattice

Why has the Aral Sea shrunk?

The Aral Sea in Central Asia was once the fourth largest inland sea on Earth. The two main rivers feeding it were dammed to irrigate farmland. The sea shrank as its water evaporated. The salts in the water became more concentrated, affecting wildlife. Now less than a quarter of the original sea remains and the dry land is covered with the salts.

FIGURE 1: A ship abandoned on a dried-out part of the Aral Sea.

Salty seas

The water, ice and snow on the Earth's surface and the water vapour in the atmosphere form the **hydrosphere**. In the water there are dissolved **salts**. When the water evaporates the salts are left as solid **crystals** with regular shapes and flat sides.

Salts are **ionic compounds** made up of particles called ions which have a positive or negative electrical charge. The ions in the crystal are arranged in a regular 3-D pattern called a **lattice**. The pattern is repeated over and over again in all directions, forming a giant ionic crystal lattice. You can see a model of the sodium chloride crystal lattice on page 124.

FIGURE 2: The oceans, seas, lakes, rivers and ice caps that make up the hydrosphere cover over three-quarters of the Earth's surface.

QUESTIONS

1 Name four types of place where water is found in the hydrosphere.

2 What must you do to seawater to form a giant crystal lattice of salt?

Did you know?

The oceans are salty because water mixes with the hot rocks at the edges of tectonic plates. This hot salty water enters the oceans in hydrothermal vents. Scientists think that life may have begun close to these vents.

Q hydrosphere

Ionic bonds

Salts have high melting and boiling points and can conduct electricity when melted or dissolved in water. We can use data about salts and our imagination to explain why they have these properties.

There is a strong force of attraction between positively charged and negatively charged ions which holds them together in the crystal lattice. We call this force an **ionic bond**.

The size and shape of the ions determines the pattern they form in the lattice when the bonding force pulls them together. The ions need a lot of energy to break out of the lattice and become a liquid. This is why ionic compounds have high melting and boiling points.

Salts are hard and cannot be compressed because within the lattice the ions are packed closely together. This also means that a solid ionic compound cannot conduct electricity. The ions are not free to move. When the salt is melted the ions become free to move, so they can conduct electricity (see Figure 4, page 125).

When an ionic compound is dissolved in water, the water molecules surround the ions so the lattice breaks up. The dissolved ions are free to move and so can conduct electricity.

FIGURE 3. The forces between positively and negatively charged ions pulls them together in a giant 3-D crystal lattice.

Watch out!

The attraction between ions acts in all directions so each ion is bonded to all its oppositely charged neighbours.

QUESTIONS

3 Explain why the melting point of sodium chloride is as high as 801 °C.

4 Describe the difference in structure of sodium chloride solution and solid sodium chloride, and explain how this makes their properties different.

Formulae of ionic compounds (Higher tier only)

An ionic compound has no overall charge. This means that the number of positive charges must just balance and cancel out the negative charges.

In sodium chloride the sodium ions have a 1+ charge and the chloride ions have a 1– charge. The charges are equal and opposite so sodium chloride is made up of equal numbers of sodium and chloride ions. The formula is written NaCl.

Magnesium ions have a 2+ charge and need two chloride ions to balance them, so the formula of magnesium chloride is $MgCl_2$.

The sulfate ion SO_4^{2-} is called a **molecular ion**. It is formed from four atoms of oxygen and one of sulfur joined together by covalent bonds. Overall it has two extra electrons so it has a charge of 2–. A sulfate ion needs two sodium ions to balance it, so the formula of sodium sulfate is Na_2SO_4.

Positively charged ions	Negatively charged ions
sodium Na$^+$	chloride Cl$^-$
potassium K$^+$	bromide Br$^-$
magnesium Mg^{2+}	iodide I$^-$
calcium Ca^{2+}	sulfate SO$_4^{2-}$

Some ions found in seawater.

QUESTION

5 Use the table to work out the formulae of the following compounds:

a sodium bromide

b calcium chloride

c magnesium sulfate

d potassium sulfate.

Q ionic bond

Testing metal ions

We are learning to:
> understand how precipitates can be formed when two solutions are mixed
> identify the metal ion in a salt
> write equations for precipitation reactions

Can testing for metals in your hair tell you how healthy you are?

Various companies offer to analyse the metal content in your hair. We eat many metals in our diets such as calcium, iron and zinc. The metal ions spread to all parts of our bodies, including hair. While analysis may show the presence of a metal, there is no proof that this gives a guide to your health.

FIGURE 1: Human hair contains metal ions absorbed by the body.

 ## Coloured ions

Ions have some properties which are the same whatever the compound they are part of, for instance compounds containing the copper ion are often blue. When an alkali, such as sodium hydroxide solution, is added to a solution containing copper ions, a blue solid is formed. The blue solid identifies that the solution contains copper ions. The solid formed when two solutions mix is called a **precipitate**.

Other metal ions can be identified from the solid formed when sodium hydroxide solution is added to solutions of their salts. These are shown in the table.

Ion	Observation
calcium, Ca^{2+}	white precipitate (insoluble in excess)
copper, Cu^{2+}	light blue precipitate (insoluble in excess)
iron(II), Fe^{2+}	green precipitate (insoluble in excess)
iron(III), Fe^{3+}	red-brown precipitate (insoluble in excess)
zinc, Zn^{2+}	white precipitate (soluble in excess, giving a colourless solution)

Tests for positively charged ions when sodium hydroxide is added.

Did you know?

Metal ions produce some of the most brilliant natural colours. The red colour of blood is caused by the iron ions in haemoglobin. Ruby is red because of chromium ions. Cobalt ions mixed with glass give it an intense blue colour.

iron(II) hydroxide   iron(III) hydroxide   copper hydroxide

FIGURE 2: Coloured precipitates are formed when an alkali is added to some metal ion solutions.

QUESTIONS

1 Why are copper sulfate and copper hydroxide blue compounds?

2 When sodium hydroxide solution is added to a solution containing an unknown metal ion a green solid is formed. What is the unknown metal ion?

Precipitates and solubility

In general, ionic compounds that are **insoluble** can be formed as a precipitate when a solution containing the positive ion of the compound is mixed with a solution containing the negative ion of the compound. This equation shows how to make a precipitate of copper hydroxide.

copper sulfate solution + sodium hydroxide solution → copper hydroxide precipitate + sodium sulfate solution

$$CuSO_4(aq) \quad + \quad 2NaOH(aq) \quad \rightarrow \quad Cu(OH)_2(s) \quad + \quad Na_2SO_4(aq)$$

This is a **precipitation reaction**.

Watch out!
Precipitation reactions can only be used to prepare insoluble compounds.

FIGURE 3: Azurite, a mineral containing copper ions, has been used as a blue pigment by painters since the Middle Ages.

QUESTIONS

3 A reddish brown precipitate is formed when sodium hydroxide solution is added to the solution of an unknown salt. Identify the metal ion in the salt and explain why the precipitate is formed.

4 Look at the first and last rows of the table on the opposite page. How could you show that an unknown compound is a zinc salt and not a calcium salt?

Ionic equations (Higher tier only)

We can write the equation for the precipitation of copper hydroxide showing all the ions present in the solutions. The charges on the ions in the solid precipitate are not shown.

$$Cu^{2+}(aq) + SO_4^{2-}(aq) + 2Na^+(aq) + 2OH^-(aq) \rightarrow Cu(OH)_2(s) + 2Na^+(aq) + SO_4^{2-}(aq)$$

If we ignore the ions that have not changed during the reaction, this leaves:

$$Cu^{2+}(aq) + 2OH^-(aq) \rightarrow Cu(OH)_2(s)$$

This is the **ionic equation** for the precipitation of copper hydroxide.

Since all metal nitrates and all sodium compounds are soluble, we can make an insoluble compound by mixing the appropriate solutions. For example, calcium carbonate is an insoluble compound. It can be precipitated from a solution containing calcium and carbonate ions.

$$Ca^{2+}(aq) + CO_3^{2-}(aq) \rightarrow CaCO_3(s)$$

Mixing calcium nitrate solution and sodium carbonate solution should give the precipitate that we want. So next we add the other ions to the ionic equation: nitrate and sodium.

$$Ca^{2+}(aq) + 2NO_3^-(aq) + 2Na^+(aq) + CO_3^{2-}(aq) \rightarrow CaCO_3(s) + 2Na^+(aq) + 2NO_3^-(aq)$$

The 2s in front of the sodium and nitrate ions are needed to balance the charges. Gathering the ions together to give the formulae for their compounds, the equation becomes:

$$Ca(NO_3)_2(aq) + Na_2CO_3(aq) \rightarrow CaCO_3(s) + 2NaNO_3(aq)$$

This is the balanced equation for the precipitation reaction.

QUESTIONS

5 Write an ionic equation for the reaction described in question 3.

6 How could you prepare a sample of insoluble lead(II) iodide?

Q precipitation chemistry GCSE   ionic equations

Analysing salts

We are learning to:
> describe and explain tests to identify the negative ion in salts
> write ionic equations for the reactions in the tests

What has photography got to do with ionic salts?

Until the arrival of the digital camera, photography relied on the sensitivity of certain salts – the silver halides – to light. A photographic film coated with tiny crystals of silver bromide reacted in light to form silver metal atoms. Developing and fixing the chemicals increased the number of silver atoms, making the image visible and permanent.

FIGURE 1: One of the first photographs taken by W H Fox Talbot, the inventor of the process.

Testing for negative ions

To test a chemical for the presence of negative ions, first add an acid. If the chemical contains the carbonate ion it will bubble and fizz. This is called **effervescence**.

Next, divide the solution of the sample into two parts. Add a few drops of silver nitrate to one part and a few drops of barium chloride or barium nitrate to the other part. The table shows what you will see if certain negative ions are present. A precipitate is a solid that makes the mixture look cloudy.

Ion	Test	Observation
carbonate CO_3^{2-}	add dilute acid	effervesces, and carbon dioxide gas produced (the gas turns lime water milky)
chloride (in solution) Cl^-	acidify with dilute nitric acid, then add silver nitrate solution	white precipitate
bromide (in solution) Br^-	acidify with dilute nitric acid, then add silver nitrate solution	cream precipitate
iodide (in solution) I^-	acidify with dilute nitric acid, then add silver nitrate solution	yellow precipitate
sulfate (in solution) SO_4^{2-}	acidify, then add barium chloride solution or barium nitrate solution	white precipitate

Tests for negatively charged ions.

FIGURE 2: A substance effervescing in an acid shows that carbonate ions are present.

QUESTIONS

1 A particular solid fizzes when you add a few drops of nitric acid to it. What does this tell you about it?

2 Nitric acid is added to a salt. There is no effervescence but when barium chloride is added the solution turns cloudy white. What does this test show?

Q test for carbonate ion   test for chloride ion

Explaining the tests

A compound containing the carbonate ion reacts with an acid to give off carbon dioxide gas. Nitric acid is used because it contains nitrate ions, which do not affect the other tests. Other salts will dissolve in nitric acid without effervescence.

calcium carbonate + nitric acid → calcium nitrate + water + carbon dioxide gas

The tests for halide and sulfate ions make use of the fact that particular compounds containing these ions are insoluble. When barium ions in solution are added to a sample containing sulfate ions, for example, insoluble barium sulfate is formed.

If chloride, bromide or iodide ions are in a sample then a precipitate is formed with silver ions but not with barium ions. As the table shows, the colour of the precipitate is different for chloride, bromide and iodide. The silver chloride is white at first but in light it soon becomes pale blue-grey.

Watch out!

The test with acid must be done before adding the silver nitrate or barium chloride solutions. This is because carbonate ions form an insoluble compound with silver ions and barium ions.

FIGURE 3: The result of a test for a sulfate ion.

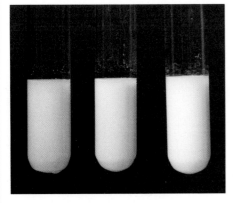

FIGURE 4: Results of tests for halide ions. From left to right, silver chloride, silver bromide and silver iodide precipitates.

Did you know?

Barium sulfate is used to obtain X-ray pictures of the digestive system. A patient drinks a suspension of the insoluble salt which coats the surface of the gut. Barium ions block X-rays, so their position shows up on X-ray photographs.

QUESTIONS

3 Describe and explain what you see when nitric acid and silver nitrate are added to a sample of sodium iodide.

4 A salt does not effervesce when nitric acid is added but forms a cream precipitate when silver nitrate is added. Identify the negative ion in the salt and explain what has happened.

Writing the equations (Higher tier only)

We can write ionic equations for the precipitation reactions used in the tests. For example:

silver nitrate solution + sodium chloride solution → silver chloride precipitate + sodium nitrate solution

$AgNO_3(aq)$ + $NaCl(aq)$ → $AgCl(s)$ + $NaNO_3(aq)$

Separate the ions in the solutions:

$Ag^+(aq) + NO_3^-(aq) + Na^+(aq) + Cl^-(aq)$
$\rightarrow AgCl(s) + Na^+(aq) + NO_3^-(aq)$

Now ignore the ions that have not changed:

$Ag^+(aq) + Cl^-(aq) \rightarrow AgCl(s)$

This is the ionic equation for the reaction. It is the same for all salts containing the chloride ion.

QUESTION

5 Write ionic equations for the formation of precipitates in the reactions of:

a silver nitrate solution and sodium bromide solution

b silver nitrate solution and potassium iodide solution

c barium nitrate solution and magnesium sulfate solution (the formula of the barium ion is Ba^{2+}).

test for sulfate ion

Preparing for assessment: Analysing, evaluating and reviewing

To achieve a good grade in science you will need to be able to use your skills and understanding to understand how scientists plan, run and evaluate investigations. These skills will be assessed in your exams and in Controlled Assessments. This activity supports you in developing the skills of evaluation of the apparatus and procedures.

✳ What is this white powder? – anion identification

1. Adding water to white powders in two beakers.

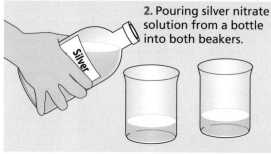

2. Pouring silver nitrate solution from a bottle into both beakers.

3. Both solutions have turned cloudy white.

Ceri has a Food Technology lesson in school and has brought the ingredients with her. Unfortunately she forgot to label the containers properly. She has two small pots containing white powders. One is common salt, sodium chloride, and the other is baking soda, sodium bicarbonate. She needs to know which is which before she starts to bake her cake. Her friend Sam says he knows a way to find out. He has learned that silver nitrate solution is used to test chlorides. Mr Williams, the chemistry teacher, agrees to supervise Ceri and Sam while they do the test during break time, but he has a set of work to mark so he has not got time to advise them.

Ceri collects two small beakers and pours one powder into one and the other powder into the other. She adds water and stirs the mixtures with a spatula. It takes a while for the solids to dissolve and time is running short.

Sam has collected a bottle of silver nitrate solution. He takes the stopper off the bottle and pours the solution into both beakers.

Both solutions turn cloudy white. "Oh, why did that happen?" Ceri says, "They can't both be sodium chloride."

Task 1

> Did Ceri and Sam carried out the chloride test correctly?
> Why was Ceri unable to decide which of the powders was sodium chloride?

 Task 2

> What other test could they have done to tell the difference between sodium chloride and sodium bicarbonate?
> Suggest the apparatus that Ceri and Sam should have used.

 Task 3

> Describe in detail how Ceri and Sam could have proved that one powder was sodium bicarbonate and the other was sodium chloride.

 Maximise your grade

Use these suggestions to improve your work and be more successful.

E

To be on target for grade E you need to:

> Comment about problems you had doing the experiment.

> Say how the equipment or the methods used prevented you from collecting all the data you needed.

C

To be on target for grades D, C, in addition, you need to:

> Suggest some improvements you could make to the apparatus or methods used

> or suggest different ways of collecting the data,

> or explain how the method used gives you enough information to write a conclusion.

A

To be on target for grades B, A, in addition, you need to:

> give a detailed set of improvements to the apparatus or the methods,

> or suggest different ways of collecting data and explain why they are better,

> or explain why the method used cannot be improved upon.

Minerals and giant molecules

Where can you find diamonds?

FIGURE 1: Cut diamonds sparkle in light.

We are learning to:

> recall which elements are commonly found in minerals in the Earth's crust

> explain the properties of some elements and compounds that have giant covalent structures

> explain the differences in structure and properties of diamond and graphite

Diamonds are the hardest natural materials. They are very beautiful and very valuable. Diamonds are formed in great heat and pressure deep below the surface of the Earth, in the layer beneath the crust. Sometimes they are carried closer to the surface by volcanic activity. They survive the heat of molten magma and may be found in the pipes below extinct volcanoes.

Minerals

We find all the naturally occurring elements in the **minerals** that make up the **lithosphere**. The lithosphere is a layer of the Earth made up of the solid rocks of the crust and the top part of the mantle below. Minerals are solid substances found naturally in which the atoms or ions are arranged in a regular crystal lattice. Rocks are usually a mixture of minerals.

Diamond is a mineral; so is graphite. They are both crystalline forms of carbon.

The table shows the elements most commonly found in the Earth's crust. Silicon and oxygen are usually found joined together in compounds such as silicon dioxide. This is found in minerals such as quartz.

Element	Percentage in the Earth's crust (%)
oxygen	47
silicon	28
aluminium	8.1
iron	5.0
calcium	3.6
sodium	2.8
potassium	2.6
magnesium	2.1
titanium	0.4
hydrogen	0.1

The abundance of the 10 most common elements in the Earth's crust.

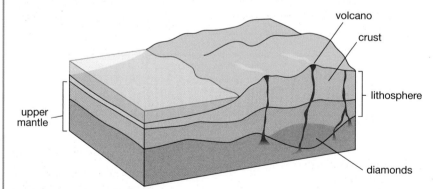

FIGURE 2: Diamonds are formed in the top of the mantle, which is part of the Earth's lithosphere.

QUESTIONS

1 Name three minerals found in the lithosphere.

2 What percentage of the Earth's crust is made up of silicon and oxygen?

lithosphere Earth's crust

Giant covalent structures

Atoms of carbon can only form bonds with each other by sharing electrons in covalent bonds. Unlike simple molecules (such as methane), diamond and graphite are made up of **giant covalent structures** in which a very large number of carbon atoms are linked together in a regular pattern.

Covalent bonds are strong. In diamond the atoms are held together rigidly so diamond is very hard. It requires a lot of energy to break the bonds to allow the carbon atoms to move, so diamond has very high melting and boiling points and does not dissolve in water. There are no free charged particles in diamond so it does not conduct electricity when solid or when melted.

Watch out!

Giant covalent and simple molecular substances both have strong covalent bonds holding atoms together.

Silicon dioxide is also a giant covalent structure. The atoms are arranged in a similar pattern to the carbon atoms in diamond, so silicon dioxide is also hard, has high melting and boiling points, does not conduct electricity and does not dissolve in water.

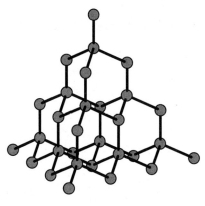

FIGURE 3: The structure of diamond. Each carbon atom is joined to four others by covalent bonds.

QUESTIONS

3 How are giant covalent structures different from simple molecules?

4 Why does silicon dioxide have a high melting point?

Diamond and graphite

Diamond and graphite are both forms of pure carbon with high melting points. They are both giant covalent structures but their different appearance and properties show that the arrangement of the atoms is different.

In diamond each carbon atom is covalently bonded to four other atoms in a tetrahedral 3-D lattice.

In graphite each atom only has three covalent bonds and the atoms are arranged hexagonally in flat sheets. The sheets are strong but there is only a weak force between the layers so they can slide over each other. This is what makes graphite a good lubricant and why graphite pencils can write on paper. Each carbon atom has one electron not used in the covalent bonding. These electrons can move easily between the layers, allowing graphite to conduct electricity.

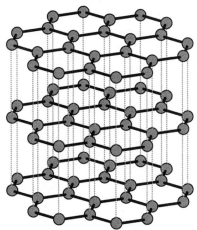

FIGURE 4: The structure of graphite. Each carbon atom is joined to three others by covalent bonds.

FIGURE 5: A sample of graphite.

Did you know?

Graphene is a material that is just a single layer of graphite about one-third of a nanometre thick. It is strong but stretchy and conducts electricity and heat well. It could be used to make touchscreen displays and other electronic components.

QUESTIONS

5 Describe the differences in the structure of diamond and graphite, and explain the resulting differences in their properties.

Extracting metals

We are learning to:
> explain why large amounts of ore are mined to extract metals
> describe the reactions used to extract metals from their ores
> explain oxidation and reduction reactions

Why was the biggest hole in the world dug?

The Bingham Canyon Mine, USA, produces copper and other metals. It is the largest man-made hole that has been dug in the Earth. Since the mine opened in 1906, 6 billion tonnes of rock have been removed, and from this 16 million tonnes of copper have been extracted.

FIGURE 1: The Bingham Canyon copper mine.

Getting metals from ores

Different minerals contain different metals. Rocks that contain minerals from which metals can be extracted are called **ores**.

Some ores contain the metal oxide. The metal oxide can be heated with carbon to produce the metal. This method is used to obtain metals such as copper, iron and zinc from their ores.

Iron oxide and carbon are heated in a blast furnace. The carbon takes away the oxygen and **reduces** the iron oxide to iron. The iron runs out of the furnace as a liquid.

iron oxide + carbon → iron + carbon dioxide

QUESTIONS

1 What is an ore?

2 Copper is extracted from copper oxide using carbon. Write a word equation for this reaction.

FIGURE 2   iron oxide   +   carbon   →   iron   +   carbon dioxide

Making metals pay

Iron is one of the most abundant elements in the Earth's crust (see the table on page 144) but it is very expensive to remove all the waste rock. It is not possible for the mining companies to make a profit if there is less than about 25% of iron in the ore. Mineralogists look for ores with a very high percentage of minerals of iron, such as haematite and magnetite. These minerals are found in many parts of the world.

Copper is a much more valuable metal and makes up a much smaller percentage of the Earth's crust. It is economic to extract copper from ores which have less than 1% of copper in them. This means that a huge amount of rock has to be mined to get at the copper.

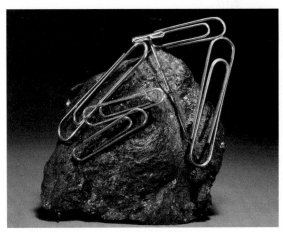

FIGURE 3: A form of magnetite called lodestone is a natural magnet.

QUESTIONS

3 Why is it rarer to find copper ores with a high percentage of copper than iron ores with a high percentage of iron?

4 How much copper can be extracted from a tonne (1000 kg) of ore if the copper makes up 1% of the ore?

Did you know?

Ancient civilisations used lodestone to create the compass. Using compasses, navigators were able to explore the whole world.

Oxidation and reduction

The extraction of zinc uses carbon to reduce zinc oxide to zinc. This is the equation for the reaction:

zinc oxide + carbon → zinc + carbon dioxide

$$2ZnO + C → 2Zn + CO_2$$

The zinc oxide loses oxygen. This process is called **reduction**. The zinc oxide has been **reduced**.

The carbon has gained oxygen. This process is called **oxidation**. The carbon has been **oxidised**.

The reaction for extracting metals from their ores is a **redox reaction**. This means it involves both oxidation and reduction. Oxidation is the gain of oxygen by a substance while reduction is the loss of oxygen by a substance.

Watch out!

In a reaction where a substance is oxidised, another substance must be reduced.

FIGURE 4: Crystals of calamine, a mineral of zinc. These are sometimes coloured blue by copper impurities.

Did you know?

Zinc is extracted by heating zinc oxide with carbon. The reaction takes place at such a high temperature that the zinc metal is formed as a gas.

QUESTIONS

5 Look at the equation for the extraction of iron from iron oxide. Which substance is oxidised and which is reduced?

6 Can you have a chemical reaction which is just reduction? Explain your answer.

oxidation reduction oxygen

Chemistry in shorthand

We are learning to:
> write word equations for chemical reactions
> understand balanced symbol equations for chemical reactions

Have chemists always used equations for reactions?

The Swedish chemist Jons Jacob Berzelius suggested a system of symbols for chemical formulae and equations in 1813. This system used letters and numbers and replaced the symbols used earlier by John Dalton. Berzelius' system was much easier to print in journals and books and so was used worldwide.

Name	Dalton's symbols	Berzelius' symbols
hydrogen		H
oxygen		O
carbon		C
water		H_2O
carbon dioxide		CO_2
zinc oxide		ZnO

FIGURE 1

Word equations

Word equations show the chemicals that reacted (the reactants) in a chemical reaction and the chemicals that were made (the products).

A reaction can be described in words, like this:

'Dilute nitric acid was added to solid sodium carbonate. There was effervescence as carbon dioxide was given off. Sodium nitrate was left in solution in water.'

This can be summarised by the word equation:

nitric acid solution + sodium carbonate solid
$\rightarrow$ sodium nitrate solution + carbon dioxide gas + water

QUESTIONS

1 What are the reactants and products of the reaction in this word equation?
copper oxide solid + carbon solid
$\rightarrow$ copper solid + carbon dioxide gas

2 Write a word equation for this reaction:
'Drops of sodium hydroxide solution are added to copper sulfate solution. Copper hydroxide precipitates, leaving a solution of sodium sulfate.'

FIGURE 2: The reaction when nitric acid is added to sodium carbonate.

Interpreting equations

Balanced symbol equations are the language of chemistry and are understood by chemists everywhere, regardless of their native language. Equations are also a shorthand code for describing reactions.

Q word equations

You need to recognise the symbols of the elements and understand how the symbols are put together to create formulae. The small letters in brackets after a formula shows the state the substance is in. A balanced equation shows the reactants and products and also the number of atoms of each element and how many covalent molecules and ionic 'formula units' are involved.

For example:

$2Fe_2O_3(s) + 3C(s) \rightarrow 4Fe(s) + 3CO_2(g)$

This equation tells us that solid iron(III) oxide and carbon react to form iron and carbon dioxide gas. It also shows that for every 2 'formula units' of iron(III) oxide, 3 atoms of carbon are needed and that this produces 4 atoms of iron and 3 molecules of carbon dioxide. The equation is balanced because there are the same number of atoms of each element on both sides (see the table).

	Substances	Number of atoms of		
		iron	oxygen	carbon
left side	$2Fe_2O_3$	4	6	
	$3C$			3
right side	$4Fe$	4		
	$3CO_2$		6	3

The number of atoms of each element on each side of the equation for the reaction of iron oxide with carbon.

QUESTIONS

3 Look at this equation:

$2CuCO_3(s) + C(s) \rightarrow 2Cu(s) + 3CO_2(g)$

a What does the formula CO_2 stand for?

b How many atoms of copper are produced for every 'formula unit' of copper carbonate ($CuCO_3$) reacted?

c How many atoms of each element are involved in the reaction?

d What does the symbol (g) mean after the CO_2?

Did you know?

In the early 19th century chemists disagreed about the formula of water. Some chemists thought the formula should be HO while others used H_2O. In the 1860s chemists agreed that H_2O was correct because experiments showed that water broke down to give twice as much hydrogen as oxygen.

Balancing equations (Higher tier only)

To write a balanced equation you must follow these steps.

> First, write a word equation for the reaction.

> Replace the words with
  – the symbol of the elements that exist as atoms (metals and elements that have giant molecules such as carbon)
  – the formulae of simple molecules
  – the formula units of ionic compounds.

> Balance the equation to make the number of atoms of each element the same on both sides of the equation. Do this by placing numbers in front of each substance. See page 115 for more detail on writing equations.

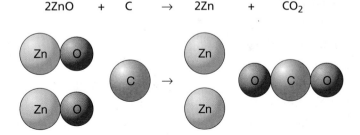

FIGURE 3: Representing the balanced equation for the reaction of zinc oxide with carbon.

Watch out!

Hydrogen, oxygen, nitrogen, fluorine, chlorine, bromine and iodine are all elements that exist naturally as simple diatomic molecules (e.g. H_2).

QUESTIONS

4 Balance this equation:

$CuO(s) + C(s) \rightarrow Cu(s) + CO_2(g)$

5 Look at question 2. Write a balanced chemical equation for the reaction described. (Formulae: sodium hydroxide, NaOH; copper sulfate, $CuSO_4$; copper hydroxide, $Cu(OH)_2$; sodium sulfate, Na_2SO_4.)

Atomic masses

We are learning to:
> use relative atomic masses to calculate the relative formula mass of a compound
> work out how much of the mass of a compound is made up by each element

What is the mass of an atom?

The mass of one atom of hydrogen is 1.67×10^{-24} g. To put it another way, about 6×10^{23} atoms of hydrogen weigh 1 g. If each of these atoms was 1 cm across they could cover Britain to a depth of 25 000 kilometres.

Scientists at Berkeley Lab in the USA have built a balance using carbon nanotubes. This can measure the mass of a single gold atom (which is about 200 times the mass of a hydrogen atom).

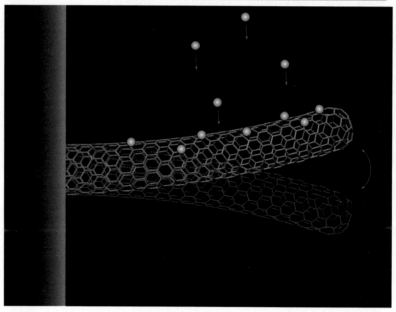

FIGURE 1: A balance for atoms. The finger-shaped nanotube vibrates like a spring. When an atom lands on it the vibration changes, allowing scientists to calculate the mass of the atom.

Comparing atoms

The **relative atomic mass** (RAM) of an atom is the mass of an atom compared to the mass of an atom of carbon, which is given the value 12. Magnesium atoms, which have twice the mass of carbon atoms, have an RAM of 24. You can find the RAM of an element in the Periodic Table. The RAM is the top number in the element's box.

K	Ca
potassium	calcium
19	20
(85)	88
Rb	**Sr**
rubidium	strontium
37	38
133	137
Cs	**Ba**
caesium	barium

FIGURE 2: The RAM of rubidium is 85.

QUESTIONS

1 Krypton atoms are seven times heavier than carbon atoms. What is the relative atomic mass of krypton?

2 Use the Periodic Table on page 309 to find the relative atomic mass of:

   a neon (Ne)

   b aluminium (Al)

   c potassium (K)

   d copper (Cu).

Formula mass

The **relative formula mass** (RFM) of a compound is the sum of the RAMs of all the atoms or ions shown in its formula. An ion has the same mass as the atom because the electrons that have been lost or gained have almost no mass.

To find the RFM of water, H_2O, we need the RAMs of hydrogen (1) and oxygen (16). The RFM of water is $2 \times 1 + 16 = 18$.

Q relative formula mass GCSE

We can measure out the number of grams of an element or compound represented by its RAM or RFM. This is the **gram formula mass**. For water it is 18g.

Example
What is the gram formula mass of sodium hydroxide, NaOH? What mass of sodium is there in it?
(RAM: Na = 23, O = 16, H = 1)

The RFM of sodium hydroxide is 23 + 16 + 1 = 40.

The gram formula mass of sodium hydroxide is 40g, of which 23g is sodium.

Watch out!
When calculating the RFM make sure you take account of the small numbers after the symbol in the formula.

FIGURE 3: The gram atomic mass of carbon is 12g.

QUESTIONS

2 Use the Periodic Table (page 309) to work out the relative formula mass of magnesium oxide (MgO), calcium chloride ($CaCl_2$), carbon dioxide (CO_2) and copper sulfate ($CuSO_4$).

Calculating the mass of metal (Higher tier only)

We can use gram formula mass and the formula to work out how much of a metal there is in any amount of a mineral.

Example
Haematite is a common mineral of iron with formula Fe_2O_3 (iron oxide). What is the percentage of iron in haematite?
(RAM: Fe = 56, O = 16)

The RFM of iron oxide is $56 \times 2 + 16 \times 3 = 160$.

The percentage of iron in iron oxide

$$= \frac{\text{total mass of iron atoms}}{\text{gram formula mass of iron oxide}} \times 100\%$$

$$= \frac{112}{160} \times 100\%$$

$$= 70\%$$

So, 70% of any mass of haematite can be extracted as iron.

The equation for a reaction also represents the ratio of the gram formula masses that react. For example:

$$2Fe_2O_3 + 3C \rightarrow 4Fe + 3CO_2$$

This shows that 2 formula units of iron oxide give 4 atoms of iron,

or $2 \times 160 = 320$g of iron oxide gives $4 \times 56 = 224$g of iron

or 1g of iron oxide gives $\frac{224}{320} = 0.7$g of iron

QUESTIONS

5 Covellite is a mineral of copper with the formula CuS. How much copper could be obtained from 100g of covellite?

6 The equation for the extraction of zinc from zinc oxide is:

$$2ZnO + C \rightarrow 2Zn + CO_2$$

What mass of zinc could be obtained from 81g of zinc oxide?

FIGURE 4: A sample of haematite, a mineral containing 70% iron.

Using electrolysis

Why is aluminium a 'modern' metal?

Aluminium is the most abundant metal in the Earth's crust but was not used in large quantities until the 20th century. This is because it clings very strongly to oxygen in its ore, aluminium oxide. Iron and copper cling much less strongly to oxygen. A powerful source of electricity is needed to break up aluminium oxide.

FIGURE 1: Aluminium ore containing aluminium oxide. Aluminium is so reactive that aluminium oxide cannot be reduced by carbon.

 What is electrolysis?

Electrolysis means passing an electric current through a liquid **electrolyte,** which is broken down into it elements. Molten ionic compounds such as sodium chloride or aluminium oxide are electrolytes. When an ionic substance is heated until it melts the ions become free to move and travel with an electric current.

Aluminium is extracted from aluminium oxide by electrolysis. An electric current is passed through molten aluminium oxide to **decompose** it. Molten aluminium is formed, which is piped out of the cell. Oxygen is also formed.

QUESTIONS

1 Write out these sentences, filling in the missing words.
When an ionic compound is .... the ions become free to .... and conduct .... The compound is .... This process is called ....

2 What are the products of the electrolysis of molten aluminium oxide?

FIGURE 2: A line of electrolysis cells for producing aluminium. A typical cell may have a current of 300000 amps flowing through it.

 Why do we use electrolysis?

The oxides of reactive metals such as sodium and aluminium are not reduced by carbon, so this method cannot be used to extract these metals from their ores. Electrolysis is a way of obtaining reactive metals from their compounds.

When molten ionic compounds are electrolysed the ions are attracted by, and move towards, the **electrodes** which carry the electric current into the electrolyte.

Did you know?

The first successful electrolysis of molten salts was carried out by Humphry Davy at the Royal Institution in London in 1807. His electric power source was a large battery. Davy produced the first samples of sodium, potassium, calcium, magnesium, strontium and barium.

Q extraction aluminium

Positive ions such as sodium (Na^+) and aluminium (Al^{3+}) move to the negatively charged electrode called the **cathode**. Metals, such as sodium and aluminium, form at the cathode.

Negative ions such as chloride (Cl^-) and oxide (O^{2-}) move to the positively charged electrode called the **anode**. Non-metals, such as chlorine and oxygen, form at the anode.

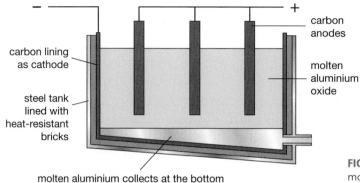

FIGURE 3: The electrolysis of molten aluminium oxide.

QUESTIONS

3 Potassium is more reactive than sodium. Would you expect potassium to be obtained by reducing its oxide with carbon or by electrolysis? Explain your answer.

4 Explain why aluminium forms at the cathode and oxygen at the anode when molten aluminium oxide is electrolysed.

Reactions at electrodes (Higher tier only)

At the cathode, metals ions gain electrons and become neutral metal atoms. For example, in the electrolysis of molten aluminium oxide, aluminium is formed at the cathode.

$$Al^{3+} + 3e^- \rightarrow Al$$

The $3e^-$ represents the electrons supplied by the cathode.

At the anode, non-metal ions lose electrons and become neutral non-metal atoms. For example, oxygen is formed in the electrolysis of molten aluminium oxide.

$$O^{2-} \rightarrow O + 2e^-$$

The oxygen atoms then combine to form oxygen molecules:
$$2O \rightarrow O_2$$

The electrons transferred to the anode flow in the circuit to the cathode, completing the electric circuit. The complete equation is:

$$2Al_2O_3 \rightarrow 4Al + 3O_2$$

Similar processes happen in the electrolysis of molten salts such as sodium chloride. Sodium and chloride ions carry the electric current through the electrolyte. At the cathode, sodium ions become neutral atoms.

$$Na^+ + e^- \rightarrow Na$$

At the anode, chloride ions become neutral atoms that combine to form chlorine gas.

$$2Cl^- \rightarrow Cl_2 + 2e^-$$

Overall the equation is:

$$2NaCl \rightarrow 2Na + Cl_2$$

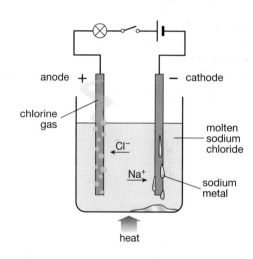

FIGURE 4: The electrolysis of molten sodium chloride.

Watch out!

Reactive metals are formed in electrolysis only when their molten ionic compounds are electrolysed and not when solutions of their salts are electrolysed.

QUESTIONS

5 Describe, with equations, what happens to the ions in aluminium oxide during electrolysis.

6 Use equations or diagrams to describe what happens when molten potassium bromide (KBr) is electrolysed.

What is special about metals?

How many metals do we use?

FIGURE 1: White light emitting diodes (LEDs) use indium and other rare metals.

Until the Middle Ages just seven metals were known and used – gold, silver, copper, tin, iron, lead and mercury. The Periodic Table includes over 70 metals. Although many of these are rare, we make use of most of them in modern technologies. For example, indium is used in white LEDs and neodymium in miniature motors.

Using metals

We have replaced metals with plastics for some uses, such as pipes and buckets, but we use metals for many purposes. Metals are used because they have the particular properties that are needed. These properties include:

> high melting point – this is needed for engines, furnaces and high-speed machines such as drills, which get very hot.

> strength – metals are strong when they are stretched, so can be used for structures like bridges and tall buildings that have to carry a large weight.

> **malleability** – metals can be hammered, bent and pressed into complicated shapes such as car bodies.

> electrical conductivity – metals conduct electricity from power stations to homes and businesses and carry energy to lights, motors, computer chips and other components.

FIGURE 2: Even when it is red hot, iron is still solid, but it can be hammered into shape.

Did you know?

Rhodium is the most expensive metal and is used in some electrical components. It is also used in jewellery because it is even shinier than gold. Mixed with platinum, it is used in catalytic converters in cars.

QUESTION

1 Write down uses for the following metals:

a copper – a very good electrical conductor

b steel – very strong

c aluminium – very malleable

d iron – has a high melting point.

Q properties of useful metals

The structure of metals

In metals there is a force called the **metallic bond** that attracts the atoms together. The atoms are held in a giant crystal lattice in which there is a repeated regular arrangement of the atoms.

The metallic bond is strong in most metals, so the atoms need a lot of energy to make them move out of their positions in the lattice. A high temperature is needed to melt most metals and a lot of force is needed to bend or stretch them.

FIGURE 3: A photograph of atoms of gold on the surface of a crystal.

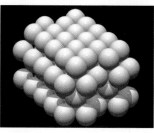

FIGURE 4: A model of the arrangement of atoms in a giant metal crystal lattice.

Watch out!

Metal atoms are packed tightly together so that they are touching. Metals cannot be squashed into a smaller volume.

QUESTIONS

2 A dock-side crane uses a thin steel cable to lift heavy crates onto ships. Explain why steel can be used for this task.

3 Titanium has a higher melting point than aluminium and is used in high-speed aircraft that become very hot in flight. Explain why titanium has a high melting point.

The metallic bond (Higher tier only)

Metal atoms can lose their outer shell electrons, leaving positively charged ions. When metal atoms are packed together in a crystal, the outer shell electrons can move freely from one atom to another. They form a 'sea of electrons' between the fixed positive ions.

The positive ions are attracted to all the free electrons around them. This force keeps the ions in the lattice – it is what makes the metallic bond. The force is strong in most metals, giving them high strength and a high melting point. The free electrons can move through the metal structure, and this allows the metal to conduct electricity.

In a pure metal all the atoms are identical. The atoms are all the same size so the layers in the giant lattice can roll across each other quite easily. The arrangement of the atoms is the same in the new position as before the movement. This means that metals can change their shape without affecting the strength of the bonds between the atoms. They are malleable.

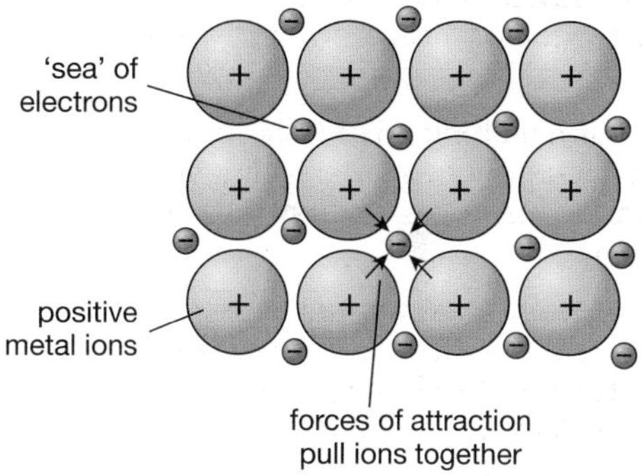

'sea' of electrons

positive metal ions

forces of attraction pull ions together

FIGURE 5: The free electrons between the ions bind them together.

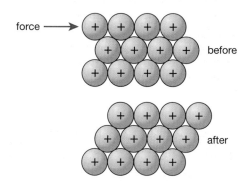

force

before

after

FIGURE 6: Applying a force to change the shape of a metal does not affect the arrangement of the atoms, so it remains strong.

QUESTIONS

4 Tungsten is one of the strongest metals. Explain why it is strong.

5 Silver is the best electrical conductor. Explain how it conducts electricity.

6 Aluminium kitchen foil can be bent and crunched up without losing its strength. Explain this property of aluminium.

Q metallic bonding and structure

Metals in the environment

We are learning to:
> discuss the risks of extracting, using and disposing of metals
> evaluate the impact on the environment of our need for metals
> consider how we can deal with undesirable effects of using metals

Are we running out of metals?

We use the whole range of metals from aluminium to zinc in everything from aircraft to zips. Metal atoms are never lost from the Earth but when we use them they can get mixed up. It is very difficult to separate and recycle them. There may only be enough of the ores of rare metals for a few more years' use.

FIGURE 1: Mobile phones use a lot of different metals. It is difficult to separate the metals when the phone is disposed of.

Danger! Contamination

People have used some metals for centuries. There are disused quarries and mines in many places. Poisonous heavy metals such as lead, mercury and cadmium have sometimes been left in the soil. People can be harmed by these metals, and it costs a lot of money to clean up the soil.

Today we are using many more metals. Mines are often huge (see page 146) and there is a lot of waste rock to dispose of. Mines destroy habitats and can damage water sources. Extracting metals uses energy and produces pollutants. Some of the pollutants are gases that can contribute to acid rain.

If metals are just dumped when they have stopped being useful, they can damage habitats.

FIGURE 2: This river is polluted by metals such as copper, nickel and zinc. The polluted water is toxic. It kills wildlife and damages habitats.

Watch out!
Even if a metal is not toxic to plants and animals, dumping a lot of it in one place may still damage habitats.

QUESTIONS

1 How does metal extraction damage the environment?

2 What problems do metals cause when they are dumped in soils and rivers?

The copper story

Copper is one of the most important metals used today. Even the best ores only contain about 1% of copper. This means that 99% of the ore is waste rock. Getting at the copper uses a lot of energy and often releases sulfur dioxide, which can cause acid rain. Copper is used for pipes and electric wiring. It can be recycled after use but about two-thirds of waste copper is left to contaminate the environment.

There are similar environmental issues with many other materials used in today's 'hi-tech' world. This poses ethical questions. We know that extracting materials damages the environment and may possibly harm the health of the people who live there. The materials extracted will benefit a large number of people. Does this justify any damage caused? Should we continue to simply throw away waste materials, or is this always wrong?

FIGURE 3: Bales of copper wire produced using recycled metal.

QUESTIONS

3 Give three ways that extracting copper can damage the environment.

4 A rare metal used in computer and TV displays has been discovered in rocks near your home. What views might people have about extracting the metal? What do you think?

The lithium story

Since the 1990s the lithium battery has become common in phones, games machines, music players and computers. Lithium batteries are also being used increasingly in electric and hybrid cars. Vehicles need vastly more power than a mobile phone, so arrays of thousands of lithium batteries are needed. Although not a rare element, not much lithium has been used until recently. New sources will have to be found to meet the increase in demand.

Lithium batteries can be a fire hazard but they are not toxic. Dumping lithium batteries in landfill may be safe, but it is a waste of the lithium and other metals used in them.

FIGURE 4: Electric cars use a lot of lithium in their batteries and also rare earth metals.

QUESTIONS

5 Describe and explain the ways that new technology has changed our use of metals.

6 Some people say that using lithium in electric cars is a waste of the resource. What arguments are there for and against this statement?

Did you know?

Rare earth metals like neodymium and lanthanum are used in 'green technologies' such as hybrid cars and wind turbines. However, separating and extracting them from their ores produces a lot of pollution. This occurs mainly in China, where most of the metals are produced.

C5 Checklist

To achieve your forecast grade in the exam you'll need to revise

Use this checklist to see what you can do now. Refer back to pages 132–157 if you're not sure. Look across the rows to see how you could progress – *bold italic* means Higher tier only.

Remember you'll need to be able to use these ideas in many ways:
> interpreting pictures, diagrams and graphs
> applying ideas to new situations
> explaining ethical implications
> suggesting some benefits and risks to society
> drawing conclusions from evidence you've been given.

Look at pages 300–306 for information about how you'll be assessed.

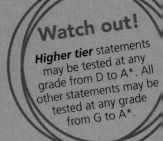

Watch out!

Higher tier statements may be tested at any grade from D to A*. All other statements may be tested at any grade from G to A*.

To aim for a grade E	To aim for a grade C	To aim for a grade A
recall the names, symbols and formulas of elements and compounds that make up air, and the percentages they make up in dry air		
recall that most non-metal elements and compounds exist as molecules	understand that in molecules of non-metallic elements the atoms are joined together by covalent bonds; understand 2-D and 3-D representations of bonds in molecules	*understand that the covalent bond is caused by the attraction between the positively charged nuclei of atoms and a shared pair of negatively charged electrons*
interpret data about the physical properties of simple molecular substances and recall that they have low melting and boiling points and do not conduct electricity	understand that as molecules are uncharged the forces between them are weak and that this explains the physical properties of molecular substances	understand that while the forces between molecules are weak the covalent bonds in the molecules are strong
recall that the hydrosphere consists largely of water which contains dissolved salts; understand that salts are ionic compounds made up of ions, which in the solid state form a regular crystal lattice	understand that the charged ions have a strong force between them called the ionic bond that results in the properties of ionic compounds; describe what happens when ionic compounds form solutions	*work out the formulas of the compounds dissolved in water, given the charges on the ions*
understand that some metal ions can be identified by the coloured precipitate formed with an alkali	understand that a precipitate of an ionic compound may be formed when solutions containing the ions are mixed	*write ionic equations for these precipitation reactions; given data on the solubility of ionic compounds, predict when a precipitate may be formed*

To aim for a grade E	To aim for a grade C	To aim for a grade A
interpret the results for tests for some negative ions in salts, given a data sheet	understand the reactions that produce an insoluble solid when reagents are added to solutions containing negative ions	*write ionic equations for these precipitation reactions; given solubility data, predict when a precipitate may be formed*
recall that the lithosphere is made up of minerals in which oxygen, silicon and aluminium are the most abundant elements; recall that diamond and graphite are made up of carbon atoms; interpret data on the abundance of elements	understand that strong covalent bonds between carbon atoms in diamond and graphite, and between silicon and oxygen in silicon dioxide, form giant covalent structures and how these different structures have particular physical properties	
recall that ores contain minerals from which metals can be obtained; recall that copper, iron and zinc can be extracted by heating their oxides with carbon	understand that in the reaction for extracting a metal, the oxide is reduced (loss of oxygen) and carbon is oxidised (gains oxygen)	explain that the extraction of metals is an example of oxidation and reduction occurring at the same time
write word equations from information about a reaction; recognise symbols of elements, understand formulas of molecules and ionic compounds, and interpret symbol equations		*balance unbalanced symbol equations and write balanced equations, including state symbols*
recall that relative atomic masses compare the masses of atoms of elements and can be read off the Periodic Table	calculate relative formula masses and calculate the mass of a metal in the formula mass of a compound	*calculate the mass of a metal that can be extracted from a mineral, given the formula of the compound or an equation*
understand that metals such as aluminium can be obtained by electrolysis of molten ionic compounds, and that in this process the compound is decomposed by electricity	understand that in electrolysis of molten ionic compounds, metals are formed at the negative electrode	*use diagrams and ionic equations to explain changes that occur at the electrodes and in the electrolyte in the electrolysis of molten salts and molten aluminium oxide*
recall the properties of metals and understand that their uses relate to these properties	explain that the properties of metals are due to the strong metallic bond holding metal atoms in a giant structure	*understand that metal crystals are made up of positive ions bound to freely moving electrons*
describe the impact that the extraction, use and disposal of metals has on the environment	evaluate, given appropriate information, the environmental impact	develop arguments on the ethics of the environmental impact

Exam-style questions

Foundation

1 AO2 **a** The sentences below show some uses of copper. Each use depends on a property. Match up each use with the property that allows the use. [2]

Use	Property
The electrical wiring in homes is made of copper.	Copper is not very reactive.
Central heating pipes in homes are made of copper.	Copper can be bent easily.
Copper (mixed with other metals) is used in coins.	Copper is a good conductor of electricity.

AO1 **b** Use ideas about the bonding in copper to explain its properties. [2]

[Total 4]

Foundation/Higher level

2 The amount of zinc extracted from ores is the fourth largest after iron, aluminium and copper. About half of the zinc produced is used to coat steel in a process called galvanising. This protects the steel against rusting. The graph shows how the price of zinc varied in the 10 years to 2011. The price increases when demand increases.

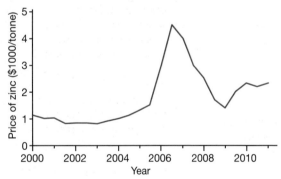

AO2 **a** Explain how the demand for galvanised steel changed during the years from 2000 to 2010. [2]

AO3 **b** Explain what the graph suggests about the impact of zinc mining on the environment during the years 2000 to 2010. [2]

AO2 **c** A mining company is planning on extracting zinc from a mineral made up of zinc carbonate, $ZnCO_3$. The mineral makes up 40 g of every kilogram of ore. What mass of zinc could be obtained from 1 kg of the ore? [Use the Periodic Table on page 309.] [2]

AO2 **d** The first stage of the process to extract zinc involves heating the solid zinc carbonate to form solid zinc oxide (ZnO) and carbon dioxide gas. Write a balanced chemical equation with state symbols for this process. [2]

AO1 **e** Complete the sentences to explain how zinc metal can be extracted from zinc oxide.

Zinc oxide is _____ with carbon.
Zinc is _____ during the reaction because it loses _____.
Carbon is _____ during the reaction because it gains _____. [2]

[Total 10]

AO1 **3** Oxygen is a molecular element present in the air. Silicon dioxide is a giant molecular compound that forms crystals in the solid state with a high melting point. Describe the similarities and differences in the bonding of oxygen and silicon dioxide and explain their different properties. The quality of written communication will be assessed in your answer to this question. [6]

Higher level

4 AO1 **a** Sodium chloride is an ionic compound. Which of the following statements is true about the bonding in sodium chloride?

A Electrons are gained or lost to form a full outer shell.

B Electrons are shared between atoms.

C The nucleus of each bonded atom attracts electrons.

D Charged ions are attracted towards one another.

E The nuclei of the atoms attract each other. [2]

AO2 **b** Lithium bromide is also an ionic compound. Molten lithium bromide conducts electricity. What will be formed at each electrode when the electrical power is turned on? [2]

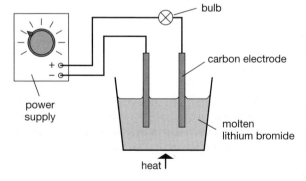

[Total 4]

Worked example

Use the data sheets (pages 307–309) to help you with these questions.

AO2 1 Read the following statements about carbon dioxide.

A Carbon dioxide is a gas at room temperature.

B Carbon dioxide does not conduct electricity in any state.

C Carbon dioxide is a simple molecular substance.

D Carbon dioxide molecules can be drawn as O=C=O where the lines represent covalent bonds.

a Which sentence(s) are reporting data on carbon dioxide? [1]

b Which sentence(s) are stating ideas that explain carbon dioxide's properties? [1]

c Which sentence(s) show where creative thinking has been used in an explanation? [1]

a A, B ✔

b C, D ✔

c D ✔

AO1
AO2 2 An unknown solution was suspected of containing dissolved zinc chloride. Describe the tests you could carry out to prove this was correct, including the expected observations. The quality of written communication will be assessed in your answer to this question. [6]

To test for the zinc ion you would add a few drops of sodium hydroxide solution to the solution. A white precipatate would show that zinc ions were present.

To test for the chlorine ion, you would add silver nitrate solution to the solution. A white precipatate shows that chlorine ions were present.

AO3 3 It is suggested that passing an electric current through the zinc chloride solution would prove that it was an ionic compound. Would this test be sufficient to show that zinc chloride was ionic? Explain your answer fully. [2]

Showing that the solution conducts electricity would show that zinc chloride is ionic. ✔ *Only ionic compounds conduct electricity when dissolved in water because they contain charged ions.* ✔

Higher level

AO1 4 A solution was thought to contain a salt. After addition of nitric acid to the solution, a few drops of barium chloride solution was added. The mixture became a cloudy white. Write an ionic equation for the reaction that took place. [3]

$Ba^+ + SO_4^- \rightarrow BaSO_4$ ✔

The answers are correct: 3 marks. It is important to be able to recognise that theories are not just based on data but involve creative and imaginative thought.

It should be mentioned that the test for zinc ions also requires excess sodium hydroxide solution to dissolve the precipitate, and that the negative ion tests should start with the addition of acid to eliminate carbonate ions. There are also some spelling mistakes and chlorine has been substituted for chloride. This answer gains just 3 marks from a possible 6.

The judgement is correct and a full explanation has been provided: 2 marks.

Here 1 mark is given for the correct formula of the product barium sulfate, but the wrong charges have been given to the ions and the state symbols have been left out.

Make sure you use the data sheet provided to get the formulae of ions correct and to identify the ions being tested for.

C6 Chemical synthesis

What you should already know...

We use many chemicals in our daily lives including acids and alkalis

The chemicals we use include polymers, drugs, paints and dyes, soaps and detergents, cosmetics, fertilisers, pesticides and food additives.

All these different substances are made up of the relatively small number of elements shown in the Periodic Table.

 Can life exist without chemicals?

Salts are ionic compounds

Ionic compounds are made up of a positively charged metal ion and a negatively charged ion which may be a single atom or a group of atoms.

When ionic compounds dissolve in water the ions move freely and independently.

 What are the ions and their charges present in solution when sodium chloride dissolves in water?

Symbols, formulas and equations are used to represent reactions

Each element has its own symbol which can represent an atom of the element and is given in the Periodic Table.

Molecules and ionic compounds can be represented by a formula which shows the number of atoms joined together.

A balanced chemical equation shows the relative number of atoms of each element in the reactants and products. The number of atoms of each element does not change in a reaction.

 What reaction does the following equation represent and how many atoms of each element take part in the reaction?

$2Mg(s) + O_2(g) \rightarrow 2MgO(s)$

In C6 you will find out about...

> the importance of chemical synthesis in making products for use as food additives, fertilisers, dyestuffs, paints, pigments and medicines

> hazard symbols and the precautions taken to reduce risk

> the stages in synthesising a new product, from deciding on the reactants to use, the quantities and the conditions, to separating the useful products and calculating the yield

> the names and properties of acids and alkalis

> the reactions of acids to form salts

> the ionic explanation of neutralisation

> writing equations for the reactions

> calculating how much of each reactant is needed and how much of a product is formed

> separating and purifying products of a reaction

> energy changes in reactions

> methods of measuring how fast reactions are

> ways of changing the rate of chemical reactions and why they work

> the importance of catalysts in speeding up reactions

Making chemicals

What do we want new chemicals for?

A new perfume or aftershave will contain a variety of substances with pleasant smells. Some of these will come from plants and some will be made for the first time in a chemistry laboratory. A lot has to happen before a new fragrance finds its way into the perfume bottle.

FIGURE 1: A new perfume may contain substances that have been manufactured for the first time.

Safety with chemicals

Did you know that your food cupboard is a fire hazard? Cooking oils, flour and sugar all burn well. They must be stored away from flames. If your house catches fire, your food can make the fire worse. Other hazardous chemicals are kept in homes. Disinfectants and cleaners contain dangerous chemicals. In factories there are rules about how these chemicals can be stored and used.

The chemists and engineers who manufacture the products need to know about hazards in the reactants that they use, such as sodium hydroxide in oven cleaners. They try to reduce risk when they are developing new products. Hazard symbols on dangerous chemicals give users a quick reminder. There are things to do to stay safe:

> Make sure chemicals are stored carefully and labelled correctly.

> Wear goggles, gloves and protective clothing when handling chemicals.   -

> Be prepared for spills.

> Do not put hazardous chemicals down the drains or in the normal rubbish.

> Think about swapping a dangerous chemical for something less hazardous or use less of it.

VECTA THICK STRONG BLEACH

IRRITANT

CONTAINS Sodium Hypochlorite and Sodium Hydroxide

WARNING! Do not use with other products. May release dangerous gases (Chlorine).

FIGURE 2: Warning signs must be displayed on hazardous chemicals.

QUESTIONS

1 What hazard symbols should be on a container of a chemical that may blow up and is poisonous?

2 What precautions would you take when using a chemical that could burn your skin?

hazard symbols

Developing new products

Chemical synthesis means combining simple substances to make a new compound. The chemical industry is always looking for new substances, such as fragrances, for new or improved products such as perfumes and shampoos. New ways of synthesising chemicals are found which are cheaper and safer. Some of the steps in chemical synthesis are looked at in more detail later in the module.

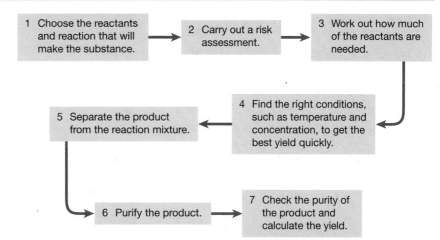

1 Choose the reactants and reaction that will make the substance.

2 Carry out a risk assessment.

3 Work out how much of the reactants are needed.

4 Find the right conditions, such as temperature and concentration, to get the best yield quickly.

5 Separate the product from the reaction mixture.

6 Purify the product.

7 Check the purity of the product and calculate the yield.

FIGURE 3: Flowchart for the synthesis of a new chemical.

QUESTIONS

3 Chemistry is a bit like cooking. What steps in the flowchart in Figure 3 would you use to design a new pizza topping?

4 A substance used in disinfectants is manufactured from nitrogen from the air and hydrogen from water. Why do we call this a synthesis reaction?

Did you know?

About 12 000 new chemicals are reported by company, university and government research laboratories every day. There are over 56 million known substances.

The chemical industry

The chemical industry is an important part of the British economy and makes up about 12% of manufacturing. There are different sectors of the chemical industry, which altogether have annual sales of about £40 billion.

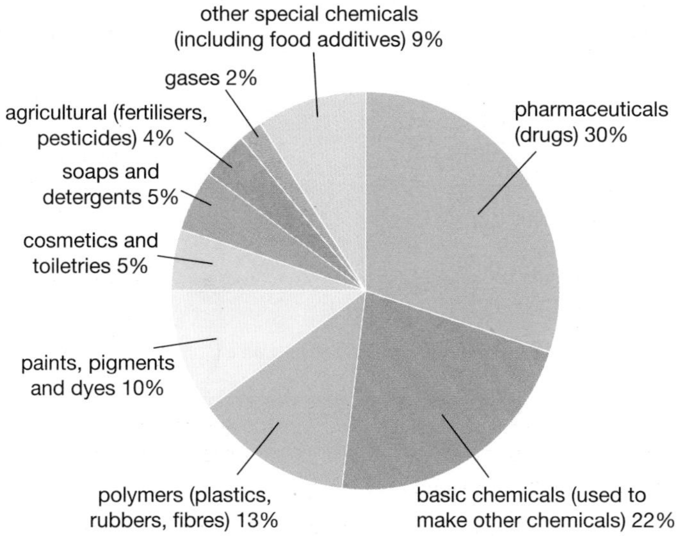

other special chemicals (including food additives) 9%

gases 2%

agricultural (fertilisers, pesticides) 4%

soaps and detergents 5%

cosmetics and toiletries 5%

paints, pigments and dyes 10%

polymers (plastics, rubbers, fibres) 13%

basic chemicals (used to make other chemicals) 22%

pharmaceuticals (drugs) 30%

FIGURE 4: Sectors of the chemical industry and the percentage contribution to sales.

Watch out!

The chemical industry covered here does not include the refining of oil into fuels, the extraction of metals from their ores, or the preparation of ceramics and glass for the construction industry.

QUESTIONS

5 'The chemical industry adds value to raw materials.' Explain why this statement is true with examples mentioned on this page.

6 Basic chemicals have a lower value than pharmaceuticals but are produced in much greater amounts. Explain this.

Acids and alkalis

What are acids used for?

Sulfuric acid is the most important industrial chemical worldwide. Each year around 160 million tonnes of sulfuric acid are produced. It is used to make fertilisers and many other chemicals, to clean and treat metals, to remove impurities from fuels and in lead–acid batteries.

The most used alkali is sodium hydroxide, with an annual production of around 60 million tonnes. Other acids and alkalis are also produced in large quantities.

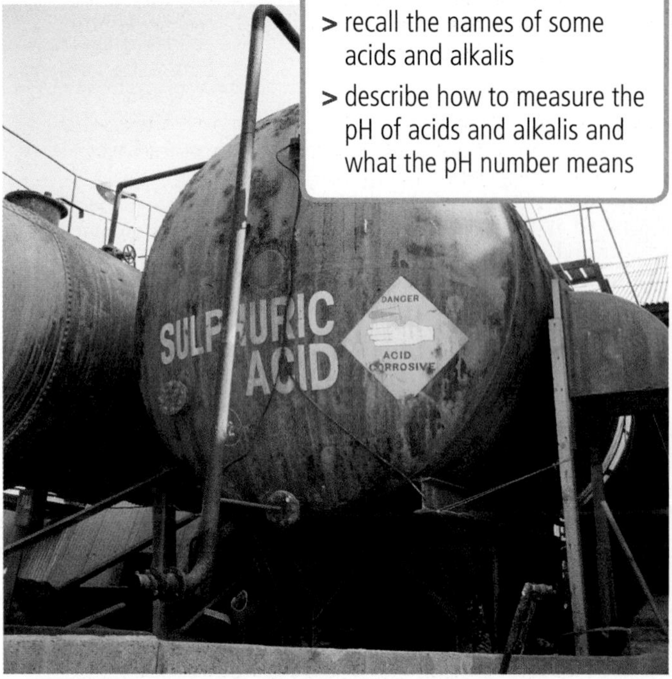

FIGURE 1: Sulfuric acid is a widely used chemical.

Recognising acids and alkalis

We use **indicators** to tell if a solution contains an **acid** or an **alkali**. Litmus is a commonly used indicator. It is available as a solution or a coloured paper. Litmus is red in an acid and blue in an alkali.

Universal indicator can also be used as a test for acids and alkalis. It is a shade of orange to red in acid and blue-green to dark blue in alkali.

Watch out!

Litmus paper and universal indicator paper must be moistened before use when testing substances. This is because acidic and alkaline properties are only shown when the substance is dissolved in water.

FIGURE 2: Litmus is an indicator of acids and alkalis.

QUESTIONS

1 When litmus paper is dipped into a solution it turns blue. What does this tell you about the solution?

2 How could you show that a liquid was an acid?

Q acids alkalis

Some acids and alkalis

Acidic and alkaline substances can be solids, liquids or gases. To affect the colour of indicators, the acids and alkalis must be dissolved in water.

Citric acid, which is extracted from fruits, is a solid. Tartaric acid is also a solid. Sulfuric acid and nitric acid are syrupy liquids when they are pure. Ethanoic acid, which is extracted from vinegar, is another acidic substance that is a liquid. Hydrogen chloride is an acidic gas but dissolves in water to form hydrochloric acid.

The commonly used alkalis sodium hydroxide, potassium hydroxide and calcium hydroxide are all solids. Ammonia is an alkaline gas.

FIGURE 3: Citrus fruits are a natural source of some acids.

QUESTION

3 Name the following:

a an acidic substance extracted from vinegar

b a solid that dissolves in water to form an acid

c an alkaline solid

d a pure liquid that forms an acidic solution when added to water.

Did you know?

As well as giving food a pleasant sharp taste, acids are also a vital part of a balanced diet. Vitamin C, which prevents scurvy, has the chemical name ascorbic acid. Vitamin B9 is folic acid, which is especially important during periods of growth.

pH

The **pH scale** is a measure of how strong an acid or an alkali is. The pH can be measured using universal indicator or a pH meter. The colour of the universal indicator can be compared to a colour chart to find the pH number of a sample. A pH meter has to be calibrated by dipping the pH probe in a solution of known pH. The probe is then washed and dipped in the test solution. After a few moments the meter reading settles and the pH number can be read.

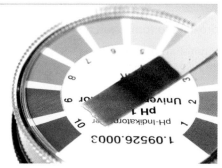

FIGURE 4: Universal indicator shows a range of colours across the pH scale from 1 (red) to 14 (dark blue).

FIGURE 5: One type of pH meter and probe used to measure the pH of solutions.

Solutions which are neither acidic nor alkaline, that is they are neutral, have a pH of 7 at room temperature. Acids have values below 7 and alkalis have pH numbers above 7. The further the number is from 7 the stronger the solution is. It is possible to have acids with a pH just less than 0 and alkalis can have a pH just over 14.

QUESTIONS

4 Why are the following precautions necessary?

a Always put a pH probe in a solution of known pH before using it.

b Wash the pH probe before use.

5 pH colour cards usually read from 1 to 14. Why is it wrong to say the pH scale is from 1 to 14?

Reactions of acids

We are learning to:

> recall patterns in the reactions of acids
> interpret chemical equations for the reactions of acids
> write chemical equations for the reactions of acids

Are salts natural or can we make them?

Salts have lots of uses. Some salts are found naturally as minerals in rocks, but many have to be manufactured by chemical reactions. Magnesium sulfate, 'Epsom salts', is found naturally but is also manufactured by the reaction of magnesium oxide with sulfuric acid.

EPSOM SALTS

natural options

250g Magnesium Sulphate Heptahydrate

FIGURE 1: Soaking feet in a bath containing magnesium sulfate will relax muscles and ease soreness: just one of the many uses of Epsom salts.

Reaction patterns

Acids react with many metals and metal compounds. In these reactions a **salt** is formed. Word equations are used to describe the reaction.

> Acids react with many metals to form a salt and hydrogen gas.

calcium + hydrochloric acid → calcium chloride + hydrogen

> Acids react with metal oxides and hydroxides to form a salt and water.

magnesium oxide + sulfuric acid → magnesium sulfate + water
sodium hydroxide + nitric acid → sodium nitrate + water

> Acids react with metal carbonates to form a salt, water and carbon dioxide gas.

calcium carbonate + hydrochloric acid
→ calcium chloride + water + carbon dioxide

In all these reactions, the first part of the name of the salt comes from the metal and the second part from the acid. Sulfuric acid produces sulfates, nitric acid produces nitrates, and hydrochloric acid produces chlorides.

FIGURE 2: Calcium metal reacts vigorously with hydrochloric acid.

QUESTION

1 What would you expect to be formed in each of these reactions:

a magnesium reacts with hydrochloric acid?

b potassium hydroxide reacts with sulfuric acid?

c magnesium oxide reacts with hydrochloric acid?

d calcium carbonate reacts with nitric acid?

Did you know?

There are hundreds of different salts in seawater. The most common is sodium chloride, which makes up 80% of the total.

Q reactions of acids

Naming salts and interpreting equations

Salts are ionic compounds made up of a positively charged metal ion and a negative ion obtained from an acid. The formula of a salt combines the symbol of the metal and the negative ion from the acid. $CaSO_4$ contains the calcium ion and the sulfate ion from sulfuric acid.

Chemical equations describe the reactions of acids.

$$Mg(s) + H_2SO_4(aq) \rightarrow MgSO_4(aq) + H_2(g)$$

This equation shows that solid magnesium reacts with sulfuric acid solution to make magnesium sulfate solution and hydrogen gas.

$$KOH(aq) + HCl(aq) \rightarrow KCl(aq) + H_2O(l)$$

In this reaction, potassium hydroxide solution reacts with hydrochloric acid solution to make potassium chloride solution and liquid water.

$$Na_2CO_3(s) + 2HNO_3(aq) \rightarrow 2NaNO_3(aq) + H_2O(l) + CO_2(g)$$

This equation shows that solid sodium carbonate reacts with nitric acid solution to make sodium nitrate solution, liquid water and carbon dioxide gas.

Acid	Formula	Negative ion
hydrochloric	HCl	chloride Cl^-
sulfuric	H_2SO_4	sulfate SO_4^{2-}
nitric	HNO_3	nitrate NO_3^-

Acids and the salts that they form.

State	Symbol
solid	s
liquid	l
gas	g
solution	aq

State symbols used in chemical equations.

Watch out!
Think of the negative ion from the acid as a single entity.

QUESTIONS

2 Name the following salts and the acid used to produce them:

  a Na_2SO_4 **b** $MgCl_2$ **c** KNO_3.

3 Describe the reaction given by the following equation:

  $$Ca(OH)_2(aq) + 2HCl(aq) \rightarrow CaCl_2(aq) + 2H_2O(l)$$

Writing formulae and equations (Higher tier only)

In the formula of a salt, the number of positive charges must equal the number of negative charges. Thus in potassium sulfate, two potassium ions (K^+) are needed to balance the charge on the sulfate ion (SO_4^{2-}), so the formula is K_2SO_4. The formula of copper sulfate is $CuSO_4$, so the charge on a copper ion must be 2+.

In a balanced chemical equation, the number of atoms of each element must be the same on both sides of the equation. For instance:

magnesium carbonate + nitric acid
$\rightarrow$ magnesium nitrate + water + carbon dioxide

Inserting the formulae gives:

$$MgCO_3 + HNO_3 \rightarrow Mg(NO_3)_2 + H_2O + CO_2$$

Nitrate ions (NO_3^-) appear on both sides of the equation. To balance the equation we need a 2 in front of the nitric acid on the left. We can also insert state symbols.

$$MgCO_3(s) + 2HNO_3(aq)$$
$$\rightarrow Mg(NO_3)_2(aq) + H_2O(l) + CO_2(g)$$

Metal	Ion	Metal	Ion	Metal	Ion
sodium	Na^+	magnesium	Mg^{2+}	aluminium	Al^{3+}
potassium	K^+	calcium	Ca^{2+}	iron(III)	Fe^{3+}
		copper	Cu^{2+}		
		zinc	Zn^{2+}		
		iron(II)	Fe^{2+}		

Formulae of some metal ions.

QUESTIONS

4 Write the formulae of the following salts: copper chloride, zinc sulfate, iron(III) nitrate.

5 Balance the following equation:

$$NaOH(aq) + H_2SO_4(aq) \rightarrow Na_2SO_4(aq) + H_2O(l)$$

6 Write a balanced chemical equation for the reaction of solid potassium carbonate (K_2CO_3) with hydrochloric acid.

chemical equations GCSE

Reacting amounts

We are learning to:

> calculate relative formula masses using the Periodic Table

> calculate the masses of reactants and products in a chemical reaction

How is baking a cake like chemical engineering?

To bake a cake you follow a recipe which lists the mass of each ingredient needed to make a cake of a certain size. Weighing out each ingredient carefully produces the cake you wanted. In the same way, manufacturing chemicals involves weighing out the correct amounts of the reactants.

FIGURE 1: Baking a cake – it's chemistry really.

Working out the mass of a compound

The **formula** of a compound tells us how many atoms of each element are joined together to make the simplest part of the compound. For instance the formula of magnesium chloride, $MgCl_2$, tells us that one magnesium atom and two chlorine atoms have joined together.

The **relative formula mass** (RFM) is the sum of the relative atomic masses of all the atoms in the formula.

We can get the relative atomic mass (RAM) of an element from the Periodic Table.

The RAM of magnesium is 24 and for chlorine it is 35.5.

So the relative formula mass of magnesium chloride, $MgCl_2$, is $24 + (2 \times 35.5) = 95$.

gen	fluorine	neo
3	9	10
2	35.5	40
5	**Cl**	A
hur	chlorine	argo
6	17	18
9	80	84

FIGURE 2: The relative atomic mass is the number above the symbol of the element. This number compares the mass of the atom with the mass of a carbon atom, which has the value 12.

> ### QUESTIONS
>
> **1** The RAM of calcium is 40. What is the RFM of calcium chloride, $CaCl_2$?
>
> **2** Use the Periodic Table on page 309 to help you work out the RFM of sodium nitrate, $NaNO_3$.

How much can we make?

A balanced chemical reaction shows the number of atoms and molecules that are involved in the reaction. The number of atoms of each element is the same on both sides of the equation. Using relative atomic mass (RAM) and relative formula mass (RFM), we can predict how much of each reactant and product there will be in a reaction.

For example, consider this reaction:

$Mg(s) + 2HCl(aq) \rightarrow MgCl_2(aq) + H_2(g)$

The table summarises what this tells us about quantities of reactants and products.

Reactant/ product	Formula	RAM/ RFM	Number of formula units in the balanced equation	Mass of reactants/ products
magnesium	Mg	24	1	24 g
hydrochloric acid	HCl	36.5	2	73 g
magnesium chloride	$MgCl_2$	95	1	95 g
hydrogen	H_2	2	1	2 g

🔍 relative formula mass

The reactants and products are always in the same proportions. For example, if we have 12 g of magnesium, then we have half the value in the table (12 g is half of 24 g). This means we will get half the amount of hydrogen. Half of 2 g is 1 g of hydrogen.

QUESTIONS

3 Use the table on page 170 to work out how much magnesium chloride would be formed if you reacted 48 g of magnesium.

4a Complete the table on the right for this reaction:

$NaOH(aq) + HNO_3(aq) \rightarrow NaNO_3(aq) + H_2O(l)$

b How much sodium nitrate would be formed if 4 g of sodium hydroxide reacted?

Reactant/product	Formula	RFM	Number of formula units	Mass
sodium hydroxide	NaOH	40	1	40 g
?	HNO_3	63	?	63 g
sodium nitrate	$NaNO_3$	?	1	?
water	H_2O	18	1	18 g

Predicting quantities (Higher tier only)

In the chemical industry the balanced equation for a process is used to calculate the minimum quantity of reactants required to produce a desired amount of a product.

Example
What mass of sodium hydroxide is needed to produce 1 tonne of sodium sulfate by reaction with sulfuric acid?

The equation for the reaction is:
$2NaOH(s) + H_2SO_4(aq) \rightarrow Na_2SO_4(aq) + 2H_2O(l)$

RFMs
NaOH
= 23 + 16 + 1
= 40

Na_2SO_4
= (2 × 23) + 32 + (4 × 16)
= 142

Substance	RFM	Reacting masses			
Na_2SO_4	142	142 g	1 g		1 tonne
NaOH	40	80 g	$\frac{80}{142} = 0.56$ g		0.56 tonnes

The table shows that to produce 1 tonne of sodium sulfate takes 0.56 tonnes of sodium hydroxide.

FIGURE 3: A chemical engineer monitors the flow of reactants in a process.

QUESTION

5 The equation describes the reaction of magnesium oxide with sulfuric acid.

$MgO(s) + H_2SO_4(aq) \rightarrow MgSO_4(aq) + H_2O(l)$

a What mass of magnesium sulfate is formed when 10 tonnes of magnesium oxide are completely reacted with sulfuric acid?

b What mass of magnesium oxide would be needed to produce 240 tonnes of magnesium sulfate?

c Which would you need the least amount of to produce a tonne of magnesium sulfate – magnesium oxide, magnesium or magnesium carbonate? Explain your answer.

Watch out!
The sum of the masses of the reactants must be the same as the sum of the mass of the products.

Neutralisation reactions

We are learning to:

> recall which reactions are neutralisation reactions

> carry out an acid–alkali titration

> interpret the results of acid–alkali titrations

How can titration solve a crime?

The forensic scientist uses a burette to add alkali to a solution in a flask. There's a colour change which tells him that the sample of rhubarb tart contained enough oxalic acid to kill the victim. Mrs Barnaby the tart-maker becomes the chief suspect and another crime is solved.

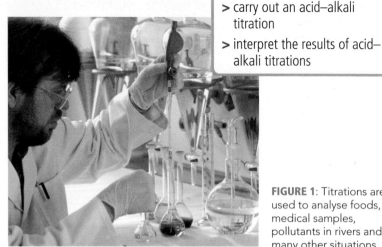

FIGURE 1: Titrations are used to analyse foods, medical samples, pollutants in rivers and in many other situations.

Describing neutralisation

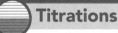

The term **neutral** means 'between acid and alkali'. Reactions where acidic and alkaline substances react together are called **neutralisation** reactions. An example is when sodium hydroxide solution reacts with hydrochloric acid.

sodium hydroxide + hydrochloric acid
→ sodium chloride + water

Hydrochloric acid will turn litmus red. As sodium hydroxide solution is added slowly the acid reacts until it is all used up. One more drop of sodium hydroxide will make the solution an alkali and the litmus will turn blue. That sudden change of colour of the indicator is called the **end-point**. A **titration** involves measuring the volumes of acid and alkali needed to reach the end-point.

QUESTION

1 Sodium carbonate solution was added a little at a time to a beaker containing a solution. At first the solution turned litmus paper turned red, but eventually it turned blue.

a How do you know the solution in the beaker is an acid?

b How do you know a neutralisation reaction has taken place?

c What would happen if more sodium carbonate solution were added?

Titrations

A titration is carried out four or five times to get a **range** of data for the volume of a solution required to reach the end-point in a reaction. There will always be **variation** between the readings because of errors in measurements. The **true value** should fall within the range of the data.

If one reading is very different from the others, then it is an **outlier**. You should see if there is a reason for the outlier. If it is caused by errors then it can be left out of the interpretation of the results. The **mean** of the remaining data can then be calculated and this should be close to the true value.

FIGURE 2: Carrying out a titration. The end-point is reached when one drop from the burette changes the colour of the indicator.

acid base neutralisation reactions

QUESTION

2 The table shows the results of a titration between hydrochloric acid and sodium hydroxide solution.

a Which burette reading is probably an outlier?

b What is the range of the remaining readings?

c What is the mean of the remaining readings?

Titration number	1	2	3	4	5
Volume of sodium hydroxide solution measured by pipette (cm³)	25.0	25.0	25.0	25.0	25.0
Volume of hydrochloric acid used at the end-point, measured by burette (cm³)	24.9	25.2	25.9	24.9	25.0

Interpreting titration results

Hydrochloric acid was titrated with sodium hydroxide solution. The end-point occurred when 20.0 cm³ of hydrochloric acid was added to 25.0 cm³ of sodium hydroxide.

The equation for the reaction is:

$$NaOH(aq) + HCl(aq) \rightarrow NaCl(aq) + H_2O(l)$$

The equation shows that one formula unit of NaOH requires one formula unit of HCl for neutralisation. The volumes of the acid and alkali measured must contain the same number of formula units of NaOH and HCl. If we doubled the amount of sodium hydroxide solution to 50.0 cm³, then twice as much hydrochloric acid, 40.0 cm³, would be required to reach the end-point.

Watch out!

The volumes obtained from a titration will always be in the same proportion if the same solutions are used.

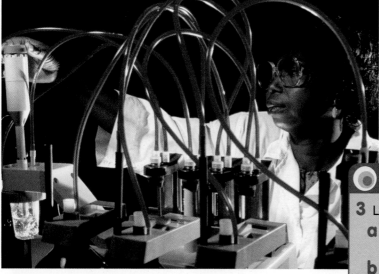

FIGURE 3: Computer-controlled titration equipment.

Did you know?

In most analytical laboratories titrations are now carried out automatically by robot and computer. The scientist just has to prepare the sample solutions, top up the solutions in the automatic burettes, sit back and interpret the results.

QUESTION

3 Look at the data in question 2.

a What does the data tell you about the two solutions?

b What volume of hydrochloric acid would be needed to neutralise each of the following:

i 100.0 cm³ of the sodium hydroxide solution?

ii 1.5 dm³ of the sodium hydroxide solution?

Q acid base titration GCSE

Explaining neutralisation

We are learning to:

> name salts given the names of acids and alkalis

> explain neutralisation as the reaction between hydrogen ions and hydroxide ions

> write formulae of salts

New theory, instant success?

In 1883, in an advanced chemistry exam, Svante Arrhenius suggested a new theory of neutralisation. But his examiners did not like his idea. They gave him the lowest pass mark possible and stopped him from getting the job in the university that he wanted. Later other scientists agreed with Arrhenius and he became a successful chemist.

FIGURE 1: Svante Arrhenius, Swedish chemist.

It's the water

All acids contain hydrogen. When an acid reacts with an alkaline compound the hydrogen reacts with hydroxide to form water. Water is formed in every neutralisation reaction between an acid and an alkaline compound. For example:

hydrochloric acid + sodium hydroxide → sodium chloride + water

The salt is formed from the other parts of the acid and alkaline compounds:

> hydrochloric acid forms salts called chlorides

> sulfuric acid forms salts called sulfates

> nitric acid forms salts called nitrates.

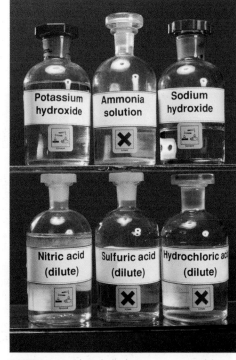

FIGURE 2: Acid and alkali: so many possible combinations – but all are the same reaction.

QUESTIONS

1 How can you tell from the formula of phosphoric acid, H_3PO_4, that it is possibly an acid?

2a What are the names of the salts formed when these compounds react:

    i zinc oxide and hydrochloric acid?

    ii magnesium hydroxide and sulfuric acid?

b What else is formed in both these reactions?

Ions combine

When an acidic compound dissolves in water it forms positive hydrogen ions ($H^+(aq)$) and a negative ion. The hydrogen ions are what make the solution an acid. The pH indicates the amount of hydrogen ions in the solution. When alkaline compounds dissolve in water, the solution contains hydroxide ions ($OH^-(aq)$) and a positive ion.

neutralisation ionic equation

In neutralisation reactions the hydrogen ions and the hydroxide ions join up to form water molecules.

$$H^+(aq) + OH^-(aq) \rightarrow H_2O(l)$$

This is the **ionic equation** for all neutralisation reactions. The negative ion from the acid and the positive ion from the alkali are left in the solution to form the salt.

So, for example, when hydrochloric acid and sodium hydroxide react together, water is formed and the chloride ions and sodium ions are left as a solution of sodium chloride.

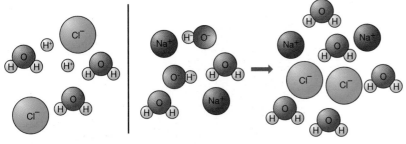

hydrochloric acid   sodium hydroxide solution   sodium chloride + water

FIGURE 3: When the ions in an acid and an alkali are mixed, water molecules are formed.

FIGURE 4: In a titration the volume of acid and alkali needed depends on the concentration of the hydrogen and hydroxide ions in the solutions.

QUESTIONS

3a Write the ionic equation for the reaction between solutions of potassium hydroxide and nitric acid.

b What ions will be left in the solution in this reaction?

4 Describe and explain the change in pH when an alkali is added to an acid.

Formulae of salts (Higher tier only)

If we know the formula of an acid and an alkaline compound, then we can work out the formula of the salt that is formed when they neutralise each other.

For example, the formula of sulfuric acid is H_2SO_4. As it contains two hydrogen ions (H^+), the sulfate ion must have a 2– charge (SO_4^{2-}). The formula of sodium hydroxide is NaOH. As the hydroxide ions have one negative charge (OH^-), the sodium ion must have a 1+ charge (Na^+).

When sodium hydroxide neutralises sulfuric acid, water is formed and the sodium and sulfate ions are left in solution. The formula of sodium sulfate is Na_2SO_4 because two sodium (Na^+) ions are needed to balance one sulfate (SO_4^{2-}) ion.

Metal oxides (which contain the oxide ion, O^{2-}) and metal carbonates (which contain the carbonate ion, CO_3^{2-}) are also alkaline compounds.

QUESTION

5 Write down the formulae of the salts formed when the following acidic and alkaline compounds react together in neutralisation reactions:

a hydrochloric acid (HCl) and magnesium hydroxide ($Mg(OH)_2$)

b nitric acid (HNO_3) and copper oxide (CuO)

c sulfuric acid (H_2SO_4) and potassium carbonate (K_2CO_3).

Did you know?

Hydrogen ions are tiny because they are just a proton. In water they are surrounded by clusters of water molecules.

Energy changes in reactions

How can we cook food outdoors without a fire?

What could be more convenient than a ready-meal that cooks itself? That is what self-heating cans do. A reaction between water and calcium oxide in the outer part of the can heats the food inside the can. The cans are used by the military and explorers, or simply by people who fancy a hot snack when they're out.

We are learning to:

> understand what is meant by exothermic and endothermic

> interpret energy diagrams for reactions

> understand the importance of the control of energy during chemical synthesis

FIGURE 1

 ## Getting hot or cold

If you drop a piece of magnesium into a test tube containing hydrochloric acid you can feel the test tube get warm. The reaction is giving out heat to the surroundings, including your hand. We say that this reaction is **exothermic**. The temperature rises in exothermic reactions.

Alternatively, if you mix sodium hydrogen carbonate, citric acid and water in a beaker you will notice that the reaction mixture becomes cold. This reaction is **endothermic**. The temperature falls in endothermic reactions.

QUESTIONS

1 An endothermic reaction is taking place in a test tube. Will the test tube feel hotter or colder?

2 Sodium hydroxide solution and hydrochloric acid are at a temperature of 22 °C. They are mixed together. A thermometer records a temperature of 31 °C. What does this tell you about the reaction?

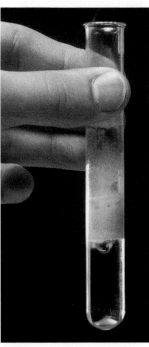

FIGURE 2: An exothermic reaction – the test tube feels warm.

FIGURE 3: An exothermic chemical reaction provides the energy of a rocket.

exothermic and endothermic reactions

Losing and gaining energy

In an exothermic reaction the reactants give out heat energy to the surroundings. The particles of the reactants themselves lose energy, so the products of the reaction have less energy than the reactants. This change is shown in an **energy level diagram** for the reaction.

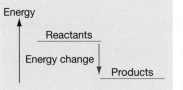

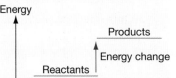

FIGURE 4: Energy level diagram for an exothermic reaction.

FIGURE 5: Energy level diagram for an endothermic reaction.

In an endothermic reaction the reactant particles take energy from the surroundings, so the energy level of the products is higher than the energy level of the reactants. This, too, is shown in an energy level diagram.

The bigger the change in energy level, the more heat energy is given out or taken in by the reaction.

Did you know?

Combustion reactions are among the most exothermic of chemical reactions, especially those used in rockets. Fuels used include oil-based fuels such as kerosene and aluminium powder.

QUESTIONS

3 Sketch an energy level diagram for the reaction in question 2.

4 What happens to the energy of the particles in an endothermic reaction?

Watch out! Make sure you can match the terms exothermic and endothermic to the correct energy level diagram.

Managing energy changes

The chemical industry uses very large quantities of reactants so a lot of energy is given out in reactions or is needed to make the reactions take place. This needs careful management. Tonnes of reactant producing heat could boil and make the reaction vessel explode. Also, the heat released is a useful resource and could be used for other stages of the process which are endothermic. For this reason industrial processes make use of **heat exchangers**. These are tubes carrying water around or through the reaction vessels. Exothermic reactions heat up the water in the heat exchanger, in the same way as heat from burning natural gas is passed to the water in a central heating boiler. The hot water is pumped to where it is needed.

While many synthesis reactions are exothermic, other processes are endothermic and a source of energy is needed. The cost of this energy is a major factor in the economics of the chemical industry.

The controllers of a chemical process aim to keep the temperature in the reaction vessels constant so that the reaction takes place at a steady rate and the energy is used efficiently.

QUESTIONS

5 Give two reasons why it is unwise to allow the reactants in a reaction vessel to react without controlling the temperature.

6 You are planning a chemical synthesis on an industrial scale. What data do you need and what steps would you take to make the process safe and efficient?

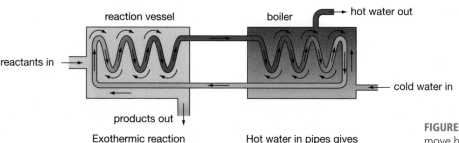

FIGURE 6: A heat exchanger can move heat from where it is produced to where it is needed.

Separating and purifying

We are learning to:
> understand methods of separating and purifying products of a chemical synthesis
> understand why the purity of a product is important
> calculate the percentage yield of product in a reaction

Why are illegal drugs sometimes lethal?

Many people have died after taking heroin or Ecstasy, but it is not always the drug that is responsible. Impurities mixed with the drug to increase profitability can be dangerous. The production of illegal drugs is not monitored and their purity is often low.

FIGURE 1: Illegal drugs may contain dangerous impurities.

The importance of purity

A **pure** substance has nothing else mixed with it. Drugs, food additives and ingredients in cosmetics must be pure. Impurities may be poisonous or could react with other ingredients to spoil a product. Manufacturers have to know if their products are pure and how to remove impurities.

When a chemical reaction is finished, the product is often mixed with left-over reactants and other substances that have been formed. All chemical processes have stages where the product is separated from the rest of the materials and its purity tested.

One way of separating one substance from others is by **filtration**. Filtering separates solids from liquids. Filtering will separate and purify the product if:

> the product is a solid and the impurities are in solution

> the product is soluble and the impurities are not.

FIGURE 2: Filtering separates a solid from a liquid.

QUESTIONS

1 What is the difference between a pure substance and an impure substance?

2 Describe how you could separate bits of sand from a salt solution.

Did you know?

Specialist chemical manufacturers can now provide compounds with less than one part per billion of impurities. This is a percentage purity of 99.9999999%.

🔍 filtration   recrystallisation

Crystallisation

If a product is an impure solid it can be purified by carrying out the following steps.

> **Dissolving** – the product is dissolved in warm water.

> Filtering – insoluble impurities will be trapped in the filter. The product is in the **filtrate**.

> **Evaporation** – some of the water is evaporated off until the product starts to **crystallise**. The solution is then cooled while the product continues to crystallise.

> Filtering – the crystals of the product are collected in the filter. Soluble impurities remain in the solution that passes through because they have not become concentrated enough to crystallise.

> Drying – the remaining water can be evaporated from the crystals of the product by placing them in an oven set at about 60 °C. Or the damp crystals can be placed In a container called a **desiccator** with a substance that absorbs water.

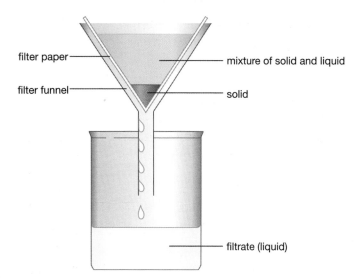

filter paper —

filter funnel —

— mixture of solid and liquid

— solid

— filtrate (liquid)

FIGURE 3: Apparatus used for filtration.

QUESTIONS

3 Suggest why the impure product is dissolved in warm water.

4 Evaporating some of the water makes the product crystallise but should leave the impurities in the solution. Why is this?

Percentage yield

The yield of a substance is the amount produced by a chemical reaction. The theoretical yield is the amount that the equation for the reaction predicts will be formed. The actual yield is the amount obtained by experiment.

$$\text{percentage yield} = \frac{\text{actual yield}}{\text{theoretical yield}} \times 100\%$$

For example, a reaction to prepare magnesium sulfate started with magnesium oxide and excess sulfuric acid. The theoretical yield was 12 g. After carrying out the experiment 9 g of magnesium sulfate was collected.

The percentage yield was $\frac{9}{12} \times 100\% = 75\%$

Watch out!

Percentage yields must be less than 100% because some product is always lost during the process.

QUESTIONS

5 A titration between sodium hydroxide solution and hydrochloric acid produced 0.250 g of sodium chloride. The results of the titration predicted that 0.290 g of sodium chloride should have been collected. What was the percentage yield?

6 A chemical company manufactures 490 000 tonnes of ammonium nitrate fertiliser a year. If the raw materials were used completely, then 500 000 tonnes of fertiliser would be formed. What is the percentage yield?

percentage yield

Preparing for assessment: Analysing, evaluating and reviewing

To achieve a good grade in science you will need to be able to use your skills and understanding to understand how scientists plan, run and evaluate investigations. These skills will be assessed in your exams and in Controlled Assessments. This activity supports you in developing the skills of using secondary data to review your confidence in your hypothesis.

✳ Chemistry Challenge – preparing a salt

As part of their school's Chemistry Week, Cheryl and Joshua's class have been set a challenge. They have to see who can produce the best yield of pure magnesium chloride. Each group will be given 100cm³ of the same hydrochloric acid solution.

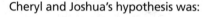

Cheryl and Joshua discover that there are three main methods of making magnesium chloride:

magnesium + hydrochloric acid → magnesium chloride + hydrogen gas

magnesium oxide + hydrochloric acid → magnesium chloride + water

magnesium carbonate + hydrochloric acid → magnesium chloride + water + carbon dioxide gas

Cheryl and Joshua's hypothesis was:

"Magnesium oxide reacted with hydrochloric acid will give the best yield of magnesium chloride because magnesium oxide is insoluble but magnesium reacts slightly with water to form magnesium hydroxide and magnesium carbonate is slightly soluble in water."

They warm their 100cm³ of hydrochloric acid and add a little magnesium oxide powder. The powder dissolves so they add some more. They do this until some of the magnesium oxide will not dissolve. Then they filter the mixture and collect the filtrate. They heat the solution until all the water has just evaporated off. They weigh a sample bottle then scrape their solid product into it and re-weigh it. The laboratory technician tests Cheryl and Joshua's sample and confirms that it is magnesium chloride.

Other groups in the class also attempted to make magnesium chloride and their yields are shown in the table below along with Cheryl and Joshua's.

Cheryl and Joshua concluded that their hypothesis was correct.

Group	Reactant	Percentage yield	Purity
Cheryl & Joshua	Magnesium oxide	82	Satisfactory
Group A	Magnesium	76	Contains some hydroxide
Group B	Magnesium	72	Contains some hydroxide
Group C	Magnesium	74	Contains some hydroxide
Group D	Magnesium oxide	84	Satisfactory
Group E	Magnesium oxide	80	Satisfactory
Group F	Magnesium carbonate	88	Contains some carbonate
Group G	Magnesium carbonate	90	Contains some carbonate
Group H	Magnesium carbonate	86	Contains some carbonate

Task 1

> How well did their result compare with the other groups that used magnesium oxide?
> Were Cheryl and Joshua right to say that magnesium oxide gives the best yield?

 ## Task 2

> What are the ranges of the percentage yield for each of the reactants?
> Do you notice any patterns in the results?

 ## Task 3

> In what ways do the other groups' results agree or disagree with Cheryl and Joshua's hypothesis?
> How does Cheryl and Joshua's hypothesis explain why some of the other samples were not pure?

 ## Task 4

> How confident can you be that the results listed are correct?
> How important are the similarities between the results obtained for each reactant?
> What other data would it be useful to have to decide if Cheryl and Joshua's hypothesis is correct?

 ## Maximise your grade

Use these suggestions to improve your work and be more successful.

E

To be on target for grade E you need to:

> Compare the similarities and differences of your results with a result from one other source.

> State where you got the secondary data from.

> Comment on whether the patterns in the data support your prediction or hypothesis.

> Use some scientific terms correctly.

C

To be on target for grades D, C, in addition, you need to:

> Use a range of secondary sources which are referenced correctly.

> Describe and explain how the secondary data supports or undermines your own data.

> Explain how your hypothesis can account for the patterns in the data or suggest how your hypothesis should be altered.

> Write a report using scientific terms and generally correct spelling, punctuation and grammar.

A

To be on target for grades B, A, in addition, you need to:

> Discuss how confident you are about the accuracy of the data used.

> Comment on similarities and differences in the data.

> Describe in detail what further work could be done to make you more confident of your hypothesis.

> Write a comprehensive and logical report using scientific terms and with very few spelling, punctuation or grammatical errors.

Measuring rates of reactions

How fast do you eat your chocolate?

When you eat a bar of chocolate, do you stuff it all in your mouth at once, or a bit at a time? Do you start with a large chunk and save smaller and smaller pieces, or do you eat the same size pieces at regular intervals? We can ask similar questions about chemical reactions.

FIGURE 1: The rate of eating is the number of squares of chocolate eaten in one minute.

What is rate of reaction?

The rate of a reaction is the amount of a product produced or the amount of reactant used up in a certain time. It is usually measured as the amount per second.

Some reactions, such as the rusting of iron, are slow and have a low rate of reaction. The chemical industry needs to make product quickly to sell. Chemical engineers look for ways to make reactions faster so that they are more economical.

An explosion is a fast chemical reaction that is not controlled. Chemical engineers look for ways to keep reactions under control so that they take place at a safe rate.

FIGURE 2: Explosions are not safe or economical ways of carrying out a chemical reaction.

QUESTIONS

1 Give two reasons why chemists in the chemical industry need to control the rate of chemical reactions.

2 Identical pieces of magnesium ribbon were added to two test tubes of hydrochloric acid. How could you tell if the rate of reaction was different in the two tubes?

Measuring rates of reaction

$$\text{mean rate of reaction} = \frac{\text{change in quantity measured}}{\text{time taken for change}}$$

To calculate the rate of a reaction we must measure a quantity that changes with the amount of reactant or product in the reaction. If one of the products is a gas, there are two ways of doing this.

> Measure the mass of the reactants and products in the reaction vessel at set times. As the gaseous product is released, the mass will decrease.

> Measure the volume of gas produced at set times.

Watch out!
The rate of reaction changes at every instant during the reaction, so the rate we calculate is the mean over a period of time.

🔍 reaction rate GCSE

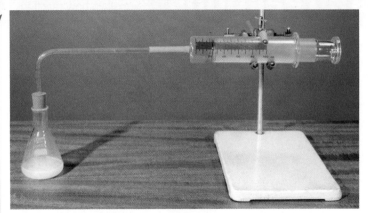

FIGURE 3: A gas syringe measures the volume of gas released by a reaction.

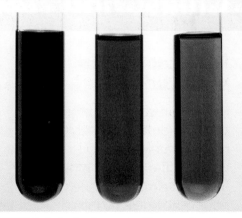

FIGURE 4: As iodine is removed in a reaction its colour in starch solution becomes lighter. This can be measured with a colorimeter.

A reaction in a liquid mixture may have a solid product. The solid product will make the mixture cloudy. The time taken for an opaque product to obscure a cross marked beneath the glass reaction vessel (glass or beaker) can give the average rate of the reaction. Alternatively, the intensity of light that passes through the mixture can be measured using a colorimeter. This instrument measures the intensity of light of a particular colour, so if a reaction produces a colour change a colorimeter can be used to measure the change.

Watch out!

All measurements should be repeated to obtain a range of results. Outliers should be noted and the mean values calculated.

QUESTIONS

3 Magnesium reacting with hydrochloric acid produces $46 \, cm^3$ of hydrogen gas in 20 seconds. What is the mean rate of reaction?

4 Lumps of calcium carbonate react with hydrochloric acid to form calcium chloride solution and carbon dioxide gas. Describe two ways of measuring the rate of this reaction.

Interpreting rates of reaction

A graph of the data from a rate of reaction experiment has time on the x-axis and the quantity measured, such as the volume of gas collected, on the y-axis. The line is steep at the start of the reaction. The line becomes horizontal when the reaction stops because all the reactants have been used up.

The gradient, or steepness, of the line at any time is the rate of the reaction at that point. To find the mean rate between any two points find the change in the quantity on the y-axis between the two times on the x-axis and calculate the rate using the formula on page 182.

Did you know?

Using lasers chemists can follow reactions that are over in a few femtoseconds. A femtosecond is $1 \times 10^{-15} \, s$, or 1 quadrillionth of a second. There are more femtoseconds in one second than there have been seconds since humans evolved.

QUESTION

5 Look at the graph.

a How long did it take for the reaction to be completed?

b What was the total volume of gas collected?

c What was the average rate for the whole reaction?

d What was the rate in the first 5 seconds?

e Which point is an outlier? Explain why.

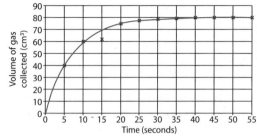

FIGURE 5: A graph showing the total volume of hydrogen gas produced in the reaction of magnesium with hydrochloric acid against the time taken.

🔍 reaction rate GCSE

Changing rates of reactions

We are learning to:
> explain how reactions occur when there are collisions between particles
> understand how changing conditions change the rate of reactions
> explain how changing conditions affect the collisions between particles

How can a solid explode?

Fires and explosions in grain silos and dusty factories are unfortunately common. When a fine powder of a flammable material, such as flour or sawdust, is mixed with air, just a spark will ignite it. The same idea is used in power stations, where coal is crushed before it is burned.

FIGURE 1: A tiny amount of powdered milk produces a fireball when sprinkled into a flame.

 ## What happens in reactions?

Reactants are made up of moving particles which collide. Sometimes the collisions result in changes in the particles and products are formed. The more collisions there are, the faster the reaction.

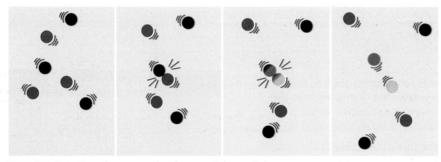

FIGURE 2: Reactions happen only when particles collide.

 **QUESTIONS**

1 Are collisions between particles in a fast reaction more frequent or less frequent than in slow reaction?

2 Why are reactions between two solids much slower than reactions involving liquids or gases?

 ## Changing the conditions

We can carry out investigations where we change one of the following factors, but control all the others:

> the temperature of the reactants

> the size of solid particles reacting

> the concentration of the reactants.

Many experiments on a variety of reactions have shown that there is a correlation between rates of reaction and each of these factors. For instance, if the temperature of the reactants is increased, the rate of reaction increases.

Watch out!

Only particles on the surface of solids can take part in reactions.

Q collision theory rates of reaction

For the same amount of material, the smaller the particle size, the higher the rate of reaction. For solid particles, the smaller the size of the particles, the larger the surface area in contact with the other reactants.

The **concentration** of a reactant is the amount of it in grams dissolved in $1\,dm^3$ of the solution. The more concentrated the reactants, the higher the rate of reaction.

FIGURE 3: Two samples of hydrochloric acid reacting with equal amounts of calcium carbonate. On the left the calcium carbonate is a lump; on the right it has been crushed into a powder.

QUESTIONS

3 Why should you only change one condition at a time in an investigation of rates of reaction?

4 Pieces of zinc metal react slowly with sulfuric acid to produce hydrogen. Describe and explain what you could do to make the reaction faster.

FIGURE 4: Equal amounts of zinc reacting with equal volumes of hydrochloric acid, but the acid on the right is more concentrated than the solution on the left.

Explaining the patterns

The conditions and rate of reaction are not simply a correlation. Collision theory is a well-researched mechanism that scientists accept shows that a change in conditions *causes* a change in rate.

Increasing the amount of surface area of a solid increases the chance that other reactant particles will collide with atoms on the surface. Increasing the frequency of collisions increases the rate of reactions.

The more particles there are in a particular volume, the more chance there is that collisions will occur. The collision frequency and hence rate of reactions increases with the concentration of the reactants. Reactions slow down as the concentration of the reactants decreases because the frequency of collisions between the reactants decreases.

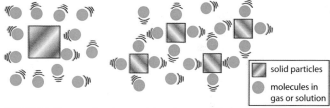

solid particles

molecules in gas or solution

FIGURE 5: The smaller the particles, the more likely there is to be a collision between reactant particles

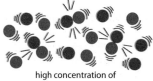

low concentration of reactants, few collisions

high concentration of reactants, more collisions

FIGURE 6: The greater the concentration of reactants, the greater the collision frequency.

QUESTIONS

5 Explain why explosions occur in grain silos.

6 The instructions on a bottle of stain remover suggest pouring it directly onto badly soiled clothes, while mixing it with water is sufficient for mild stains. Explain why this is.

Did you know?

The movement of particles and collision frequency has been used to model the behaviour of crowds of people, for example at football matches. Vehicles in traffic jams can also behave like particles, but a different type of collision is involved.

concentration rates of reaction

Catalysts

We are learning to:
> understand how catalysts can speed up reactions
> interpret information about controlling rates of reaction

What can we do when reactions are very slow?

Hydrogen peroxide solution in a bottle on a shelf will do very little. If a little black powder is added to it, froth forms immediately. The hydrogen peroxide decomposes to oxygen gas and water. The black powder is still there but it has made a reaction happen in seconds that would normally take months.

FIGURE 1: Hydrogen peroxide decomposes rapidly when a black powder, manganese dioxide, is added.

What are catalysts?

A **catalyst** is a substance that speeds up a chemical reaction but is not used up in the reaction itself. **Catalytic converters** in cars and lorries speed up reactions between pollutant gases to form less harmful substances. The catalyst works for years before it needs replacing. The rare metals in the catalytic converter can be recovered to use again.

Catalysts are very important in the chemical industry. They are used to speed up synthesis reactions that are slow and uneconomical. Many different substances are used as catalysts.

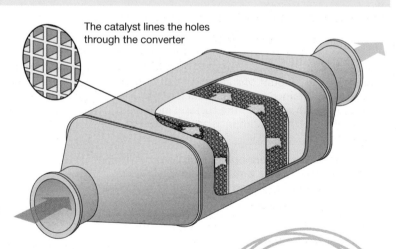

The catalyst lines the holes through the converter

FIGURE 2: The catalytic converter contains just a few grams of catalyst but helps to reduce the pollutants in the air.

Watch out!
Do not say 'catalysts are not involved in a reaction'. It is more correct to say 'they return to their original form at the end of the reaction'.

QUESTIONS

1 Why is a catalyst needed in some chemical processes?

2 Some of the catalysts used in the chemical industry are very expensive. Why is this not a big problem for chemical companies?

Q catalyst rates of reaction

Investigating catalysts

Catalysts speed up reactions because the reactant particles react more easily when they collide with the catalyst particles. The catalyst collides with many reactant particles, so a small amount of catalyst can have a big effect on the rate of a reaction. Increasing the surface area of the catalyst increases the rate of reaction. The catalyst can be in tiny pieces or spread out over a large area as in catalytic converters, or the catalyst can be dissolved in a solution with the reactants.

Often there is one substance that is the best catalyst for a particular reaction. Manganese dioxide is a very good catalyst for decomposing hydrogen peroxide to oxygen, but other substances are catalysts too.

FIGURE 3: Reactions happen when reactant particles collide with catalyst particles.

 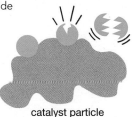

products

reactant

catalyst particle

QUESTIONS

3 Ahmed and Chloe carried out an investigation to find which substances catalysed the decomposition of hydrogen peroxide. Their results are shown in the table.

Catalyst used	Volume of oxygen gas given off in 30 s (cm³)
none	0
zinc oxide powder	2
manganese dioxide lump	22
copper oxide powder	23

a Which substances acted as a catalyst?

b Does the data show which is the 'best' catalyst for the reaction? Explain your answer.

c What should Ahmed and Chloe do to improve their investigation?

Controlling rates of reaction

Chemical engineers can control the rate of a chemical reaction in different ways. They can change the temperature, change the concentration of the reactants, change the particle size of solid reactants or use a catalyst.

Engineers also have to consider safety and the cost of the process. Increasing the temperature may increase the yield but the cost of the energy may make the process uneconomic. Concentrated acids are corrosive and are a hazard. Chemical engineers have to examine the data for a reaction and decide the best conditions to use for an industrial process.

Did you know?

Enzymes are large protein molecules in living cells. They act as catalysts in many different reactions. Chemists are now investigating the use of enzymes in industrial processes. They are safer and cheaper to use because they work at lower temperatures than their chemical counterparts.

QUESTION

4 Chemical engineers want to manufacture zinc chloride. They investigate the reaction of zinc and hydrochloric acid. The reaction gives off hydrogen gas. Here are the results they obtained. Answer the questions that follow, giving explanations.

a What other factors may have affected the outcome of the investigation?

b Which factor had the most effect on the rate of reaction?

c What conditions would produce the fastest reaction?

d What conditions would be safest and most economical for the industrial process?

Reactants	Volume of hydrogen gas collected (cm³) after		
	30 s	60 s	120 s
zinc lumps and dilute acid	5	10	20
zinc powder and dilute acid	10	20	40
zinc powder and concentrated acid	28	45	60
zinc powder and hot dilute acid	30	50	60
zinc powder, dilute acid and a little copper powder catalyst	25	40	55

Synthesising a product

We are learning to:

> apply our understanding of acid–alkali reactions and factors affecting rates of reaction to the synthesis of a new chemical product

Why make magnesium sulfate?

Magnesium sulfate has a huge number of uses. Known as Epsom Salts, it is used as bath salts and relaxes the muscles. Some people think it has amazing health benefits. It certainly has many different medical uses. It is used to improve nutrient-deficient soil, it is useful for keeping foods such as biscuits dry. It can also be used in the production of tofu.

Magnesium sulfate crystals can be found naturally but can also be manufactured.

FIGURE 1

Choosing the reactants

We can make magnesium sulfate by reacting certain substances with sulfuric acid. Sulfuric acid reacts with:

> magnesium

> magnesium oxide

> magnesium hydroxide

> magnesium carbonate.

Magnesium carbonate is found in rocks. The other substances must be made from other materials and so are expensive. In the example here we will use magnesium carbonate.

Magnesium carbonate reacts with sulfuric acid to make magnesium sulfate, water and carbon dioxide gas. Sulfuric acid is corrosive. Magnesium carbonate is not a hazard.

FIGURE 2: Dolomite is a mineral that contains magnesium carbonate.

QUESTIONS

1 Write a word equation for the reaction of magnesium carbonate with sulfuric acid.

2 What safety precautions should be taken when using sulfuric acid?

🔍 chemical synthesis GCSE

Getting the conditions right

To make the reaction go faster we could warm the acid before starting the reaction. The acid could be warmed using heat taken from the products by a heat exchanger. In a chemical factory pipes may carry steam, which transfers heat from one part of the process to another (see page 177).

Magnesium carbonate is a solid. The reaction will go faster if it is crushed into a powder. The higher the concentration of sulfuric acid, the faster the reaction. However, concentrated sulfuric acid is a bigger risk. It will be best if the acid is dilute.

If we add enough magnesium carbonate all the acid will be used up and some solid magnesium carbonate will be left at the end. Some impurities in the magnesium carbonate will be left as solids and can be separated from the magnesium sulfate solution. Magnesium sulfate crystallises from the solution and can then be washed and dried.

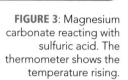

QUESTIONS

3 Why are the products of the reaction hotter than the reactants?

4 What steps are taken to make the reaction go as fast as possible?

5 Describe how the magnesium sulfate is separated and purified.

FIGURE 3: Magnesium carbonate reacting with sulfuric acid. The thermometer shows the temperature rising.

Finding the yield

The equation for the reaction is:

$$MgCO_3(s) + H_2SO_4(aq) \rightarrow MgSO_4(aq) + H_2O(l) + CO_2(g)$$

The relative formula masses are magnesium carbonate 84 and magnesium sulfate 120.

This means that 84 g of magnesium carbonate will react with sulfuric acid to form 120 g of magnesium sulfate.

The magnesium sulfate solution formed in the reaction may contain some unreacted sulfuric acid. We can find out how much sulfuric acid is present by titrating a measured volume of the solution with sodium hydroxide solution.

Did you know?

Ignoring metal extraction and the oil and plastics industry, the most important chemicals produced by the chemicals industry are sulfuric acid, sodium hydroxide, chlorine and ammonia. These chemicals are used in a huge variety of processes.

Watch out!

There are many steps in designing the synthesis of a chemical. The cost of each step is an important factor.

QUESTIONS

6 We can sell 240 tonnes of magnesium sulfate. What mass of magnesium carbonate will be needed to make this if we could get a 100% yield?

7 A test showed that when 84 g of magnesium was reacted, only 108 g of magnesium sulfate was collected instead of 120 g. What was the percentage yield?

8 The table shows the results of a titration between sodium hydroxide solution and sulfuric acid before and after the reaction with magnesium carbonate. The same sodium hydroxide solution was used for both sets of titrations and the same volume of sulfuric acid was used for each titration.

a What was the mean volume of sodium hydroxide used to neutralise the sulfuric acid after the reaction?

b What do the results show about the concentration of the sulfuric acid after the reaction with magnesium carbonate?

Titration number	Volume of sodium hydroxide solution required to neutralise sulfuric acid	
	Before reaction with magnesium carbonate (cm³)	After reaction with magnesium carbonate (cm³)
1	45.2	4.5
2	45.1	4.4
3	45.3	4.6
mean	45.1	

C6 Checklist

To achieve your forecast grade in the exam you'll need to revise

Use this checklist to see what you can do now. Refer back to pages 164–189 if you're not sure. Look across the rows to see how you could progress – **bold italic** means Higher tier only.

Remember you'll need to be able to use these ideas in many ways:
> interpreting pictures, diagrams and graphs
> applying ideas to new situations
> explaining ethical implications
> suggesting some benefits and risks to society
> drawing conclusions from evidence you've been given.

Look at pages 300–306 for information about how you'll be assessed.

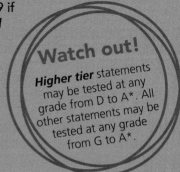

Watch out!

Higher tier statements may be tested at any grade from D to A*. All other statements may be tested at any grade from G to A*.

To aim for a grade E	To aim for a grade C	To aim for a grade A
recall hazard symbols and give precautions for handling hazardous chemicals		
understand the importance of chemical synthesis in providing a variety of products	identify the stages in the synthesis of a chemical compound; interpret data from various sectors of the chemical industry	
recall the use of indicators to test for acidity and alkalinity; recall some solid, liquid and gaseous acidic substances and some common alkalis; recall the use of universal indicator and pH meters to measure the pH of a solution		
recall the reactions of acids with metals, metal oxides, metal hydroxides and metal carbonates, and write word equations for the reactions	recall the formulae of the reactants and products of some of these reactions; interpret balanced chemical equations including state symbols	*work out the formula of salts given the charge on the ions and work out the charge on an ion given the formula of the salt and the charge on the other ion*
use the Periodic Table to obtain relative atomic masses and calculate the relative formula mass of compounds; understand that the relative atomic mass compares the mass of an atom with other atoms	understand that a balanced equation shows the relative number of atoms of each element in the reactants and products; substitute relative formula masses and data into a given mathematical formula to calculate the mass of a reactant or product	*use balanced equations and given data to calculate the mass of reactants or products in a reaction*
recall that the reaction of an acid with an alkali is a neutralisation reaction; describe how to accurately carry out a titration		interpret titration results by substituting data into a given mathematical formula

To aim for a grade E	To aim for a grade C	To aim for a grade A
write down the name of the salt formed from a named acid and alkali in a neutralisation reaction	understand that when dissolved in water, acids form hydrogen ions and alkalis form hydroxide ions; understand that in neutralisation reactions the hydrogen ions and hydroxide ions join together to form water	*write down the formula of a salt given the formulae of the acid and alkali that react together*
understand the terms exothermic and endothermic	use and interpret energy level diagrams for exothermic and endothermic reactions	understand the importance of energy changes in managing and controlling chemical reactions such as in chemical synthesis
understand the importance of the purity of chemicals and how to check this; understand the use of filtration to separate a solid from a liquid	understand how the processes of dissolving, filtration, evaporation, crystallisation and drying are used to purify a chemical	calculate the percentage yield of a reaction given the actual and theoretical yields
understand what is meant by rate of reaction, and understand the need to control reaction rate	describe methods for measuring rates of reactions, including measuring volumes of gases, changes in mass and the formation or loss of a colour or precipitate	interpret data obtained from rates of reaction experiments
use ideas about collisions between particles to explain how reactions take place; understand how concentration, temperature, and size of particles affect reaction rates		explain how the frequency of collisions affects the rate of reaction when concentration or particle size changes
understand the effect of catalysts on rates of reaction and that catalysts are not used up		interpret data about the control of the rate of reactions in chemical synthesis
understand the need to choose reactants and a suitable reaction, and assess risk, in chemical synthesis	understand the need to calculate quantities of reactants, choose suitable conditions and plan how to separate and purify products of chemical synthesis	note methods of determining the yield of a chemical synthesis and checking the purity of the product

Exam-style questions

Foundation level

1 AO1 **a** Which of the following is an acidic compound that is a gas?

sulfuric acid   citric acid
hydrogen chloride   ethanoic acid   [1]

AO1 **b** Tom tested a solution with a pH meter. Which of the following results would he have got if the solution was an acid?

13   9   7   4   [1]

AO2 **c** Marie was investigating the reactions of acids. She added some sodium carbonate to sulfuric acid. A gas was given off and she was left with a solution of a salt.

Write a word equation for the reaction.   [2]

[Total 4]

Foundation/Higher level

AO1

AO2 **2** Calcium carbonate reacts with hydrochloric acid to give off carbon dioxide gas. Carla predicts that the carbon dioxide gas is given off more quickly if smaller pieces of calcium carbonate are used.

Describe how you could collect reliable data to test this prediction and use collision theory to explain why it could be true.

The quality of written communication will be assessed in your answer to this question.   [6]

[Total 6]

3 a Ahmed wanted to make a sample of magnesium chloride by reacting magnesium oxide with hydrochloric acid. The equation for the reaction is

$$MgO(s) + 2HCl(aq) \rightarrow MgCl_2(aq) + H_2O(l)$$

AO1 **(i)** What do the letters (aq) mean?   [1]

AO2 **(ii)** How many atoms of hydrogen are involved in the reaction?   [1]

AO2 **(iii)** Ahmed added 4 g of magnesium oxide to excess hydrochloric acid. What mass of magnesium chloride might he expect to make? Use the Periodic Table (page 309) to find the relative atomic masses.   [2]

AO1 **b** Eve wanted to separate pure crystals of a salt from a solution which contained some solid impurity. Sort the following instructions into the correct order for her to do this.

A Leave the evaporating dish for crystallisation to take place.

B Heat the evaporating dish to evaporate off water until crystals start to form.

C Pour the crystals and remaining solution into a filter paper and funnel.

D Pour the impure solution through a filter paper in a filter funnel.

E Collect the crystals on the filter paper and spread them out to dry.

F Collect the filtrate in an evaporating dish.   [3]

[Total 7]

Higher level

4 Alex wants to use a solution of sodium hydroxide to make a salt. He needs to check that the alkali is the correct concentration so he decides to check it by doing a titration with hydrochloric acid.

AO1 **a** Which of the following pieces of apparatus should Alex use to measure out accurately 20 cm³ of the sodium hydroxide solution?

100 cm³ beaker   100 cm³ measuring cylinder
50 cm³ pipette   20 cm³ pipette   [1]

AO1 **b** Which of the following is the formula of the particle present in all acid solutions?

$H^+(aq)$ $H(aq)$ $H_2(aq)$ $H_2(g)$ [1]

AO1 **c** Alex places the 20 cm³ of sodium hydroxide in a conical flask, adds a few drops of an indicator. He fills a burette with the hydrochloric acid. What should Alex do to measure accurately how much of the hydrochloric acid is needed to react with the sodium hydroxide?   [2]

d Alex thinks the sodium hydroxide solution has 4.00 g of sodium hydroxide dissolved in 100 cm³ of solution. The hydrochloric acid has 3.65 g of hydrogen chloride dissolved in 100 cm³ of acid.

The equation for the reaction is

$$NaOH(aq) + HCl(aq) \rightarrow NaCl(aq) + H_2O(l)$$

Alex did the titration four times. His results are shown in the table

Volume of sodium hydroxide solution used (cm³)	20.0	20.0	20.0	20.0
Volume of hydrochloric acid used (cm³)	21.4	20.1	19.9	20.0

AO3 **(i)** Is Alex's first result an outlier? Explain your answer. What should he do about it?   [2]

AO2 **(ii)** Show that 20 cm³ of the sodium hydroxide should react with 20 cm³ of hydrochloric acid. Use the Periodic Table on page 309 for Relative Atomic Masses.   [2]

AO3 **(iii)** Do Alex's results suggest that the sodium hydroxide is the correct concentration? Explain your answer.   [2]

[Total 10]

AO1   recall the science   AO2   apply your knowledge   AO3   evaluate and analyse the evidence

Worked example

AO1

AO3 **a** Wilson measured the temperature of a two samples of a citric acid solution. To one sample he added some magnesium powder and to the other some sodium hydrogen carbonate. He measured the temperatures of both mixtures after stirring for 10 seconds.

Temperature of solution (°C)	Citric acid + magnesium	Citric acid + sodium hydrogen carbonate
Before mixing	19	19
After mixing	22	17

Wilson says both reactions are exothermic because the temperature changes. Explain whether he is correct. [3]

Wilson is correct about the citric acid/magnesium reaction because the temperature has risen. ✔ *The reaction is exothermic because it gives out energy.* ✔

He is wrong about the other reaction because the temperature has fallen. It is endothermic because it is taking in energy from the surroundings. ✔

> **How to raise your grade**
>
> Take note of the comments from examiners – these will help you to improve your grade.

> This question requires a judgement about the data provided and knowledge of the terms exothermic and endothermic: 3 marks.

AO1 **b** Draw an energy level diagram for the reaction of citric acid with magnesium. [2]

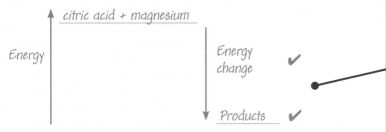

> This answer receives 2 marks; 1 mark for correctly showing the products at a lower energy level than the reactants in an exothermic reaction, and 1 mark for correctly labelling the energy change.

c A scientist thinks that he has found a new catalyst to speed up a reaction that could provide a cheap renewable energy source.

AO1 **(i)** Why is only a small amount of the catalyst needed? [1]

The catalyst is reformed at the end of each reaction and can be used over and over again. ✔

> This is a correct explanation of the action of catalysts at this stage: 1 mark.

AO3 **(ii)** What should the scientist do next? Choose the best actions from the list below.
  A Do his experiments again to get more data.
  B Announce his discovery to a newspaper.
  C Put his results on the internet.
  D Submit a report on his experiments to a peer-reviewed journal. [2]

A ✔ *and C* ✗

> This answer gains 1 mark only. A is correct as repeating experiments makes the data more reliable. C is not correct as there is no check on the accuracy of material posted on the internet. D is the correct action to take. Peer-review ensures that expert scientists check the data and the conclusions carefully.

P4 Explaining motion

What you should already know...

Energy is needed to make things happen

Energy cannot be created or destroyed.

Energy can be stored.

Energy can be transferred between objects.

Energy exists in different forms.

Energy can be dissipated so that it is less useful.

 What energy transfers take place when electricity is generated?

Forces are 'pushes' or 'pulls'

Forces act between objects.

Forces can change an object's shape.

Forces can affect an object's motion, speeding it up or slowing it down.

Forces can change the direction of a moving object.

 What different types of forces are there?

Speed is the distance travelled by an object in a certain time

We usually measure speed in metres per second (m/s), but sometimes we use km/s or km/hour.

Distance travelled can be calculated by using the formula: distance = speed × time.

 The speed of light in space is 300 000 km/s. How far does light travel in an hour?

In P4 you will find out about...

> how we calculate speed

> what we mean by acceleration and how we calculate it

> how we represent motion on a graph

> the difference between speed and velocity

> how forces act between objects

> the effect of friction on motion

> reaction forces

> how rockets and jets work

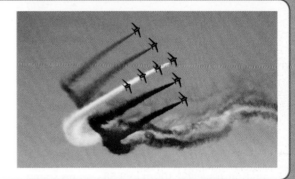

> what is meant by momentum and how we calculate it

> the effect of a change in momentum in a collision

> how car design can improve safety

> how seat-belts, air bags and safety helmets help to reduce injuries

> why moving objects have a top speed

> what scientists mean by work

> how potential energy and kinetic energy are connected

> how to calculate kinetic energy

> how to calculate potential energy

> the motion of falling objects

Measuring speed

How fast can humans run?

The fastest athletes are the 100 m sprinters. In 1912 the fastest runner in the world took 10.6 s to run 100 m. In 2011 the world record holder is the Jamaican sprinter, Usain Bolt, who ran the distance in just 9.58 s. It has taken 100 years to take one second off the record time. Some people believe we may be approaching the limit of human performance.

FIGURE 1: Usain Bolt easily winning the 100 m sprint.

Calculating speed

The **speed** of a moving object tells us how far it will travel in a certain time. In science we measure the distance travelled in metres (m) and the time taken in seconds (s). We can calculate the speed in metres per second (m/s) by using the equation:

$$\text{speed (m/s)} = \frac{\text{distance travelled (m)}}{\text{time taken (s)}}$$

Usain Bolt travelled 100 m in 9.58 s, so his speed was:

$$\text{speed} = \frac{100}{9.58} = 10.4 \, \text{m/s}$$

Usain Bolt's speed was not the same throughout the race. He started from a standstill and got faster. The equation above tells us Usain Bolt's **average speed** over the whole 100 m of the race.

Did you know?

The Bugatti Veyron is the world's fastest car that can drive on normal roads. Its top speed is 408 km/h. For faster objects, like this car, speed is measured in km/h rather than m/s.

QUESTIONS

1 What is your average speed if you walk 50 m in 20 seconds?

2 The world record for running 1500 m is 3 minutes and 56 seconds. What average speed is this?

Watch out!

Time is usually measured in seconds, so always convert minutes to seconds. 1 minute = 60 seconds.

Average speed and instantaneous speed

Sprinters start the race slowly and then speed up. Coaches measure their 'split-times' for each 20 m distance. The split-times for Usain Bolt are shown in the table. Bolt ran fastest between 60 and 80 m, taking 1.61 s to run 20 m. This is a speed of 20/1.61 = 12.4 m/s. This is still an average speed, but taken over a shorter time interval. If we could measure the distance travelled over a *very* short time interval, we could get close to the speed at that moment. This is called the **instantaneous speed**.

Distance (m)	Time (s)
0–20	2.89
20–40	1.75
40–60	1.67
60–80	1.61
80–100	1.66

Split-times for Usain Bolt's record run.

In the early days of athletics, timing was done manually using stopwatches. Even though race officials were trained, their results could vary and times were only accurate to 1/10 of a second, for example a time of 10.6 s. To increase the accuracy of the readings, several timekeepers were used and the mean of their results was used. The mean was closer to the true value than any individual reading.

Nowadays fully automatic electronic timers are use, which are started when the starting pistol is fired and stopped when the runner crosses the line. This method is more accurate and times are given to 1/100 of a second, for example a time of 9.68 s.

FIGURE 2: Modern timing system use high-speed digital cameras linked to computers.

QUESTIONS

3 Which is more important for a 100 m sprinter, a high instantaneous speed or a high average speed? Which is more important for a long jumper?

4 Suggest some reasons why the results from several timekeepers might vary.

Displacement (Higher tier only)

When a journey is a simple straight line, as in a 100 m race, the distance travelled tells you how far from the start you are. This is not always true. A 400 m race is one complete circuit of a running track. At the end of the race, the runners have travelled 400 m, but are back where they started. We say that their **displacement** is zero. If you travel between two villages along a country lane that twists and turns, the total distance travelled will be much further than your displacement.

The displacement of an object is the difference between its current position and its starting position. It is expressed as a distance *and* a direction, e.g. 150 m due west or 5 m vertically. Quantities such as displacement, which need both a size (magnitude) and a direction to define them, are called **vectors.**

QUESTION

5 There are other quantities (things you can measure) in physics that need a direction *and* a size to fully describe them. Suggest some examples of these vector quantities.

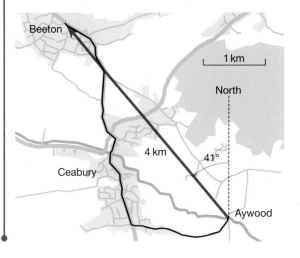

FIGURE 3: The displacement is shown by the red line, the distance by road is shown by the black line. The displacement of Beeton from Aywood is 4 km in a direction 41° west of north.

Distance–time graphs

We are learning to:
- > draw and interpret distance–time graphs
- > understand the significance of the gradient on a distance–time graph

How can we keep moving in our cities?

Travelling around London can be difficult. The average speed of the traffic is only 10 miles an hour, the same as it was 100 years ago. A personal rapid transport system may be the answer. These electrically powered vehicles run on a computer-controlled network with no congestion and very little pollution.

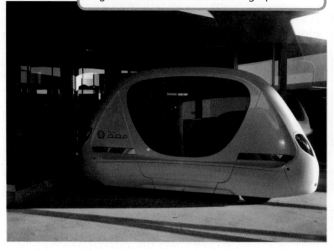

FIGURE 1: An idealised personal pod rapid transport system.

Plotting a journey

A journey by bus or by train is a series of stops and starts with fast and slow sections. One way to show this is a **distance–time graph.** The time for the journey is plotted on the horizontal axis (the *x*-axis). The distance travelled is plotted on the vertical axis (the *y*-axis).

Figure 2 shows a distance–time graph for a bus journey. A straight line, such as the section labelled C, means that the bus covers the same distance in each second. *A straight line means that the bus is travelling at a constant speed.*

A horizontal line, like the section labelled B, means that the bus is not changing its distance from the start: it has stopped. *A horizontal line means that the bus is stationary.*

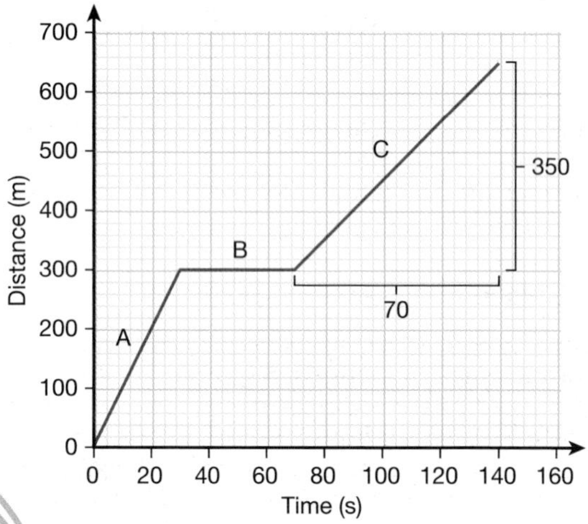

FIGURE 2: A distance–time graph for a bus journey.

QUESTION

1 Look again at the distance–time graph for the bus journey in Figure 2.

a How far does the bus travel altogether?

b Between which times is it stationary?

Watch out!

Use 'constant speed' or 'uniform speed' to mean 'steady speed'. The word 'stationary' means 'not moving'.

Speed on a distance–time graph

We can find the average speed of the bus during any part of its journey if we know the distance travelled and the time taken. For each section of the graph in Figure 2, the distance travelled is the difference in the *y* values, and the time taken is the difference in the *x* values.

$$\text{speed} = \frac{\text{distance travelled}}{\text{time taken}} = \frac{\text{difference in } y}{\text{difference in } x}$$

distance-time graph

The calculation for speed is therefore the same as the calculation for the **gradient** (slope) of a straight line on a distance–time graph. So, for uniform speed, *the gradient of the distance–time graph gives the speed*.

In Figure 2, the line labelled A is steeper than the line labelled C. This shows that the bus is travelling at a higher speed during this part of the journey.

Watch out!

Remember to label your graph axes with a quantity such as distance, and an appropriate unit, such as metres, m. The label should be written like this: Distance (m).

⬤ QUESTION

2 Sketch a distance–time graph for a cyclist who starts at a low constant speed, increases to a higher constant speed, reverts to the initial slow speed, and then stops.

Calculating the speed (Higher tier only)

To find the value of speed in section C of Figure 2 on the opposite page, we need to find the gradient of the line in section C. First find the difference in the y values, which is $650 - 300 = 350$ m. The difference in the x values is $140 - 70 = 70$ s. The speed is calculated from:

$$\text{gradient} = \frac{\text{difference in } y}{\text{difference in } x} = \frac{350}{70} = 5 \text{ m/s}$$

In reality, a bus would gradually increase its speed as it left a bus stop. On a distance–time graph, a curved line means that the bus is changing its speed. The steeper the gradient of the curve, the faster the bus is travelling. See Figure 3.

Displacement–time graphs

Some journeys are return journeys. We can visualise such a journey by using a **displacement–time graph** (Figure 4). This has displacement, that is the distance *and* the direction from the start, on the y-axis. The displacement can be zero, meaning that the object has returned to its starting point. The displacement can even be negative, showing that the object has travelled behind its starting point.

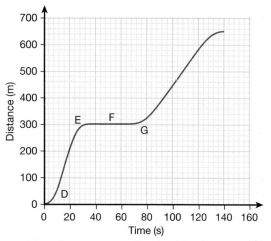

FIGURE 3: The curves D and G show that the bus is getting faster.

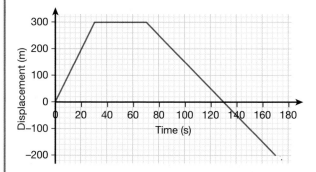

FIGURE 4: Displacement–time graph: the object moves away at constant speed for 30 s, stops for 40 s and then travels back in the opposite direction for 100 s. It ends up 200 m behind its starting point.

⬤ QUESTIONS

3 a Calculate the speed of the bus in section A of Figure 2.

   b How would you find the average speed for the whole journey, including any stops, from a distance–time graph?

   c Calculate the average speed of the bus in Figure 2 over its whole journey.

4 What does the curve labelled E in Figure 3 show about the motion of the bus?

5 a What is the displacement at the end of the journey in Figure 4?

   b What is the total distance travelled?

   c Calculate the speed between 70 s and 170 s.

   d Your answer to part c should be negative. Explain why.

Acceleration

We are learning to:
> explain what is meant by acceleration
> use an equation to calculate acceleration

What are the fastest cars on Earth?

In theory drag racing is a simple sport. The cars, called dragsters, race in a straight line from a standing start. The winner is the car that can cover a quarter of a mile in the shortest time. In practice, it is far from simple. Dragsters use high-performance engines to reach speeds of over 500 km/h (320 mph) in under five seconds.

FIGURE 1: A top dragster can accelerate to 140 m/s from a standing start in 5 s.

Speeding up

Cars in a drag race must have a high top speed. A winning car has to reach that top speed in a very short time. The rate at which the car changes speed is known as its **acceleration**. This is the change in speed in a given time interval, which can be written as:

$$\text{acceleration} = \frac{\text{change in speed}}{\text{time taken}}$$

If the speed is measured in metres per second (m/s), the change in speed is also in metres per second (m/s). Acceleration tells us how many metres per second an object speeds up in one second. So acceleration is measured in metres per second, per second. We write this as m/s^2, spoken as 'metres per second squared'.

$$\text{acceleration (m/s}^2) = \frac{\text{change in speed (m/s)}}{\text{time taken (s)}}$$

The acceleration of the drag car in Figure 1 is:

$$\text{acceleration (m/s}^2) = \frac{\text{change in speed (m/s)}}{\text{time taken (s)}}$$
$$= \frac{\text{final speed} - \text{starting speed}}{\text{time taken}}$$
$$= \frac{140 - 0}{5} = 28 \text{ m/s}^2$$

QUESTIONS

1 A cyclist can accelerate from rest at 1 m/s^2. How fast will she be travelling after 1 second? After 2 seconds? What speed will she reach after 5 seconds?

2 A cheetah can accelerate from standstill to a speed of 25 m/s in 5 s. Calculate its acceleration.

Watch out!

The correct unit for acceleration is m/s^2. It is a common mistake to forget the squared symbol.

Did you know?

On Earth, gravity makes all falling objects accelerate at 9.8 m/s^2. This acceleration is known as g. The acceleration of drag cars is almost three times this value. We write this as $3g$.

Slowing down

At the end of the race a dragster needs to slow down quickly. The speed might change from 140 m/s to a stop in only 3.5 s. This slowing down is also acceleration, though it has a negative value.

$$\text{acceleration (m/s}^2) = \frac{\text{change in speed (m/s)}}{\text{time taken (s)}} = \frac{\text{final speed} - \text{starting speed}}{\text{time taken (s)}}$$
$$= \frac{0 - 140}{3.5} = -40 \text{ m/s}^2$$

Watch out!

If you are taking the Higher tier paper you'll need to be able to rearrange equations like this.

Negative acceleration is sometimes called *deceleration*, or retardation.

FIGURE 2: Dragsters decelerate so quickly that their drivers have suffered injuries, such as detached retinas.

Cornering

A dragster is raced in a straight line, but a Formula One car has to take corners at high speed. Although the speed of the racing car may not be changing, the direction of its motion is. We call the instantaneous speed of a car in a certain direction, its instantaneous **velocity**.

Acceleration is more correctly defined as:

$$\text{acceleration (m/s}^2) = \frac{\text{change in velocity (m/s)}}{\text{time taken (s)}}$$

If the object is travelling in a straight line, then this definition is exactly the same as the tinted equation opposite. However, this definition of acceleration takes into account any change in direction as well as any change in speed.

FIGURE 3: When a car goes round a corner it is accelerating, even if it does not change its speed.

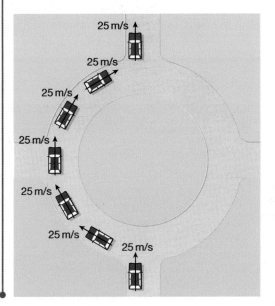

25 m/s
25 m/s
25 m/s
25 m/s
25 m/s
25 m/s
25 m/s

FIGURE 4: The car travels at constant speed, but its direction changes. That means its velocity changes, and so it is accelerating.

Speed–time graphs

We are learning to:
> draw and interpret speed–time graphs
> determine acceleration from a speed–time graph

How can we make driving safer?

Looking down at the speedometer takes a driver 0.8 s. At 70 mph, the car will travel 25 m in this time. New technology can provide a 'head-up' display, projecting road speed, road warnings and GPS information into the driver's field of view.

FIGURE 1: Head-up displays have been used for fighter pilots and are now being installed in cars.

Plotting speed

A car's speed changes during a journey. A **speed–time graph** can be used to show these changes. Speed is plotted on the y-axis with time on the x-axis. Figure 2 shows a speed–time graph for a short car journey. The car starts from rest (point A) and then speeds up for the next 40 s. It reaches a speed of 20 m/s (point B) and stays at this speed for the next 30 s. It then slows down to 15 m/s (from point C to point D).

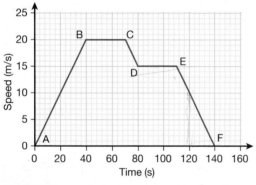

FIGURE 2: A speed–time graph for a short car journey.

> **Watch out!**
> Do not confuse speed–time graphs with distance–time graphs. They can look similar but they tell you different things. In an exam, always check whether it is speed or distance on the y-axis.

QUESTIONS

1 In Figure 2, describe the car's motion between points D and E.

2 How fast is the car travelling after 120 s?

What speed–time graphs tell us

A speed–time graph provides information about an object's motion.

> A horizontal line means that the object is travelling at steady speed.

> A straight line going up (/) tells you that the object is speeding up (accelerating) at a constant rate.

> A straight line going down (\) tells you that the object is slowing down (decelerating) at a constant rate.

> A steeper line means a quicker change of speed. That means greater acceleration.

Speed–time graphs tell you how fast an object is travelling. They do not tell you about its direction.

QUESTIONS

3 In Figure 2, what is happening to the car between E and F?

4 Sketch a speed–time graph for a cyclist who starts from rest, accelerates uniformly and then cycles at a low constant speed for a while, then accelerates uniformly again and remains at a higher constant speed for a while, then slows down at a constant rate and stops.

Velocity–time graphs (Higher tier only)

Velocity is the speed *in a certain direction*, so a **velocity–time graph** can show which way the object is travelling. A positive velocity means that the object is going in one direction; a negative velocity means it is travelling the opposite way.

Figure 3 shows the velocity–time graph for a shuttle train between two stations at an airport. It accelerates at a constant rate until it reaches 12 m/s. It then travels at constant speed until 130 s. The train then decelerates for 30 s, coming to a stop at 160 s. It remains stationary for 60 s. Its velocity then becomes negative. This shows that the train is travelling back the other way.

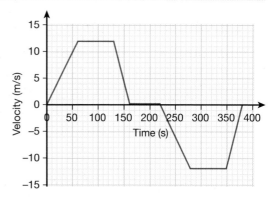

FIGURE 3: Velocity–time graph for an airport shuttle train.

Calculating acceleration

The slope of a line on a velocity–time graph gives the acceleration. The steeper the line, the greater the acceleration. We can calculate the acceleration from the gradient of the line.

Ejector seats in military aircraft have saved thousands of lives, but the high acceleration can cause injuries to the pilot. Figure 4 shows a velocity–time graph for a pilot as he ejects. To calculate the acceleration, we need to find the gradient:

$$\text{gradient} = \frac{18.5 - 0}{100 - 0} = \frac{18.5}{100}$$

But the scale on the x-axis is in milliseconds, not seconds. One millisecond is 1/1000th of a second, so 100 ms is 100/1000 = 0.1 s.

$$\text{acceleration} = \frac{18.5}{0.1}$$

$$= 185 \text{ m/s}^2$$

This is about 19g, 19 times the acceleration due to gravity. For that short time the pilot is pressed into his seat with a force of 19 times his own weight.

Watch out!

Time is usually measured in seconds. 1 millisecond (1 ms) is one-thousandth of a second (not to be confused with a speed of 1 m/s).

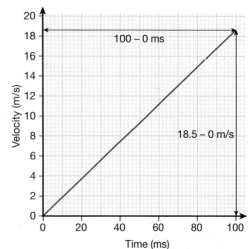

FIGURE 4: Calculating acceleration.

FIGURE 5: Pilots who have to use their ejector seat experience such high accelerations that they are often injured.

QUESTIONS

5 a When does the shuttle train in Figure 3 have the greatest acceleration? When is it speeding up? When it is braking?

b Calculate the acceleration of the shuttle train during the first 60 s of its journey.

c Calculate the acceleration of the same train over the last 30 s of its journey. Is it speeding up or slowing down?

6 A negative slope on a velocity–time graph (a line that goes this way, \) could mean that an object is slowing down. What else could it mean?

Forces

Can humans fly?

A personal jet-pack might be the way to beat the traffic. The latest model can reach a speed of 60 miles per hour and can fly for 30 minutes before refuelling.

FIGURE 1

Forces between objects

Whether you are travelling by jet-pack, or just walking, you need a **force** to get you going. A force is a push or a pull that acts between two objects. In Figure 1, the jet-pack pushes air downwards, and the air pushes up on the jet-pack with an equal force.

Sometimes the force between two objects pushes them apart, like the **repulsive** force between the trampoline and the girl in Figure 2.

Sometimes the force between two objects pulls them towards each other, like the **attractive** force of gravity between the Earth and the Moon.

FIGURE 2: The girl exerts a downwards force on the trampoline. The trampoline exerts an equal force back on the girl, acting upwards.

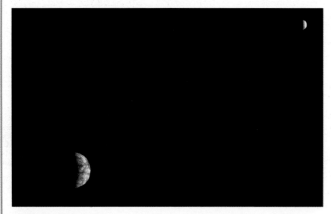

FIGURE 3: The Earth and the Moon as seen from Mars. The Earth pulls on the Moon, holding it in orbit, and the Moon pulls back on the Earth, causing tides. It took Newton's genius to realise that gravity acted equally on both objects.

QUESTIONS

1 Look at Figure 2. The forces on the girl and on the trampoline are the same size. Why is the girl that moves and not the trampoline?

2 When the trampolinist is falling back down, what is the object that is interacting with her? Does she exert a force on that object?

Equal and opposite forces

When two objects interact, the *size* of the force is always the same on each object. The forces on the objects act in opposite directions. Look at the situations in the table on the next page.

Q forces GCSE   force pairs

Situation	Force	Direction	What is happening
ship floating on water	upthrust (buoyancy)	repulsive	The ship pushes down on the water, which pushes back on the ship.
bungee jumper hanging on a cord	tension	attractive	The cord pulls up on the jumper, who pulls down on the cord.
apple falling to the ground	gravity (weight)	attractive	The Earth pulls the apple down. The apple pulls the Earth up.
student sat on a lab stool	reaction (contact force)	repulsive	The student pushes down on the stool, which pushes up on the student.
a bicycle skidding to a stop	friction	attractive	Atoms in the bicycle tyres pull on atoms in the road, and vice versa.

FIGURE 4: The world's fastest train runs in Shanghai, China. Magnets in the train repel magnets in the track, lifting it up. This reduces friction and allows the train to reach a speed of 431 km/h (268 mph).

Did you know?

Scientists believe there are only four fundamental forces: gravity, electromagnetic force, strong nuclear force and weak nuclear force. All the forces in the table, except gravity, are examples of the electromagnetic force.

● QUESTION

3 Identify the force acting between these objects.

a A cricket *bat* striking a *ball*.

b A *meteorite* falling to *Earth*.

c A hot-air *balloon* rising through the *atmosphere*.

d A *car* accelerating along a *road*.

Drawing forces

Forces are **vector** quantities. They have a magnitude (size) and a direction. On a diagram we represent a force by an arrow. Often drawn to scale, the length of the arrow represents the magnitude of the force. The direction of the arrow shows which way the force acts.

FIGURE 5: The car pushes backwards on the road through the force of friction between the tyres and the road (yellow arrow). The road pushes the car forward with an equal but opposite force (red arrow).

FIGURE 6: Rockets (and jets) push gas out of the back of the engine with a large force (yellow). The gas pushes back on the engine with an equal but opposite force (red), propelling the rocket forward

Watch out!

Remember that the forces in a force pair act on *different* objects. If equal, but opposite, forces always acted on the same object, then nothing would ever move!

● QUESTION

4 Draw simple diagrams to represent the objects in question 3. Draw and label arrows to represent the forces that act between the objects.

Friction

What happens when there is no friction?

There is no such thing as a frictionless surface, but the icy track of a bob-sled run comes close. In the skeleton bob, the athlete sprints for 20–30 m before diving aboard the sled. Top athletes reach speeds of 135 km/h (84 mph) as they race down the 1.5 km track.

FIGURE 1: Amy Williams won a gold medal for the UK in record time in the 2010 Winter Olympics.

Sliding

Push a book across the desk. If you stop pushing, the force of friction quickly brings the book to rest. The size of the frictional force depends on the roughness of the surfaces. There is less friction between two smooth surfaces but there is always some friction, even between polished surfaces like ice and the bob-sled runners.

The frictional force also depends on how hard the surfaces are pushed together. A heavier book would push the surfaces together more and lead to a larger frictional force.

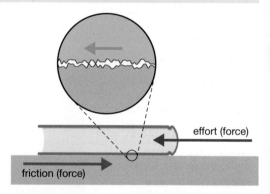

FIGURE 2: Both surfaces have bumps which collide with each other or even stick together.

effort (force)

friction (force)

QUESTIONS

1 Suppose you had to find the maximum frictional force between a book and the desk. Explain how you would carry out the experiment.

2 If you carried out the experiment several times, you would probably get different answers. Why would the value of friction be slightly different each time? (Look at Figure 2.)

Limiting friction

Suppose an object is placed on a surface, like a book on a table, and a small force is applied to the book to try to slide it along. Friction will be equal to the applied force and will act in the opposite direction. This will stop the book from moving. If the applied force is gradually increased, the force of friction will increase too, preventing sliding. Eventually the friction reaches a maximum value and the book will start to slide. The force at which this happens is called the **limiting friction**.

Q friction GCSE

Friction and energy

As the surfaces of two objects slide across each other, friction acts to oppose the motion. The effect of this is to transfer kinetic energy from the objects into internal energy. In other words, they heat up. Rub your hands together quickly and you will notice the heating effect. This can be a problem. In machinery, like a car engine, closely fitting metal parts rub against each other at high speed. Without oil to reduce the friction, the engine would quickly wear out.

FIGURE 3: If a car brakes heavily whilst turning the wheels can 'lock' and the car may skid. Modern cars have ABS (anti-lock braking systems), which helps to stop this happening.

QUESTIONS

3 How does oil reduce friction?

4 Give two examples where friction is a problem and two examples where friction is useful.

Reaction force

When you are standing on the ground the **reaction force** stops gravity pulling you through the floor. If you are not accelerating up or down, the reaction force will balance your weight. If you jump upwards, by pushing harder on the floor, the reaction force will increase. It will be greater than your weight, and push you up.

Walking (Higher tier only)

Friction does not always prevent motion. Without friction you would not be able to walk because your feet would just slide across the floor. You need friction so that you can push backwards against the floor. The floor then pushes you forward.

The overall or **resultant**, force between an object and the surface is a combination of friction and reaction (see Figure 5). It is this resultant force that pushes your foot up and forward when you walk.

FIGURE 4: The gravitational pull of the Earth on the dancer (her weight) is balanced by the reaction force of the ground pushing on her shoe.

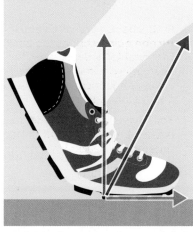

FIGURE 5: The reaction force (red) and the friction force (blue) combine to push the foot in the direction of the resultant force (black).

Did you know?

The force that acts upwards on the ballet dancer in Figure 4 is electromagnetic. It is due to the charges in the atoms in the ground repelling the charges in her foot. The electromagnetic force is much stronger than gravity. The relatively small number of atoms in contact can balance the gravitational attraction of every atom in the Earth.

QUESTIONS

5 A car accelerates away from traffic lights. What forces are acting on the car?

6 Imagine you are standing in the middle of an ice-rink. There is no friction at all. How would you get to the side?

🔍 friction GCSE

Forces and their effects

We are learning to:
> explain what happens to an object when several forces act on it
> understand what is meant by momentum

How does a kite-surfer stay in control?

Kite-surfers use kites with large surface area to pull them across the waves at speeds of up to 90 km/h. They use their weight and the forces from the wind on the kite and the waves on the board to stay upright.

FIGURE 1: There are several different forces acting on the kite-surfer.

Adding forces

Most objects are acted upon by several different forces at the same time. The effect of a combination of forces depends on the size and direction of the forces. Forces can be added together to find the total, or **resultant** force. Because forces have size *and* direction, we have to take both of these into account when we add them together.

We add forces together by drawing them to scale as arrows, drawn nose to tail (see Figure 2). The resultant force is found by drawing an arrow from the tail of the first force to the nose of the last one.

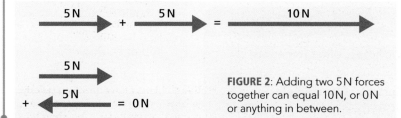

FIGURE 2: Adding two 5 N forces together can equal 10 N, or 0 N or anything in between.

QUESTIONS

1 A car is pushed forward with a force of 1000 N. There is a backward force due to drag and friction of 600 N. Draw this on a diagram and find the resultant force.

2 Two people lift a box. One lifts with a force of 300 N and one with a force of 200 N. The box weighs 400 N. What is the resultant force on the box?

Q resultant forces GCSE

Balanced forces

Sometimes the forces on an object add together to give a resultant of zero. We say that the forces are **balanced**. In this case the object will not accelerate. It will maintain its original speed and direction.

This means that if you give something a push, and there are no other forces, it should move off in the direction of the force and then keep moving. On Earth this is not obvious. Friction or air resistance (drag) soon bring the object to a stop. Without friction or any other force acting, the object would keep going forever.

FIGURE 3: Rear passengers should wear a seat belt. If the car crashes, they will keep moving at constant speed, until acted on by a force. This could be when they hit the driver at 60 mph.

◯ QUESTIONS

3 Draw diagrams to show how three 10 N forces can be added together to make these resultant forces:

a 30 N **b** 10 N **c** 0 N

4 A newspaper article says 'When the train crashed, all the passengers were thrown forward'. Rewrite this using correct physics.

5 Aristotle (384 BCE) thought that a force was needed to keep objects moving, like an arrow fired from a bow. Explain why he was wrong.

Did you know?

The spacecraft Voyager 1 was launched in 1977. It is now 17 billion kilometres from the Sun, and is the most distant man-made object. It will keep going at a constant speed of 38 000 mph until it is acted upon by a force.

Momentum

An unbalanced, or resultant, force on an object will change its motion. It will make the object speed up, slow down or change direction. Suppose that a lorry travelling down the motorway applies its brakes. The resultant force will slow the lorry down. The force needed will depend on the mass, m, and the velocity, v, of the lorry. The product of mass and velocity is called the **momentum**.

Momentum is defined by the equation:

momentum (kg m/s) = mass (kg) × velocity (m/s)

In symbols this is written $p = mv$. A resultant force will change an object's momentum, in the direction of that resultant force.

◯ QUESTIONS

6 Estimate your momentum when you are running at your top speed.

7 Describe in terms of momentum will happen to the box in question 2.

Watch out!

Momentum is measured in kg m/s. Do not forget to include units with every quantity.

FIGURE 4: A heavy lorry travelling quickly has a large momentum. It would take a large force to slow it down in a short time.

Reaching top speed

We are learning to:

> describe how forces affect moving vehicles and falling objects

> understand that a scientific hypothesis makes predictions that can be tested

How fast do raindrops and hailstones fall?

The top speed of a raindrop depends on the size of the drop. Drizzle drops are only around 0.5 mm in diameter, and fall at about 2 m/s. Large raindrops, around 6 mm in diameter, reach 10 m/s. Hailstones can be up to 8 cm across, reach 50 m/s (110 mph), and pose a risk to aircraft, crops and buildings.

FIGURE 1: Hailstones are formed in thunderclouds, where they grow until they get too heavy.

Falling through the air

Raindrops and hailstones fall slowly at first but they accelerate towards the ground due to the force of gravity. If the hailstones were falling through a vacuum, they would keep accelerating at the same rate, around 9.8 m/s², until they hit the ground. But on Earth the atmosphere gets in the way. The hailstones have to push air molecules aside. This exerts an upwards force known as **air resistance** or **drag** on the hailstones.

It was about 400 years ago that Galileo put forward the hypothesis that falling objects accelerate, rather than fall at a steady speed. He tested this by timing a ball as it rolled down a slope. Galileo is sometimes called the first scientist, because he tested his ideas by experiment. He also suggested that, without air resistance, all objects would accelerate at the same rate, whatever their mass. The Apollo 15 astronaut, David Scott, tested this on the Moon, where there is no air. He dropped a hammer and a feather at the same time. They fell at the same rate and hit the Moon's surface together.

QUESTIONS

1 Why does the drag force increase as the hailstone moves faster?

2 Why do you think hailstones fall quicker than raindrops?

Terminal velocity

The maximum speed reached by a raindrop or hailstone is known as its **terminal velocity**. Any object falling through a gas, like air, or through a liquid, will eventually reach terminal velocity.

Figure 2 shows a sky-diver in free-fall.

A At first the force of gravity, or weight, is larger than the drag and the sky-diver accelerates.

B As the speed increases, so does the drag. The resultant downwards force is less. The sky-diver's acceleration is smaller. He is still speeding up, but at a lower rate.

C At a certain speed the drag is equal to the weight. There is no resultant force and so the sky-diver stops accelerating. He continues to fall at this speed, the terminal velocity.

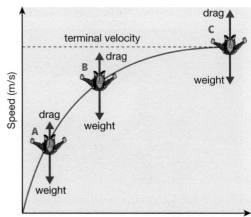

FIGURE 2: Speed–time graph for a sky-diver.

🔍 terminal velocity GCSE

Objects that are relatively light and have a big surface area have a lower terminal velocity, because drag has a greater effect on them. The terminal velocity for a free-fall sky-diver is around 55 m/s (124 mph), but using a parachute reduces this to 5 m/s (just 12 mph).

Figure 3 shows a ball being thrown up in the air and coming down again. The same forces act on the ball, whether it is travelling upwards or falling down. These forces are gravity and air resistance. Gravity always acts down, towards the Earth. Air resistance always acts in the opposite direction to the ball's velocity.

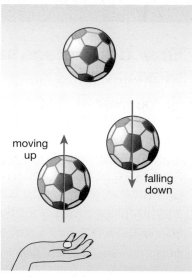

FIGURE 3

QUESTIONS

3 Look at Figure 3. Sketch a diagram showing the direction of the forces on the ball at each position. Explain what is happening to the motion of the ball at each position.

4 Explain why you do not notice air resistance when you are walking, but it is very noticeable when you are cycling.

Top speed

Vehicles have a top speed too. A car travelling along a road is propelled forwards by the driving force caused by the road pushing against the tyres. There are **counter forces**, such as friction and drag, which act against the motion of the car.

When a car starts to move along a straight road, the driving force is greater than the counter force and the car speeds up. The total counter force increases with the speed of the car and eventually balances the driving force. When this happens, the car travels at constant velocity.

At some point the driver will reduce the driving force, and apply the brakes. The counter force will be larger than the driving force and the car will slow down.

Cyclists also reach their top speed when the counter forces become equal to the maximum driving force.

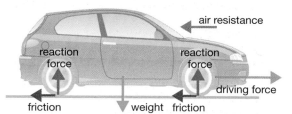

FIGURE 4: This car is travelling at a steady speed. The driving force between the road and the car is balanced by the counter forces, which are the drag and some resistance at the tyres.

Did you know?

Air resistance is a massive problem for racing cyclists, but they can reduce the drag, and save 30% of their energy, by riding immediately behind another rider. This is called slipstreaming.

FIGURE 5: Racing cyclists reduce drag by using drop-handlebars, getting rid of spokes and wearing tight-fitting clothing and an aerodynamic helmet.

QUESTIONS

5 What factors do you think would determine the top speed of a car?

6 A cyclist sets off from rest at the top of a long steep hill. Sketch a speed–time graph for the motion. Explain the shape of your graph.

Force and momentum

We are learning to:
> understand how forces and momentum are linked
> apply this to car safety measures

How do air bags save lives?

When a car crashes, it may come to a stop in a very short time. The driver and passengers keep moving at high speed until a force stops them. This could be when their head hits the dashboard or the windscreen. An air bag has to be inflated in time to prevent this. The air bag has to be in place just 50 milliseconds after the crash. That is less time than it takes you to blink your eye.

FIGURE 1: Air bags save thousands of lives each year, cutting the chance of dying in a head-on collision by about 30%.

Forces in a crash

People in a car crash are subject to large forces as the car stops. Modern cars have a number of safety features that are designed to reduce the force on the occupants.

The force on a person in a crash depends on two things:

> the person's initial **momentum**, which depends on their mass and the speed of the car

> how quickly they are brought to a stop – the quicker the person is brought to rest, the larger the force.

In a car crash, only the second factor can be altered by the design of the car. Seat-belts and air bags are designed to stop the people inside the car more slowly than if they had hit the dashboard or windscreen. If the time taken to stop is increased, the force is reduced.

FIGURE 2: A crash barrier is designed to bend and stretch so as to stop the car more slowly and reduce the force on the car and its occupants.

QUESTIONS

1 Seat-belts are designed to stretch a little in a crash. Why is that a good thing?

2 If you drop a glass on a hard floor it will probably break, but if you drop it on a carpet, it may well survive. Explain why.

Reducing the force

The passenger's momentum depends on their mass, in kilograms (kg), and on their velocity, in metres per second (m/s). These two quantities are multiplied together to calculate the momentum.

| momentum = mass × velocity |
| (kg m/s)   (kg)   (m/s) |

This is written in symbols as: $p = mv$

The momentum of a person with a mass of 70 kg, travelling at 20 m/s, is therefore:

momentum = mass × velocity = 70 kg × 20 m/s = 1400 kg m/s

Q momentum GCSE   how air bags work

After the collision, the person's final momentum will be zero, since their velocity will be zero.

change of momentum = final momentum − initial momentum
                   = 0 − 1400
                   = −1400 kg m/s.

This change of momentum is caused by a resultant force, from the seat-belt and air bag, acting for the time it takes the person to come to a halt.

change of momentum = resultant force × time for which it acts   (1)
      (kg m/s)   (N)   (s)

If the passenger hit a hard surface, they could be brought to a stop in just 0.01 s. The force acting would then be 140 000 N (since the change in momentum is 1400 kg m/s, which equals force × time = 140 000 N × 0.01 s).

The only way to reduce the size of the force is to make it act for a longer time. Air bags and seat-belts together increase the stopping time by a factor of about ten. The force is reduced by the same factor.

FIGURE 3: Cycle and motorcycle helmets extend the time of a collision, as they are deformed. This reduces the force on the head and reduces the risk of serious head injury.

QUESTIONS

3 When a gymnast lands they bend their knees. Explain why.

4 When a tennis player plays a shot, they follow-through with the action. Explain why.

Changing momentum (Higher tier only)

A resultant force is required to change an object's momentum. If the force is large, or acts for a long time, there will be a large change in momentum.

The supertanker in Figure 4 has a mass of 400 000 tonnes when fully loaded with oil. It has a top speed of 25 km/h. Putting the engines in reverse leads to a resultant force of 3.3 MN. How long will it take to stop?

We first need to calculate the change in momentum.

initial momentum = mv
                 = $(400\,000 \times 1000)$ kg $\times \left(\dfrac{25\,000}{60 \times 60}\right)$ m/s
                 = 2.78×10^9 kg m/s

final momentum = 0 kg m/s   (as the tanker has stopped)

So the change in momentum is 2.78×10^9 kg m/s

Rearranging equation 1 (see above) gives:

$$\frac{\text{change of momentum (kg m/s)}}{\text{resultant force (N)}} = \text{time for which it acts (s)}$$

$$\frac{2.78 \times 10^9}{3.3 \times 10^6} = 842\,\text{s} \text{ or } 14.0 \text{ minutes}$$

Watch out!

Always work in units of kilograms for mass, metres for length and seconds for time. In the supertanker example, 1 tonne is converted to 1000 kg and 1 km/h to 1000 metres per hour, then divided by (60×60) to convert to metres per second.

FIGURE 4: A large supertanker can be 300 m long. At top speed it has enormous momentum. It needs a large reverse force to act for a long time to change its momentum and bring it to a stop.

QUESTION

5 It is illegal to hold a baby on your knee in a car. In a car crash at 25 m/s, what force would you need to exert on the baby to stop it in 0.05 s?

Preparing for assessment: Planning and collecting

To achieve a good grade you will need to be able to apply your skills and knowledge to understand how scientists plan, run and evaluate investigations. These skills will be assessed in your exams and in Controlled Assessments. This activity supports you in developing the skills of formulating a hypothesis, planning an investigation and choosing equipment.

✳ Crumple zones save lives

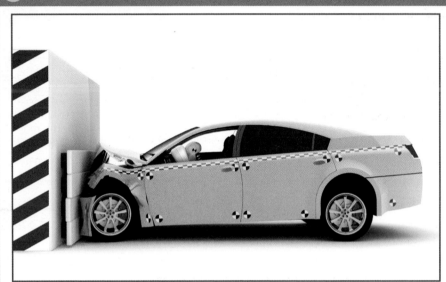

Crumple zones are designed to absorb energy by deforming the car while the passenger compartment stays intact.

How could the front of a car be designed so that, in a collision, the energy is absorbed by the car, instead of being transferred to the occupants? This is one of the challenges facing car designers. Surprisingly, they don't make the whole car as rigid as possible. The solution is to have 'crumple zones' that deform relatively easily at the front and back of the car. This absorbs the energy of impact instead of transferring it to the occupants. Design engineers test their designs to show that occupants will be protected inside a rigid 'passenger cage' while energy is transferred to the crumple zone. This is actually safer than making the whole car very rigid. However, the crumple zone has to blend in with the design of the car; a car in which the crumple zones are bigger than the passenger compartment may not sell very well.

A group of students decide to investigate crumple zones. They set up an investigation using a toy car on a track. In the top of the car is a small hole. They put a piece of dry spaghetti into the hole and a wooden bead on the spaghetti; this represents the head and neck of a person in the car. They roll the car down the track and let it hit an obstacle. When

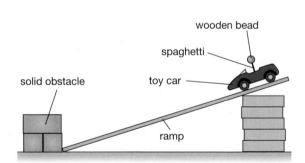

they do so, the car comes to a sudden stop and the spaghetti snaps. They then design a crumple zone to go on the front of the car and repeat the experiment to see if the spaghetti still snaps. A successful crumple zone is one that keeps the spaghetti 'neck' from breaking.

The students have a number of materials to try out, including foam rubber, expanded polystyrene, bubble wrap and corrugated cardboard. They are going to predict how big the crumple zone will need to be for each of the materials.

☀ Task 1

> Which of the material(s) do you think will work as a crumple zone and stop the spaghetti from snapping?

> Which material do you think the students could use to make the smallest effective crumple zone?

> What would the students need to be careful about when conducting the experiment?

☀ Task 2

> What do you think the students will find out as they experiment with crumple zones of different sizes and made from different materials?

> What kind of scientific terms should they use?

> What equipment might they find useful?

> What hazards would there be in their investigation?

☀ Task 2

> What variables are there in this investigation?

> Suggest a hypothesis relating to one of the variables that the students could test out.

> Suggest a procedure they might adopt that would produce useful data, including safety precautions.

☀ Task 2

> Considering the hypothesis, what quantitative prediction could they make about what the data might show?

> What equipment should they use to produce data that is precise and reliable?

> Suggest a suitable risk assessment.

☀ Maximise your grade

Use these suggestions to improve your work and be more successful.

E

To be on target for grade E you need to:

> Suggest how the students should work safely.

> Offer a testable prediction for the students and justify it, using relevant scientific terms.

> Specify equipment the students could use to collect data, identifying and commenting on hazards.

C

To be on target for grades D, C, in addition, you need to:

> Identify major factors and scientific knowledge the students should use to make a testable hypothesis about how one factor will affect the outcome.

> Suggest techniques and equipment the students should use which are appropriate for the range of data required.

> Identify any significant risks and suggest some precautions.

A

To be on target for grades B, A, in addition, you need to:

> Suggest one factor the students could investigate, propose a testable hypothesis and a quantitative prediction.

> Suggest equipment and techniques the students should use to achieve precise and reliable data.

> Produce a full and appropriate risk assessment.

Work

We are learning to:
> understand what physicists mean by 'work'
> understand the link between work and energy
> calculate how much work is done

Can the gym make us slim?

Over the last 20 years, gym membership has boomed and yet, as a nation, we are getting fatter! Research suggests several reasons for this. Some gym members do not go very regularly, and others tend to eat more because the exercise makes them hungry. More important is the fact that, on average, people use less energy in their jobs, walk less and eat more than they used to.

FIGURE 1: There is no doubt that regular exercise is good for your health, but it may not make you slim.

Work done

A work-out at the gym needs energy. Energy from your food is transferred to movement energy as you run on the treadmill, or to potential energy as you lift a weight. We can calculate how much energy is needed for a particular exercise by using the idea of **work**. Work is done when the force on an object moves its point of action. The movement has to be in the same direction as the force. We use this equation to calculate how much work is done.

| work done by a force (joules, J) | = | force (newtons, N) | × | distance moved in the direction of the force (metres, m) |

When you lift a weight, you have to exert an upward force to overcome the force of gravity on the weight. You would do one joule of work if you lifted a weight of one newton (an average apple) through a height of one metre (1 J = 1 N m).

Work is done against friction when an object, such as a car, is pushed along. In Figure 3:

work done = force × distance moved = 300 N × 10 m = 3000 J

FIGURE 2: Work is done when the weight is lifted. More work is done if the weight is larger, or if it is lifted further.

300N

10m

FIGURE 3

> **Watch out!**
> In a gym the 'weights' are often marked in kilograms. This is really their mass. To convert from mass to weight, you have to multiply by the gravitational field strength, which is 9.8 N/kg on Earth. So a mass of 10 kg is a weight of 10 kg × 9.8 N/kg = 98 N.

Q work done GCSE

QUESTIONS

1 If you are sitting down reading this, then you are exerting a force on your chair. Are you doing any work?

2 How many joules of work would you do if you lifted a book weighing 10 N through a height of 2 m?

Work and energy

Work done is measured in joules, the same unit that is used to measure energy. In fact **energy** is defined as the ability to do work. When work is done on an object, like pushing a car or lifting a weight, we transfer energy to that object.

amount of energy transferred = work done on the object
(joules, J)   (joules, J)

Sometimes it is the object that does the work, and energy is transferred from the object to something else. For example, when a car brakes it does work against friction and its movement energy is transferred by heat to the brakes and surroundings.

work done by the object   =   energy transferred from the
(joules, J)   object to another object
                                    (joules, J)

QUESTIONS

3 Suppose you do some work lifting a weight in the gym. In what form is the energy transferred to the weight?

4 Explain why a stretched elastic band is said to have energy.

How much energy?

When you do work in a gym, say lifting a weight, you are transferring energy stored in your body to the weight. How many weights do you have to lift to transfer all the energy you gained from eating a biscuit?

Suppose that you are lifting a weight of 98 N through a height of 0.5 m. Then:

work done = 98 N × 0.5 m = 49 J

The energy available from a chocolate chip cookie is about 200 kJ. So, in theory, you would have to lift the weight 200 000 ÷ 49 = 4082 times to transfer all the energy from a cookie! However, the energy from the cookie is also transferred in other ways, for example as heat.

All forms of energy have the potential to do work. The energy in a beam of light or in a lump of coal may seem very different but, using the right equipment, they could both be used to do work, such as lifting a weight. For example, the beam of light could be shone onto a solar cell, which would generate electricity. This electricity could be used to drive an electric motor, which could lift a weight.

But energy cannot be entirely transferred as work. There is always some **dissipation** of energy as heat.

QUESTIONS

5 Estimate how many steps you could climb if you were just using the energy available from a bag of crisps, about 650 kJ.

6 Explain why the real answer to question 6 is a lot less than this.

7 How could the energy in lump of coal be used to lift a weight?

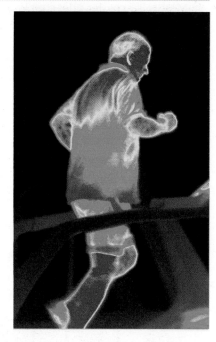

FIGURE 4: Not all of the energy from food is transferred as work – some is transferred as heat. This thermogram shows the temperature of the body as a colour code from pink (hottest), through red, yellow and green to blue (coldest).

energy transfer work done

Kinetic energy and potential energy

What is the biggest roller coaster in the world?

The world's tallest roller coaster is Kingda Ka in the USA. A hydraulic launch system accelerates the train to 128 mph in only 3.5 seconds. The train then climbs to the top of a 139 m high tower, before plunging down the other side at 120 mph.

FIGURE 1: The tallest, and second fastest, roller coaster in the world.

Potential energy

Most roller coaster rides start with a long, slow drag up a steep hill. A motor beside the track does work on the train as it pulls it up the slope. As the train is pulled higher, its energy increases.

The energy that an object gains due to its increase in height is called **gravitational potential energy**. The amount of gravitational potential energy gained depends on the weight of the object and on the height increase.

change in gravitational potential energy (joules, J)	=	weight (newtons, N)	×	vertical height difference (metres, m)

As you climb a flight of stairs you do work against the force of gravity. This work is used to raise your gravitational potential energy. If you weigh 700 N and the stairs are 4 m high, the change in gravitational potential energy is given by 700 × 4 = 2800 J.

FIGURE 2: The trains are launched along the horizontal track before climbing the vertical tower known as the 'Top-Hat'.

QUESTIONS

1 A cricket ball weighing 1.5 N is thrown 5 m into the air. What is the change in the gravitational potential energy?

2 How much work was done on the cricket ball?

potential energy GCSE

Kinetic energy

The Kingda Ka roller coaster is launched at high speed along a track before climbing to the top of the tower. The motor does work on the train to increase its speed to 209 km/h (58 m/s). This increase in speed gives the train the energy to climb the tower. This movement energy is called **kinetic energy**. The amount of kinetic energy depends on the mass of the train and on its speed. The kinetic energy is transferred to gravitational potential energy as the train climbs the tower.

When the train goes over the top of the tower, it begins to lose height. The force of gravity on the train makes it speed up and increases its kinetic energy. Some of the gravitational potential energy is transferred to kinetic energy. At the bottom of the 127 m drop, the train is travelling at 54 m/s (120 mph).

QUESTIONS

3 Sometimes the train does not have enough kinetic energy to reach the top of the tower and it rolls back, quite fast, to the start. What could cause the train to roll back?

4 After the drop from the tower, the train is not going quite as fast. Why do you think this is?

Energy transfers

As the roller coaster train travels round the track, rising and falling, its energy changes from kinetic to potential and back again. The total energy of the train at any time is the sum of its kinetic energy and its potential energy.

This transfer of kinetic energy to potential energy and back again is very important in physics. It happens to atoms vibrating in a solid and to a pendulum swinging back and forth.

Without resistive forces, the total energy (kinetic plus potential) stays the same. The roller coaster train has to do work against friction and air resistance, which results in energy being transferred to the surroundings by heat. For example, when the train is falling, the gain in kinetic energy will be less than the work done on it by the force of gravity, because some energy is dissipated through heating.

Did you know?

Comets orbit the Sun in a highly elliptical orbit. As they get closer to the Sun they lose potential energy, but they gain kinetic energy. Comets move faster when they are close to the Sun. As a comet moves further away from the Sun, kinetic energy is transferred to potential energy and the comet slows down again.

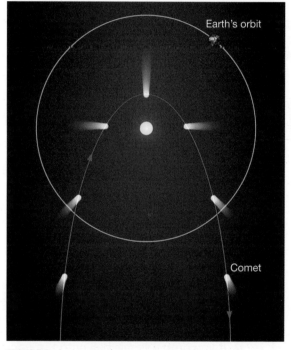

FIGURE 3: A comet orbit.

QUESTIONS

5 Look at Figure 4. When does the swing have maximum kinetic energy? When does the swing have maximum potential energy?

6 Why doesn't a swing keep going forever?

FIGURE 4: Kinetic energy transfers to potential energy as the swing rises. Gravitational potential energy transfers back to kinetic energy as it falls.

Q kinetic energy GCSE

Energy transfers

We are learning to:
> understand that energy is conserved
> calculate the kinetic energy of a moving object
> use the conservation of energy to solve problems

Could an asteroid destroy life on Earth?

Sixty-five million years ago a massive asteroid, about 10 km across, hit the Earth at a speed of 20 km/s. According to one theory, this impact led to a mass extinction. This is thought to have wiped out most of the species alive on Earth at that time, including the dinosaurs. Most scientists now agree that there is enough evidence to support this theory. The question is, could it happen again?

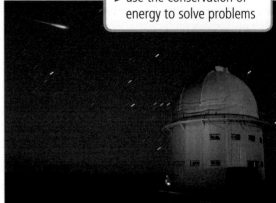

FIGURE 1: Every day about 100 tonnes of rock falls to Earth. Small rocks, known as meteors, burn up in the atmosphere.

Conservation of energy

Meteors speed up as they fall through space towards Earth. In space there are no resistive forces. A meteor gains kinetic energy as its gravitational potential energy gets less. The total energy of a meteor stays the same. This is an example of the **conservation of energy**, which applies to all processes. It means that the total energy is unchanged by any event or process.

The conservation of energy means that energy cannot be created or destroyed. Energy can be transferred between objects and can change from one form, like kinetic, to another, like gravitational potential, but throughout any process the total energy stays the same.

As the meteor reaches the Earth's atmosphere, it heats up. Some energy is transferred as work is done against air resistance. This energy causes the meteor, and the air around it, to heat up. The conservation of energy still applies. The total energy, which is the sum of the thermal energy, gained by the meteor and the air, and the kinetic energy and potential energy of the meteor, is still the same.

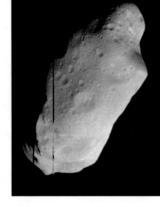

FIGURE 2: Scientists are watching out for large asteroids that might hit the Earth. Large asteroids have enormous kinetic energy because of their mass and high speeds.

QUESTION

1 Explain how the conservation of energy applies in these situations.

   a If you drop a tennis ball onto the floor, the ball loses potential energy as it falls.

   b The ball bounces several times, before coming to rest.

Calculating the kinetic energy

Kinetic energy depends on the mass of the object and its speed, or velocity. The formula for calculating the kinetic energy of a moving object is:

$$\text{kinetic energy (KE)} = \frac{1}{2} \times \text{mass} \times [\text{velocity}]^2$$
$$\text{(J)} \qquad\qquad \text{(kg)} \quad ([\text{m/s}]^2)$$

Watch out!

When you calculate the kinetic energy, make sure that you only square the velocity. You could use a calculator to work out kinetic energy, like this.
$0.5 \times$ mass $\times$ velocity $\times$ velocity =

Q conservation of energy GCSE   kinetic energy GCSE

For example, the kinetic energy of a 10000 kg lorry travelling at 20 m/s would be:

$$\text{kinetic energy } = \frac{1}{2} \times 10\,000 \times [20]^2 = 5000 \times 400$$

$$= 2\,000\,000\,\text{J} \quad \text{or} \quad 2\,\text{MJ}$$

This kinetic energy is due to work done by the driving force on the lorry.

If we ignore the work done against friction, then:

work done by an applied force = change in kinetic energy of the object

If the driving force on the lorry was 20 kN and the lorry moved through 100 m, then:

work done = force × distance moved
= 20 000 × 100 = 2 000 000 J

In reality the lorry would gain less kinetic energy than this. Some energy would be transferred by work done against friction and air resistance. This would cause the lorry, the road and the surrounding air to heat up.

FIGURE 3: The kinetic energy is large because of the lorry's mass and speed. The work done in stopping the lorry will also be large.

◉ QUESTIONS

2 A car and a bicycle are both travelling at their top speed. Explain why the car will have more kinetic energy than the bicycle.

3 Find the kinetic energy of a runner of mass 90 kg who is running at 10 m/s.

4 A bicycle is pushed forward with a force of 400 N for a distance of 10 m. How much kinetic energy will it gain?

Falling (Higher tier only)

When an object falls, its potential energy is transferred to kinetic energy. We can use this to calculate the final speed of a falling object, but we have to ignore energy transferred due to friction or air resistance. Suppose someone drops an apple off the top of a skyscraper. How fast will the apple hit the ground?

The skyscraper is 180 m tall and the apple has a mass of 100 g.

loss in gravitational potential energy = weight × height loss

The weight of the apple is its mass (in kg) multiplied by the gravitational field strength (9.8 N/kg), so:

weight of apple = 0.100 kg × 9.8 N/kg = 0.98 N

Therefore:

loss of gravitational potential energy = 0.98 N × 180 m = 176 J

This is equal to the gain in kinetic energy (ignoring air resistance). We can use this to calculate the speed:

$$176 = \frac{1}{2} \times 0.100 \times [v]^2$$

$$176 = 0.050 \times [v]^2$$

$$\frac{176}{0.050} = 3520 = [v]^2$$

So $v = \sqrt{3520} = 59$ m/s

In practice, air resistance would reduce this speed.

FIGURE 4: One Canada Square (Canary Wharf) is 235 m tall. An object dropped from near the top of this building will be travelling very fast when it reaches the ground.

◉ QUESTIONS

5 An asteroid crashing to Earth has a kinetic energy of 5×10^{14} J and a mass of 2.5×10^6 kg. How fast would it be travelling?

6 If a stone is dropped from near the top of Canary Wharf (see Figure 4), how fast will it be travelling when it hits the ground?

Did you know?

If you throw an object up fast enough, it will not come down again. It will have enough kinetic energy to escape from the Earth's gravitational pull. The 'escape velocity' for Earth is 11 km/s.

P4 Checklist

To achieve your forecast grade in the exam you'll need to revise

Use this checklist to see what you can do *now*. Refer back to pages 196–221 if you're not sure. Look across the rows to see how you could progress – *bold italic* means Higher tier only.

Remember you'll need to be able to *use* these ideas in many ways:
> interpreting pictures, diagrams and graphs
> applying ideas to new situations
> explaining ethical implications
> suggesting some benefits and risks to society
> drawing conclusions from evidence you've been given.

Look at pages 300–306 for information about how you'll be assessed.

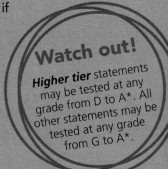

Watch out!

Higher tier statements may be tested at any grade from D to A*. All other statements may be tested at any grade from G to A*.

To aim for a grade E	To aim for a grade C	To aim for a grade A
recall that speed is the distance travelled in a certain time, and use this relationship to calculate the average speed of a journey	***explain the difference between displacement and distance travelled;*** use *and rearrange* the equation: speed = distance/time	
explain the difference between average speed and instantaneous speed for a journey during which the speed changes		
draw a distance–time graph for an object that is stationary or moving at steady speed; describe the motion of an object by looking at a distance–time graph	***calculate speed from straight sections of a distance–time graph; interpret curved sections***	
read information from a speed–time graph and identify when the object is stationary, moving at steady speed, slowing down or speeding up	explain the difference between speed and velocity; ***interpret and draw velocity–time graphs, including negative velocities, and calculate acceleration from the graph***	
recall that the acceleration of an object is the change in its speed in a certain time, and use this relationship to calculate the acceleration	use the equation: acceleration = change in velocity/time taken to calculate acceleration, using the correct units, ***and rearrange it as necessary to solve problems***	
identify the forces acting between two objects, show these on a diagram, and use the idea of equal and opposite forces to explain the motion of specific objects, such as rockets and jets		
describe how friction acts between two surfaces	explain in detail how the frictional force acts in a specific context, e.g. a car being pushed along	

To aim for a grade E	To aim for a grade C	To aim for a grade A
understand what is meant by the reaction force; apply the ideas of friction and reaction to explain the driving force on a car	*apply the ideas of friction and reaction to explain the forces on us as we walk*	
find the resultant force on an object when the forces act along the same line; identify the horizontal forces acting on a moving object; explain how the relative sizes of the forces on an object affect its motion		explain how the various forces acting on a moving object determine its acceleration and why a car has a top speed
recall what is meant by momentum and use the equation: momentum (kg m/s) = mass (kg) × velocity (m/s) in calculations, using the correct units		
describe how car safety measures, such as air-bags, reduce the force in a crash	use the equation: change of momentum = resultant force × time taken to explain car safety measures	explain how the change in momentum, force and time are related and use this to solve problems in unfamiliar contexts
recall that work is done when a force moves an object, and calculate work done using the equation: work done = force × distance moved in the direction of the force; understand that when work is done on an object energy is transferred to it, and when work is done by an object energy is transferred from it to something else, and that energy transferred = work done		
recall that a raised mass has gravitational potential energy, and calculate this for a given height change	apply *and rearrange* the equation: change in gravitational potential energy = weight × vertical height difference to solve problems	
identify the forces acting on an object thrown up in the air, and sketch a diagram showing the direction of these forces		explain how the forces acting on a falling object affect the motion of the object
recall that the energy of a moving object is called its kinetic energy, and calculate this when given relevant information	use *and rearrange* the equation: kinetic energy = ½ × mass × [velocity]² to solve problems *including finding the speed of a falling object*	
recall that energy is always conserved	describe how energy is conserved in situations such as a falling object; describe how friction and air resistance can lead to some energy being dissipated through heating	

Exam-style questions

Foundation Level

1 AO1 **a** A sandbag is dropped from a hot-air balloon. Which row in the table correctly describes how the energy of the sandbag changes?

A	Kinetic energy decreases	Gravitational potential energy decreases
B	Kinetic energy decreases	Gravitational potential energy increases
C	Kinetic energy increases	Gravitational potential energy decreases
D	Kinetic energy increases	Gravitational potential energy increases

[1]

AO2 **b** The sandbag weighs 20 N. The balloon lifted the sandbag 50 m above the ground before it was dropped. Use the equation:

work done by a force = force × distance moved in the direction of the force

to calculate how much work was done in lifting the sandbag. [2]

AO2 **c** When the sandbag hits the ground it comes to rest. Jonathan says "All the energy has been destroyed." State whether this is correct and explain your reasoning. [2]

[Total 5]

Foundation/Higher Level

AO3 **2** A car is driving along a straight, level road. The diagram below shows the forces acting on the car.

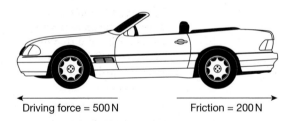

Driving force = 500 N   Friction = 200 N

Year 10 students Claire and Sarah disagree about the effect of friction on the car. Claire says friction is holding the car back. Sarah says that without friction the car wouldn't go forward at all.

a Do you agree with Claire? Explain your answer. [2]

b Do you agree with Sarah? Explain your answer. [2]

[Total 4]

AO2 **3** The diagram below shows a distance–time graph for a cyclist on a journey to work.

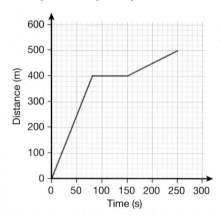

a How far does the cyclist travel altogether? [1]

b The cyclist had to stop at traffic lights. Between what times was he stationary? [1]

c When was the cyclist moving at his highest speed? [1]

d Calculate the average speed for the whole journey. [2]

[Total 5]

Higher level

AO1

4 AO2 **a** A stone of mass 5 kg is dropped down a well. The stone falls through a vertical distance of 10 m. Calculate the change in gravitational potential energy of the stone. (Take the acceleration due to gravity to be 9.8 m/s^2) [3]

AO1

AO2 **b** How fast will the stone be travelling when it reaches the bottom of the well? [3]

AO2 **c** Explain why the actual speed may be slightly smaller than your answer above. [2]

[Total 8]

AO2 **5** The foam in a cycle helmet is designed to collapse in a collision.

a Explain how the cycle helmet helps to prevent injury. [2]

b A report claims that wearing a cycle helmet reduces the risk of serious head injury by 85%.

  (i) Explain why this is not in itself scientific evidence for making helmets compulsory. [2]

  (ii) Suggest how scientists might verify such a claim. [1]

[Total 5]

AO1 recall the science   AO2 apply your knowledge   AO3 evaluate and analyse the evidence

Worked example

AO1 **a**

A glider is launched by pulling it with a cable attached to a winch. Over the first 50 m, just before the glider takes off, the cable exerts a force of 350 kN on the glider.

Physicists would say that the cable does **work** on the glider.

(i)   State what is meant by the word **work**.   [1]

Work is done when a force moves through a distance ✔

(ii) Explain the effect of the work done on the glider, over the first 50 m.   [1]

The work will increase the kinetic energy of the glider ✔

AO1
AO2 **b** How much work does the cable do on the glider over the first 50 m?   [3]

Work done = force x distance moved ✔

$$= 350 \times 50 \text{ ✘}$$

$$= 17\,500 \text{ J ✔}$$

AO1
AO2 **c** Just before take-off the glider is moving at a speed of 20 m/s. How much kinetic energy does it have? (The mass of the glider is 500 kg)   [3]

Kinetic Energy = ½ mv² ✔

$$= 0.5 \times 500 \times 20^2 \text{ ✔}$$

$$= 25,000,000 \text{ J ✘}$$

AO2 **d** In practice the work done by the cable is always greater than the kinetic energy gained by the glider. Explain why this is.   [2]

Some energy is lost due to friction. ✘

How to raise your grade

Take note of the comments from examiners – these will help you to improve your grade.

This defines the scientific term, work, precisely: 1 mark.

This accurately describes what happens using the correct physical terms, and is much better than just saying "It goes faster". 1 mark.

It is a good idea to write down the equation you are using first. The data has been correctly identified from the question, but the force is 350 kN and needed to be converted to N (1kN = 1000 N). One mark was dropped here but the other two awarded because the formula and calculation were correct.

The correct formula was given and the correct data identified, but the student has squared (0.5 x 500 x 20) instead of just the 20: 2 marks out of 3.

This gains no marks. It is incorrect to say that energy is lost. Work has been done against the forces of friction and air resistance. This will result in the heating of the air, the glider and the ground. The total energy is the same before and after the glider is launched.

P5 Electric circuits

What you should already know...

Electric circuits transfer energy

Energy is transferred from the power supply to components in a circuit and then to the environment.

Power is the rate at which energy is transferred.

We can use power = voltage × current to calculate the rate of energy transfer.

 What makes electricity so useful in modern life?

A current is a flow of charge in an electric circuit

Components in circuits can be connected in series or in parallel.

We use circuit symbols to represent electric circuits.

Current and voltage are measured using ammeters and voltmeters.

 What is the difference between the way that current flows in a series circuit and in a parallel circuit?

Electricity can be generated in large amounts and transmitted across long distances

In generators a magnet spins near a coil and electricity is generated.

Mains voltage in our homes is 230 V.

 In a power station, what is used to drive the spinning generators?

In P5 you will find out about...

> static electricity and how charges behave

> how charge can be transferred by friction

> how charge flows as a current in electric circuits

> the relationship between voltage and energy

> how current and voltage vary in series and parallel circuits

> electrical resistance and how voltage, current and resistance are interrelated

> the increasing resistance of a wire as it gets hotter

> how the resistance of LDRs varies with light level

> how the resistance of thermistors varies with temperature

> how electricity can be produced in part of a circuit that moves relative to a magnetic field

> the use of alternating current (a.c.) in the generation and distribution of electricity

> the details of how electricity is generated and how the alternating voltage can be increased or decreased

> how a current in a magnetic field produces a force

> how motors work

Static electricity

Why does cling film cling?

Cling film is not sticky but will cling to itself, to pottery and to plastic containers. It does not cling well to metals.

When you unwrap cling film from its roll, electrons are pulled away from the atoms. This leaves positive areas of cling film where the electrons have been removed and negative areas of cling film where the 'rubbed off' electrons now are. These two areas attract each other.

FIGURE 1

Attraction and repulsion

When your hair is attracted to a charged comb or charged balloons move away from each other, there must be a force acting. In both these examples the force is an **electrostatic force** caused by positive and negative charges.

In Figure 3, the girl's hair is acquiring *positive charge* from the Van de Graaf generator. Each hair has extra *positive* charge and each hair is repelling its neighbour.

When you rub two balloons together, electrons will rub off one and move *onto* the other. One balloon will be negatively charged and the other positively charged. They will be attracted and move together.

The rule for the way charges behave is:

> Like charges attract; unlike charges repel.

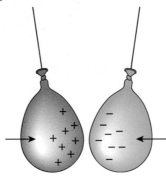

FIGURE 2: Electrostatic attraction.

FIGURE 3: Electrostatic repulsion.

Where do these charges come from?

Atoms are made up of charged particles. They have a positive nucleus with negative electrons orbiting it.

Atoms have no overall charge. We say they are **neutral**.

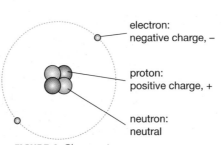

electron:
negative charge, −

proton:
positive charge, +

neutron:
neutral

FIGURE 4: Charges in an atom.

QUESTIONS

1 Does an electron carry positive or negative charge?

2 The charged particles in the nucleus of an atom are protons. Are they positively or negatively charged?

Q static electricity GCSE

Charging by friction

FIGURE 5: Charging by friction.

Each electron is held in the atom by an electrostatic force between the positive nucleus and the negative electron. The further the electron is from the nucleus, the weaker this force. Sometimes some of the outer electrons can be removed by rubbing. If you rub a balloon on your jumper, electrons will be rubbed onto the balloon, making it negatively charged.

Each of the two rubbed objects will become oppositely charged.

QUESTIONS

3 The jumper in Figure 5 will have lost electrons. Will the jumper be negatively or positively charged?

4 You will notice that after you have rubbed the balloon on your jumper, the balloon will be attracted to it. Explain this.

Static electricity every day

Have you noticed that when you take clothes from a tumble dryer they often cling together? The clothes have been rubbing together in the dryer and charge has been redistributed, leaving some clothes positively charged and some clothes negatively charged.

Sometimes there is a crackle or spark when you separate the clinging clothes. This is caused by electrons moving through the air to a positive part of the clothes.

Lightning is a very spectacular example of electrostatics. Charge is built up by friction in the clouds. When it becomes large enough to break down the insulation of the air, the charge flows between the cloud and the earth. The release of energy appears as a flash of light.

QUESTIONS

5 Explain why some clothes taken from a tumble dryer will stick together but others will not.

6 An internet article says that if you put a crumpled ball of aluminium foil into the dryer the clothes will not become charged. Suggest reasons why this may work.

FIGURE 6

Q static electricity GCSE

Moving charges

We are learning to:

> understand that in metal conductors there are lots of charges free to move but in an insulator there are few charges free to move
> recall that electric current is a flow of charge
> understand that the charges flowing in an electric circuit are not used up

Why do we cover electric wires with plastic?

Wires are covered with plastic for safety. Copper conducts electricity but plastic does not. The plastic covering prevents electricity in a wire from flowing through us or through parts of the structures of our homes. It prevents electrocution and reduces the risk of fires.

FIGURE 1

 ## Conductors and insulators

Whether a material is an insulator or a conductor depends on its structure at an atomic level. The outer electrons of atoms of materials that are good conductors of electricity – usually metals – are loosely held and can break free easily. They are then free to move in the metal. These electrons are known as **free electrons**.

Metals are electrical **conductors**. Plastic is an electrical **insulator**, as it has few charges that are free to move.

The circuit in Figure 3 can be used to test if a material is a conductor or an insulator. The crocodile clips are attached to the sample.

When the bulb is lit there is an **electric current** in the circuit. The testing circuit needs a power supply to provide the energy (the cell or 'battery'), conducting wires to provide a pathway and a bulb to indicate when the current is flowing.

The circuit could include a switch. When the switch is open, it creates a gap in the circuit that stops the current flowing. When the switch is closed, the current flows.

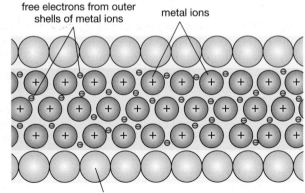

free electrons from outer shells of metal ions

metal ions

plastic layer with no free electrons

FIGURE 2: Free electrons in the metal cannot pass through the plastic layer.

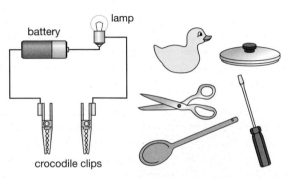

lamp

battery

crocodile clips

FIGURE 3: The bulb will light if the sample is a conductor and will not light if it is an insulator.

QUESTIONS

1 Sort the samples shown in Figure 3 into conductors and insulators.

2 How did you decide which material would conduct and which would not?

Q electrons current GCSE

What is an electric current?

Good conductors have free electrons. When a circuit is complete the power supply provides the energy, or push, which makes all the free electrons in the components and wires flow in one direction. Electrons carry a negative electric charge. This flow of charge is the **electric current**.

In an electric circuit there are free electrons everywhere, so as soon as the circuit is completed, there is a movement of electrons at all points in the circuit. As soon as a switch is closed and the circuit completed, the light goes on or the motor starts moving.

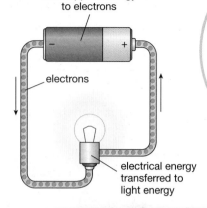

cell: supplies energy to electrons

electrons

electrical energy transferred to light energy

FIGURE 4: The moving electrons, or electric current, transfer energy to light the bulb.

Watch out!

The positively charged particles in the metal (see Figure 2) will also have a force on them, but they are massive and not free to move. It is the movement of electrons that is important in electric circuits.

Did you know?

Electrons do not move very fast or very far in a circuit. In a simple circuit to light a bulb they might be moving about 8 cm in an hour.

QUESTIONS

3 What makes it possible for a current to flow in a metal?

4 If electrons move so slowly, why does a light come on the instant the switch is turned on?

Increasing the current

How fast the electrons move depends on the amount of push they get from the power supply. As the electrons go through the power supply they gain energy. The more energy they gain, the faster they travel and the larger the current.

Current is the **rate of flow of charge**, or the charge flowing per second. Current is measured in **amperes**, or amps for short.

Charge is not used up in an electric circuit. When electrons flow through a bulb, for example, their energy is transferred to the surroundings as heat and light. They need a push from the battery to keep moving and keep transferring energy to the bulb to keep it lit. The electrons flow in a continuous loop around the circuit.

In an electric circuit *charge is conserved* and *energy is transferred*.

QUESTIONS

5 Joe and Emma have connected the circuit shown in Figure 5 for their model lift. They want the motor to move the lift up and a light to come on inside the lift. Where do the transfers of energy occur? For each transfer, state where the energy is at the start and at the end.

6 For a current of one ampere, 90 000 000 000 000 000 electrons need to flow past a point each second. A circuit has an electric current of 200 mA (or 0.2 A) through it. How many electrons are flowing through each component per second?

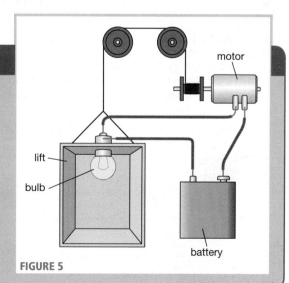

motor

lift

bulb

battery

FIGURE 5

Measuring current and voltage

How can moving electrons do work?

Batteries do work by pushing the electrons around the circuit. The electrons gain energy. In Figure 1, energy is transferred to the electric motor-driven pulley. The pulley lifts the weight – it does work on the weight.

The higher the voltage, the more energy is transferred, and the more work is done.

FIGURE 1

Using ammeters and voltmeters

An **ammeter** is connected in series with the components in the circuit so that it can measure the current *through* the circuit, in amperes (amps). The circuit symbol for an ammeter is ──(A)──.

In an electric circuit the current gains energy from the power supply (such as an electric cell) and transfers (gives out) energy when it passes through **components** such as lamps, motors and so on. The larger the voltage of the power supply (such as a battery), the larger the current and so the more energy is transferred to the components.

A **voltmeter** measures how much energy is transferred in a particular part of the circuit, for example in an electrical device such as a motor. We call this the **voltage** across the motor, and the unit we use is the **volt**. Voltmeters are connected *across* the device (in parallel). The circuit symbol for a voltmeter is ──(V)──.

Watch out!

Always use the word 'through' to describe the flow of current and 'across' to describe voltage.

FIGURE 2: There are different types of ammeters and voltmeters. The meter with the pointer is an analogue meter. The pointer can take any position on the dial according to the size of the current or voltage being measured. A digital meter gives the size of the current or voltage as a number. Digital meters are easier to read but both types can be very accurate.

QUESTION

1 In this circuit, which is the correct position for a voltmeter to measure the voltage across the lamp?

FIGURE 3

Q measuring current

Energy in a circuit

In an electric circuit the charges (free electrons) are energy carriers. There are charges throughout the circuit and these charges can accept energy from a battery and transfer energy to a component. The battery does work, giving the charges a 'push' and they gain energy, just as a swing gains energy when it is pushed. This means that charges leaving the battery have more energy than charges entering the battery on the other side.

At the bulb the reverse happens. The charges do work. They transfer their energy to heat and light, which is radiated from the circuit to the surroundings. The charges will have more energy on one side of the bulb than on the other side of the bulb. The exhausted charges are then pushed back towards the battery.

Voltmeters measure this difference in energy between the terminals of a battery or a bulb.

The number of charges flowing in the circuit always remains the same: there is nowhere else for them to go.

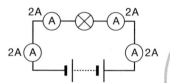

FIGURE 4: The ammeters in this circuit all give the same reading. Current is a flow of charge, and charge is conserved in a circuit.

Watch out!

A battery is one or more cells in series.

QUESTIONS

2 Draw the circuit (shown in Figure 4 on page 231) using circuit symbols.

3 If a higher voltage battery is used in the circuit, explain in terms of energy what will happen to the current in the circuit.

Potential difference

At the top of the slide the child has more potential energy than at the bottom. In much the same way, the charges on either side of a battery have a different amount of energy: electrical potential energy. This is because the battery gives the charges energy as they flow through it. This difference in energy per charge is the **potential difference (p.d.)**. This is another term for voltage. It is measured in volts.

Similarly the charges either side of a lamp in a circuit will have different amounts of electrical potential energy. There is a potential difference between the terminals of the lamp, measured in volts by a voltmeter.

The p.d. between two points in a circuit is one volt if one joule of electrical energy is transferred to another form of energy when one unit of charge passes between the points.

FIGURE 5: The child gains potential energy as she climbs to the top of the slide. As she goes down the slide, she loses potential energy and gains kinetic energy.

Did you know?

Electromotive force (e.m.f.) is another term for voltage (or p.d.) of a battery. It reinforces the idea of charge being given 'push' by the battery.

QUESTIONS

4 The voltmeter across a device reads 3 V. How many joules of energy is being transferred from each unit of charge?

5 Write the story of an electron as it goes around a circuit that has a battery and a motor. Try to use all the following words: potential difference, volts, energy, charge.

Electrical resistance

We are learning to:
> understand how resistance is used to control current
> use the equation relating resistance, current and voltage
> interpret experimental data

How do we know lightning is a giant spark?

In 1752, to prove that lightning is electricity, Benjamin Franklin flew a kite in a thunderstorm. Current passed down the string and he collected the charge in a metal can.

This is not a safe experiment and several other people who did it were killed. It should not be attempted.

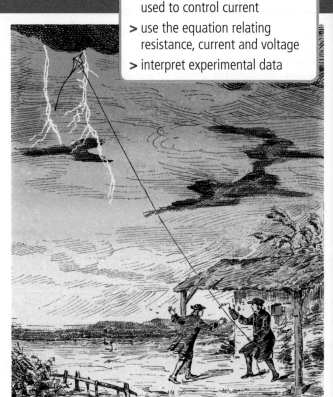

FIGURE 1

Controlling current

In electric circuits the current can be controlled by changing the number of cells in the circuit. If there are more cells, then more energy will be supplied. This means that there will be a faster flow of charge and therefore a bigger current. In other words, the larger the voltage of the power supply, the larger the current.

The current is also affected by the amount of **resistance** in the circuit. All components resist the current flowing through them. If there is more resistance in a circuit then the charges move slower and the current will be lower.

QUESTIONS

1 Use the words *increases* and *decreases* to complete the sentence:

The current _____ if you add resistance but it _____ if you add cells.

2 Describe how you could demonstrate these effects using circuits in the laboratory.

Resistance

A **variable resistor** is a device that allows you to vary the amount of resistance in a circuit by moving a slide or rotating a knob, so that more or less resistance wire is connected into the circuit.

This is its circuit symbol:

Resistance is a measure of how much a conductor opposes the current. Its unit is the **ohm** (Ω).

Good conductors, like copper, have low resistance. The resistance of copper connecting wires is so small it can be ignored.

FIGURE 2: A linear variable resistor.

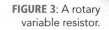

FIGURE 3: A rotary variable resistor.

There is an important relationship between current, voltage and resistance.

> When a current flows through a conductor the size of the current is affected by the voltage. The greater the voltage applied, the more current flows.

> The size of the current is also affected by the resistance of the conductor. The greater the resistance, the less current flows.

Resistance, voltage and current are related by the formula:

$$\text{resistance} = \frac{\text{voltage}}{\text{current}} \quad \text{or} \quad R = \frac{V}{I}$$

where the resistance R is in ohms, the current I is in amps and the voltage V is in volts.

Consider the two resistors in Figure 4. Each has a voltage of 6 V across them. The one with a current of 3 A through it has a resistance of $6 \div 3 = 2\,\Omega$. The other with a current of 2 A through it has a resistance of $6 \div 2 = 3\,\Omega$. The current is smaller when the resistance is larger.

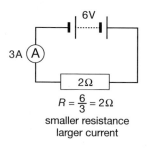

$R = \frac{6}{3} = 2\,\Omega$
smaller resistance
larger current

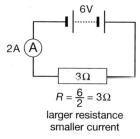

$R = \frac{6}{2} = 3\,\Omega$
larger resistance
smaller current

FIGURE 4

Watch out!

You must have current in amps and voltage in volts to get the resistance in ohms.

◯ QUESTION

3 What is the resistance of a motor when the voltage across it is 12 V and the current through it is 4 A?

Ohm's law

If you plot the graph of current against voltage for a fixed resistor it will (within the range of experimental error) give a straight line. The red line in Figure 5 is the graph for a small fixed resistance.

The straight line through the origin shows that current through the resistor is directly proportional to the voltage across it. This means that the resistance is constant. You can use the gradient of the graph to calculate the resistance:

$$\text{resistance} = \frac{1}{\text{gradient of the graph}}$$

A higher resistance gives a lower gradient (green line).

Ohm's law describes this current–voltage relationship. It states that the current through a metallic conductor is directly proportional to the voltage across its ends if the temperature and other conditions are constant.

This only applies to some components, such as resistors. For other components the value of the resistance changes as the current increases.

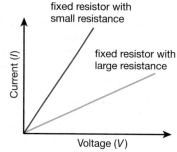

fixed resistor with small resistance

fixed resistor with large resistance

FIGURE 5: Plot of voltage against current for two fixed resistors.

◯ QUESTIONS

4 Why is it better to find resistance using a graph than by a one-off measurement of current through and voltage across the resistor?

5 Calculate the p.d. across a motor that has a resistance of $10\,\Omega$ and with a 3 A current flowing through it.

Watch out!

You can use the formula triangle to help solve these problems, but you must remember that resistance is not constant for all components as the current increases.

Series and parallel circuits

We are learning to:
> explain how current behaves in series and parallel circuits
> explain how voltage behaves in series and parallel circuits

Can you play computer games on your breakfast plate?

Computers the size of dust are being developed, which you could sprinkle on a plate while eating your breakfast. When lots of them are clustered together, they communicate with each other and may be able to create entertainment devices. So, one day, you may be able to sprinkle them on a plate and play games while eating your boiled egg.

FIGURE 1: Smart dust on a coin.

Series circuits

In the 'smart dust' there are electric circuits. Despite these being very small, they have parts where components are connected **in series** and other places where components are connected **in parallel**.

Components connected in series are in a line.

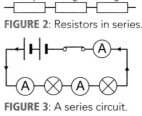
FIGURE 2: Resistors in series.

In the circuit in Figure 3, two cells and two lamps are connected in series with a switch. If the circuit is broken (perhaps by one bulb blowing), both the lamps will go out. The current is the same everywhere in a series circuit: all the ammeters read the same. Remember that current is the flow of charge through the circuit. There is only one path through the circuit, so all the charge has to follow it.

FIGURE 3: A series circuit.

In a series circuit, the supply voltage, or potential difference, is shared between the components. In Figure 4:

FIGURE 4

> battery p.d. = p.d. across lamp + p.d. across resistor

In general, for two components in a series circuit:

> supply p.d. = $V_1 + V_2$

For each component the resistance is given by $R = \dfrac{V}{I}$, which can be rearranged as: $\boxed{V = IR}$

Since the current I is the same through all the components, if the resistance of the lamp is twice the resistance of the resistor, then the p.d. across the lamp will be twice the p.d. across the resistor.

If the resistance in the whole circuit is increased, the current will be smaller. Resistances in series (Figure 2) add up.

> $R_{total} = R_1 + R_2 + R_3$

The resistance in the whole circuit increases because the battery has to move charge through more resistors and so the extra work will mean that the charges will flow slower.

If another identical battery is added to the circuit in Figure 4, the overall voltage of the battery will double and this will increase the rate of flow of charge round the circuit. The current will also double.

Watch out!

We can use the relationship $V = IR$ to calculate individual currents, voltage and resistances in any circuit.

QUESTIONS

1 a Calculate the total resistance R_{total} in circuit A.

b Using $I = V \div R_{total}$ calculate the current supplied to the circuit by the battery in circuit A and in circuit B.

c Explain why the current is different in each circuit.

2 a Using $V = IR$, calculate the voltage across each resistor in circuit A.

b Add up the voltages of the resistors in circuit A.

c Explain what you found in part **b**.

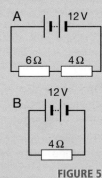
FIGURE 5

Q Crocodile Clips   electric circuits GCSE

Parallel circuits

Components connected in parallel are each connected separately to the power supply.

In a parallel circuit such as the simple one in Figure 7, the current from the battery is shared between each branch. The charge travelling through the circuit it has a choice of pathways. The current to and from the battery is the sum of the current through the branches.

$$I_{total} = I_1 + I_2 + I_3$$

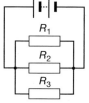

FIGURE 6: Resistors in parallel.

The total current from the battery is greater than if any of these resistors were alone in the circuit. This is because the parallel circuit provides more pathways for the charges to move in and so overall increases the rate of flow of charge to and from the battery. Seen from the battery, connecting more resistors in parallel decreases the overall resistance in the circuit.

In Figure 7 you can see that the 4 Ω resistor has half as much current flowing though it than the 2 Ω resistor. The current is *inversely proportional* to the resistance and so the current is largest through the component with the smallest resistance.

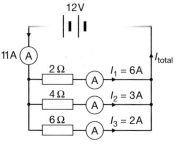

FIGURE 7: A parallel circuit.

> ### Watch out!
> Although we know that electrons move towards the positive (+) terminal of a battery, conventional current flow is towards the negative(–) terminal of a battery.

> ### Did you know?
> Engineers use resistors in parallel to make components with very small resistances, for example in an ammeter.

● QUESTIONS

3 Redraw the parallel circuit in Figure 7 without the 6 Ω resistor. Calculate the current through each of the remaining resistors and the current from the battery.

4 a Explain why connecting three lamps in parallel across a battery, rather than in series, will result in brighter bulbs, but the battery will run down faster.

b What will happen if one of the lamps blows?

Understanding more about circuits (Higher tier only)

Branches in parallel circuits behave like individual circuits: each branch gets the full p.d. provided by the battery. The current through each branch is the same as if each branch was a series circuit connected separately to the battery. For example in Figure 7 the 4 Ω and the 2 Ω resistors have the same battery p.d. across them. We can apply $I = V \div R$ to each branch, and see why the current through the 2 Ω resistor is twice the current through the 4 Ω resistor.

Circuits and energy

In an electric circuit work is done transferring energy to and from the charges in the circuit. In a series circuit such as that in Figure 4, work is done by the battery to provide energy to the charge flowing in the circuit. The lamp then uses some of this energy to do work to provide heat and light, and work is done in the resistor and heat is produced. The amount of work done providing energy to the charge by the battery is equal to the energy transferred out of the circuit by the components. In general in a series circuit, this results in the expression:

supply p.d. = $V_1 + V_2 + V_3 + \dots$

More work is done moving charge through a large resistance than a small resistance. This leads to the largest p.d. being across the largest resistance in a series circuit.

> ### Watch out!
> Remember that p.d. is a measure of how much energy is transferred per unit charge.

● QUESTIONS

5 Cells can be connected in parallel (Figure 8). The p.d. across each cell will be the same, but now there are two cells providing energy for the circuit. Explain how will this affect:

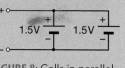

FIGURE 8: Cells in parallel.

a the current in the circuit

b the time before the battery runs down.

Useful components

We are learning to:
> explain how components such as the thermistor and the light dependent resistor can affect an electric circuit
> describe what happens to the resistance of a metal when it gets hot
> identify the effect of different factors on the resistance of a component

How do we protect sensitive electronics in spacecraft?

Space travel involves extremes of temperature that many devices cannot cope with. A thermistor, however, is an electrical component made of materials that can cope with a large range of temperatures. Thermistors can monitor temperatures and control cooling systems.

FIGURE 1: The Messenger probe entered orbit around Mercury in March 2011. It needs to withstand very high temperatures since Mercury is close to the Sun.

The thermistor and the LDR

The **thermistor** is a semiconductor device. Its resistance changes with temperature.

In the most common thermistors the resistance decreases as the temperature increases. Thermistors are used as temperature sensors, for example in digital thermometers. They can be used with a thermostat to control temperature, for example to switch on a heater when the temperature of an incubator falls below a certain value.

The **light dependent resistor (or LDR)** is another semiconductor device. Its resistance varies with the amount of light falling on it. In bright light its resistance is low but in darkness it has a high resistance. An LDR can be used to switch on street lighting when night falls.

Watch out!
Sometimes an LDR symbol is shown with a circle around the resistor symbol.

FIGURE 2: A thermistor and its circuit symbol.

FIGURE 4: An LDR and its circuit symbol.

FIGURE 3: An egg incubator is controlled by a thermistor circuit.

FIGURE 5: Can you see where the LDR is attached to this street light? Do you think that is a good position?

Did you know?

Pure semiconductors are insulators at room temperature but can conduct an electric current if their temperature increases. Electrons absorb the extra energy and become free to move and to conduct an electric current.

QUESTIONS

1 Suggest a use for an LDR to make something happen when it gets light.

2 You want to invent a device that will open the greenhouse windows when it gets too hot inside. What components would you need in the circuit?

thermistor GCSE   LDR GCSE

How does the resistance vary?

The temperature of a thermistor thermometer can be calibrated with temperature by heating it in a beaker of water and noting the temperature at regular temperature intervals. A graph of resistance against temperature it will look like this.

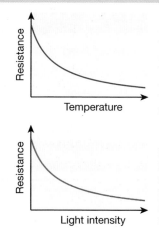

FIGURE 6: At low temperatures, the resistance of a thermistor is high and at high temperatures, the resistance is low.

The resistance of an LDR is highest in the dark. The resistance falls as the surroundings get brighter. A graph of resistance with light level will look like this.

FIGURE 7: At low light intensities, the resistance of an LDR is high, and at high light intensities its resistance is low.

QUESTIONS

3 Explain what will happen to the current in a thermistor as it gets hotter.

4 Explain what will happen to the current in an LDR circuit as night falls.

Explaining varying resistance

A conventional light bulb filament gets very hot when a current flows through it. The filament is a thin metal wire. Is its resistance affected by temperature?

When the current I through a lamp is measured with increasing potential difference V across it, a graph of I against V look like this.

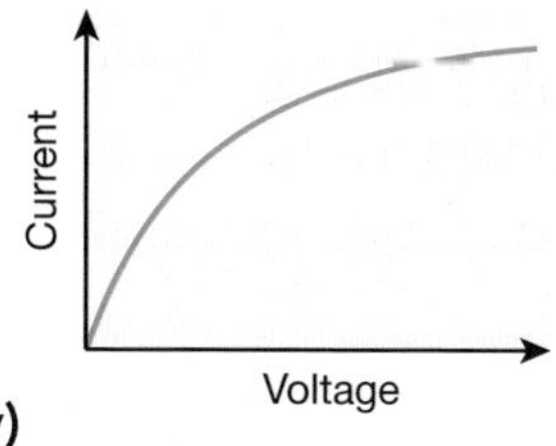

FIGURE 8: The varying gradient of the graph shows that the resistance (V/I) is varying. Is the resistance increasing or decreasing as the current increases?

What is happening in the filament (Higher tier only)

All metals behave like the light bulb filament when they get hot. As the metal gets hot its resistance increases. This is because the positive ions in the metal structure have more energy and jiggle about more. The free electrons collide more often with them and so their overall speed is slower. There is a smaller rate of flow of charge (carried by the negative electrons) through the metal.

This is opposite to the thermistor and LDR, where the extra heat or light energy provides more free electrons. In these semiconductor devices there is a greater rate of flow of charge because there is more charge available. Their resistance decreases.

A varying resistance in a series circuit (Higher tier only)

The basis of a device that would open your curtains without you getting out of bed might be an LDR in series with a motor, as in Figure 9.

When it gets light the resistance of the LDR will decrease. This will reduce the p.d. across it. Since the total p.d. across the components ($V_1 + V_2$) must equal the p.d. of the supply, this will increase the p.d. across the motor. The overall resistance in the circuit will fall and the current will increase. This may be sufficient to get the motor to work and open the curtains.

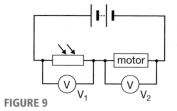

FIGURE 9

QUESTIONS

5 Have you noticed if that light bulbs 'blow' it is often when you first switch them on? When they 'blow' the filament has melted. Why might this be?

6 Look at the circuit in Figure 10.

a If the variable resistor is kept at a constant value, what will happen to the current in the circuit as the temperature increases?

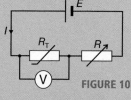

FIGURE 10

b What will happen to the p.d. across the thermistor as the temperature increases?

c How could you alter the value of the variable resistor to bring the current back to the original value?

Preparing for assessment: Analysing, evaluating and reviewing

To achieve a good grade you will need to be able to use your skills and knowledge to understand how scientists plan, run and evaluate investigations. These skills will be assessed in your exams and in Controlled Assessments. This activity supports you in developing the skills of analysing data.

✳ Some like it hot – investigating the resistance of a filament bulb

When a voltage is applied to a light bulb, current flows through it and it glows. Increasing the voltage will make more current flow and the bulb glow brighter. The bulb has a resistance, which can be calculated by dividing voltage by current for any pair of values. What happens to the resistance as the voltage is increased?

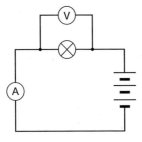

Josh and Donna have been gathering data to try and answer this question. They set up a circuit with a variable power supply, bulb, ammeter and voltmeter. Their results table is below.

Voltage (V)	0	1	2	3	4	5	6	7	8	9	10
1st current reading (A)	0	0.14	0.22	0.25	0.31	0.35	0.38	0.44	0.45	0.48	0.54
2nd current reading (A)	0	0.13	0.20	0.25	0.30	0.36	0.39	0.40	0.44	0.46	0.51
3rd current reading (A)	0	0.19	0.21	0.28	0.28	0.36	0.38	0.39	0.45	0.47	0.48

Task 1

> How did Josh and Donna get the data to complete the table?

> They took three readings of the current for each voltage. Explain how these readings should be processed.

> Explain whether or not you think any of the readings are outliers.

Task 2

> Construct a graph of voltage against resistance using appropriate axes and scales.

> Draw in a line of best fit.

Task 3

> Look at the trend in the figures you calculated for the average current flow.

> What does this say about the accuracy and the repeatability of the data?

Task 4

> Comment on the spread of the readings, accounting for any outliers.

> What does this say about the repeatability of the data?

Maximise your grade

Use these suggestions to improve your work and be more successful.

E

To be on target for grade E you need to:

> Explain how the students collected the data.

> Display the data appropriately.

> Comment on the general accuracy or repeatability.

> Correctly identify outliers or justify a claim that there are no outliers.

C

To be on target for grades D, C, in addition, you need to:

> Correctly select scales and axes and plot data for a graph, including an appropriate line of best fit.

> Use the general pattern of results or degree of scatter between repeats as a basis for assessing accuracy and repeatability.

A

To be on target for grades B, A, in addition, you need to:

> Indicate the spread of data.

> Consider critically the repeatability of the evidence, accounting for any outliers.

Producing electricity

We are learning:

> how a voltage can be induced from relative movement between a magnet and a wire

> how to maximise an induced voltage

> how an outcome might alter when a factor in electromagnetic induction is changed

How do pigeons find their way home?

Scientists have done experiments that seem to indicate that some migratory birds navigate using the Earth's magnetic field. One idea is that they see the magnetic field as a faint colour gradient, which tells them its strength and direction.

FIGURE 1

Looking at effects of magnetic fields

A **field** is a space in which a particular force acts. If you put a magnetic material in the space around a magnet it will experience a force. We use the idea of field lines to help visualise this **magnetic field**.

Magnetic field lines may be imaginary, but they are a useful model. Remember that they go from the north pole to the south pole and they never cross. Where they are closer together, the magnetic field strength is greater.

Magnets may be 'permanent' magnets or **electromagnets**. An electromagnet only acts as a magnet while a current is flowing, so is called a 'temporary' magnet. Electromagnets can be very strong.

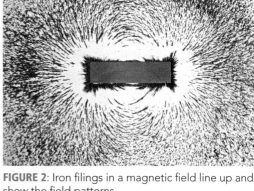

FIGURE 2: Iron filings in a magnetic field line up and show the field patterns.

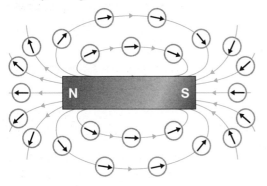

FIGURE 3: The needles of plotting compasses line up along the magnetic field lines, pointing towards the south pole.

Making an electric current

In the 1830s Michael Faraday discovered that if he moved a magnet near to a piece of wire then a voltage was **induced** between the ends of the wire. If the ends of the wire were joined to complete the circuit a current flowed. The wire can be moved instead – by moving the wire up and down between the poles of a very strong magnet a current will register on a sensitive meter.

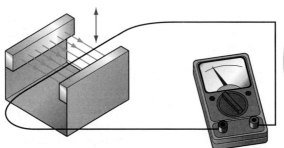

FIGURE 4: Moving the wire up induces a current; moving it down induces a current in the other direction.

Watch out!

Micro or μ means a millionth part of something. One microamp, or 1 μA, is a millionth of an amp – a very small current.

Q electromagnetic induction GCSE

FIGURE 5: Michael Faraday, English physicist (1791–1867).

QUESTIONS

1 a Where is the field strongest for a bar magnet?

 b The magnetic field between the poles of the magnet in Figure 4 is uniform (the same at all points). How is it shown in the diagram?

2 What do we mean by an induced current?

Induced voltage and current

Faraday found that:

> the direction of the current changed if the motion of the wire was reversed

> if the wire was kept still, then no current flowed at all.

Faraday also used coils of wire instead of a single wire. He found that the more turns of wire he used, the bigger the induced voltage and therefore the bigger the current on the ammeter. Using a stronger magnet induced a bigger current too.

Enough current can be induced to light a small bulb by moving a bar magnet in and out of a coil of a few hundred turns. The magnet needs to be moved rapidly. The slower it goes, the smaller the current produced.

When the magnet is pulled out of the coil the current flows in the opposite direction to when the magnet is pushed in. If the magnet is reversed, so is the current flow.

A voltage is induced whenever there is *relative* movement between the magnet and the coil. Either the magnet or the coil could move, or both. The coil could spin in the magnetic field, or the magnet could spin in front of one end of the coil. Faster relative motion induces a bigger current and having an iron core in the coil also makes the current bigger.

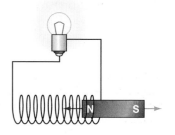

FIGURE 6: Lighting a bulb with an induced current.

QUESTIONS

3 What determines the direction of the induced voltage?

4 Make a list of the factors that increase the size of the induced voltage.

Electromagnetic induction

Faraday introduced the idea of visualising a magnetic field using magnetic field lines. He used it to explain the induced voltage, which he called **electromagnetic induction**. Field lines need to 'cut' through the electrical conductor to induce a voltage, and the greater the rate at which the field lines cut, the bigger the voltage induced.

Imagine the field lines around a bar magnet. They will 'cut' through the turns of the coil if the magnet (or the coil) is moving and will cut faster if the movement is faster or if there are more turns to cut through.

QUESTIONS

5 Explain, using Faraday's idea of 'cutting' magnetic field lines, why no current is induced if there is no relative motion of the conductor and magnet.

6 Looking at Figure 4, explain what would happen if the wire were moved across, horizontally, parallel to the magnetic field lines.

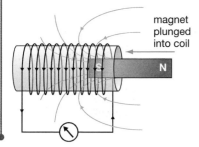

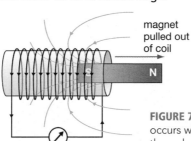

FIGURE 7: Electromagnetic induction occurs when magnetic field lines cut through an electrical conductor.

Faraday and electromagnetic induction

Generating mains electricity

When did houses first have electric lights?

The first house in UK was fitted with carbon filament lights in 1880. These electric light bulbs were the first kind of practical, safe light bulbs, invented by Thomas Edison just a year before. But the house had to run its own generator. The first council-owned power station was opened in Bradford in 1889. The National Grid supply network was not developed until the 1930s.

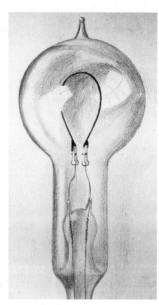

FIGURE 1: Thomas Edison's carbon-filament light bulb.

Did you know?

In the 1880s it cost about 20 times the average weekly wage to have your house converted from gas lighting to electric lighting.

Generators

A bicycle dynamo acts like a mini electrical generator. The bicycle wheel spins the wheel on the dynamo, which in turn makes a magnet spin inside a coil in the dynamo. The induced voltage powers the bike's lights.

We have previously (page 000[P5.07]) seen how an electric pulse can be induced by relative movement between a magnetic field and a metal wire. A continuous supply of electricity can be induced by relative rotation of a magnet and a coil. In a model generator such as that in Figure 4, a coil rotates continuously in a magnetic field.

The poles of the magnets are on their large flat sides. The north and south poles are positioned so that they face each other. There is a magnetic field between the poles of the magnets. Imagine straight parallel field lines between the magnets. When the coil is made to rotate, the magnetic field lines 'cut through' wire. A voltage is induced across the ends of the coil. This is called **electromagnetic induction**.

FIGURE 2: This dynamo powers the bike's lights.

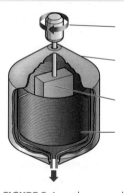

FIGURE 3: In a dynamo, the spinning magnet causes a voltage to be induced.

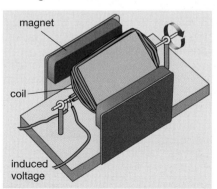

FIGURE 4: A model generator.

⬤ QUESTIONS

1 Make a sketch of the magnetic field lines between the faces of the magnets in Figure 4. Label north (N) and south (S) poles.

2 Explain (using the idea of the magnetic field lines and moving a conductor) why a voltage is generated when the coil is spun.

🔍 a.c. generator GCSE

The size of the induced voltage

A model generator like that in Figure 4 can be used to investigate the size of the voltage and current produced. Some results are shown in the table.

These results show that the size of the current produced depends on the rate at which the coil rotates, that is the rate at which the magnetic field lines are cut. It also depends on the number of turns of the coil, the strength of the magnet and whether there is an iron core in the coil.

Factors altered	Current induced (mA)
First attempt rotating with fingers	1.5
Use cotton for faster rotation	2.0
Increasing the number of turns	2.5
Adding more magnets to original	2.25
Winding the coil on an iron core	2.75

But current depends on the induced voltage. So, this experiment also tells us that the size of the induced voltage can be increased by:

> increasing the strength of the magnet

> increasing the number of turns in the coil

> increasing the rate at which the coil is turned

> placing an iron core inside the coil.

QUESTIONS

3 An electromagnet is a magnet whose strength depends on an electric current. Why do commercial power stations use electromagnets?

4 Suggest why winding the coil on an iron block will affect the voltage induced.

Alternating current

The model generator produces an **alternating current (a.c.)**. The direction of an alternating current changes at regular intervals. Our mains electricity in UK is a.c., generated at 230 V and a frequency of 50 Hz, which means the direction of the current changes 50 times a second. This is the frequency of rotation of the coils in the power station.

Why does the generator induce an alternating current? (Higher tier only)

The size of the voltage induced in a generator depends on the rate at which the coil in the generator cuts through the magnetic field lines.

In the model generator in Figure 4, the magnetic field is the same strength at all points between the poles. This is called a **uniform** field and is shown on the diagram by parallel, evenly spaced lines.

Look at Figure 5a, which shows the short edge of the coil, end-on, in the magnetic field. Consider the red end of the coil. The magnetic field is uniform but red end of the coil is cutting through different numbers of lines in each position. In positions A, C and E it is cutting no lines, so no p.d. is induced. In positions B and D it is cutting through the maximum number of lines, so a maximum p.d. is induced. Its direction in D is reversed, so a negative p.d. is induced, as shown in Figure 5b.

This varying p.d. will result in an alternating current when the circuit is completed. The frequency of the alternating current will be the same as the frequency of the rotating coil that induced it.

> **Watch out!**
> The free electrons that make up an alternating current vibrate backwards and forwards 50 times a second.

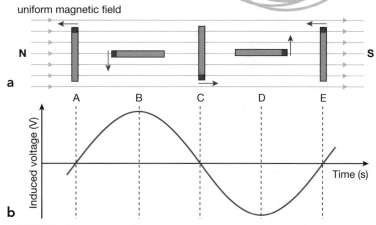

FIGURE 5: Generation of a.c.

QUESTIONS

5 In The USA the mains electricity is 120 V and 60 Hz. What is the frequency of rotation of the generators in US power stations? Why will a British hairdryer take longer to dry someone's hair if they use it in USA?

6 Draw an energy transfer diagram to show the energy transfer in a generator.

Motors

We are learning to:
> identify how widely used motors are
> describe the motor effect
> explain how motors work

Is there a bike that makes going uphill easier?

It is easier to go uphill on an electric bike. These bikes have an electric motor that can switch in when the going gets hard. The motor might make a roller rotate directly on the tyre, or drive the chain, or work directly on the hub. The downside is that, because the motor needs a battery, the bike will be heavier.

FIGURE 1

The magnetic effect of a current

Think of all the electric appliances in the home that make something move. In all these there is a **motor**, which has an axle that is attached to the part that needs to move. In a hairdryer it is attached to the fan, in a DVD player it rotates the disc drive, and in a food mixer it is attached to the blades in the bowl. Motors convert electrical energy to kinetic energy.

To understand how a motor works, we need to start with the magnetic effect of a current. When an electric current flows through a wire, it produces a circular magnetic field around the wire. If the wire is made into a coil, the magnetic field pattern becomes similar to the field around a bar magnet. We know there is a magnetic field because, near the wire or coil, a force is exerted on a magnet, or on another current-carrying wire or coil.

QUESTION

1 Why can a current-carrying wire or coil exert a force on a magnet, or on another current-carrying wire or coil nearby?

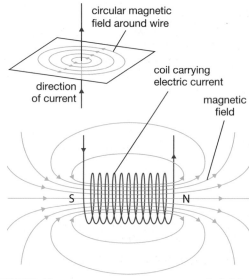

FIGURE 2: Electric currents generate magnetic fields.

The motor effect

When a current flows through a wire in a region where there is *another* magnetic field, the wire experiences a force. If it is free to move, it moves. This is called the **motor effect**.

The biggest force is felt when the magnetic field and the current are perpendicular (at 90°) to each other. No force is felt if the current-carrying wire is along a magnetic field line.

The force is bigger if the current is larger or if the magnetic field is stronger.

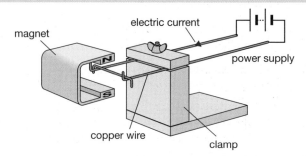

FIGURE 3: The motor effect causes the short piece of copper wire to move towards the clamp.

Q motor effect animation   motors GCSE

The force on the current-carrying wire in a magnetic field is at right angles to both the magnetic field and to the current in the wire. If either are reversed, the direction of the force – and hence the movement – is reversed.

A motor uses the motor effect but is assembled so that the force gives continuous rotation. It is like a generator (page 244) but is used in reverse. The coil is connected to a power supply and a force is produced that makes the coil turn. This can be understood by considering a rectangular coil (Figure 4). Each side of the coil in the field experiences a force: on one side the force is upwards and the other side it acts downwards. This makes the coil turn.

The motor will turn faster if:

> the current is bigger

> there are more turns on the coil

> the magnets are stronger

> there is a soft iron core in the coil.

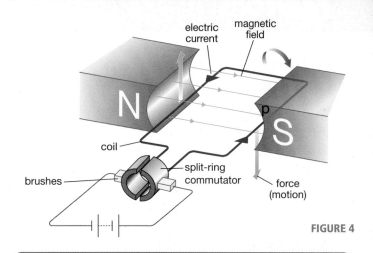

FIGURE 4

Did you know?

All charges experience a force when in a magnetic field. This is how protons are made to travel in a circle in the Large Hadron Collider.

QUESTIONS

2 The copper wire in Figure 3 is thick. Will it be carrying a large or small current? What effect will that have on the force?

3 a Will the coil in Figure 4 turn clockwise or anticlockwise?

   b The current in the coil is reversed. What happens?

4 Why do opposite poles need to be facing each other across the motor? Will the motor work if they are not?

Explaining how the motor works

The motor effect works because the magnetic field around the current-carrying wires and the magnetic field of the permanent magnet combine.

The fields reinforce each other above the wire and cancel each other out below the wire. The right-hand diagram shows the combined effect and the resultant force on the wire. This happens to each long side of the coil in the motor.

Why does the motor keep turning? In Figure 4 the left-hand side of the coil experiences an upwards force and the right-hand side experiences a downward force. When the sides reach the top and bottom (that is, when the plane of the coil is vertical) the fixed **commutator** (a metal ring split into two halves) swaps contacts with the coil to reverse the current through the coil. This happens each half cycle and ensures that the turning effect is always in the same direction and the coil rotates continuously.

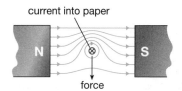

FIGURE 5: Combining magnetic fields.

QUESTIONS

5 What would happen to a model motor if a commutator was not used?

6 Figure 6 shows two current-carrying coils close to one another. Explain, by thinking about their magnetic fields, whether the coils will attract or repel each other.

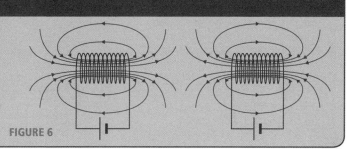

FIGURE 6

Q motor effect animation   motors GCSE

Transformers

We are learning to:
> describe what a transformer does
> explain how a transformer works by electromagnetic induction
> identify practical uses of electromagnetic induction

Why doesn't my laptop blow up?

My laptop needs 19.5 V but when I charge it up I plug it into the 230 V mains. Why doesn't it blow up?

The black box on the mains lead of the laptop is a transformer. This is device that changes one voltage to another. The laptop transformer changes 230 V to 19.5 V so that it is safe for the laptop to use.

FIGURE 1

What's inside a transformer?

The diagram shows the transformer in the mains adapter for an appliance such as an electric screwdriver. It will convert mains voltage (230 V) to 3 V. It is made up of two separate copper wire coils with iron core inside and surrounding the coils. The mains a.c. current is fed into the **primary coil** on the left. The smaller voltage is induced in the **secondary coil** on the right, and this is connected to the appliance.

QUESTIONS

1 Notice the difference in width of the wires in the two coils in Figure 2. Which coil will be carrying the larger current?

2 Why are transformers quite heavy?

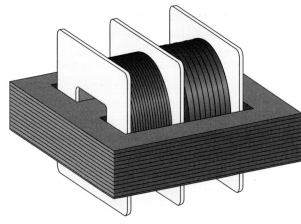

FIGURE 2: Inside a transformer.

Stepping up and stepping down

In the circuit shown in Figure 3, ten turns of wire are wound on a soft iron core and connected to an a.c. power supply. This is the primary coil. The secondary coil has 25 turns and is connected to a small bulb. The two coils have been clipped together so that the soft iron makes a complete loop. Another small bulb has been connected across the primary supply.

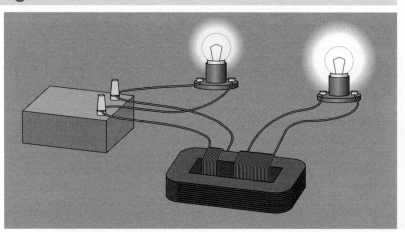

FIGURE 3

Q transformer GCSE

When the alternating voltage is applied, both bulbs light. The brighter secondary bulb indicates that the secondary voltage is greater than the primary voltage. This is a **step up** transformer.

If the coils are reversed so that the one with the larger number of turns is the primary coil and the 10 turn coil as the secondary the transformer will decrease the voltage and the secondary bulb will be dimmer. This is a **step down** transformer.

Watch out!

Transformers get very hot because they are transferring a large amount of electrical energy to thermal energy.

QUESTIONS

3 What is the purpose of the soft iron core in a transformer?

4 Is the screwdriver transformer in Figure 2 a step up or a step down transformer?

How a transformer works

The coils of a transformer are not connected, so how can a current in one coil induce another current in a nearby coil?

The a.c. voltage in the primary coil creates an ever-changing magnetic field around it (see page 246). The magnetic soft iron core channels the field through the secondary coil. This repeatedly changing magnetic field cuts through the secondary turns and an a.c. voltage is produced across the ends of the secondary coil.

The size of the output voltage (Higher tier only)

A changing current in one coil of the transformer will cause a changing magnetic field in the iron core. This in turn induces a changing p.d. across the other transformer coil.

If the number of turns in the secondary coil is doubled, then the output voltage will be doubled. If the number of turns in the secondary coil is halved, then the output voltage will be halved. The turns ratio is equal to the voltage ratio:

$$\frac{\text{voltage across primary coil}}{\text{voltage across secondary coil}} = \frac{\text{number of turns in primary coil}}{\text{number of turns in secondary coil}} \quad \text{or} \quad \frac{V_p}{V_s} = \frac{N_p}{N_s}$$

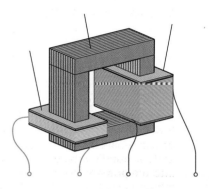

FIGURE 4: A step up transformer.

QUESTIONS

5 If the screwdriver transformer is stepping down 230 V to 3 V and has 20 turns on the secondary coil, how many should there be on the primary coil?

6 The transformer for a laptop needs to step down 230 V to 19.5 V. If the primary coil has 300 turns, how many turns will the secondary coil need?

7 An electric toothbrush is charged using a transformer with one coil in the charger and one in the base of the toothbrush.

  a Which is the primary coil?

  b Transformers only work with a.c. Where does this a.c. come from?

  c Explain how the current is induced in the toothbrush coil.

FIGURE 5

Did you know?

Spot welding uses a step down transformer with a turns ratio of about 120 : 1. This gives a huge current and lots of heat for the weld.

Watch out!

Transformers only work with alternating voltages and currents.

Distributing mains electricity

Could I power my house with a big battery?

A house could run on battery power, and then there would be no ugly power lines going across the country. But the battery would have to be replaced frequently when it ran out. Using a battery, it would not be possible to transform voltages to all the different voltages that our appliances use, as batteries only produce direct current.

We are learning to:

> understand the difference between alternating and direct current

> understand why our mains supply is alternating

> apply the formula
electrical power = current × voltage

Alternating current

In some circuits the current flows in one direction all the time. This is called **direct current**, or d.c. Torches use d.c. and so does the electrical system in a car. In other circuits the current keeps changing direction. This is called **alternating current**, or a.c. Mains appliances, such as TVs and hair dryers, run on a.c.

The mains electricity in UK has a frequency of 50 hertz. This means it changes direction 50 times a second.

QUESTIONS

1 What is the difference between alternating and direct current?

2 What devices produce:

a alternating electricity? b direct electricity?

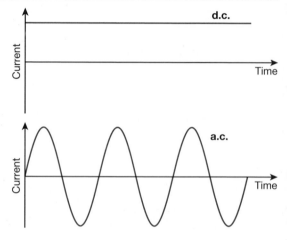

FIGURE 1: Direct and alternating current.

At the power station

There are good reasons for using alternating electricity as our electricity supply. Generators like the one in Figure 2 generate alternating electricity. They produce far more power than other forms of electricity production. Solar panels large enough to generate an equivalent amount of power would take huge amounts of land (and sunshine). An equivalent battery would be huge, expensive and impractical. Another advantage of generators is that many different fuels can be used to turn the large turbines.

Watch out!
Power station generators are sometimes called alternators.

FIGURE 2: The turbine hall of Drax power station in Yorkshire. The generator is the large purple object in the centre of the picture.

Q generating electricity GCSE

Transmitting the electricity

Another important reason for using alternating electricity as our mains supply is that, both at the power station and at the consumer end, transformers are used to achieve the required voltage. Transformers only work with alternating electricity.

At the power station transformers are used to step up to the high voltage used for transmission. Pylons and aluminium cables are used to transmit the electricity across the country. There is less energy lost at high voltages, making the transmission of electricity across the country more efficient.

Outside a town you may see substations like the one in Figure 4. Here transformers change the high transmission voltage to low domestic voltage. By using several transformers different voltages can be delivered to various consumers. Factories can have 30 kV delivered while 230 V is delivered to homes. Some appliances, such as computers, use d.c. The a.c. can be converted to d.c.

FIGURE 3: Pylons carry electricity from the power station to industry, towns and houses.

FIGURE 4: An electricity substation changes high voltage electricity to a low voltage domestic supply.

QUESTIONS

3 What is the advantage of alternating electricity at the power station?

4 What is the advantage of alternating electricity when transmitting electricity across the country?

Electrical power

Power is the rate at which energy is transferred. The formula for **electrical power** is:

power = voltage × current

Power is measured in watts, current in amps and voltage in volts.

A power station of power 1 MW generates a.c. at 25 000 volts. Using this information, we can calculate the current:

$$I = \frac{P}{V} = \frac{1\,000\,000}{25\,000} = 40\,A$$

If a step up transformer steps the voltage to 400 kV, the current will now be:

$$I = \frac{P}{V} = \frac{1\,000\,000}{400\,000} = 2.5\,A$$

The current is much lower at the higher voltage. Much less energy will be lost through heating the cables with this lower current, so the transmission will be more efficient.

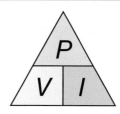

FIGURE 5: The formula triangle can be used to help rearrange the equation.

QUESTION

5 Mains domestic voltage is 230 V.

a A kettle has a power rating of 3 kW. How much current flows in it?

b A light bulb is rated at 3 V, 10 W. How much current flows in it?

P5 Checklist

To achieve your forecast grade in the exam you'll need to revise

Use this checklist to see what you can do now. Refer back to pages 228–251 if you're not sure. Look across the rows to see how you could progress – **bold italic** means Higher tier only.

Remember you'll need to be able to use these ideas in many ways:
> interpreting pictures, diagrams and graphs
> applying ideas to new situations
> explaining ethical implications
> suggesting some benefits and risks to society
> drawing conclusions from evidence you've been given.

Look at pages 300–306 for information about how you'll be assessed.

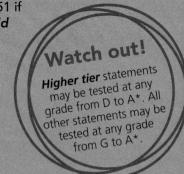

Watch out!

Higher tier statements may be tested at any grade from D to A*. All other statements may be tested at any grade from G to A*.

To aim for a grade E	To aim for a grade C	To aim for a grade A
describe effects of electrostatic charge	explain charging by friction in terms of electron transfer	use the idea of attractive and repulsive forces to explain electrostatic phenomena
explain the properties of electrical conductors and insulators; explain that in an electric circuit the power supply does work and transfers energy to the charges	explain that the more energy provided by the power supply, the faster the charge will flow and the larger the current	
explain that voltage, also referred to as potential difference (p.d.) supplied by a power supply is a measure of the 'push' or work done in making a current flow in a circuit, and a larger voltage produces a large current	understand that the potential difference (p.d.) between two points in a circuit is the work done per unit charge moving through the points	

recall that ammeters are connected in series and voltmeters in parallel with a component; know how to use circuit symbols to draw circuits

| explain how current in a circuit is controlled by changing the resistance, and calculate this from:

resistance = voltage/current | use **and rearrange** the equation: resistance = voltage/current;

describe how to set up a circuit to explore the relationship between voltage and current in a component; calculate resistance from voltage–current graphs | |
| recall that resistors get hot when a current flows; recall how LDRs and thermistors behave in relevant circuits | interpret resistance graphs for resistors, LDRs and thermistors; **explain why the resistance of a wire increases with temperature** | |

To aim for a grade E	To aim for a grade C	To aim for a grade A
understand that the same current flows through components connected in series to a battery; understand that the p.ds across the components add up to the p.d. across the battery	understand that in a series circuit the p.d. is largest across the component with the greatest resistance	*understand that the work done on each unit of charge by the battery equals the work done by it on the components; understand that more work is done by charge moving through a large resistance than through a small one*
understand that in a parallel circuit the total current from the battery is the sum of the currents through each of the components; and that the current is largest through the component with the smallest resistance		*explain the relationships between the p.ds across and the currents through components connected in parallel*
understand that electricity can be induced in a wire that moves in a magnetic field; recall that the induced voltage depends on the speed of movement and the strength of the magnetic field	understand the size of the voltage induced by considering the rate at which magnetic field lines are cut	
describe how electricity can be generated by spinning a coil of wire in a magnetic field; predict changes in the voltage induced if changes are made to the magnetic field, the number of turns in the coil, or the rate at which the coil is turned		*explain how a generator produces an alternating voltage or current*
recall that electric currents generate magnetic fields; recall that a current flowing in a conductor in a magnetic field will result in a force called the motor effect		explain how the commutator ensures that the motor keeps turning in the dame direction
describe the construction of a transformer; recall that a transformer can change the size of an alternating voltage	*explain how a changing current in one coil of a transformer will induce a changing p.d. across the other coil; use the equation: $V_p/V_s = N_p/N_s$*	
recall that power (in watts, W) is a measure of the rate at which a power supply transfers energy to a device and its surroundings	use *and rearrange* the equation: power = voltage × current	
recall that a.c. is used for mains electricity	*understand that a.c. is used because it is easier to generate large amounts of power and more efficient to distribute across long distances*	

Exam-style questions

Foundation level

1 Static electricity is sometimes used when spray painting cars.

AO1 a The fine spray of paint rubs against the nozzle of the spray can and electrons are rubbed onto the drops of paint. Electrons have a _____ charge. [1]

AO1 b The car is also given a charge so that the paint is attracted to it. The car would need a _____ charge. [1]

AO2 c Explain how charging the paint drops helps produce a fine spray. [2]

[Total 4]

AO1 2 Saul moves a bar magnet in and out of a coil of wire. The ends of the coil are connected to a sensitive ammeter. He sees that as he pushes the magnet into the coil, the meter needle moves to one side. What happens to the meter reading if Saul:

a pushes the magnet in quicker? [1]

b leaves the magnet in the coil? [1]

c pulls the magnet out of the coil? [1]

[Total: 3]

Foundation/Higher level

3 Each of the resistors in these circuits has a resistance of 2 ohms and the voltage supply for each circuit is 12 V.

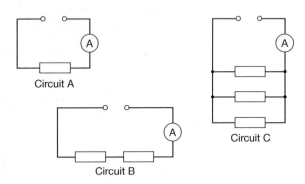

Circuit A

Circuit B

Circuit C

AO1 a In which circuit(s) are the components wired in series? [1]

b **AO1 (i)** In which circuit will the current be smallest? [1]

AO2 (ii) Explain your answer in terms of resistance, current and voltage. [2]

AO2 c Calculate the current in circuit A. [2]

[Total: 6]

4 Faith's bedside light has a power rating of 60 W. It is plugged into the mains circuit of the house.

AO1 a What is the voltage at which electricity is delivered to houses in UK? [1]

AO2 b Calculate the current flowing in the circuit. [2]

[Total: 3]

5 Toby has made a model to show the motor effect. On the right is a battery he has taped to the wooden base. The terminals of the battery are connected to a loop of wire which passes between a pair of magnets on the left.

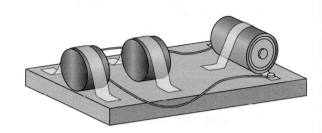

AO2 a Explain how this arrangement could be used to demonstrate the motor effect. [3]

AO3 b Toby's friend Will tries to copy this but his experiment doesn't work. Suggest the possible causes. [3]

[Total: 6]

Higher level

6 Farzina sets up two coils of wire around an iron core to investigate how a transformer works. She wants to use it to convert 12 V alternating current (a.c.) into 3 V a.c.

AO1 a What has to be true about the number of turns on the secondary coil compared to the primary coil? [1]

AO2 b How could the same arrangement be used to convert 12 V a.c. into 48 V a.c.? [1]

[Total: 2]

7 John wants to recreate Faraday's experiment in which he induced an electric current using a coil of wire and a magnet. John wants to demonstrate how the size and direction of the current can be changed. Describe how he should set about doing this. The quality of written communication will be assessed in your response. [6]

[Total: 6]

AO1 recall the science   **AO2** apply your knowledge   **AO3** evaluate and analyse the evidence

✳ Worked example

Higher level

1 A transformer consists of two coils wrapped around a soft iron core. The purpose of a transformer is to change voltage.

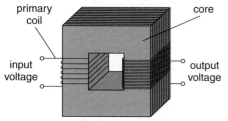

primary coil • core • input voltage • output voltage

AO1 **a** Is the transformer in the picture a step-up or a step-down transformer? [1]

Step-up. ✔

AO1 **b** Explain your answer. [2]

It has more turns in the secondary coil than in the primary coil. ✔

AO1 **c** Explain the purpose of the core. [2]

To conduct the magnetic field from the primary to the secondary coil. ✔ ✔

AO1 **d** Why it is usually made of soft iron? [1]

Soft iron is magnetic material. ✔

AO1 **e** Explain why a transformer needs to be used with alternating current. [3]

The magnetic field threading through the secondary coil must be continuously changing. A changing magnetic field in the secondary will induce a voltage across the ends of the coil. ✔ ✔

AO1
AO2 **f** A transformer has 5000 turns on its primary coil and 8000 turns on its secondary coil. If the input voltage is 230 V find the output voltage. [3]

$Np/Ns = Vp/Vs$ ✔
$8000/5000 = 230/Vs$
$Vs = 143.75 V$ ✔

How to raise your grade

Take note of the comments from examiners – these will help you to improve your grade.

> Correct: 1 mark.

> Correct: 2 marks.

> Correct. For 2 marks you need not only to mention the magnetic field, but how it gets from the primary coil where it is generated to the secondary where it needs to induce the secondary voltage.

> Correct: 1 mark.

> This answer gets 2 of the 3 marks. For 3 marks you need to make three points in the explanation. Start the explanation at the start of the process – the primary current creating the changing magnetic field in this case. Explain each step in a logical order.

> The formula is correct but the voltages have been incorrectly substituted (it should have been 5000/8000). However as the calculation was otherwise correct it gets 2 of the 3 marks.

P6 Radioactive materials

What you should already know...

Energy is transferred by electromagnetic radiation

The electromagnetic spectrum transfers energy in packets called photons.

It includes gamma rays, X-rays, ultraviolet, visible light, infrared, microwaves, TV and radio.

Electromagnetic waves with shorter wavelengths, such as gamma waves, have higher energy.

 Which types of electromagnetic radiation harm living tissue?

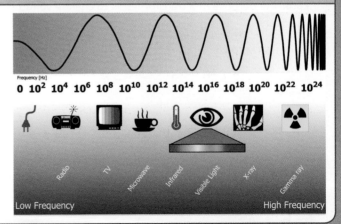

Frequency [Hz]

0 10^2 10^4 10^6 10^8 10^{10} 10^{12} 10^{14} 10^{16} 10^{18} 10^{20} 10^{22} 10^{24}

Radio TV Microwave Infrared Visible Light X-ray Gamma ray

Low Frequency   High Frequency

High-energy electromagnetic waves are ionising

High-energy electromagnetic waves such as gamma waves can cause ionisation.

Ionisation can damage living cells.

Excess exposure to ionising radiation can lead to cancer or cell death.

 What is ionisation and why can it be dangerous?

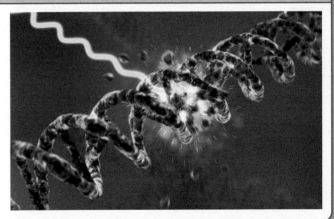

Nuclear energy can be used to generate electricity

Heat is produced by nuclear fuels in nuclear reactors.

The waste products are radioactive, which means they emit ionising radiation.

Irradiation by ionising radiation is not the same as contamination by radioactive material, and there are different consequent risks.

 Compare and contrast a nuclear power station with a coal fired power station.

In P6 you will find out about...

> the evidence for a nuclear model of the atom

> emission of ionising radiation from radioactive nuclei

> the properties of alpha, beta and gamma radiation

> the random nature of radioactive decay

> the decrease in activity with time, and the concept of radioactive half-life

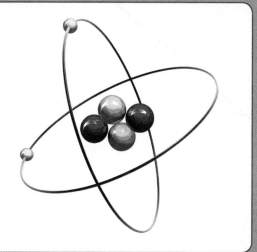

> ionisation as the production of ion pairs

> the risks to living organisms of ionising radiation, its harmful effect on cells and how it can be handled safely

> the beneficial uses of ionising radiation in medicine and in industry

> interpreting data on risk and evaluating risks and benefits

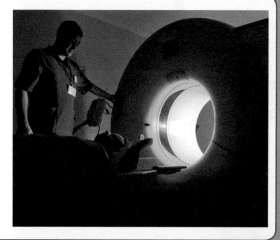

> how large amounts of energy are produced by nuclear fission

> how fission is controlled in a reactor

> the protective measures for workers in the nuclear industry

> how low-level, intermediate-level and high-level radioactive waste is dealt with

> nuclear fusion of hydrogen nuclei

The nuclear atom

How small is the Atom?

The Atom is a superhero who can shrink himself and his assistant down to subatomic size. In one adventure, his assistant asks how they can breathe when they are much smaller than an oxygen molecule. The Atom replies, 'Well, I'm not sure about that.'

FIGURE 1: The Atom.

What is in an atom?

An atom is the smallest part of an element. It can only be split by a nuclear reaction. For many years, it was thought that atoms were solid, but experiments in the 20th century showed that they are made up of tiny particles.

Outside the nucleus

Electrons are the smallest particle with a mass of $\frac{1}{2000}$ of a proton. This is so small that we often consider electrons to have no mass. They move at high speeds around the nucleus in orbits and they carry a negative charge.

Inside the nucleus

Protons have a mass that is 2000 times greater than an electron. They have a positive charge which is the same size, but opposite in sign, to the charge on an electron.

Neutrons have the same mass as the proton and no charge.

The large mass of protons and neutrons means that nearly all the mass of the atom is concentrated in the **nucleus**.

The atom is neutral because there is the same number of protons in the nucleus as electrons orbiting it.

Watch out!

You don't need to know the masses of particles in kilograms, just their relative mass compared with a mass of a proton. 2000 electrons equal the mass of 1 proton.

FIGURE 2: An atom of helium.

Did you know?

Imagine Figure 2 had been drawn to scale. If you had a nucleus the size of a pea, the outer electrons would be orbiting with a radius of 1 km. Most of the atom is empty space!

QUESTIONS

1 Copy the table and fill in the gaps with the relative charges and masses of the particles.

Particle	Mass	Charge
electron		−1
proton	1	
neutron		

2 Uranium has 92 protons in its nucleus. How many electrons are there in an atom of uranium?

Q Build an atom animation

How do we know that the atom has a massive, positive nucleus?

In 1909 Ernest Marsden, under the supervision of Professor Ernest Rutherford, fired positive alpha particles at a very thin sheet of gold foil. He made observations using a particle detector designed by Hans Geiger. The results were completely unexpected. At the time, it was thought that the positive charge of the atom was spread out. But a significant number of the alpha particles bounced backwards from the foil. This could not be explained using that model of the atom.

As shown in Figure 3, what Marsden found was that:

> Most of the alpha particles passed straight through the foil without deviation (A).

> The path of a few particles was bent by a small angle (B).

> A few particles bounced back from the foil (C).

What Rutherford concluded from these results was that:

> The atom is mostly empty space because most of the alpha particles passed straight through the gold foil.

> There is a concentration of mass and positive charge at the centre of the atom.

This was the discovery of the atomic nucleus. Rutherford knew the nucleus was positive because some of the positive alpha particles were repelled by it. He knew the nucleus was massive because when an alpha particle hit it directly, the alpha particle bounced back.

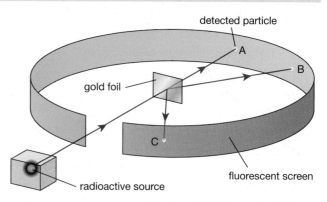

FIGURE 3: The Rutherford–Geiger–Marsden scattering experiment.

QUESTIONS

3 What would happen if we repeated this experiment but fired neutrons at the gold foil?

4 Suggest why some of the alpha particles were deflected through a small angle.

What holds the nucleus together? (Higher tier only)

Protons are positively charged and would normally repel each other. Neutrons are neutral and cannot be held together by electrostatic forces. However, there is a **strong nuclear force** which holds all the particles in the nucleus together.

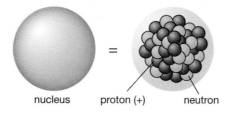

FIGURE 4: The strong nuclear force balances the repulsive electrostatic forces between the protons.

Isotopes

The number of protons in a nucleus determines the element and its chemical properties. However, atoms of the same element can have a different number of neutrons.

Isotopes are atoms with the same number of protons, but different numbers of neutrons. Isotopes are different forms of the same element. There are three isotopes of hydrogen:

> Hydrogen has one proton.

> Deuterium has one proton and one neutron.

> Tritium has one proton and two neutrons.

Most elements have isotopes. Carbon has 15 isotopes. They are named by the number of nucleons (protons and neutrons) in the nucleus, for example carbon-12 and carbon-14. All the isotopes of carbon have six protons.

QUESTIONS

5 Oxygen has three stable isotopes – oxygen-16, oxygen-17 and oxygen-18. Oxygen has eight protons. What is the other particle in the nucleus? How many of this particle is in each isotope?

6 Elements can exist as different isotopes. How does this affect the mass and chemical properties of elements?

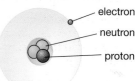

hydrogen deuterium tritium

FIGURE 5: There are three isotopes of hydrogen.

Radioactive elements

We are learning to:

> describe how some elements are radioactive and emit ionising radiation

> describe how radiation is around us all the time

> explain what contributes most to background radiation

Are bananas radioactive?

Bananas contain low levels of radioactive potassium. Don't worry, our bodies also contain this and we can cope with the radioactivity of a banana.

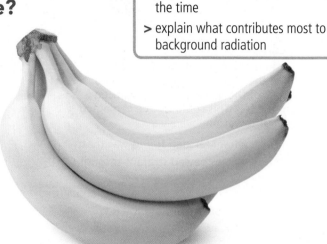

FIGURE 1

Ionising radiation

In 1896 a French scientist called Henri Becquerel discovered a form of radiation coming from a lump of uranium ore. A Polish–French scientist called Marie Curie decided to investigate this and processed tons of rock. First, she isolated two radioactive elements – polonium and uranium – but realised that in the ore there was an element which emitted much more radiation than the other two. Eventually, she isolated radium.

Radioactive elements have unstable nuclei which emit radiation. This changes them to a more stable state. Radioactive elements occur naturally and some are made in nuclear reactors.

All radioactive elements emit **ionising radiation**.

When ionising radiation, which can be either high-energy particles or high-energy electromagnetic waves, meets an atom it knocks out an outer electron. This produces a (negative) electron and a positive **ion** (the remains of the atom).

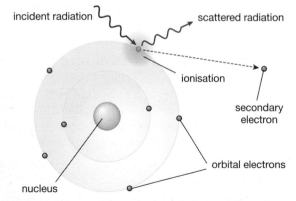

FIGURE 3: Ionising radiation knocks out electrons from atoms.

FIGURE 2: Marie Curie discovered radioactive elements.

Did you know?

Marie Curie was the first woman to win a Nobel Prize and the only person to be awarded Nobel Prizes in both Physics and Chemistry.

QUESTIONS

1 Draw the two particles that remain after the ionisation shown in Figure 3. Label their charges.

2 Name three naturally occurring radioactive elements.

FIGURE 4: The Geiger–Muller tube (also known as a G–M tube, or Geiger counter) detects the ionising properties of radioactivity.

Background radiation

If you take a Geiger counter reading at any location some radioactivity will be detected. We call this **background radiation**. It is low-level radiation that is around us all the time. Where does background radiation come from?

Some of the background radiation comes from outer space as cosmic rays, but most of it comes from rocks and soil. We use rock materials to build with, so our buildings may emit radiation. Radiation can be absorbed by plants from the soil.

Radioactive sources have many medical uses and these also account for some background radiation.

A small percentage comes from human activity such as fallout from nuclear explosions and accidents or from nuclear waste.

The level of background radiation varies depending on where you live. Granite releases radon gas, so people whose houses are built on granite, such as in Dartmoor or Aberdeen, can experience higher levels of background radiation. Radon can be dispersed by ensuring good ventilation.

Aeroplane travel increases the level of cosmic rays you are exposed to, as does going deep into mines.

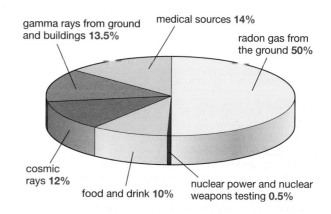

gamma rays from ground and buildings **13.5%**

medical sources **14%**

radon gas from the ground **50%**

cosmic rays **12%**

food and drink **10%**

nuclear power and nuclear weapons testing **0.5%**

FIGURE 5: The various sources of background radiation.

QUESTIONS

3 Name three occupations that expose a person to higher levels of background radiation.

4 What can be done to prevent radon gas building up in a house?

Radioactivity is a random process

Marie Curie noted in her diary that the amount of radioactivity given off was dependent only on the amount of element present, not on whether it was wet, dry, hot or cold, crushed or solid or mixed with other elements.

If you listen to the pings on a Geiger counter, they do not come at regular intervals. We never know when an individual unstable atom will decay and there is nothing that will hurry up the process. When a radioactive atom does decay, it changes into another element.

QUESTIONS

5 Scientists monitoring background radiation in Scandinavia were the first people outside Russia to realise that there had been a nuclear accident at Chernobyl. Explain how they detected this.

6 Why do you need to allow the counter to count for a few minutes when taking a reading of background radiation?

Three types of ionising radiation

How can you tell the time when it's completely dark?

A hundred years ago, some watches had the numbers and hands painted with radium, a radioactive material, mixed with a luminescent substance. When the particles emitted by the radium hit the luminescent substance it glowed.

The radium has now been replaced with tritium, an isotope of hydrogen.

FIGURE 1

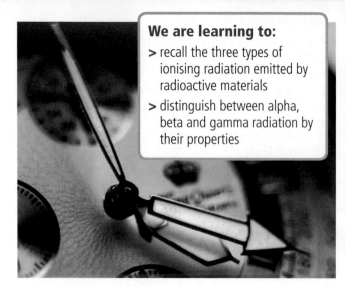

We are learning to:

> recall the three types of ionising radiation emitted by radioactive materials

> distinguish between alpha, beta and gamma radiation by their properties

 Alpha, beta, gamma

There are three types of nuclear radiation. These are called **alpha** (α), **beta** (β) and **gamma** (γ) radiation. They can be distinguished by their different properties.

Alpha particles

> Have a positive charge and are deflected by electric and magnetic fields.

> Are relatively big and heavy and so are good ionisers; their bulk means that they can easily knock electrons out of atoms.

Beta particles

> Have a negative charge and are deflected by electric and magnetic fields (in the opposite direction to alpha particles).

> Are relatively much smaller, faster and lighter and so are not as good ionisers as alpha particles.

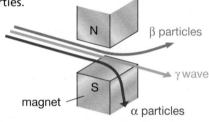

FIGURE 2: Ernest Rutherford applied a strong magnetic field to the radiation from some radium.

Gamma rays

> Are short-wavelength electromagnetic waves.

> Have no charge and so are not deflected by electric and magnetic fields.

> Are weak ionisers because they tend to pass through things, but when they do contact an atom they will knock out an electron.

● QUESTIONS

1 There are two ways of deflecting alpha and beta rays in opposite directions. What are they?

2 Why are alpha particles better at ionising atoms than beta particles or gamma rays?

 How far does ionising radiation go?

When alpha, beta and gamma radiation go through air they interact with the air molecules. Alpha particles, being larger, have more interactions than beta particles or gamma rays. They lose energy quicker and travel less far.

A Geiger–Muller tube will stop detecting alpha radiation about 3 cm from the source. It will detect beta radiation up to 1 m away from the source. Gamma rays are not stopped at all by air, although they do spread out and become less intense.

Watch out!
Alpha radiation is not safer than the other types because it is less penetrating; when it does contact other atoms it has strong ionising power.

Q properties of alpha beta and gamma radiation

Alpha particles can be stopped by a sheet of paper and do not penetrate the skin.

Beta radiation is stopped by about 3mm of aluminium.

These properties of alpha and beta radiation are used to monitor the thickness of paper and metal sheets when they are being manufactured.

A lot of dense metal is needed to stop gamma radiation. Thick lead is used when transporting nuclear waste from power stations to reprocessing plants. Very thick concrete is used around nuclear reactors to stop gamma rays.

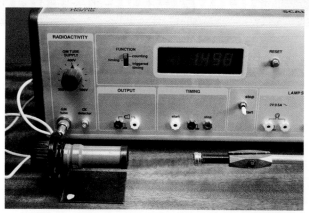

FIGURE 3: Measuring the range of ionising radiation in the lab.

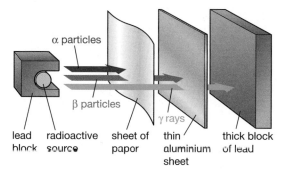

FIGURE 4: Alpha, beta and gamma have different penetrating properties.

lead block · radioactive source · sheet of paper · thin aluminium sheet · thick block of lead

α particles · β particles · γ rays

QUESTIONS

3 Devise an experiment to detect whether a piece of radioactive rock is emitting alpha, beta or gamma radiation.

4 When alpha particles have travelled through about 3cm of air they have just run out of energy. Where has this energy gone?

What are alpha and beta radiation? (Higher tier only)

Alpha particles are helium nuclei, meaning that an alpha particle is positive and consists of two protons and two neutrons. Alpha particles, therefore, have a **nucleon number**, or mass number, of 4 and a charge of +2.

Beta particles are very fast-moving electrons. But they are not orbital electrons from the outer atom – they come from the nucleus. Electrons do not exist in the nucleus, but in some unstable nuclei a neutron changes into a proton and an electron. The electron is emitted as beta radiation.

Scientists have devised a symbolic way to indicate the number of protons and neutrons in any nucleus. They put the nucleon number, or mass number, as a superscript and the number of protons as a subscript. For example:

$$^{\text{mass number}}_{\text{proton number}} \text{particle symbol}$$

So an alpha particle is written: $^{4}_{2}\text{He}$

Although a beta particle is not a nucleus, it can also be represented in this way: $^{0}_{-1}\text{e}$

Nuclear symbol notation is useful for representing isotopes, for example $^{1}_{1}\text{H}$ for hydrogen, $^{2}_{1}\text{H}$ for deuterium and $^{3}_{1}\text{H}$ for tritium.

alpha particle

beta particle

gamma ray

FIGURE 5: What constitutes alpha, beta and gamma.

Watch out!

Alpha particles are helium nuclei, not helium atoms.

Did you know?

In a supernova explosion, which occurs at the end of a massive star's life, protons and electrons are squeezed together and turn into neutrons. This is the reverse of what happens to produce beta radiation.

QUESTIONS

5 Explain why $^{0}_{-1}\text{e}$ represents a beta particle.

6 The element carbon has six protons. Three of the isotopes of carbon have six neutrons, eight neutrons and 16 neutrons. Write these isotopes in nuclear symbol form.

Radioactive decay

Is radioactive decay the alchemists' dream?

Alchemists tried to change base metals, such as lead, into gold. During radioactive decay one element is changed into another, which may in turn decay into another. Unfortunately for the alchemists, most decay chains end in lead, not gold.

FIGURE 1: Alchemy was a serious challenge before the science of elements was understood.

Radioactive decay

Used nuclear fuel from nuclear power stations is radioactive. It is sometimes put under water for storage and the radioactivity is monitored; it decreases over time.

When a radioactive nucleus has emitted alpha or beta radiation, the number of protons and neutrons changes producing a new element. Therefore, the amount of original radioactive source has decreased. It is said to have decayed, or undergone **radioactive decay**.

Marie Curie found that the amount of radiation emitted, or the **activity**, depends on the number of radioactive nuclei present in a sample.

 QUESTION

1 After a period of time, used fuel rods from nuclear power stations can be taken out of the water tanks where they are stored and moved to a processing plant. Why are they now able to be moved?

Q radioactive decay GCSE

Three methods of decay

Alpha decay

Many large nuclei tend to be unstable. For example, uranium-238 is a large unstable atom that decays to the element thorium with the emission of an alpha particle.

Beta decay

Carbon-15 is an example of an isotope that undergoes beta decay. It is an unstable form of carbon. The carbon decays into nitrogen and emits a beta particle.

Gamma decay

Often alpha or beta decay is accompanied by gamma emission. Gamma radiation is an electromagnetic wave. Emitting gamma radiation does not change one element into another.

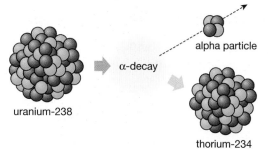

FIGURE 2: Alpha decay.

 QUESTION

2 Why can the emission of gamma radiation not change one element into another?

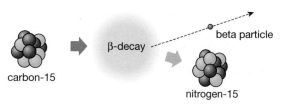

FIGURE 3: Beta decay.

Instability of the nucleus (Higher tier only)

When we say a nucleus is unstable, we mean that it is in an energetic state. It has excess energy and to become stable it needs to lose some energy.

Alpha and beta decay are both ways of changing a large unstable nucleus into a more stable nucleus. However, after alpha or beta decay the new nucleus is often still in an energetic state. Emitting a photon of gamma radiation reduces this energy.

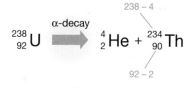

FIGURE 4: Alpha decay of uranium-238.

Decay equations

Alpha and beta decay can be written as an equation using the nuclear shorthand introduced on page 263.

An alpha particle $^4_2$He has a mass of 4 and a charge of +2. When a nucleus loses an alpha particle, the mass of the new nucleus will be lighter by 4. The charge also decreases by 2. This means that a new element is produced. You need to consult a periodic table to find out which element is made.

Beta decay does not affect the mass, but leaves an extra proton in the new nucleus. So the charge increases by 1.

The total mass and total charge on the left-hand side of the equation should equal the total mass and total charge on the right-hand side of the equation. In other words the total charge is conserved and the total number of protons and neutrons is also conserved.

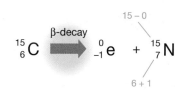

FIGURE 5: Beta decay of carbon-15.

QUESTIONS (Use the Periodic Table on page 309 for questions 5 and 6)

3 Neptunium-217 decays to protactinium-213. What type of radioactive emission has been emitted?

4 When uranium decays to thorium it emits an alpha particle and also a gamma photon. What effect does the gamma emission have on the new nucleus?

5 Radium-226 decays to radon by emitting an alpha particle. Write the decay equation.

6 Iodine-131 is used as a medical tracer. It emits beta radiation to become xenon. Write the decay equation.

Preparing for assessment: Analysing, evaluating and reviewing

To achieve a good grade you will need to be able to use your skills and knowledge to understand how scientists plan, run and evaluate investigations. These skills will be assessed in your exams and in Controlled Assessments. This activity supports you in developing the skills of analysing data and evaluating an investigation.

✸ Investigating radioactive decay

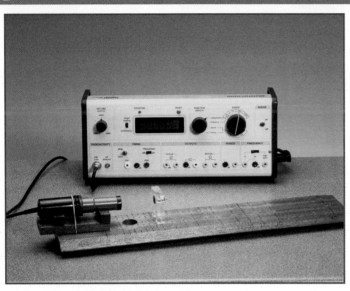

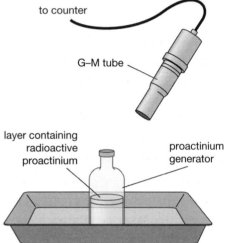

to counter

G–M tube

layer containing radioactive proactinium

proactinium generator

A class of GCSE students are studying radioactivity and finding out about what happens when one element decays into another. Their teacher has set up a demonstration using a material called protactinium and a G–M tube.

The protactinium decays and emits ionising radiation, which is detected by the G–M tube and displayed on the counter. The counter is allowed to run for 10 seconds, then stopped and the reading recorded. After a further 10 seconds, it is started again and run for another 10 seconds.

Finally, the source is put back in the store and a reading taken of the background count. This value is subtracted from each of the readings; the adjusted values are displayed in a table.

Time (s)	count per 10 seconds	Time (s)	count per 10 seconds	Time (s)	count per 10 seconds	Time (s)	count per 10 seconds
10	204	130	63	250	28	370	1
30	168	150	53	270	14	390	0
50	131	170	38	290	22	410	12
70	107	190	32	310	20		
90	93	210	28	330	17		
110	77	230	29	350	15		

✹ Task 1

> If the experiment was repeated, how similar do you think the results would be?

> How good do you think this experiment is at producing accurate data?

> Explain whether or not you think any of the readings are outliers.

✹ Task 2

> Construct a graph of count rate against time using appropriate axes and scales.

> Draw in a line of best fit.

✹ Task 3

> Suggest how the experiment could be modified to improve the quality of the data gathered.

✹ Task 4

> Look at the trend in the figures, accounting for any outliers.

> What does this say about the repeatability of the data?

> Comment on the spread of the readings.

✹ Maximise your grade

Use these suggestions to improve your work and be more successful.

E

To be on target for grade E you need to:

> Comment on how the students collected the data and its accuracy or repeatability.

> Comment on the limitations to accuracy or range of data due to their techniques and equipment.

> Identify individual results which are outliers, or justify a claim that there are no outliers.

C

To be on target for grades D, C, in addition, you need to:

> Suggest improvements to their apparatus or techniques, or alternative ways to collect data.

> Use the general pattern of their results as a basis for assessing accuracy and repeatability.

A

To be on target for grades B, A, in addition, you need to:

> Describe and justify improvements to their apparatus or techniques, or alternative ways to collect the data.

> Consider critically the repeatability of their evidence, accounting for any outliers.

Half-life

We are learning to:
> understand the meaning of half-life in radioactive decay
> understand that radioactive elements have a wide range of half-lives

How can we tell the age of old skeletons?

The remains of a skeleton were found by the Columbia River in USA and named Kennewick Man after the area. Initially assumed to be around 150 years old and from a Native American tribe, radiocarbon dating showed that Kennewick Man was around 9300 years old. Radiocarbon dating uses the fact that the unstable isotope carbon-14 is present in all organic material and decays over time.

FIGURE 1

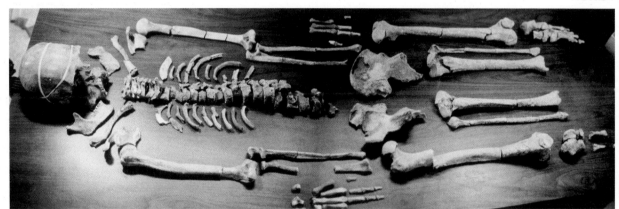

Half-life

Radioactive decay is random. We cannot know the exact moment at which an unstable nucleus will emit radiation. But we know that the activity of any radioactive source decreases with time. When the activity of a mass of radioactive element is measured over a period of time, the same pattern always emerges.

No matter how many undecayed atoms you start with, it takes the same amount of time for half of the radioactive atoms to decay. It then takes the same amount of time for half of the remaining radioactive atoms to decay, and so on. This period of time is specific to each radioactive element and is called the **half-life** of that element.

> The half-life of a radioactive element is the time taken for half of the atoms in a sample to decay.

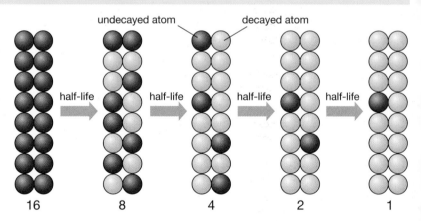

FIGURE 2: Half of the radioactive nuclei present decay in a period of time called the half-life.

QUESTIONS

1 The half-life of carbon-14 is 5730 years and the half-life of iron-59 is 44.53 days. If you start with a sample of each with equal activities, which will lose its radioactivity first?

2 If you start with a sample of a pure radioactive element explain why, after a period of time, the sample is no longer pure.

🔍 radioactive half-life   radioactive decay chains

A range of half-lives

Half-lives may be as short as seconds or as long as thousands of years. Some radioactive rocks are still radioactive today, millions of years after they were formed. Many radioactive elements belong to a **decay chain**: the initial element decays into a **daughter product** that is also a radioactive element, and this decays to another element, and so on until a stable nucleus results.

The activity of a radioactive source – the amount of radiation emitted – is a measure of the rate of decay of the radioactive material. A pure sample of a radioactive element consists of undecayed atoms. Initially, the rate of decay is rapid but this rate falls as the number of undecayed atoms decreases.

In theory, radioactivity never reaches zero. However it is continually decreasing and eventually reaches a negligible value.

> The half-life is the time taken for the activity of a sample to fall by half.

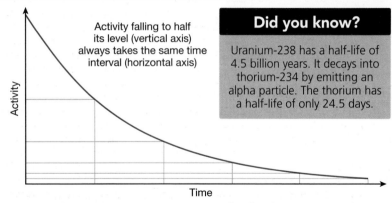

Activity falling to half its level (vertical axis) always takes the same time interval (horizontal axis)

FIGURE 3: The same pattern occurs over time for all radioactive materials.

Did you know?

Uranium-238 has a half-life of 4.5 billion years. It decays into thorium-234 by emitting an alpha particle. The thorium has a half-life of only 24.5 days.

QUESTIONS

3 The age of archaeological finds can be found by calculating how much the activity of Carbon-14 has decreased over time. What does this suggest about the half-life of carbon-14?

4 A radioactive source has a half-life of 15 minutes. At a particular time the activity of the source is 16000 counts/sec. What is the activity of the source 1 hour later?

Calculating half-life (Higher tier only)

Scientists can find the half-life of a substance by monitoring the count rate over a period of time and drawing a graph of count rate on the y-axis and time on the x-axis.

In the example shown in figure 4 the activity falls from 80 counts per minute to 40 counts per minute in 2 days.

It also takes two for the count rate to halve from 40 to 20 counts per minute and from 20 to 10 counts per minute.

So, the half-life of this sample is 2 days.

To calculate the fraction of sample remaining after 6 days, first consider how many half-lives have been completed. In this case it is three half-lives.

After one half-life $\frac{1}{2}$ will be left.

After two half-lives $\frac{1}{2} \times \frac{1}{2} = \frac{1}{4}$ will be left.

After three half-lives $\frac{1}{4} \times \frac{1}{2} = \frac{1}{8}$ will be left.

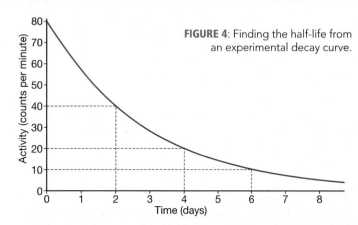

FIGURE 4: Finding the half-life from an experimental decay curve.

QUESTIONS

5 In an experiment to find the half-life of radioactive iodine the count rate falls from 400 counts per second to 50 counts per second in 75 minutes. What is the half-life?

6 Sketch the decay graph for a sample that is twice as big, showing how the count rate changes. (You will need to put numbers on the axes.)

Hazards of ionising radiation

How can you tell if shoes really fit?

In the 1950s it was commonplace for shoe shops to have X-ray machines. The customer put the shoes on and then put a foot into the machine. Looking into the viewer, they could see an X-ray image of their foot in the shoe. The practice was ended when it was decided that the risk of damage to living tissue was greater than the benefit of seeing if shoes fitted properly.

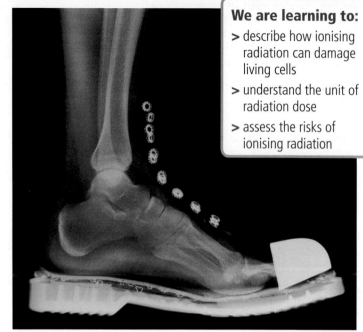

FIGURE 1

How ionising radiation affects living cells

The effects of ionising radiation on living cells depend on the type of radiation, its intensity, the duration of irradiation and the type of cells. When ionising radiations enter the body, they collide with living cells and knock electrons out of atoms leaving positive **ions**, a bit like a snooker ball colliding with a group of other snooker balls.

High intensity radiation can kill living cells causing tissue damage and leading to radiation sickness.

Lower intensities can affect cells' genetic make-up, causing **mutations**. These mutated cells sometimes reproduce rapidly, leading to cancer. Some damaged cells can repair themselves and there are no ill effects.

Watch out!

Be careful with the words you use when assessing the risk of ionising radiation. For example, say 'there is an increased risk of developing cancer' not 'cancer will result'; developing cancer is not inevitable.

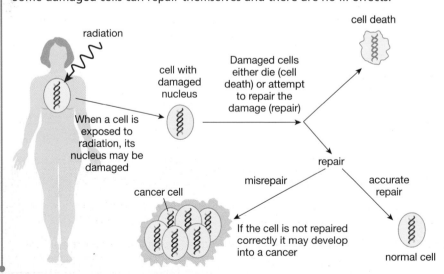

radiation

cell with damaged nucleus

When a cell is exposed to radiation, its nucleus may be damaged

Damaged cells either die (cell death) or attempt to repair the damage (repair)

cell death

repair

misrepair

accurate repair

cancer cell

If the cell is not repaired correctly it may develop into a cancer

normal cell

FIGURE 2: The effects of radiation on our body cells.

QUESTIONS

1 What is produced when an atom is ionised?

2 Are damaging results a certain outcome when a living cell is irradiated?

Q dose equivalent

Assessing radiation risk

Which is the most damaging type of radiation? This depends on the location of the radiation source. If it is inside the body, alpha radiation causes the most damage as it is a very good ioniser. However, it doesn't penetrate far. From outside the body, it doesn't penetrate the skin.

Beta and gamma radiation are much more penetrating and can go through the skin into the body. Therefore, if the source is outside the body, beta and gamma are more dangerous despite being poorer ionisers. Most gamma radiation just passes straight through the body.

People working with ionising radiation need a measure to compare equivalent doses of different sources of radiation. The **sievert (Sv)** is the SI unit of **equivalent dose** of absorbed radiation. This means that 1 sievert of alpha, beta or gamma radiation produces the same biological effect in a specified tissue.

Radiation dose (millisieverts per year, mSv/yr)	Effect
2	Typical background radiation experienced by most people
9	Exposure of airline crew flying from New York to Tokyo via the polar route
20	Current limit for nuclear industry employees
50	Former nuclear industry limit
100	Lowest level at which an increase in cancer is clearly evident
1000	Causes temporary radiation sickness, not death
5000	Would kill half of those receiving this dose within a month

QUESTIONS

3 The highest dose equivalent measurement taken on the perimeter of the Fukushima power station after the earthquake in Japan in 2011 was 11.9 mSv per hour. Compare this to the background radiation level in the tables above and write a sentence about the risks to people.

4 Explain why alpha radiation is most dangerous when in the form of a gas.

Did you know?

The sievert is named after a Swedish medical physicist called Rolf Maximilian Sievert who researched the biological effects of radiation.

Ionisation of water molecules in the body (Higher tier only)

We have seen that alpha, beta and gamma radiation can produce a positive ion when they collide with an atom. Because the ion is charged, it can break chemical bonds and form new bonds with other atoms and molecules. The resulting molecules may change cellular activity in a harmful way.

Oxygen, hydrogen, nitrogen and carbon are vulnerable to ionisation. They are present in large quantities in the body.

The picture shows ionising radiation hitting a water molecule (made of hydrogen and oxygen). The resulting positive ion goes on to interfere with the cell's DNA. This may be repaired or may go on to behave incorrectly.

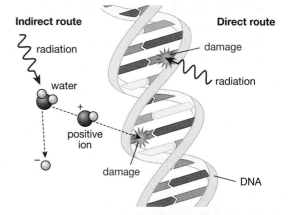

FIGURE 3: DNA damage caused by ionisation.

QUESTIONS

5 A CT scan (a specialised medical X-ray procedure) has an equivalent dose of 10 mSv per hour. Is this higher or lower than the dose equivalent for airline crew flying from New York to Tokyo?

6 Explain why scientists have monitored people involved in the nuclear explosion at Chernobyl for many years after the event.

Useful radiation

How do you know that factory waste is not polluting this beach?

A radioactive substance can be added to the outfall from a factory. It then moves with the waste. Boats with detecting apparatus can monitor the radiation given off and check that the waste is taken well away from beaches by tides and currents.

FIGURE 1

Destroying cells

Treating cancer

More than 100 years ago, Marie Curie realised that cancers could be destroyed by radiation. She put some radium on a small tumour and found that the radiation destroyed the tumour.

Ionising radiation, if sufficiently intense, will kill cancer cells. If all the cells in the tumour are destroyed, there will be no cancerous cells left to grow out of control. Killing cancer cells in this way is called **radiotherapy**. Usually gamma radiation is used in radiotherapy.

As the radiation will also kill healthy cells around the tumour, the radiographer ensures that the radiation is focused on the tumour. The radiographer also carefully works out the intensity and duration of the radiation dose.

Sterilising medical instruments

Medical instruments for operations need to be **sterile**, meaning that there are no bacteria on them. This used to be achieved by boiling or soaking in chemicals.

Now all instruments can be irradiated with gamma radiation. They can be sterilised inside their packaging and will remain sterile until the packet is opened. This has led to the worldwide use of disposable plastic syringes instead of heavy glass or metal ones.

Sterilising food

As soon as fresh fruits, such as strawberries, are picked ready for transport to shops, microorganisms start the decay process.

If the food is packed and then irradiated with gamma radiation, the microorganisms will be killed. This means that the food will stay fresh until the packaging is opened. The shelf-life of the food will be extended without altering the food itself.

This method is not suitable for all foods and in UK all irradiated foods have to be clearly labelled.

FIGURE 2: The radiographer is using the lights and measurements to line up the radiation beam accurately.

Q uses of radiation GCSE

Watch out!
Irradiated food does not become radioactive.

FIGURE 3: The strawberries on the left have been irradiated; those on the right have not.

QUESTIONS

1 a Why do radiographers have to focus the beam carefully?

b Why would alpha radiation be useless for radiotherapy?

2 State the advantages of using gamma rays to sterilise medical instruments.

3 When might food benefit from irradiation?

Detecting brain tumours

If a surgeon wants to diagnose the extent of a brain tumour they can use some technetium-99. This is a gamma emitter with a half-life of about 6 hours. When injected into a patient, it is being used as a **radioactive tracer**. It accumulates in the brain-tumour tissues and a radiographer can detect it from outside the body using a gamma camera. They can use a computer to build up a 3D picture of the brain tumour. Other tracers can be used to diagnose abnormalities in other parts of the body. Radioactive tracers are also used to monitor where the waste from factories goes.

Did you know?

Some cancers can be cured with gold. Gold-198 is a radioactive isotope of gold with a half-life of 2.7 days. It can be injected into a tumour to kill the cancer cells.

QUESTION

4 Describe how surgeons, together with radiographers, can build up pictures of brain tumours.

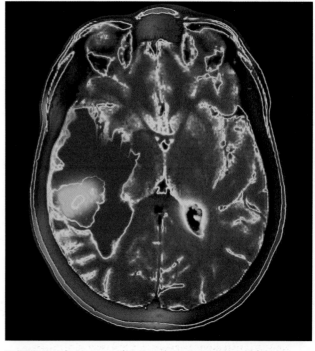

FIGURE 4: A brain scan showing the concentration of the radioactive tracer technetium-99 in a tumour (orange).

Choosing the radioactive source (Higher tier only)

The type and strength of radiation are carefully selected according to the application. To sterilise instruments or irradiate food, the radiation has to penetrate the packaging and be capable of killing bacteria. Gamma radiation is suitable for this.

Tracers for medical imaging are usually beta or gamma emitters, as the radiation needs to exit the body to reach the detector. These generally have a half-life of a few hours. This allows the tracer to reach the affected part of the body in sufficient quantities to make a picture, but means that it does not last long enough to cause damage.

QUESTION

5 Explain the properties of a good radioactive tracer for medical use.

Keeping people safe

We are learning to:

> understand that risks need to be evaluated by assessing the level of risk and the consequences of harm

> describe the risks to people from irradiation and contamination

> explain how the time taken for a radioactive source to become safe depends on its half-life

> recall that exposure is regulated in certain occupations

How do we know 'cosmic rays' come from space?

In 1912 an Austrian scientist called Victor Hess went up in a hot air balloon during a total eclipse of the Sun. He measured the ionisation by cosmic rays and found that it increased with his distance from the Earth and did not come from the Sun. His conclusion was that cosmic rays came from space.

Risks from irradiation

Exposure to radiation is called **irradiation**. Cosmic radiation bombards the Earth all the time and some rocks are radioactive. Look back at the pie chart on page 261, which shows the background radiation we are exposed to and where most of it comes from. The risk to our health is usually insignificant, but it does depend on the level of radiation and the length of exposure. In turn, this depends on where we live and what job we do. For example, miners may be exposed to higher levels of background radiation than others.

In risk assessment, the first step is to identify the hazards. The next step is to evaluate the risk to the person.

> A **hazard** is anything that may cause harm.

> The **risk** is the chance, high or low, that somebody could be harmed by the hazard.

In the case of irradiation, the hazard is the background radiation and any additional exposure to radiation is due to individual circumstances, such as working with radioactive materials or undergoing medical procedures. The dose equivalent in sieverts (see page 271) can be used to evaluate the level of risk and what harm may be done. A decision can then be made about whether that risk is worth taking, considering the benefits of the work or the medical treatment.

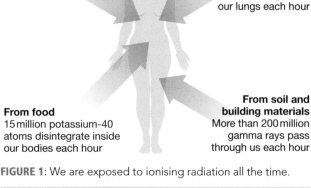

From the sky
About 400 000 cosmic rays pass through us each hour

From the air
30 000 atoms of radioactive gases breathed in disintegrate in our lungs each hour

From food
15 million potassium-40 atoms disintegrate inside our bodies each hour

From soil and building materials
More than 200 million gamma rays pass through us each hour

FIGURE 1: We are exposed to ionising radiation all the time.

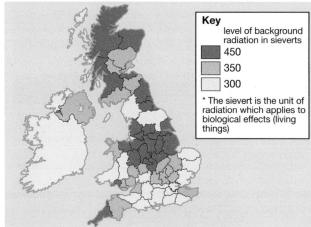

Key
level of background radiation in sieverts

■	450
■	350
□	300

* The sievert is the unit of radiation which applies to biological effects (living things)

FIGURE 2: The level of background radiation varies across the country.

FIGURE 3: This sign warns about the presence of something that is radioactive.

QUESTIONS

1 What are the possible consequences of exposure to ionising radiation?

2 Is this a high risk if you are only exposed to background radiation?

Q safety working with radioactive material

Contamination

Irradiation means exposure to ionising radiation, but irradiation does not make a person or object radioactive. **Contamination** means that something has come into direct contact with a radioactive material. Radioactive contamination may happen following an accident involving the production or use of radioactive materials.

Contained radioactive waste materials from nuclear power stations are not classed as contamination. If waste cannot be contained, it may be diluted to safe concentrations.

Low levels of contamination pose little risk. Radioactive material with a short half-life of a few hours or a few days may be allowed to decay naturally. To avoid exposure over a long period of time, radioactive material with a longer half-life, such as several months or more, should be cleaned up. It is the job of health physicists to monitor contamination levels to ensure that they stay within safe boundaries.

Radioactive material can be considered safe when its activity approaches the level of the background radiation. For most radioactive materials used in the nuclear industry this occurs after five half-lives. In this time the activity will have decayed to about 3% of its original value.

Higher levels of contamination, following fallout from a nuclear explosion, need huge interventions. One such treatment is to give iodine pills to people at risk from contamination with radioactive iodine. The thyroid takes up iodine. If the thyroid is full of non-radioactive iodine, it will not be able to take up the radioactive iodine.

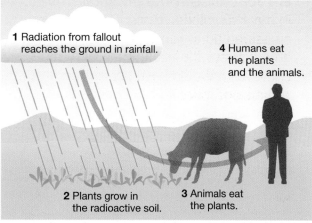

1 Radiation from fallout reaches the ground in rainfall.

4 Humans eat the plants and the animals.

2 Plants grow in the radioactive soil.

3 Animals eat the plants.

FIGURE 4: How our food can become contaminated.

QUESTIONS

3 Iodine-131 has a half-life of 8 days. After how long can we consider it to be at a safe level?

4 Look at Figure 4 and explain how radioactive contamination can get into the food chain.

Monitoring risk

Many people work with radioactive isotopes both in medicine and industry. Their levels of exposure have to be monitored and there are strict guidelines as to how much radiation they may experience in a year. This can be monitored using a film badge which workers wear all the time. Radiation falls on the film in the badge and exposes it. The level of radiation exposure is measured by assessing how black (exposed) the film in the badge has become. Different thicknesses of plastic allow the medical physicist to determine whether the exposure was to alpha, beta or gamma radiation.

Lead, either incorporated in protective walls or lead-lined aprons, is used to shield workers from radioactive isotopes. Radiographers wear lead-lined aprons when dealing with patients and always go out of the room or behind a lead screen when radiotherapy is taking place.

FIGURE 5: Film badge for determining radiation exposure.

QUESTION

5 To make a judgement (risk assessment) about a possible outcome you need to ask two questions:

• What is the chance of the outcome happening?

• What is the consequence of that outcome?

Consider a case in which someone has been exposed to radiation levels that increase the risk of cancer. Use the questions above to make a statement about the possible outcome.

Energy from the nucleus

We are learning to:

> understand that nuclear reactions produce energy

> explain the difference between nuclear fission and nuclear fusion

> recall that nuclear reactions release much more energy than chemical ones

Would a nuclear-powered car help reduce global warming?

The Ford Nucleon was designed in the 1950s to have no CO_2 emission and to run for a long time without the need to refuel. However, it would have been very heavy; it would have needed heavy lead lining around the reactor. And its waste products would have been radioactive.

FIGURE 1: Nuclear power has advantages and disadvantages.

Energy from the nucleus

There are two ways in which energy can be obtained from the nucleus of an atom:

> **Nuclear fission** is a process in which a heavy nucleus such as uranium is split into two lighter nuclei of almost equal mass. Energy is released when this change happens.

> **Nuclear fusion** is a process where two light nuclei such as hydrogen combine to create a larger nucleus. Energy is also released when this change happens.

Materials that can provide energy by either of these different processes are called **nuclear fuels**.

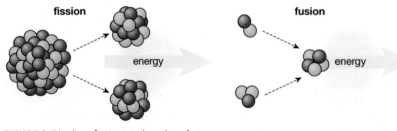

FIGURE 2: Nuclear fission and nuclear fusion.

Watch out!

Fission and fusion are very similar words. Be careful that you do not write one when describing the other.

QUESTION

1 What is the difference between fission and fusion? What is similar?

Nuclear fuels and energy

The energy released in nuclear fission and fusion is much greater than that released by any chemical reaction. This is because the energy that holds particles together in a nucleus, called the **binding energy**, is much greater than the energy that holds electrons in an atom. In both fission and fusion it is some of this binding energy that is released.

Q nuclear fission simulation

The energy released from the fission of one uranium nucleus is 32×10^{-11} J. As 1 kg of uranium contains many atoms, the energy released from 1 kg of uranium is 6.1×10^{13} J.

For comparison, the energy released by burning 1 kg of coal is 3.5×10^8 J.

The energy released from the fusion of two hydrogen atoms is 2.8×10^{-12} J. This occurs in stars and an estimate of the energy released by the Sun when 1 kg of hydrogen is fused is about 9×10^{16} J.

QUESTIONS

2 How many times greater is the energy released from 1 kg of uranium undergoing fission than from 1 kg of coal undergoing combustion?

3 Why is far more energy released in nuclear reactions than in chemical reactions?

4 Why is this fact a challenge as well as an opportunity?

Obtaining energy from fission (Higher tier only)

Uranium-235 is used as a nuclear fuel. A neutron is needed to initiate the fission process. It hits the uranium-235 nucleus and is absorbed. The resulting unstable nucleus splits into two other nuclei of almost equal mass. In this example the nuclei are krypton-92 and barium-141. Three neutrons also result and much energy is produced.

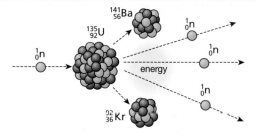

$$^{235}_{92}\text{U} + ^{1}_{0}\text{n} \rightarrow ^{141}_{56}\text{Ba} + ^{92}_{36}\text{Kr} + 3\,^{1}_{0}\text{n} + \quad \text{energy}$$

Many different products may result, but the total mass number on each side of the equation is constant.

FIGURE 3: The fission process involves neutrons.

Chain reactions

The neutrons produced in the fission of one nucleus are available to initiate fission in other nuclei. A **chain reaction** is set up.

The number of neutrons increases at each stage of the chain reaction. If this is not controlled, a huge number of neutrons and lots of energy are produced in a very short amount of time.

This rapid production of energy is what happens in a nuclear bomb. In nuclear reactors, such as those at power stations, the number of available neutrons has to be limited.

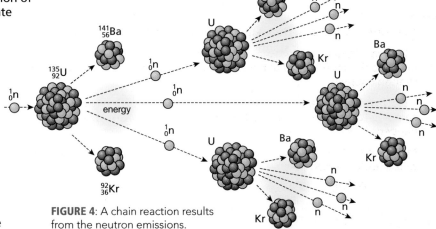

FIGURE 4: A chain reaction results from the neutron emissions.

Plutonium-239 undergoes a similar process of fission. A nucleus struck by a neutron splits into two fission fragments, nuclei of lighter elements, and two more neutrons. Each of these neutrons can then strike other plutonium nuclei.

Did you know?

It is necessary to have a critical mass of uranium for a chain reaction to be viable. If the mass is too small, neutrons leak out instead of causing fission in another uranium nucleus. The critical mass of uranium is about the size of a baseball (diameter 10 cm).

QUESTIONS

5 In this reaction the uranium-235 has fissioned into caesium and rubidium. Complete the equation and say how many neutrons were released.

$$^{235}_{92}\text{U} + ^{1}_{0}\text{n} \rightarrow ^{140}_{55}\text{Cs} + ^{93}_{37}\text{Rb} + \text{X}\,^{1}_{0}\text{n} + \text{energy}$$

6 If a chain reaction started with one fission reaction and three neutrons are produced per fission, how many neutrons would there be at the fourth fission stage?

nuclear fission simulation

Harnessing fission energy

Where was the world's first nuclear power station?

Calder Hall in Cumbria, the world's first full size nuclear power station, opened in 1957. At its peak it generated 196 MW of electricity. It was decommissioned (closed down) in 2003.

FIGURE 1: Calder Hall nuclear power station.

Nuclear power stations

About a sixth of the UK's electricity is generated in nuclear power stations. There are currently ten working nuclear power stations in various locations around the UK.

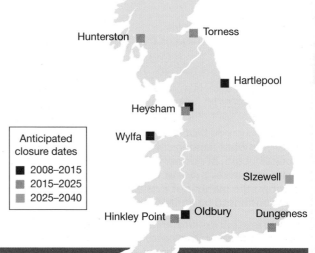

FIGURE 2: Nuclear power stations operating in England, Wales and Scotland.

Hunterston   Torness

Hartlepool

Heysham

Wylfa

Slzewell

Hinkley Point   Oldbury   Dungeness

Anticipated closure dates	
■	2008–2015
■	2015–2025
■	2025–2040

QUESTIONS

1 What do you notice about the location of the power stations?

2 How many will still be operational in 2025?

Radioactive waste

Nuclear fission produces radioactive waste. There are various ways of dealing with this depending on whether the activity of the waste is high, intermediate or low. People who have to deal with any kind of radioactive waste need protective clothing.

Low-level waste is made up of contaminated paper and clothing, for example. It is not dangerous to handle but must be disposed of with care. It is burned and placed in closed containers before being buried in landfill sites.

Q nuclear reactors   energy from fission

Intermediate-level waste consists of chemical sludges and reactor components, as well as contaminated materials from reactor decommissioning. It is more radioactive and must be shielded. Waste with a longer half-life is buried deep underground, whereas the short half-life waste, which will become safe quickly, is buried in shallow landfill sites.

High-level waste, such as spent (used up) fuel rods, contains highly radioactive fission products and requires shielding. Some of this waste is mixed with molten glass and contained in stainless steel drums before careful storage. Spent fuel rods can be reprocessed to produce more fuel, cutting down the amount of waste.

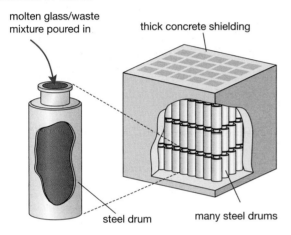

molten glass/waste mixture poured in

thick concrete shielding

steel drum

many steel drums

FIGURE 4: One method of dealing with high-level radioactive waste is in a concrete store above ground.

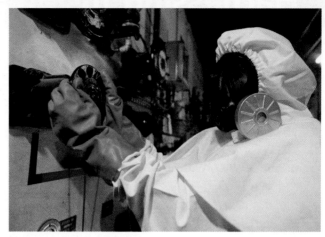

FIGURE 3: Workers at risk of exposure to high levels of radiation need full protective clothing, including breathing apparatus.

Did you know?

If the UK's reactors all operate until their shutdown dates, they will have produced enough intermediate- and high-level waste to fill 14 Olympic-sized swimming pools.

QUESTIONS

3 How do we deal with high-level radioactive waste?

4 What constitutes low-level waste? How do we deal with this?

Controlling the fission process in power stations

In a nuclear reactor the fuel, such as uranium-235, is in pellet form inside a thin **fuel rod** about 3 to 4 m long. There are many of these fuel rods in the reactor. Neutrons cause the fuel to undergo a controlled fission chain reaction (see page 277). The energy is released as kinetic energy of the resulting particles – effectively as heat. The **coolant** – gas or liquid – circulates around the reactor, absorbs the heat and transfers it, by means of a heat exchanger, to a steam generator. The rest of the process to make electricity is the same as in any other power station, using turbines and generators.

Control rods are designed to absorb neutrons and are often made of boron. In order to control the chain reaction, excess neutrons are absorbed by the control rods. Only a limited number of neutrons are allowed to continue the chain reaction. The control rods are raised or lowered to control the fission rate. If all the control rods are lowered into the reactor core, all the neutrons are absorbed and the fission process stops.

QUESTIONS

5 Explain the purpose of the coolant in a reactor core.

6 Explain the purpose of the control rods in a nuclear reactor.

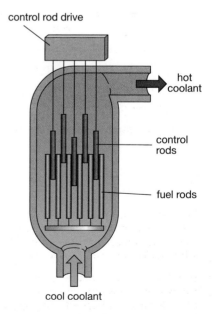

control rod drive

hot coolant

control rods

fuel rods

cool coolant

FIGURE 5: The core of a nuclear reactor.

Harnessing fusion energy

Could we use nuclear fusion to generate our electricity?

The JET project at Culham in Oxfordshire is the home of the world's first working fusion reactor. Inside the reactor, high temperature hydrogen plasma is contained magnetically, accelerated and collided to produce fusion reactions. Energy of 16 MW has been produced from this fusion.

FIGURE 1: The 'tokamak' in which the high temperature fusion fuel is contained by magnetic fields.

Fusion of hydrogen to helium

Nuclear fusion is the joining of two light nuclei to form a heavier product. Hydrogen-2 and hydrogen-3 are forms of hydrogen. (Normal hydrogen is hydrogen-1.) Under conditions of very high temperature and very high density, nuclei of hydrogen-2 and hydrogen-3 are travelling very fast, are close together, and collide frequently. Some pairs fuse, forming helium-4 and releasing a neutron. A lot of energy is released, mostly in the form of kinetic energy of the neutron.

Fusion is the process which produces energy in stars. The fusion processes in our Sun provide the Earth with light and heat energy, sustaining life.

FIGURE 2: The fusion of hydrogen-2 and hydrogen-3.

Did you know?

All heavier elements, such as carbon, are produced in fusion processes in stars. Heavy elements are formed in final stages of massive stars and are thrown out into the universe in supernovae explosions.

QUESTION

1 How do the nuclei of hydrogen-1, hydrogen-2 and hydrogen-3 differ?

Fusion and power generation

A worldwide research programme is underway to try to harness the energy of fusion in a controlled way on Earth. The challenge now is to prove that fusion can work at power-station size. The advantages of fusion energy are:

> the by-products of fusion are not radioactive

> fusion does not contribute CO_2 to the atmosphere

> it produces a lot more energy per kilogram than fossil fuels

> fuel supplies will last for millions of years; hydrogen-2 comes from water and hydrogen-3 from the Earth's crust

> the small amount of fuel needed makes this a relatively safe process.

Q Culham Centre for Fusion Education

Problems to overcome if fusion is to provide our energy

For fusion to occur, a high temperature of about 100 million °C is required. The problem is containing the hydrogen (which is **plasma** or ionised gas) at these temperatures. The tokomak is a device that does this using magnetic fields. The high-temperature plasma is contained in a doughnut shape (Figures 1 and 3) and does not touch the sides of the reactor.

At the moment it takes more energy to produce a fusion reaction, due to the high temperature and magnetic fields that are needed, than the energy it generates, but research is continuing. The research costs are enormous so the project is an international collaboration. A large fusion reactor, ITER, is being constructed in France to continue the work started at JET in the UK.

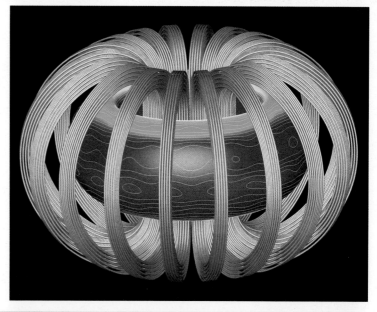

FIGURE 3: A computer model showing how the fusion reaction plasma is contained at ITER.

QUESTIONS

2 State three advantages of fusion power.

3 How can the problem of the containment of high-temperature plasmas be overcome?

Mass loss in fusion and fission (Higher tier only)

The equation for the fusion of hydrogen-2 (deuterium) and hydrogen-3 (tritium) is:

$$^2_1H \quad + \quad ^3_1H \quad \rightarrow \quad ^4_2He \quad + \quad ^1_0n \quad + \quad \text{energy}$$

deuterium + tritium → helium + neutron + energy

As we have seen (page 276), the energy produced in fusion is due to the release of some of the binding energy of the original nuclei. But what does this mean and how can we measure it?

If the total mass of the initiating particles is compared with the final total mass in a fusion or a fission reaction it will be found that there is more mass at the beginning than at the end. Where has this mass gone? According to Einstein, it has been converted to energy and we can use his equation to calculate how much energy is produced.

$E = mc^2$ is Einstein's famous equation, which defines the interchangeability of mass and energy.

E is the energy in joules, m is the mass in kilograms and c is a constant which is equal to the speed of light in a vacuum, or 3×10^8 m/s.

Finding the energy released in the deuterium–tritium fusion reaction

Total initial mass of deuterium and tritium is $8.3500523 \times 10^{-27}$ kg

Final mass of helium and neutron is $8.3187065 \times 10^{-27}$ kg

Therefore the mass lost is $0.0313458 \times 10^{-27}$ kg

To find out how much energy is released, substitute in $E = mc^2$

$E = 0.0313458 \times 10^{-27} \times (3 \times 10^8)^2 = 2.82 \times 10^{-12}$ J

QUESTIONS

4 In fission and fusion reactions, what happens to the mass?

5 In fission and fusion, the mass loss is converted to energy. Where is most of the energy after a fusion reaction? What do we use to calculate that energy?

P6 Checklist

To achieve your forecast grade in the exam you'll need to revise

Use this checklist to see what you can do now. Refer back to pages 257–281 if you're not sure. Look across the rows to see how you could progress – **bold italic** means Higher tier only.

Remember you'll need to be able to use these ideas in many ways:
> interpreting pictures, diagrams and graphs
> applying ideas to new situations
> explaining ethical implications
> suggesting some benefits and risks to society
> drawing conclusions from evidence you've been given.

Look at pages 300–306 for information about how you'll be assessed.

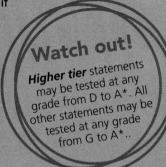

Watch out!

Higher tier statements may be tested at any grade from D to A*. All other statements may be tested at any grade from G to A*..

To aim for a grade E	To aim for a grade C	To aim for a grade A
describe how the Rutherford–Geiger–Marsden scattering experiment gave evidence for the atomic nucleus		
recall that protons and neutrons make up the nucleus of an atom and that electrons orbit the nucleus	*recall that the strong force holds the nucleus together; understand that isotopes of an element have the same number of protons but different number of neutrons*	
recall that radioactive elements give off ionising radiation; recall that background radiation is everywhere and describe the different sources		
recall that the three types of nuclear radiation are alpha, beta and gamma; recall their penetration properties and describe how to distinguish between alpha, beta and gamma radiation	*understand that alpha is a helium nucleus, beta is an electron and gamma is an electromagnetic wave*	
understand that radioactivity is a random process, unaffected by physical or chemical conditions	*describe how unstable nuclei decay to form new nuclei by alpha or beta and gamma radiation; represent isotopes using nuclear symbols*	*write complete nuclear equations for alpha and beta decay*
understand that over time the activity of radioactive sources decreases; recall that the half-life of a radioactive element is the time taken for half of the nuclei in a sample to decay	*calculate half-life from data or graphs*	

To aim for a grade E	To aim for a grade C	To aim for a grade A
recall that ionising radiation can damage living cells: higher levels may kill the cells and lower levels can cause mutations	understand that when certain atoms in the body are ionised the resulting charged ion can break apart DNA in a cell and cause damage	

use data to compare the radiation dose from different sources, interpret data on risk related to dose, and describe measures taken for the safety of people who work with radioactive sources

recall that there is a wide range of half-life values, and understand that how long a radioactive source will be considered a danger is related to its half-life

describe how ionising radiation can be used to kill cancer cells; explain the advantages of sterilising medical instruments and food	describe the beneficial uses of ionising radiation, including how tracers are used to diagnose medical conditions; understand that the best sources for various uses are selected based on their nature and half-life	
understand that a nuclear fuel releases energy; recall that the energy released by nuclear fission is much greater than that released in chemical reactions	*describe the fission reaction; explain the conditions for a chain reaction; understand the functions of fuel rods, control rods and coolant in a nuclear reactor*	*write a complete nuclear equation for a fission reaction*

recall that all nuclear power stations produce radioactive waste, and describe how low-, intermediate- and high-level wastes are dealt with

describe nuclear fusion of hydrogen nuclei	*use $E = mc^2$ to explain that the mass lost in nuclear fission and nuclear fusion results in the release of energy*	

Exam-style questions

Foundation level

1 Stewart is carrying out an experiment to find what type of radiation is emitted by a source. He carries out three tests as shown in the diagram.

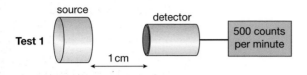

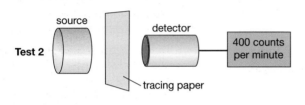

Test 3

detector — 50 counts per minute

AO3 **a** Conclude what type of radiation Stewart can be certain the source is emitting, and explain your answer. [2]

AO3 **b** How does he know that another type of radiation is being emitted? [1]

AO1 **c** Explain why the counter shows a reading when the source is removed. [1]

AO1 **d** Give one cause for this reading. [1]
[Total 5]

AO1 **2** People who work with radioactive materials on a regular basis need to be protected from their harmful effects.

a Identify three precautions they could take to reduce the risk. [3]

b State two occupations that involve a greater than average exposure to radiation. [2]
[Total 5]

Foundation/Higher level

AO1 **3** When a nuclear power station reaches the end of its useful working life it is closed down and dismantled. This is called decommissioning. Describe the kind of materials that need to be disposed of and explain how they are classified and dealt with. The quality of written communication will be assessed in your answer. [6]
[Total 6]

4 A radioactive tracer with a half-life of 30 minutes is being considered for use in medical imaging. If selected, it will be injected into patients to diagnose problems.

AO1 **a** Describe how a medical tracer works. [2]

AO3 **b** Explain the advantage of using a tracer with this half-life. [2]

AO3 **c** Explain the disadvantage of using a tracer with this half-life. [2]
[Total 6]

Higher level

5 Carbon-14 is a radioactive isotope of carbon.

AO1 **a** Explain what an isotope is. [1]

AO2 **b** Carbon-14 has a half-life of nearly 6000 years. How does this make it useful when dating archaeological specimens? [2]
[Total 3]

6 When an alpha or a beta particle is emitted, the nucleus changes into that of another atom.

	Mass	Charge	Nuclear symbol
alpha	4	2	
beta	0	−1	

AO1 **a** Copy and complete the table to show how alpha and beta radiation can be represented in nuclear notation. [2]

AO2 **b** Uranium-238 ($^{238}_{92}$U) decays by emitting an alpha particle, leaving thorium (Th). Write down the nuclear equation. [2]
[Total 4]

AO2 **7** The count rate from a radioactive source is shown in the table:

Minutes	1	2	3	4	5	6	7	8	9
Count rate/min	146	120	94	76	66	55	45	38	27

a Plot a graph of count rate against time and draw a line of best fit. [4]

b Calculate the half-life of the source. [3]
[Total 7]

AO1 recall the science   AO2 apply your knowledge   AO3 evaluate and analyse the evidence

Worked example

1 Many smoke detectors contain a small radioactive source as shown in the diagram. There is a loud alarm connected to the circuit.

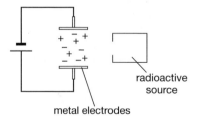

radioactive source

metal electrodes

AO1 a What type of radiation is emitted by the source? [1]

Alpha. ✔

AO2 b The radiation causes the air particles to become charged. Explain this process. [2]

The alpha particle knocks electrons from atoms in the air. ✔

AO2 c Explain what happens between the electrodes in the smoke detector when there is no smoke. [2]

A current will flow in the circuit. ✔

AO2 d Describe what changes will occur when there is smoke between the source and the electrodes. [3]

The alpha particles will be stopped by the smoke. ✔

2 Nuclear power stations can be a cause of irradiation and contamination.

AO1 a Distinguish between irradiation and contamination. [2]

Irradiation is exposure to radiation emitted by radioactive sources. The radiation is around us but does not make us radioactive. ✔

AO1 b Contaminated wastes from power stations can be of a low or a high level. Both need to be disposed of carefully but differently. What is classed as low-level waste? How can it be disposed of? [2]

Low-level waste includes clothing, paper, and other articles contaminated with short half-life radioactivity. ✔

AO1 c Explain how ionising radiation can be harmful to people. [2]

It will damage or destroy living tissue. ✔

AO3 d Considering risk and benefit, justify allowing a higher dose equivalent for workers in the nuclear industry. [2]

It is still a relatively low dose compared with doses which will cause the body harm. ✔

How to raise your grade

Take note of the comments from examiners – these will help you to improve your grade.

> Correct. Make sure you learn the properties of the different types of radiation.

> This gets 1 of the 2 marks. It should be added that this will leave positive ions.

> This is correct (1 mark) but doesn't explain why. It should state that the negative electrons will be attracted to the positive plate.

> This is true (1 mark), but insufficient detail is given for 3 marks. It should be said that no ionisation occurs, so no current will flow and the alarm will sound.

> This gets 1 mark – it explains what irradiation is but doesn't compare the two terms or identify the difference between them.

> This is an incomplete answer getting just 1 mark – it needs to include method of disposal.

> This gets just 1 mark – it doesn't explain how this happens by the formation of charged particles.

> This is true (1 mark) but doesn't refer to the benefits. It could be added that, economically, it could be considered a risk worth taking for the benefits of nuclear energy or medicine.

Carrying out practical work in GCSE Additional Science

Introduction

As part your GCSE Science course, you will develop practical skills and will carry out investigative work in science.

Investigative work can be divided into several parts:

planning, researching and formulating a hypothesis for your investigation → carrying out a risk assessment → carrying out the practical work → recording observations and measurements you have made → processing and analysing your data → drawing conclusions → evaluating your investigation → comparing your findings with those of other scientists → discussing whether you findings support your hypothesis or prediction

✳ Planning and researching your investigation

A scientific investigation usually begins with you considering an idea, answering a question, or trying to solve a problem.

Researching what other people know about the idea or problem should suggest some variables that have an effect on the problem.

From this you should develop, or 'formulate', a hypothesis. For example you might notice that plants grow faster in a heated greenhouse than an unheated greenhouse.

Your hypothesis would be that 'the rate of photosynthesis is affected by the temperature of the environment of the plant'.

You would then plan how you will carry out an investigation to test this hypothesis.

To formulate a hypothesis you may have to research some of the background science.

First of all, use your lesson notes and your textbook. The topic you've been given to investigate will relate to the science you've learnt in class.

Also make use of the internet, but make sure that your internet search is closely focused on the topic you're investigating.

Definition

A **hypothesis** is a possible explanation that someone suggests to explain some scientific observations.

Tip

When formulating a hypothesis, it's important that it's testable. In other words, you must be able to test the hypothesis in the school lab.

✔ The search terms you use on the internet are very important. 'Investigating temperature and photosynthesis' is a better search term than just 'photosynthesis', as it's more likely to provide links to websites that are more relevant to your investigation.

✔ The information on websites also varies in its reliability. Free encyclopaedias often contain information that hasn't been written by experts. Some question and answer websites might appear to give you the exact answer to your question, but be aware that they may sometimes be incorrect.

✔ Most GCSE Science websites are more reliable, but if in doubt, use other information sources to verify the information.

As a result of your research, you may be able to extend your hypothesis and make a prediction that's based on science.

Example 1

Investigation: Plan and research an investigation into the effect of temperature on the change in height of a plant over 2 weeks

Your hypothesis might be 'When I increase the temperature, the percentage increase in the height of the plant will be greater'.

You should be able to justify the hypothesis by some facts you have found. For example, 'growing lettuces in greenhouses halves the time it takes for them to be ready to sell'.

> **Tip**
> You need to use your research to explain why you made your hypothesis.

✺ Choosing a method and suitable apparatus

As part of your planning, you must choose a suitable way of carrying out the investigation.

You will have to choose suitable techniques, equipment and technology, if this is appropriate. How do you make this choice?

For most of the practical work you are likely to do, there will be a choice of techniques available. You must select the technique:

✔ that is most appropriate to the context of your investigation, and

✔ that will enable you to collect valid data, for example if you are measuring the effects of light intensity on photosynthesis, you may decide to use an LED (light-emitting diode) at different distances from the plant, rather than a light bulb. The light bulb produces more heat, and temperature is another independent variable in photosynthesis.

Your choice of equipment, too, will be influenced by measurements you need to make. For example:

✔ you might use a one-mark or graduated pipette to measure out the volume of liquid for a titration, but

✔ you may use a measuring cylinder or beaker when adding a volume of acid to a reaction mixture, so that the volume of acid is in excess to that required to dissolve, for example, the calcium carbonate.

> **Tip**
> Technology, such as data-logging and other measuring and monitoring techniques, for example heart sensors, may help you to carry out your experiment.

> **Tip**
> Carrying out a preliminary investigation, along with the necessary research, may help you to select the appropriate technique to use.

 Variables

In your investigation, you will work with factors which may affect an outcome.

The factors you choose, or are given, to investigate the effect of are called input variables or **independent variables**.

What you choose to measure, as affected by the independent variable, is called the outcome variable or **dependent variable**.

Independent variables

In your practical work, you will be provided with an independent variable to test, or will have to choose one – or more – of these to test. Some examples are given in the table.

Investigation	Possible independent variables to test
activity of amylase enzyme	> temperature > sugar concentration
rate of a chemical reaction	> temperature > concentration of reactants
stopping distance of a moving object	> speed of the object > the surface on which it's moving

Independent variables can be **discrete** or **continuous**.

> When you are testing the effect of different disinfectants on bacteria you are looking at discrete variables.

> When you are testing the effect of a range of concentrations of the same disinfectant on the growth of bacteria you are looking at continuous variables.

Range

When working with an independent variable, you need to choose an appropriate **range** over which to investigate the variable.

You need to decide:

✔ which variables you will test, and/or

✔ the upper and lower limits of the independent variable to investigate.

Once you have defined the range to be tested, you also need to decide the appropriate intervals at which you will make measurements.

The range you would test depends on:

✔ the nature of the test

✔ the context in which it is given

✔ practical considerations, and

✔ common sense.

Definition

Variables that fall into a range of separate types are called **discrete variables**.

Definition

Variables that have a continuous range, or are numeric, are called **continuous variables**.

Definition

The **range** defines the extent of the independent variables being tested, for example from 15 cm to 35 cm.

Example 2

1 Investigation: Investigating the factors that affect how quickly a weak acid works to remove limescale from an appliance

You may have to decide which acids to use from a range you're provided with. You would choose a weak acid, or weak acids, to test, rather than a strong acid, such as concentrated sulfuric acid. This is because of safety reasons, but also because the acid might damage the appliance you were trying to clean. You would then have to select a range of concentrations of your chosen weak acid to test.

2 Investigation: How speed affects the stopping distance of a trolley in the lab

The range of speeds you would choose would clearly depend on the speeds you could produce in the lab.

Temperature as an independent variable

You might be trying to find out the best temperature for growing tomatoes.

The 'best' temperature will differ, depending on the value of a number of other variables that, taken together, would produce tomatoes as fast as possible whilst not being too costly.

You should limit your investigation to just one variable, temperature, and then consider other variables such as fuel cost later.

✳ Dependent variables

The dependent variable may be clear from the problem you're investigating, for example the stopping distance of moving objects. But you may have to make a choice.

Example 3

1 Investigation: Measuring the rate of photosynthesis in a plant

There are several ways in which you could measure the rate of photosynthesis in a plant. These include:

> counting the number of bubbles of oxygen produced in a minute by a water plant such as *Elodea* or *Cabomba*

> measuring the volume of oxygen produced over several days by a water plant such as *Elodea* or *Cabomba*

> monitoring the concentration of oxygen in a polythene bag enclosing a potted plant using an oxygen sensor

> measuring the colour change of hydrogencarbonate indicator containing algae embedded in gel.

2 Investigation: Measuring the rate of a chemical reaction

You could measure the rate of a chemical reaction in the following ways:

> the rate of formation of a product

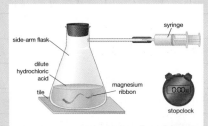

> the rate at which the reactant disappears

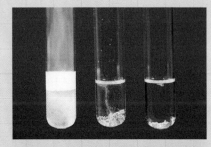

> a colour change

> a pH change.

✳ Control variables

The validity of your measurements depends on you measuring what you're supposed to be measuring.

Other variables that you're not investigating may also have an influence on your measurements. In most investigations, it's important that you investigate just one variable at a time. For a 'fair test', other variables, apart from the one you're testing at the time, must be kept constant. These are called **control variables**.

Some of these variables may be difficult to control. For example, in an ecology investigation in the field, factors such as varying weather conditions are impossible to control.

Experimental controls

Experimental controls are often very important, particularly in biological investigations where you're testing the effect of a treatment.

Example 4

Investigation: The effect of temperature on the growth of tomato plants

The tomato plants grow most at 35 °C, but some plants at lower temperatures grow just as well. You need to be certain that the effect is caused by the temperature. There are lots of things that affect plant growth, so you should make sure these variables are controlled. These include the volume of water they receive, the soil that the plants are grown in, the nutrients present in the soil, and that the plants are as genetically similar as possible. Farmers often use f1 hybrid seeds as the plants are virtually genetically identical and will be ready to harvest at the same time.

> **Definition**
>
> An **experimental control** is used to find out whether the effect you obtain is from the treatment, or whether you get the same result in the absence of the treatment.

✳ Identifying hazards and managing risk

Before you begin any practical work, you must assess and minimise the possible risks involved.

Before you carry out an investigation, you must identify the possible **hazards**. These can be grouped into biological hazards, chemical hazards and physical hazards.

Biological hazards include:	**Chemical hazards can be grouped into:**	**Physical hazards include:**
> microorganisms > body fluids > animals and plants.	> irritant and harmful substances > toxic > oxidising agents > corrosive > harmful to the environment.	> equipment > objects > radiation.

Scientists use an international series of symbols so that investigators can identify hazards.

Hazards pose **risks** to the person carrying out the investigation.

A risk posed by chlorine gas produced in the electrolysis of sodium chloride, for example, will be reduced if you increase the ventilation of the process, or devise a method to remove the gas so that workers cannot inhale it.

When you use hazardous materials, chemicals or equipment in the laboratory, you must use them in such a way as to keep the risks to an absolute minimum. For example, one way is to wear eye protection when using hydrochloric acid.

> **Definition**
>
> A **hazard** is something that has the potential to cause harm. Even substances, organisms and equipment that we think of as being harmless, used in the wrong way may be hazardous.

Hazard symbols are used on chemical bottles so that hazards can be identified.

> **Definition**
>
> The **risk** is the likelihood of a hazard to cause harm in the circumstances of its use.

✹ Risk assessment

Before you begin an investigation, you must carry out a risk assessment. Your risk assessment must include:

✔ all relevant hazards (use the correct terms to describe each hazard, and make sure you include them all, even if you think they will pose minimal risk)

✔ risks associated with these hazards

✔ ways in which the risks can be minimised

✔ whether or not it is appropriate to proceed with the investigation as planned, bearing in mind the hazards, the risks and the necessary management procedures

✔ results of research into emergency procedures that you may have to take if something goes wrong.

You should also consider what to do at the end of the practical. For example, used agar plates should be left for a technician to sterilise; solutions of heavy metals should be collected in a bottle and disposed of safely.

Tip

To make sure that your risk assessment is full and appropriate:

> remember that for a chemical reaction, the risk assessment should be carried out for the products and the reactants

> when using chemicals, make sure the hazard and ways of minimising risk match the concentration of the chemical you're using; many acids, for instance, while being corrosive in higher concentrations, are harmful or irritant at low concentrations.

✹ Collecting primary data

✔ You should make sure that observations, if appropriate, are recorded in detail. For example, it is worth recording the colour of your precipitate when making an insoluble salt, in addition to any other measurements you make.

✔ Measurement should be recorded in tables. Have one ready so that you can record your readings as you carry out the practical work.

✔ Think about the dependent variable and define this carefully in your column headings.

✔ You should make sure that the table headings describe properly the type of measurements you've made, for example 'time taken for magnesium ribbon to dissolve'.

✔ It's also essential that you include units – your results are meaningless without these.

✔ The units should appear in the column head, and not be repeated in each row of the table.

Definition

When you carry out an investigation, the data you collect are called **primary data.** The term 'data' is normally used to include your observations as well as measurements you might make.

✹ Repeatability and reproducibility of results

When making measurements, in most instances, it's essential that you carry out repeats.

	Test 1	Test 2	Test 3

These repeats are one way of checking your results. One set of results from your investigation may not reflect what truly happens. Carrying out repeats enables you to identify any results that don't fit.

Results will not be repeatable of course, if you allow the conditions the investigation is carried out in to change.

Definition

A reading that is very different from the rest, is called an anomalous result, or **outlier**.

Definition

If, when you carry out the same experiment several times, and get the same, or very similar results, we say the results are **repeatable**.

You need to make sure that you carry out sufficient repeats, but not too many. In a titration, for example, if you obtain two values that are within 0.1 cm³ of each other, carrying out any more will not improve the reliability of your results.

This is particularly important when scientists are carrying out scientific research and make new discoveries.

✳ Processing data

Calculating the mean

Using your repeat measurements you can calculate the arithmetical mean (or just 'mean') of these data. We often refer to the mean as the 'average'.

You may also be required to use formulae when processing data.

Significant figures

When calculating the mean, you should be aware of significant figures.

For example, for the set of data below:

18	13	17	15	14	16	15	14	13	18

The total for the data set is 153, and ten measurements have been made. The mean is 15, and not 15.3.

This is because each of the recorded values has two significant figures. The answer must therefore have two significant figures. An answer cannot have more significant figures than the number being multiplied or divided.

Using your data

When calculating means (and displaying data), you should be careful to look out for any data that don't fit in with the general pattern.

An outlier might be the consequence of an error made in measurement, but sometimes outliers are genuine results. If you think an outlier has been introduced by careless practical work, you should ignore it when calculating the mean. But you should examine possible reasons carefully before just leaving it out.

Example 5

Here are the results of an investigation into the energy requirements of three different mp3 players. The students measured the energy using a joulemeter for ten seconds.

mp3 player	Energy used in joules (J)			
	Trial 1	Trial 2	Trial 3	Mean
Viking	5.5	5.3	5.7	5.5
Anglo	4.5	4.6	4.9	4.7
Saxon	3.2	4.5	4.7	4.6

Note that one result (3.2) has been excluded from the mean calculation because it was more than 10% lower than the other values, and so considered an outlier.

Displaying your data

Displaying your data – usually the mean values – makes it easy to pick out and show any patterns. And it also helps you to pick out any anomalous data.

It is likely that you will have recorded your results in tables, and you could also use additional tables to summarise your results. The most usual way of displaying data is to use graphs. The table will help you decide which type to use.

Type of graph	When you would use the graph	Example
Bar charts or bar graph	Where one of the variables is discrete	'The energy requirements of different mp3 players'
Line graph	Where independent and dependent variables are both continuous	'The volume of carbon dioxide produced by a range of different concentrations of hydrochloric acid'
Scatter graph	To show an association between two (or more) variables	'The association between length and breadth of a number of privet leaves' In scatter graphs, the points are plotted, but not usually joined

It should be possible from the data to join the points of a line graph using a single straight line or using a curve. In this way, graphs can also help you to understand the relationship between the independent variable and the dependent variable.

Tip

Remember when drawing graphs, plot the independent variable on the x-axis, and the dependent variable on the y-axis.

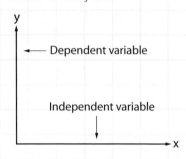

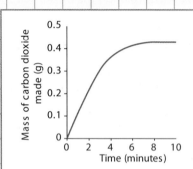

We can calculate the rate of production of carbon dioxide from the gradient of the graph.

✹ Variation in data

Plotting a graph of just the means doesn't tell you anything about the spread of data that has been used to calculate the mean.

You can show the spread or range of the data on your graphs using error bars or range bars.

Range bars are very useful, but they don't show how the data are spread between the extreme values. It is important to have information about this range. It may affect the analysis you do of the data, and the conclusions you draw.

Scientists use a number of techniques to look at the spread of data. You could refer to the work that you've done in Maths to look at some of these techniques.

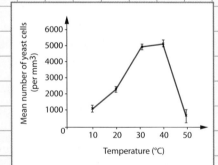

Range bars indicate the spread or range of values.

Conclusions from differences in data sets

When comparing two (or more) sets of data, we often compare the values of two sets of means.

Example 6

Investigation: Comparing the braking distance of two tyres

Two groups of students compared the braking distance of two tyres, labelled A and B. Their results are shown in the table.

Tyre	Braking distance (m)										Mean (m)
	1	2	3	4	5	6	7	8	9	10	
A	15	13	17	15	14	16	15	14	13	18	15
B	25	23	24	23	26	27	25	24	23	22	24

When the means are compared, it appears that tyre A will bring a vehicle to a stop in a shorter distance than tyre B. The difference might have resulted from some other factor, or could be purely by chance.

Scientists use statistics to find the probability of any differences having occurred by chance. The lower this probability is, which is found out by statistical calculations, the more likely it is that tyre A is better at stopping a vehicle than tyre B.

Statistical analysis can help to increase the confidence you have in your conclusions.

> **Tip**
>
> You have learnt about probability in your Maths lessons.

> **Definition**
>
> If there is a relationship between dependent and independent variables that can be defined, we say there is a **correlation** between the variables.

Drawing conclusions

Observing trends in data or graphs will help you to draw conclusions. You may obtain a linear relationship between two sets of variables, or the relationship might be more complex.

Example 7

Conclusion from graph A: The higher the concentration of acid, the shorter the time taken for the magnesium ribbon to dissolve.

Conclusion from graph B: The higher the concentration of acid, the faster the rate of reaction.

When drawing conclusions, you should try to relate your findings to the science involved.

> In investigation A in Example 7, your discussion should focus on the greater possibility/increased frequency of collisions between reacting particles as the concentration of the acid is increased.

> In investigation B in Example 7, there's a clear scientific mechanism to link the rate of reaction to the concentration of acid.

But we sometimes see correlations between data in science which are coincidental, where the independent variable is not the *cause* of the trend in the data.

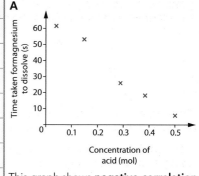

This graph shows **negative correlation**.

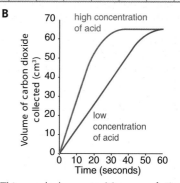

This graph shows **positive correlation**.

✳ Evaluating your investigation

Your conclusion will be based on your findings, but must take into consideration any uncertainty in these introduced by any possible sources of error. You should discuss where these have come from in your evaluation.

The two types of errors are:

✔ random error   ✔ systematic error.

Errors can occur when the instrument you're using to measure lacks sufficient sensitivity to indicate differences in readings. They can also occur when it's difficult to make a measurement. If two investigators measure the height of a plant, for example, they might choose different points on the compost, and the tip of the growing point to make their measurements.

Measurements can be either consistently too high or too low. One reason could be down to the way you are making a reading, for example taking a burette reading at the wrong point on the meniscus. Another could be the result of an instrument being incorrectly calibrated, or not being calibrated.

The volume of liquid in a burette must be read to the bottom of the meniscus.

Definition

Error is a difference between a measurement you make, and its true value.

Definition

With **random error**, measurements vary in an unpredictable way, for example when measuring the length of an object that is moving.

Definition

With **systematic error**, readings vary in a controlled way, for example, measuring the length of something with a ruler that was incorrectly calibrated.

Tip

What you shouldn't discuss in your evaluation are problems introduced by using faulty equipment, or by you using the equipment inappropriately. These errors can, or could have been, eliminated, by:

> the checking of equipment

> practising techniques beforehand

> taking care and being patient when carrying out the practical.

✳ Accuracy and precision

When evaluating your investigation, you might mention accuracy or precision. But if you use these terms, it's important that you understand what they mean, and that you use them correctly. The terms accuracy and precision can be illustrated using shots at a dartboard.

precise but not accurate

precise and accurate

imprecise and inaccurate

Definition

When making measurements:
> the **accuracy** of the measurement is how close it is to the true value

> **precision** is how closely a series of measurements agree with each other.

✳ Improving your investigation

When evaluating your investigation, you should discuss how your investigation could be improved. This could be by improving:

✔ the reliability of your data. For example, you could make more repeats, or more frequent readings, or 'fine-tune' the range you investigate, or refine your technique in some other way

✔ the accuracy and precision of your data, by using more precise measuring equipment.

In science, the measurements you make as part of your investigation should be as precise as you can, or need to, make them. To achieve this, you should use:

✔ the most appropriate measuring instrument
✔ the measuring instrument with the most appropriate scale.

The smaller the scale divisions you work with, the more precise your measurements. For example:

✔ in an investigation on how your heart rate is affected by exercise, you might decide to investigate this after a 100 m run. You might measure out the 100 m distance using a trundle wheel, which is sufficiently precise for your investigation

✔ in an investigation on how light intensity is affected by distance, you would make your measurements of distance using a metre rule with millimetre divisions; clearly a trundle wheel would be too imprecise

✔ in an investigation on plant growth, in which you measure the thickness of a plant stem, you would use a micrometer or Vernier callipers. A metre rule would be too imprecise.

✳ Using secondary data

Another method of evaluation is to compare your data – primary data – with **secondary data**. One of the simplest ways of doing this is to compare your data with data from other members of your class who have carried out an identical practical investigation. In your controlled assessment you will be provided with a data sheet of relevant secondary data.

You should also, if possible, search through the scientific literature – in textbooks, the internet, and databases, to find data from similar or identical practical investigations so that you can compare the data with yours.

Ideally, you should use secondary data from a number of sources, carry out a full analysis of the data you have collected, and compare the findings with your own. You should critically analyse any evidence that conflicts with yours, and suggest what further data might help to make your conclusions more secure.

You should review secondary data and evaluate it. Scientific studies are sometimes influenced by the **bias** of the experimenter.

✔ One kind of bias is having a strong opinion related to the investigation, and perhaps selecting only the results that fit with a hypothesis or prediction.

✔ Or the bias could be unintentional. In fields of science that are not yet fully understood, experimenters may try to fit their findings to current knowledge and thinking.

In other instances the 'findings' of experimenters have been influenced by organisations that supplied funding for the research.

You must reference secondary data you have used (see page 298).

Definition

Secondary data are measurements or observations made by anyone other than you.

Referencing methods

The two main conventions for writing a reference are the:

✔ Harvard system
✔ Vancouver system.

In your text, the Harvard system refers to the authors of the reference, for example 'Smith and Jones (1978)'.

The Vancouver system refers to the number of the numbered reference in your text, for example '... the reason for this hypothesis is unknown[5]'.

Though the Harvard system is usually preferred by scientists, it is more straightforward for you to use the Vancouver system.

Harvard system

In your references list a book reference should be written:

> Author(s) (year of publication). *Title of Book*, publisher, publisher location.

The references are listed in alphabetical order according to the authors.

Vancouver system

In your references list a book reference should be written:

> 1 Author(s). *Title of Book*. Publisher, publisher location: year of publication.

The references are numbered in the order in which they are cited in the text.

> **Tip**
>
> Remember to write out the URL of a website in full. You should also quote the date when you looked at the website.

Do the data support your hypothesis?

You need to discuss, in detail, whether all, or which of your primary data, and the secondary data you have collected, support your original hypothesis. They may, or may not.

If your data do not completely match your hypothesis, it may be possible to modify the hypothesis or suggest an alternative one. You should suggest any further investigations that can be carried out to support your original hypothesis or the modified version.

It is important to remember, however, that if your investigation does support your hypothesis, it can improve the confidence you have in your conclusions and scientific explanations, but it can't prove your explanations are correct.

> **Tip**
>
> Make sure you relate your conclusions to the hypothesis you are investigating. Do the results confirm or reject the hypothesis? Quote some results to back up your statement, for example 'My results at 35 °C and 65 °C show that over a 30 degree change in temperature the time taken to produce $50\,cm^3$ of carbon dioxide halved'.

> **Tip**
>
> Communicate your points clearly, using the appropriate scientific terms, and checking carefully your use of spelling, punctuation and grammar. Your quality of written communication is important, as well as your science.

Controlled assessment in GCSE 21st Century Science

Introduction

The controlled assessment task for each of these GCSE courses: Additional Science, Biology, Chemistry and Physics, is a practical investigation. It is worth 25% of the total marks, so it is important to do it well.

Investigations are central to the nature of science as an evidence-based activity, and practical investigations provide an effective assessment method. Your ability to formulate a hypothesis and to explain patterns in results will be related to your knowledge and understanding of the topic.

✳ Controlled assessment

In the controlled assessment you will need to:

✔ develop a hypothesis

✔ plan practical ways to test your hypothesis

✔ do and record a risk assessment for the procedures you plan to use

✔ manage the risks when carrying out the practical work

✔ collect primary data

✔ process, analyse and interpret your primary data and also secondary data

✔ draw evidence-based conclusions

✔ evaluate the reliability of your data and review the effectiveness of your procedures

✔ review your hypothesis in the light of your results.

The task provided will be open-ended and investigative in nature. At the start of a task, you will be given a sheet about the topic of the investigation, putting the task into a wider context. You need to use the information provided to plan how to collect data, including any preliminary work required, and to develop a testable hypothesis before carrying out the investigation.

After you have collected primary data, you will be given a sheet of secondary data for analysis. You need to interpret and evaluate your own data, and also analyse relevant secondary data. As well as the sheet of secondary data provided, you may include experimental results from other students, as well as information from textbooks and websites.

You need to use your results and your comparison of these with secondary data to develop and evaluate your conclusions, and finally review your original hypothesis.

Your written report of the completed work will be presented for assessment.

Tip

Pages 286–298 give guidelines on all these investigative skills.

Tip

Work through the 'Preparing for assessment' tasks in each module of this book to help build your skills for your controlled assessment.

How to be successful in your GCSE Additional Science exam

Introduction

OCR uses assessments to test your understanding of scientific ideas, how well you can apply your understanding to new situations and how well you can analyse and interpret information you've been given. The assessments are opportunities to show how well you can do these things.

To be successful in exams you need to:

✔ have a good knowledge and understanding of science

✔ be able to apply this knowledge and understanding to familiar and new situations, and

✔ be able to interpret and evaluate evidence that you've just been given.

You need to be able to do these things under exam conditions.

✺ The language of external assessment

When working through an assessment paper, make sure that you:

✔ re-read the question enough times until you understand exactly what the examiner is looking for

✔ highlight key words in the question. In some instances, you will be given key words to include in your answer

✔ look at how many marks are allocated for each part of the question. In general, you need to write at least as many separate points in your answer as there are marks.

✺ What verbs are used in the question?

A good technique is to see which verbs are used in the wording of the question and to use these to gauge the type of response you need to give. The table lists some of the common verbs found in questions, the types of responses expected and then gives an example.

Verb used in question	Response expected in answer	Example question
> write down > state > give > identify	These are usually more straightforward types of question in which you're asked to give a definition, make a list of examples, or select the best answer from a series of options	'Write down three types of microorganism that cause disease' 'State one difference and one similarity between radio waves and gamma rays'
calculate	Use maths to solve a numerical problem	'Calculate the percentage of carbon in copper carbonate'

estimate	Use maths to solve a numerical problem, but you do not have to work out the exact answer	'Estimate from the graph the speed of the car after 3 minutes'
describe	Use words (or diagrams) to show the characteristics, properties or features of, or build an image, of something	'Describe how meiosis halves the number of chromosomes in a cell to make egg or sperm cells'
suggest	Come up with an idea to explain information you're given	'Suggest why eating fast foods, rather than wholegrain foods, could increase the risk of obesity'
> demonstrate > show how	Use words to make something evident using reasoning	'Show how enzyme activity changes with temperature'
compare	Look for similarities and differences	'Compare aerobic and anaerobic respiration'
explain	Offer a reason for, or make understandable, information you're given	'Explain why alpha and beta radiations are deflected in opposite directions by a magnetic field'
justify	Give reason(s) for a conclusion, or statement(s) to back up an opinion	'Which person's idea gives the best explanation? Justify your response'
evaluate	Examine and make a judgement about an investigation or information you're given	'Evaluate the evidence for vaccines causing harm to human health'

✳ What is the style of the question?

Try to get used to answering questions that have been written in lots of different styles before you sit the exam. Work through past papers, or specimen papers, to get a feel for these. The types of questions in your assessment fit the three assessment objectives shown in the table.

Assessment objective	Your answer should show that you can...
AO1 Recall the science	Recall, select and communicate your knowledge and understanding of science
AO2 Apply your knowledge	Apply skills, knowledge and understanding of science in practical and other contexts
AO3 Evaluate and analyse the evidence	Analyse and evaluate evidence, make reasoned judgements and draw conclusions based on evidence

Tip

Of course you must revise the subject material adequately. But it's as important that you are familiar with the different question styles used in the exam paper, as well as the question content.

☀ How to answer questions on: AO1 Recall the science

These questions, or parts of questions, test your ability to recall your knowledge of a topic or a process. There are several types of this style of question:

✔ Fill in the spaces (you may be given words to choose from)

✔ Tick the correct statements or use lines to link a term with its definition or correct statement

✔ Add labels to a diagram or complete a table

✔ Describe a process

✔ Explain observations

✔ Write a full account or explanation of a topic or a process

To revise for these types of questions, make sure that you have learnt definitions and scientific terms. Produce a glossary of these, or key facts cards, to make them easier to remember. Make sure your key facts cards also cover important practical techniques.

> **Tip**
>
> Don't forget that mind maps – either drawn by you or by using a computer program – are very helpful when revising key points.

Example 1

1 What is meant by the term *exothermic reaction*?

Tick (✓) **one** box.

☐ a reaction that gives out heat energy

☐ a reaction that takes in energy form the surroundings

☐ a reaction that can go in either direction

2 Describe how to measure the resistance of an electrical component.

☀ How to answer questions on: AO2 Apply skills, knowledge and understanding

Some questions require you to apply basic knowledge and understanding in your answers.

You may be presented with a topic that's familiar to you, but you should also expect questions in your Additional Science exam to be set in an unfamiliar context.

Questions may be presented as:

✔ experimental investigations

✔ data for you to interpret and analyse

✔ a short paragraph or article.

The information required for you to answer the question might be in the question itself, but for later stages of the question, you may be asked to draw on your knowledge and understanding of the subject material in the question.

You may be expected to describe patterns in data from graphs you are given or that you have drawn from given data.

Practice will help you to become familiar with some contexts that examiners use and common question styles. But you will not be able to predict all of the contexts used. This is deliberate; being able to apply your knowledge and understanding to different and unfamiliar situations is a skill the examiner tests.

Practise doing questions where you are tested on being able to apply your scientific knowledge and on your ability to understand new and unfamiliar situations. In this way, when this type of question comes up in your exam, you will be able to tackle it successfully.

Example 2

Look at the graph showing the volume of gas collected when 10g of calcium carbonate is reacted with three different concentrations of hydrochloric acid.

a What is the maximum volume of gas that can be produced using 1 mole per dm^3 of hydrochloric acid?

b Explain why this volume of gas is produced quicker when using 2 moles per dm^3 of hydrochloric acid.

c Suggest why 0.5 mole per dm^3 of hydrochloric acid does not produce this volume of gas.

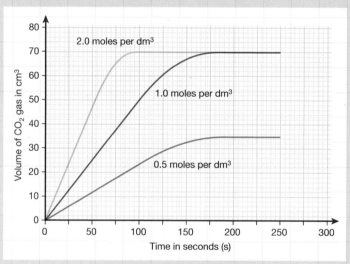

You will also need to analyse scientific evidence or data given to you in the question. Analysing data may involve drawing graphs and interpreting them, and carrying out calculations. Practise drawing and interpreting graphs from data.

When drawing a graph, make sure you:

✔ choose and label the axes fully and correctly

✔ include units, if this hasn't been done for you already

✔ plot points on the graph carefully – the examiner will check individual points to make sure that they are accurate

✔ join the points correctly; usually this will be by a line of best fit.

When reading values off a graph you have drawn or one given in the question, make sure you:

✔ do it carefully, reading the values as accurately as you can

✔ double-check the values.

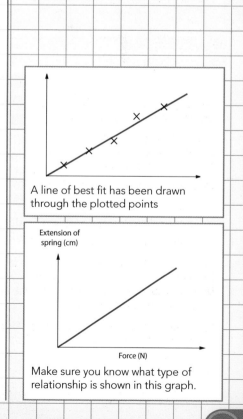

A line of best fit has been drawn through the plotted points

Make sure you know what type of relationship is shown in this graph.

When describing patterns and trends in the data, make sure you:

✔ write about a pattern or trend in as much detail as you can

✔ mention anomalies where appropriate

✔ recognise there may be one general trend in the graph, where the variables show positive or negative correlation

✔ recognise the data may show a more complex relationship. The graph may demonstrate different trends in several sections. You should describe what's happening in each

✔ describe fully what the data show.

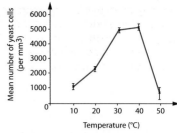

What type of relationship does this graph show?

✳ How to answer questions needing calculations

✔ The calculations you're asked to do may be straightforward, for example the calculation of the mean from a set of practical data.

✔ Or they may be more complex, for example calculating the yield of a chemical reaction.

✔ Other questions will require the use of formulae. These are often given to you on the question paper, but sometimes you will be expected to recall and use these.

Remember, this is the same maths that you learnt in your Maths lessons.

Example 3

A parachutist with a mass of 75 kg is taken up 3000 metres in an aircraft. Calculate the parachutist's gravitational potential energy on leaving the plane. Assume the gravitational field strength is 9.8 N/kg.

Tip

Check the specification, or with your teacher, to make sure that you know the formulae that you have to learn and remember.

Tip

Remember, when carrying out any calculations, you should include your working at each stage. You may get credit for getting the process correct, even if your final answer is wrong.

Tip

When completing your calculation, make sure you include the correct units.

✳ How to answer questions on: AO3 Analysing and evaluating evidence

For these types of questions, in addition to analysing data, you must also be able to evaluate the information you're given. This is one of the hardest skills. Think about the validity of the scientific data: did the technique(s) used in any practical investigation allow the collection of accurate and precise data?

Your critical evaluation of scientific data in class will help you to develop the evaluation skills required for these types of questions.

Example 4

Explain reasons why it may be beneficial to produce chlorine gas by the electrolysis of a sodium chloride solution, rather than the electrolysis of molten sodium chloride.

You may be expected to compare data with other data, or come to a conclusion about its reliability, its usefulness or its implications. Again, it is possible that you won't be familiar with the context. You may be asked to make a judgement about the evidence or to give an opinion with reasons.

✳ The quality of your written communication

Scientists need good communication skills to present and discuss their findings. You will be expected to demonstrate these skills in the exam. Some questions will end with the sentence: The quality of written communication will be assessed in your answer to this question. It will be worth 6 marks.

✔ You must try to make sure that your writing is legible and your spelling, punctuation and grammar are accurate, so that it's clear what you mean in your answer. Examiners can't award marks for answers where the meaning isn't clear. When describing and explaining science, use correct scientific vocabulary.

✔ You must present your information in a form that suits its purpose: for example, a series of paragraphs, with lists or a table if appropriate, and a conclusion if required. Use subheadings where they will be helpful.

✔ You must use a suitable structure and style of writing: ensure that in continuous text you use complete sentences. Remember the writing skills you've developed in English lessons. For example, make sure that you know how to construct a good sentence using connectives.

Practise answering some 'quality of written communication (QWC)' questions. Look at how marks are awarded in mark schemes. You'll find these in the specimen question papers, and past papers.

> **Tip**
>
> You will be assessed on the way in which you communicate science ideas.

> **Tip**
>
> There are worked examples of these questions on pages 129 and 161.

Example mark scheme

For 5–6 marks:
Ideas about the topic are correctly described and correctly used to explain it. All information in answer is relevant, clear, organised and presented in a structured and coherent format. Specialist terms are used appropriately. Few, if any, errors in grammar, punctuation and spelling.

For 3–4 marks:
Some aspects of the topic are correctly described, but only some are made use of in explaining it. For the most part information is relevant and presented in a structured and coherent format. Specialist terms are used for the most part appropriately. There are occasional errors in grammar, punctuation and spelling.

For 1–2 marks:
Some aspects of the topic are correctly described, but not used to explain it. Answer may be simplistic. There may be limited use of specialist terms. Errors of punctuation, grammar and spelling hinder communication of the science.

0 marks:
Insufficient or irrelevant science. Answer not worthy of credit.

Revising for your Additional Science exam

You should revise in the way that suits you best. But it's important that you plan your revision carefully, and it's best to start well before the date of the exams. Take the time to prepare a revision timetable and try to stick to it. Use this during the lead up to the exams and between each exam.

When revising:

✔ find a quiet and comfortable space in the house where you won't be disturbed. It's best if it's well ventilated and has plenty of light

✔ take regular breaks. Some evidence suggests that revision is most effective when you revise in 30 to 40 minute slots. If you get bogged down at any point, take a break and go back to it later when you're feeling fresh. Try not to revise when you are feeling tired. If you do feel tired, take a break

✔ use your school notes, textbook and possibly a revision guide. But also make sure that you spend some time using past papers to familiarise yourself with the exam format

✔ produce summaries of each module

✔ draw mind maps covering the key information in a module

✔ make revision cards containing condensed versions of your notes

✔ ask yourself questions, and try to predict questions, as you're revising modules

✔ test yourself as you're going along. Try to draw important labelled diagrams, and try some questions under timed conditions

✔ prioritise your revision of topics. You might want to allocate more time to revising the topics you find most difficult.

> **Tip**
>
> Try to make your revision timetable as specific as possible – don't just say 'science on Monday, and Thursday', but list the topics that you'll cover on those days.

> **Tip**
>
> Start your revision well before the date of the exams, produce a revision timetable, and use the revision strategies that suit your style of learning. Above all, revision should be an active process.

How do I use my time effectively in the exam?

Timing is important when you sit an exam. Don't spend so long on some questions that you leave insufficient time to answer others. For example, in a 60-mark question paper, lasting one hour, you will have, on average, one minute per question.

If you're unsure about certain questions, complete the ones you're able to do first, then go back to the ones you're less sure of.

If you have time, go back and check your answers at the end of the exam.

✹ On exam day...

A little bit of nervousness before your exam can be a good thing, but try not to let it affect your performance in the exam. When you turn over the exam paper keep calm. Look at the paper and get it clear in your head exactly what is required from each question. Read each question carefully. Don't rush.

If you read a question and think that you have not covered the topic, keep calm – it could be that the information needed to answer the question is in the question itself or the examiner may be asking you to apply your knowledge to a new situation.

Finally, good luck!

Data sheet

Fundamental physical quantity	Unit(s)
length	metre (m); kilometre (km); centimetre (cm); millimetre (mm); nanometre (nm)
mass	kilogram (kg); gram (g); milligram (mg)
time	second (s); millisecond (ms); year (a); million years (Ma); billion years (Ga)
temperature	degree Celsius (°C); kelvin (K)
current	ampere (A); milliampere (mA)

Derived physical quantity	Unit(s)
area	cm^2; m^2
volume	cm^3; dm^3; m^3; litre (l); millilitre (ml)
density	kg/m^3; g/cm^3
speed, velocity	m/s; km/h
acceleration	m/s^2
momentum	kg m/s
force	newton (N)
energy	joule (J); kilojoule (kJ); megajoule (MJ); kilowatt hour (kWh); megawatt hour (MWh)
power	watt (W); kilowatt (kW); megawatt (MW)
frequency	hertz (Hz); kilohertz (kHz)
information	bytes (B); kilobytes (kB); megabytes (MB)
p.d. (voltage)	volt (V)
resistance	ohm (Ω)
radiation dose	sievert (Sv)

Prefixes for units

nano (n)	one thousand millionth	0.000 000 001	$\times 10^{-9}$
micro (μ)	one millionth	0.000 001	$\times 10^{-6}$
milli (m)	one thousandth	0.001	$\times 10^{-3}$
kilo (k)	× one thousand	1 000	$\times 10^{3}$
mega (M)	× one million	1 000 000	$\times 10^{6}$
giga (G)	× one thousand million	1 000 000 000	$\times 10^{9}$
tera (T)	× one million million	1 000 000 000 000	$\times 10^{12}$

Useful equations

speed = distance travelled ÷ time taken

acceleration = change in velocity ÷ time taken

momentum = mass × velocity

change of momentum = resultant force × time it acts

change in gravitational potential energy = weight × height difference

kinetic energy = ½ × mass × [velocity]^2

resistance = voltage × current

energy transferred = power × time

electrical power = voltage × current

efficiency = (energy usefully transferred ÷ total energy supplied) × 100%

continued

Tests for negatively charged ions

Ion	Test	Observation
carbonate CO_3^{2-}	add dilute acid	effervesces, and carbon dioxide gas produced (the gas turns lime water milky)
chloride (in solution) Cl^-	acidify with dilute nitric acid, then add silver nitrate solution	white precipitate
bromide (in solution) Br^-	acidify with dilute nitric acid, then add silver nitrate solution	cream precipitate
iodide (in solution) I^-	acidify with dilute nitric acid, then add silver nitrate solution	yellow precipitate
sulfate (in solution) SO_4^{2-}	acidify, then add barium chloride solution or barium nitrate solution	white precipitate

Tests for positively charged ions

Ion	Test	Observation
calcium Ca^{2+}	add sodium hydroxide solution	white precipitate (insoluble in excess)
copper Cu^{2+}	add sodium hydroxide solution	light blue precipitate (insoluble in excess)
iron(II) Fe^{2+}	add sodium hydroxide solution	green precipitate (insoluble in excess)
iron(III) Fe^{3+}	add sodium hydroxide solution	red-brown precipitate (insoluble in excess)
zinc Zn^{2+}	add sodium hydroxide solution	white precipitate (soluble in excess, giving a colourless solution)

Formulae of some common molecules and compounds*

H_2	hydrogen gas	CH_4	methane	KCl	potassium chloride
O_2	oxygen gas	NH_3	ammonia	MgO	magnesium oxide
N_2	nitrogen gas	H_2SO_4	sulfuric acid	$Mg(OH)_2$	magnesium hydroxide
H_2O	water	HCl	hydrochloric acid	$MgCO_3$	magnesium carbonate
Cl_2	chlorine gas	HNO_3	nitric acid	$MgCl_2$	magnesium chloride
CO_2	carbon dioxide	NaCl	sodium chloride	$MgSO_4$	magnesium sulfate
CO	carbon monoxide	NaOH	sodium hydroxide	$CaCO_3$	calcium carbonate
NO	nitrogen monoxide	Na_2CO_3	sodium carbonate	$CaCl_2$	calcium chloride
NO_2	nitrogen dioxide	$NaNO_3$	sodium nitrate	$CaSO_4$	calcium sulfate
SO_2	sulfur dioxide	Na_2SO_4	sodium sulfate		

* These will not be provided in your exam. You need to learn them.

Periodic Table

Key

| relative atomic mass |
| **atomic symbol** |
| name |
| atomic (proton) number |

Example:
| 1 |
| **H** |
| hydrogen |
| 1 |

1	2											3	4	5	6	7	0
																	4 **He** helium 2
7 **Li** lithium 3	9 **Be** beryllium 4											11 **B** boron 5	12 **C** carbon 6	14 **N** nitrogen 7	16 **O** oxygen 8	19 **F** fluorine 9	20 **Ne** neon 10
23 **Na** sodium 11	24 **Mg** magnesium 12											27 **Al** aluminium 13	28 **Si** silicon 14	31 **P** phosphorus 15	32 **S** sulfur 16	35.5 **Cl** chlorine 17	40 **Ar** argon 18
39 **K** potassium 19	40 **Ca** calcium 20	45 **Sc** scandium 21	48 **Ti** titanium 22	51 **V** vanadium 23	52 **Cr** chromium 24	55 **Mn** manganese 25	56 **Fe** iron 26	59 **Co** cobalt 27	59 **Ni** nickel 28	63.5 **Cu** copper 29	65 **Zn** zinc 30	70 **Ga** gallium 31	73 **Ge** germanium 32	75 **As** arsenic 33	79 **Se** selenium 34	80 **Br** bromine 35	84 **Kr** krypton 36
85 **Rb** rubidium 37	88 **Sr** strontium 38	89 **Y** yttrium 39	91 **Zr** zirconium 40	93 **Nb** niobium 41	96 **Mo** molybdenum 42	[98] **Tc** technetium 43	101 **Ru** ruthenium 44	103 **Rh** rhodium 45	106 **Pd** palladium 46	108 **Ag** silver 47	112 **Cd** cadmium 48	115 **In** indium 49	119 **Sn** tin 50	122 **Sb** antimony 51	128 **Te** tellurium 52	127 **I** iodine 53	131 **Xe** xenon 54
133 **Cs** caesium 55	137 **Ba** barium 56	139 **La*** lanthanum 57	178 **Hf** hafnium 72	181 **Ta** tantalum 73	184 **W** tungsten 74	186 **Re** rhenium 75	190 **Os** osmium 76	192 **Ir** iridium 77	195 **Pt** platinum 78	197 **Au** gold 79	201 **Hg** mercury 80	204 **Tl** thallium 81	207 **Pb** lead 82	209 **Bi** bismuth 83	[209] **Po** polonium 84	[210] **At** astatine 85	[222] **Rn** radon 86
[223] **Fr** francium 87	[226] **Ra** radium 88	[227] **Ac*** actinium 89	[261] **Rf** rutherfordium 104	[262] **Db** dubnium 105	[266] **Sg** seaborgium 106	[264] **Bh** bohrium 107	[277] **Hs** hassium 108	[268] **Mt** meitnerium 109	[271] **Ds** darmstadtium 110	[272] **Rg** roentgenium 111							

Elements with atomic numbers 112–116 have been reported but not fully authenticated

* The lanthanoids (atomic numbers 58–71) and the actinoids (atomic numbers 90–103) have been omitted.

Bad Science for Schools

When the evidence doesn't add up

Sometimes people use what sound like scientific words and ideas to sell you things or persuade you to think in a certain way. Some of these claims are valid, and some are not. The activities on these pages are based on the work of Dr Ben Goldacre and will help you to question some of the scientific claims you meet. Read more about the work of Ben at www.badscience.net.

Brown goo

You may have seen adverts for a foot spa that can remove toxins from your body. They are sometimes used in beauty salons or you might even buy one to use at home. The basin is filled with water, a sachet of special salts is added and then it is plugged in. You put your feet in to soak and the water turns brown!

It looks impressive, but is that because toxins have left your body through your feet?

Now, the advertisers of these products would tell us that we are being 'detoxed' and that horrible chemicals, toxins, which have accumulated in our bodies are at long last being released. It's perhaps not surprising that people are keen to be cleansed. However the talk doesn't match the facts. The chemicals in the water didn't come from your body which (as you know) is quite capable of getting rid of substances it doesn't need without using special equipment.

We are learning to:

> Use primary and secondary evidence to investigate scientific claims
> Apply scientific concepts to evaluate 'health products'
> Explore the implications of these evaluations

✴ CAN YOU DETOX VIA YOUR FEET?

Read the leaflet – it sounds scientific but is it? Think about what you have learnt in science.

> Human metabolism is complex with the 'building blocks' of molecules being reshaped into new arrangements. The same molecule can be a waste product or a valued ingredient, depending on when and where it is in the body. There is no such thing as a 'detox system' in any medical textbook. Sometimes the body does need to dispose of waste but it does so by well-known ways.

> Electrolysis occurs when a direct electric current is passed through a liquid containing mobile ions, resulting in a chemical reaction at the electrodes.

Can you come up with a hypothesis about what's going on? How would you prove it? Ben came up with a good idea and gave his Barbie™ a foot bath – you might get a chance to replicate his experiment. Can you predict what might happen?

What would happen if you gave this toy a detoxifying foot spa?

310

Collins Detox Foot Bath

Before

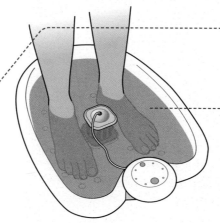

After 30 minutes

This looks like a serious piece of equipment.

This brown water looks horrible but is it brown because of toxins from the body?

This explanation sounds scientific, but is it?

The patented Collins Detox Foot Bath stimulates the active release of tingling ions that surge back and forth around your feet generating a flow of both negative and positive energy. This refreshes and renews the tissues, cleansing your body of accumulated toxins, readjusting the balance of energy at a bio-cellular level and removing excretory residues.

The centrally located micro-voltaic electrodes cause the flow of bi-polar ions producing an energy field that carries essential nutrients and life-giving oxygen. The release of toxins takes places through the myriad of microscopic pores in the soles of your feet. Graduated colour changes in the water present conclusive evidence of the beneficial effects.

The many enthusiastic users report a range of exhilarating effects including a heightened sense of awareness, improved circulation and relief of arthritic pain. The results are personal to each user as their toxin levels and combinations vary, but all report positive outcomes. One recent example of enthusiastic feedback said "The colour of the water shocked me in the realisation of what had accumulated in my body but the lightness I felt lasted for days!"

The people who tested it were impressed but did they enjoy the effects of detox or a relaxing foot bath?

✳ DETOX SELLS!

Words like 'toxins' and 'detoxification' (the removal of toxins) are sometimes used to promote products and techniques. Nobody likes to think of toxins accumulating in their body but we must consider whether there's any scientific basis for these ideas.

> Can you think of other products that claim to 'detox'?

> Why do you think that 'detoxing' can be used to sell these products?

> These treatments could all be said to be a little theatrical. How does this help to convince people that they're effective?

Bad Science for Schools

When the evidence doesn't add up

Sometimes people use what sound like scientific words and ideas to sell you things or persuade you to think in a certain way. Some of these claims are valid, and some are not. The activities on these pages are based on the work of Dr Ben Goldacre and will help you to question some of the scientific claims you meet. Read more about the work of Ben at www.badscience.net.

Bad news

In science you learn about ideas that scientists have developed by collecting evidence from experiments; you are also learning to collect and evaluate evidence yourself. You can use this outside of the laboratory to weigh up information you come across every day. Let's look at this example about how data can be used to support a story for a newspaper.

When data are produced you might think that there's only one way they can be used, and only one meaning that can be supported. This isn't always true.

We are learning to:
> understand how data can be used to make a good news story
> understand how science reports may be distorted to make headlines
> consider why science reports may be represented in various different ways

✱ GOOD ADVICE?

If a woman wants to be sexually active but doesn't want to get pregnant, one of the contraceptive methods available to her is to use a contraceptive implant. There are a number of factors to take into account; one of the most important ones is, of course, 'how well does it work?' Think about the headline on the right. What kind of questions might you ask that would reveal whether this method is, in fact, a failure?

600 pregnancies despite contraceptive implant

✱ STICKING TO THE NUMBERS

One of the questions we might want to consider is 'over what timescale?' Is this 600 over the last month, last year or since records began? In fact, the contraceptive implant had been available for ten years when this data was released, so it's 60 unintended pregnancies per year, on average. Still not ideal, but maybe not as disastrous as at first thought.

We might also want to know how widespread the use of the implant was. If the 60 pregnancies a year was out of say, 1,000 people, then that's not very good: it would mean that 6 out of every hundred women with an implant had got pregnant over a year.

If it was out of 100,000 then that means 6 out of every 10,000 women got pregnant over a year, so this method of contraception would compare well with other methods.

In fact, around 1.3 million implants have been used over the last ten years, and each lasts for three years. This works out as 1.4 unwanted pregnancies for every 10,000 women using the method per year if we assume that each implant lasts for the full 3 years.

Making the headlines

Four students are talking about this story.

Jo says

I think the journalists were doing a good job here to tell people about the fact that 600 women who thought that they couldn't get pregnant, then did. They got hold of the facts and then reported them.

Adam says

The journalists didn't write this up very well. Most of the people reading this story would be women who would be wondering if this method of contraception was one that they should use. The headline suggests that it's not safe and it is. Well, most of the time.

Will says

Journalists have to be responsible. If this story frightens women off one of the safest methods of contraception they've let people down.

Emma says

The main job of journalists is to be entertaining. Boring stories don't get read. '600 women using contraceptive get pregnant' makes you read the story. '0.014% of women using contraceptive get pregnant' looks boring.

- Look at these comments. Who do you think is right?

- Do you think the main purpose of a journalist is:
  - To be informative, even if it's sometimes boring?
  - To be engaging, even if it may sometimes give a false impression?

- If you had been the journalist assigned to this story, what headline would you have used?

✱ NUMBERS IN THE REAL WORLD

A useful way of presenting data like this is to use what's called the natural frequency. Out of a set number, this indicates how many will have a changed outcome as a result of this. In this case it's 1.4 out of 10 000. The figure of 60 per year isn't wrong, neither is the 0.014%, but 1.4 in 10 000 puts it in a simple form that people can make sense of and use to assess the likely impact on them.

When the evidence doesn't add up

Sometimes people use what sound like scientific words and ideas to sell you things or persuade you to think in a certain way. Some of these claims are valid, and some are not. The activities on these pages are based on the work of Dr Ben Goldacre and will help you to question some of the scientific claims you meet. Read more about the work of Ben at www.badscience.net.

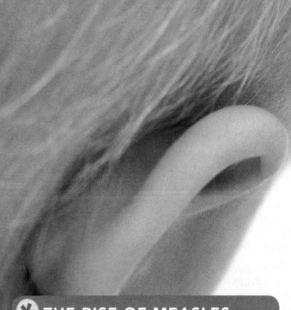

MMR – don't die of ignorance

Autism is a condition which affects between one and two people in every thousand, affecting neural development and causing restricted and repetitive behaviour. It affects social behaviour and language. It is usually diagnosed from the age of three onwards.

In Britain, as in many countries, the majority children are vaccinated against measles, mumps and rubella using a combined vaccine (MMR) between the ages of one and two. In 1998 a British doctor wrote a report on 12 children who had been vaccinated with the MMR vaccine and were subsequently diagnosed as autistic. The result of this report was that media interest was raised, many anti-MMR stories appeared and there was a significant fall in the number of children who were given the MMR vaccine.

Consider these questions:

> Does the fact that the children in the report were diagnosed with autism after being given the MMR vaccine prove that the vaccine caused the autism?

> At the time of the report being written well over 90% of children had the MMR vaccine. Why should it not be a surprise if some of those children are diagnosed with autism?

> What kind of survey would have helped to identify whether the MMR vaccine caused autism?

✱ THE RISE OF MEASLES

As the number of MMR vaccinations fell, the number of measles cases rose. Measles is a very dangerous disease that even in developed countries kills one in every 3000 people and causes pneumonia in one in 20.

It was subsequently established beyond reasonable doubt that there is no causal link between MMR vaccination and autism. The doctor had a commercial interest in the alleged link and was subsequently struck off. The scare affected no other countries. MMR vaccination rates in Britain are rising again. Doctors are still not sure why some children develop autism; its causes are unknown.

Consider these points of view:

"The doctor who wrote the report was right to alert people to his concerns and suggest that more research should be carried out."

"The media got hold of the story and turned it into a huge scare. It's their fault."

"There was never any evidence to prove a link. Thousands of children have caught diseases that could otherwise have been avoided."

We are learning to:

> Understand the difference between correlation and cause and effect
> To apply this understanding to a variety of contexts
> To explore the professional dilemma facing scientists who have concerns and whose actions have serious consequences

✱ THE RISE OF MEASLES

One of the things this story illustrates is what can happen when you look at only a very small sample and the importance of working with large-scale surveys wherever possible. Such a study was carried out in Denmark: the Madsen study. Because Denmark tracks patients and the care they receive on a central system they have been able to study the correlation between vaccination and illness. The data clearly shows that there is no correlation between MMR vaccination and the incidence of autism.

The study was based on data from over half a million children: over 440,000 had been vaccinated and there was no greater incidence of autism in children vaccinated than in those not vaccinated.

> Identify the features of this study that make its findings reliable.

> What might you say to someone who still wasn't convinced by this study and decided to 'play it safe' by not having their child vaccinated for MMR?

Cause and effect?

Sometimes it looks like something causes something else, perhaps because they both happen at the same time. But scientists need to be very careful before saying that one thing causes another.

• Often you need to use common sense and extra information to help decide if there is true causation. For example, cocks crow in the morning, but nobody thinks that cocks crowing causes the sun to come up, because there's no conceivable mechanism for that, and it conflicts with everything we know about the sun and the earth. On the other hand, we can observe that when it gets warmer, people wear fewer clothes, and it seems reasonable to say that the warm weather causes people to wear less.

• Sometimes two things are correlated, but it's harder to say what causes what, and there might be a third factor causing both of the things that we are observing. Let's say, for example, that a study finds that there is a strong correlation between a child's IQ and their height: perhaps both height and IQ are themselves related, through a complex causal pathway, to something else, like general health, or diet, or social deprivation

• Often, although things happen at the same time, there is no link at all. For example, Halley's Comet appears once every 76 years. Previous appearances have coincided with King Harold's defeat at the Battle of Hastings, Genghis Khan's invasion of Europe and both the birth and death of great American novelist Mark Twain, author of Tom Sawyer.

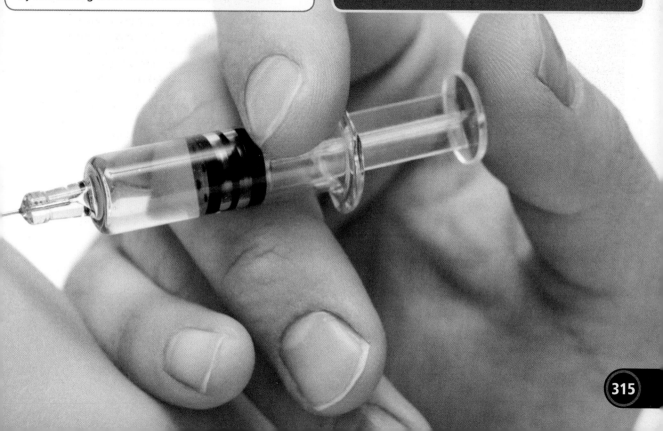

Glossary

abundance   a measure of how common a species is in an area

acceleration   the rate at which the velocity of an object changes

acid   a chemical substance that has a pH of less than 7

active (genes)   genes that are turned on and control how a cell behaves and looks

active site   part of an enzyme where a substrate can fit neatly into it

active transport   the movement of chemicals into or out of a cell from areas of low concentration to high concentration, where the cell controls the direction in which chemicals move rather than the difference in concentration

activity (radioactivity)   the amount of radiation emitted from a material

adaptations   the ways in which an organism has evolved to become better able to survive in its environment

adrenal gland   found above the kidneys, produces the hormone adrenaline

adrenaline   a hormone that helps prepare your body for action in the 'fight or flight' response

adult stem cells   unspecialised body cells that can develop into some other specialised cells that the body needs

aerobic respiration   respiration that requires oxygen

air resistance   the upwards force exerted by air molecules on an object

alkali   a chemical substance that has a pH of more than 7

alkali metal   very reactive metal in Group 1 of the Periodic Table, for example sodium

alpha particles (α)   radioactive particles which are helium nuclei – helium atoms without the electrons (they have a positive charge)

alternating current (a.c.)   an electrical current in which the direction of the current changes at regular intervals

amino acids   small molecules from which proteins are built

ammeter   a device that measures the amount of current running through a circuit in amperes

amperes (amps)   the unit of measurement used for the flow of electrical current or charge

anaerobic respiration   respiration that does not need oxygen

antidepressant   a prescribed drug that makes synapses in the brain more sensitive to certain types of transmitter substances

attractive   a force that pulls two objects together

auxin   a plant hormone that affects the rate of growth

average speed   distance travelled divided by the time taken

axon   a long projection from a nerve fibre that conducts impulses away from the body of a nerve cell

background radiation   low-level radiation that is found all around us

balanced symbol equation   a symbolic representation showing the kind and amount of the starting materials and products of a chemical reaction

base   (1) solid alkali; any substance that neutralises an acid (2) one of the three molecules that makes up a single unit of DNA

base pair   in a DNA double helix, the two strands are held together by bases in base pairs

behaviour   the way in which an organism reacts to changes in its environment

beta blockers   a prescribed drug that blocks the adrenaline receptors in the synapses and stops the transmission of impulses

beta particles (β)   particles given off by some radioactive materials (they have a negative charge)

binding energy   the energy that holds particles together in a nucleus

catalyst   substance added to a chemical reaction to alter the speed of the reaction

catalytic converter   the section of a vehicle's exhaust system that converts pollutant gases into harmless ones using a catalyst

cathode   negatively charged electrode

cell body   the part of a nerve cell that contains the nucleus

cell membrane   layer around a cell which helps to control substances entering and leaving the cell

cellulose   large polysaccharides made by plants for cell walls

central nervous system (CNS)   collectively the brain and spinal cord

cerebral cortex   the outer layer of the brain

chain reaction   a fission reaction that is maintained because the neutrons produced in the fission of one nucleus are available to initiate fission in other nuclei causing a rapid production of energy

chemical synthesis   combining simple substances to make a new compound

chlorophyll   the green chemical in plants that absorbs light energy

chloroplasts   structures characteristic of plant cells and the cells of algae where photosynthesis takes place

chromosomes   thread-like structures in the cell nucleus that carry genetic information – each chromosome consists of DNA wound around a core of protein

commutator   a device that, in a motor, ensures the direction of the current in the coil causes the motor to rotate in one sense continuously

components   devices such as lamps and motors on an electrical circuit to which energy is transferred

conditioned (response)   a learned response that occurs when animals link two or more stimuli that are not connected

conditioned reflex   see conditioned response

conductor   a substance in which electric current can flow freely

conservation of energy   when energy can not be created or destroyed

contamination (radioactivity)   something that comes into contact with radioactive material

control processes   the name given to the way information is transferred as part of the multi-store model

control rods   absorb excess neutrons in order to control a chain reaction

coolant   gas or liquid that circulates around a reactor to keep it cool

co-ordinator   something that works together, e.g. the brain is the co-ordinator of the body

corrosive   a substance that can destroy or eat away other substances by a chemical reaction, e.g. it will burn skin

counter forces   forces which act against another force

covalent bonds   these join together the atoms inside a molecule

crystal lattice   crystals formed by ionic compounds, such as sodium chloride, which have a regular repeating pattern and shape

crystallise   when a liquid undergoes evaporation the product left behind cools and starts to form crystals

crystals   the solid residue left after salts evaporate, they have regular shapes and flat sides

cytoplasm   a jelly-like substance within a cell where most of the chemical reactions take place

daughter cells   in mitosis a cell splits to form two daughter cells which are identical to each other

daughter product   the name given to the radioactive element formed from the decayed initial radioactive element

decay chain   a series of radioactive decays of an unstable nucleus to the nucleus of a different element, until a stable nucleus is formed

decompose   in chemistry, separation of a chemical compound into simpler compounds

denaturing   when an active site is destroyed and the enzyme molecules are broken apart

dendrite   a short thread of cytoplasm on a neuron, carrying an impulse towards the cell body

desiccator   a container that contains a substance which absorbs water

diatomic molecules   atoms that are joined together in pairs

differentiated (cells)   cells that may change their shape and structure to become adapted to do a particular job

diffusion   the movement of molecules or particles from regions of high concentration to low concentration

direct current (d.c.)   an electric current that flows in one direction only

displacement   the distance moved in a specific direction

displacement reactions   the difference in the reactivity of halogens. Where one halogen will take the place of another in its compounds

displacement–time graph   a visual way of showing the displacement (distance and direction from a starting point) of an object against time

dissolving   the act of a solid mixing into a liquid to form a solution

distance–time graph   a visual way of showing the time taken for a journey and the distance travelled

DNA   polymer molecule found in the nucleus of all body cells – its sequence determines genetic characteristics, such as eye colour, and gives each one of us a unique genetic code

double helix   two strands of the DNA molecule face each other in a way that looks like a ladder, these are then twisted around each other to form a double helix – like a spiral staircase

drag   *see* air resistance

dry air   air that has had all water vapour removed

ecstasy   an illegal drug that affects the working of the chemical transmitter substance in nerve synapses in a similar way to antidepressants

effector   part of the body that responds to stimuli

effervescence   the fizzing and bubbling effect that occurs e.g. when an acid reacts with a carbonate ion

egg   female sex cell of an animal

electric current   a negative flow of electrical charge through a medium, carried by electrons in a conductor

electrical power   a measure of the amount of energy supplied each second

electrodes   solid electrical conductors through which the current passes into and out of the liquid during electrolysis – and at which the electrolysis reactions take place

electrolysis   decomposing an ionic compound by passing an electric current through it while molten or in solution

electrolyte   the liquid in which electrolysis takes place

electromagnet   a magnet which is magnetic only when a current is switched on

electromagnetic induction   a term used by Faraday to explain induced voltage

electron   tiny negatively charged particle within an atom that orbits the nucleus – responsible for current in electrical circuits

electron arrangement   the configuration of electrons in shells, or energy levels, in an atom

electrostatic force   a force caused by positive and negative charges

element   substance made out of only one type of atom

embryo   an organism in the earliest stages of development which began as a zygote and will become a foetus

embryonic stem cells   cells in or from an embryo with the potential to become any other type of cell in the body

endothermic   a reaction that reduces the temperature of the surroundings. The temperature falls in endothermic reactions

end-point   the sudden change of colour of an indicator in e.g. titration

energy   the ability to do work

energy level   describes the arrangement of electrons in an atom in shells

energy level diagram   visual way of showing the change in energy level during a chemical reaction

enzyme pathway   splits a complex reaction into a series of simpler steps

enzymes   proteins found in living things that speed up or catalyse reactions

equivalent dose   a measure of radiation dose to biological tissue

evaporation   change of state where a substance changes from liquid to gas at a temperature below its boiling point

exothermic   a reaction that gives out heat to the surroundings. The temperature rises in exothermic reactions

feral (children)   children who have been isolated during their development are said to be 'feral'. Feral means wild or untamed

fermentation   the conversion of carbohydrates to alcohol and carbon dioxide by yeast or bacteria

fertilisation   the moment when the nucleus of a sperm fuses with nucleus of an egg

field   in physics, a space in which a particular force acts

filtrate   the insoluble products that remain trapped in a filter

filtration   a method of separating one substance out from others. Filtering separates solids from liquids

force   the push or pull that acts between two objects

formula   (for a chemical compound) group of chemical symbols and numbers, showing elements, and how many atoms of each, a compound is made up of

free electrons   the outer electrons of atoms of materials that are good conductors which are loosely held and can break free easily so they can move freely

fuel rod   long narrow tube in a nuclear reactor which contains nuclear fuel in pellet form

gametes   the male and female sex cells (sperm and eggs)

gamma rays (γ)   ionising high-energy electromagnetic radiation from radioactive substances, harmful to human health

gene   a section of DNA that codes for a particular characteristic by controlling the production of a particular protein or part of a protein by cells

genetic code   the information contained in a gene which determines the type of protein produced by cells

giant covalent structures   an element made with very strong covalent bonds between atoms in which a large number of carbon atoms are linked together in a regular pattern

gland   organ that secretes a useful substance

glucagon   hormone produced by the pancreas that promotes conversion of glycogen to glucose

glucose   a simple sugar

gradient   the degree of slope of a line

gram formula mass   the number of grams of an element or compound represented by its RAM or RFM

gravitational potential energy   the energy an object gains due to its height

groups   within the Periodic Table the vertical columns are called groups

growth hormone   a hormone produced by the pituitary gland that controls the rate of growth in humans

half-life   the time taken for half of the atoms in a radioactive element to decay

halides   compounds formed when halogens react with alkali metals and other metals

hazard   something that is likely to cause harm, e.g. a radioactive substance

heat exchangers   tubes that carry water around or through a reaction vessel. Exothermic reactions heat the water and it is pumped away to be used elsewhere

high-level waste   for example, (radioactive) spent fuel rods, with a long half-life, which need to be disposed of carefully

hormones   substances produced by animals and plants that regulate activities; in animals, hormones are produced by and released from endocrine tissue into the blood to act on target organs, and help coordinate the body's response to stimuli

hydrosphere   made up of the water, ice and snow on the Earth's surface and the water vapour in the atmosphere

identification key   a way to find a scientific name for an organism by answering yes/no questions

impulse   an electrical signal that travels along an axon

in parallel   when components are connected across each other in a circuit

in series   when components are connected end-to-end in a circuit

indicators   used to tell if a solution contains acid or alkali

induced   a term used to mean 'created'

inert   an element that does not react with any other elements

insoluble   not soluble in water (forms a precipitate)

instantaneous speed   the speed at a particular moment in time

instinctive response   behaviour that comes from reflex responses and does not have to be learned

insulator   a substance in which electric current cannot flow freely

insulin   hormone produced by the pancreas that promotes the conversion of glucose to glucagon

intermediate-level waste   for example, (radioactive) chemical sludge and reactor components, with short or longer half-lives that have to be disposed of with care

intermolecular   the forces between molecules

intramolecular   the forces within molecules

involuntary   not under the control of the will, an action done without choice

ion   atom (or groups of atoms) with a positive or negative charge, caused by losing or gaining electrons

ionic bond   chemical bond between two ions of opposite charges

ionic compounds   salts made up of particles called ions which have a positive or negative electrical charge

ionic equation   a chemical equation that describes changes that occur in aqueous solutions

ionising radiation   electromagnetic radiation that has sufficient energy to ionise the material it is absorbed by

irradiation   exposure to waves of radiation

isotopes   atoms that have the same number of protons, but different numbers of neutrons. Different forms of the same element

kinetic energy   the energy an object has due to its motion

lattice   a repeating pattern formed by the regular 3-D arrangement of ions

learned response   behaviour that can be learned

light dependent resistor (LDR)   a semiconductor device, where resistance changes with the amount of light

limiting factor   a lack of something that prevents a reaction from increasing any further

limiting friction   the maximum amount of force that can be applied to an object before it will move

line spectrum   a set of different coloured lines produced when the light from a burning element is passed through a prism

lithosphere   the rocky outer section of Earth, consisting of the crust and upper part of the mantle

long-term memory   information from our earliest memories onwards, which is stored for a long period of time

low-level waste   for example, contaminated (radioactive) paper and clothing that is not very dangerous, with a short half-life, but still needs to be disposed of carefully

magnetic field   a space in which a magnetic material exerts a force

malleability   the capability of a metal to be shaped or bent

MDMA   3,4-methylenedioxymethamphetamine the scientific name for ecstasy

mean   an average of a set of data

meiosis   cell division that results in the formation of gametes

melting point   the temperature at which a solid becomes a liquid

membrane   (of a cell), the layer around a cell which helps to control substances entering and leaving the cell

memory   the storage and retrieval (bringing back or remembering) of information

meristems   special regions in a plant where cells are able to divide

messenger RNA (mRNA)   a molecule that copies the base sequence of the DNA and carries it out of the nucleus of the ribosomes

metallic bond   the force in metals that attracts atoms together

minerals solid metallic or non-metallic substances found naturally in the Earth's crust

mitochondria found in the cytoplasm, where respiration takes place

mitosis cell division that takes place in normal body cells and produces identical daughter cells

molecular ion a charged ion composed of two or more atoms joined together by covalent bonds

molecule two or more atoms held together by strong chemical bonds

momentum the product of mass and velocity; momentum (kg m/s) = mass (kg) × velocity (m/s)

motor an electric motor converts electrical energy into mechanical energy

motor effect a term used to describe the force experienced when a current flows through a wire in a region where there is a magnetic field. If it is free to move this is known as the motor effect

motor neuron nerve carrying information from the central nervous system to muscles and glands

multicellular consisting of many cells

multi-store model a type of model used by scientists to help explain how we remember and retrieve information

mutation a change in the DNA in a cell

myelin a fatty sheath that surrounds an axon, it acts as an insulator and makes an impulse travel faster

nerve a group of nerve fibres

nervous system sends messages between body cells using neurons; includes the central nervous system (brain and spinal cord) and the peripheral nervous system (network of neurons)

neuron a nerve cell that carries nerve impulses

neuron pathway neurones linked to pass nerve impulses

neuroscientists scientists who study the nervous system

neutral (1) in chemistry the term neutral means 'between acid and alkali' (2) in physics, an atom with no overall charge

neutralisation reaction between H⁺ ions and OH⁻ ions (acid and base react to make a salt and water)

neutron small particle that does not have a charge – found in the nucleus of an atom

nuclear fission a chain reaction employed in nuclear power reactors in which atoms are split, releasing huge amounts of energy

nuclear fuel radioactive fuel, such as uranium or plutonium, used in nuclear power stations

nuclear fusion reaction in which two small atomic nuclei combine to make a larger nucleus, with a large amount of energy released

nucleon number the total number of neutrons and protons in an atomic nucleus

nucleotide the basic unit of DNA, consisting of a sugar, a phosphate and a base

nucleus (1) the central core of an atom, which contains protons and neutrons and has a positive charge (2) a distinct structure in the cytoplasm of cells that contains the genetic material

oestrogen female hormone secreted by the ovary and involved in the menstrual cycle

Ohm's law law that states that the current through a metallic conductor is directly proportional to the voltage across its ends, if the conditions are constant

optimum the best or most suitable conditions for a reaction to occur

orbits electrons are arranged in orbits (or shells) around the nucleus of an atom

ores rocks that contain minerals, including metals, e.g. iron ore

organ a part of the body made up of different tissues that work together to do a particular job

organ systems different organs that work together to do a particular job

osmosis the diffusion of water molecules through a partially permeable membrane

outlier a measurement that does not follow the trend of other measurements

ovary organ in females which makes oestrogen and produces eggs

oxidation gain of oxygen by a compound – the opposite of reduction

oxidised a substance that has undergone oxidation

oxygen debt the amount of oxygen required to clear lactic acid from the body

palisade cells photosynthetic plant cells found near the top of the leaves where they receive a lot of light from the Sun

pancreas organ that produces hormones insulin and glucagon (from endocrine tissue) and digestive enzymes (from exocrine tissue)

partially permeable membrane a cell membrane that lets small molecules pass through but not large ones

period a horizontal row in the periodic table

Periodic Table a table of all the chemical elements based on their atomic number

peripheral nervous system (PNS) network of neurons leading to and from the brain and spinal cord

pH scale a measure of how strong an acid or alkali is

phloem cells plant cells that carry dissolved substances to every part of the plant

photosynthesis process carried out by green plants where sunlight, carbon dioxide and water are used to produce glucose and oxygen

photosynthesise the act of photosynthesis

phototropism a plant's growth towards or away from the stimulus of light

pituitary gland found at the base of the brain, produces hormones that control other endocrine glands

plasma (ionised gas) a gas that contains positive ions and free electrons and has no overall electric charge

positively phototropic plant shoots that grow towards a light source

potential difference (p.d.) another term for voltage, a measure of the energy carried by the electrical charge

power amount of energy that something transfers each second, measured in watts (or joules per second)

precipitate insoluble solid formed in a solution during a chemical reaction

precipitation reaction an ionic substance produced from a solution forming an insoluble solid

primary coil the input coil of a transformer

products chemicals produced at the end of a chemical reaction

progesterone   hormone produced by the ovary that prepares the uterus for pregnancy

proton   small positively charged particle found in the nucleus of an atom

proton number   the number of protons in an atom

pure   a substance that has nothing else mixed with it

quadrat   a frame, usually square, of wood or metal, that ecologists put on the ground and count the number of plants within it

qualitative (data)   data that describes and compares the qualities of a substance

quantitative (data)   numerical data

radioactive   a material that randomly emits ionising radiation from its atomic nuclei

radioactive decay   the disintegration of a radioactive substance, the process by which an atomic nucleus loses energy

radioactive tracer   a radioactive isotope with a short half-life that can be ingested and traced through a patient's body or to monitor the movement of waste products in industry

radiotherapy   a technique that uses ionising radiation to kill cancer cells in the body

range   in a series of data, the spread from the highest number to the lowest number

rate of flow of charge   the current, or charge, that flows per second, measured in amperes

rate of reaction   the speed with which a chemical reaction takes place

reaction force   an equal force that acts in the opposite direction to the action force

receptor   part of a neuron that detects stimuli and converts them into nerve impulses

receptor molecules   found on the membrane of cells, they allow transmitter substances to bind to them

redox reaction   the reaction for extracting metals from their ores, involving both oxidation and reduction

reduced   a substance that has undergone a chemical reaction

reduces   when the atoms of a substance are oxidised resulting in the reduction of another substance

reduction   process that reduces the amount of oxygen in a compound, or removes all the oxygen from it – the opposite of oxidation

reflex   a muscular action that we make without thinking

reflex arc   pathway taken by nerve impulse from receptor, through the nervous system to effector, bringing about a reflex response

relative atomic mass (RAM)   the mass of an atom compared to the mass of an atom of carbon (which has a value of 12)

relative formula mass (RFM)   the sum of the RAMs of all the atoms or ions in a compound

relay neurons   found in the CNS they connect sensory neurons to motor neurons and so co-ordinate the body's response to stimuli

repulsive   a force that pushes two objects apart

resistance   (in an electrical circuit) a measure of how hard it is for an electric current to flow through a material

respiration   the chemical reaction used by all living organisms to produce the energy they need

response   the action taken as the result of a stimulus

resultant (force)   the overall forces acting on an object added together

ribosomes   small structures in the cytoplasm that make proteins

risk   the likelihood of a hazard causing harm

salt   (1) in chemistry, an ionic compound formed when an acid neutralises a base (2) generically, the dietary additive sodium chloride

secondary coil   the output coil of a transformer

sensory neuron   nerve cell carrying information from receptors to the central nervous system

serotonin   a transmitter substance found at the synapses in the brain

sex cells   the male and female gametes (sperm and eggs)

shells   electrons are arranged in shells (or orbits) around the nucleus of an atom

short-term memory   information from our most recent experiences, which is only stored for a short period of time

sievert (Sv)   the SI unit of equivalent dose

specialised (cells)   a cell that has a particular function

speed   how fast an object travels, calculated using the equation: speed (metres per second) = distance/time

speed–time graph   a visual way of showing how an object's speed changes over a period of time

sperm   male sex cell of an animal

state symbols   symbols used in equations to show whether something is solid (s), liquid (l), gas (g) or in solution in water (aq)

step down (transformer)   device used to change the voltage of an a.c. supply to a lower voltage

step up (transformer)   device used to change the voltage of an a.c. supply to a higher voltage

sterile   containing no living organisms

stimulus (pl stimuli)   a change in the environment that causes a response by stimulating receptor nerve cells, e.g. a hot surface

stores   the name given to different types of memory storage in the multi-store model

strong nuclear force   a force that holds all the particles together in a nucleus of an atom

substrates   the chemicals that enzymes work on

switched off   genes in body cells that are not active

switched on   genes that are active, or turned on and control how a cell behaves and looks

synapse   the gap between two adjacent neurons

synthesis   the building up of larger molecules through chemical reactions

tarnish   the reaction that occurs when a metal reacts with oxygen in the air

terminal velocity   the maximum speed achieved by any object falling through a gas or liquid

testes   organs in males which produce testosterone and make sperm

testosterone   a hormone that controls the development of male characteristics in puberty

therapeutic cloning   a procedure in which a nucleus is removed from an egg and is replaced with a nucleus from a body cell in order to produce new cells with identical genes

thermistor   a semiconductor device in which resistance changes with temperature

thyroid gland   a gland found in the neck that produces thyroxin

thyroxin   a hormone that controls the rate of chemical reactions in the body

tissue a group of cells that work together and carry out a similar task, such as lung tissue

tissue culture (in plants) a method of cloning by taking small pieces of plant tissue from the root or stem and treating it with enzymes to separate the cells, which then grow into separate identical plants

titration common laboratory method used to determine the unknown concentration of a known reactant

toxic a poison or hazardous substance that can cause serious medical conditions or death

transect a line of quadrats

transmitter substance a chemical that passes across a synapse

trend the changes in a property across a period of the Periodic Table

true value a theoretically accurate value that could be found if measurements could be made without errors

unicellular consisting of a single cell

variable resistor a device that allows the amount of resistance in a circuit to be varied

variation differences between individuals belonging to the same species

velocity the speed of an object in a certain direction

velocity–time graph a visual way of showing direction of travel and acceleration

volt the unit of voltage

voltage a measure of the energy carried by an electric current (*see* potential difference)

voltmeter a device used to measure the voltage across a component

work work is done when a force moves an object

xylem cells plant cells that carry water and mineral salts to where they are needed

zygote the cell formed by the fusion of a male and female gamete

Index

Acknowledgements

Acknowledgements

The publishers wish to thank the following for permission to reproduce photographs. Every effort has been made to trace copyright holders and to obtain their permission for the use of copyright material. The publishers will gladly receive any information enabling them to rectify any error or omission at the first opportunity. (t = top, b = bottom, c = centre, l = left, r = right)

cover & p.1 GustoImages/Science Photo Library, p.8t Laurence Gough/Shutterstock, p.8c Gareth Price, p.8b Howard Barlow/Alamy, p.9t Dirk Ott/Shutterstock, p.9c holbox/Shutterstock, p.9b Subbotina Anna/Shutterstock, p.10 Caroline Green, p.11 Specialist Stock/Corbis, p.12 Muellek Josef/Shutterstock, p.13 Peter Arnold, Inc./Alamy, p.14t James Brunker/Alamy, p.14b Adrian Sherratt/Alamy, p.16t Thomas Imo/Alamy, p.16b Tree of Life/Shutterstock, p.18 Maximilian Weinzierl/Alamy, p.20t Paul Glendell/Alamy, p.20b Emily Hooton, p.21 Chris Howes/Wild Places Photography/Alamy, p.22t Pictorial Press Ltd/Alamy, p.22b Gareth Price, p.23t withGod/Shutterstock, p.23b think4photop/Shutterstock, p.24 Gregory Johnston/Shutterstock, p.25t Gareth Price, p.25bl Craig Hansen/iStockphoto, p.25br tella_db/iStockphoto, p.26t Fotokostic/Shutterstock, p.26b Photographer, Visuals Unlimited /Science Photo Library, p.28t Richard Cooke/Alamy, p.28b Power and Syred/Science Photo Library, p.30t nick willshaw/iStockphoto, p.30b Gareth Price, p.32 Yuri Arcurs/Shutterstock, p.33t Gareth Price, p.33b Ian Pritchard, p.38t Juergen Berger/Science Photo Library, p.38c Smart-foto/Shutterstock, p.38b Professor Miodrag Stojkovic/Science Photo Library, p.39t Martin Shields/Science Photo Library, p.39c Dr G. Moscoso/Science Photo Library, p.39b Falko Matte/Shutterstock, p.40 Edelmann/Science Photo Library, p.41 Sebastian Kaulitzki/Shutterstock, p.42t craftvision/iStockphoto, p.42b Francis Leroy, Biocosmos/Science Photo Library, p.43t Steve Gschmeissner/Science Photo Library, p.43b Juergen Berger/Science Photo Library, p.44l Elena Elisseeva/Shutterstock, p.44r Christopher Meder - Photography/Shutterstock, p.45 Dr. Keith Wheeler/Science Photo Library, p.46t Alex Gumerov/iStockphoto, p.46b clearviewstock/Shutterstock, p.47 Chorthip Saesalub/iStockphoto, p.48 bofotolux /Shutterstock, p.50 Cathy Melloan/Alamy, p.51 Bojan Bogdanovic/Shutterstock, p.52 Power and Syred/Science Photo Library, p.53 Dimarion/Shutterstock, p.54 Zvonimir Atletic/Shutterstock, p.55 Fabio Bianchini/iStockphoto, p.56t Aptyp_koK/Shutterstock, p.56b Michael Abbey/Science Photo Library, p.58 StockLite/Shutterstock, p.60t Sinisa Botas/Shutterstock, p.60b Taylor Jackson/Shutterstock, p.61t Vo Trung Dung/Look At Sciences/Science Photo Library, p.61b Jeff Banke/Shutterstock, p.62t Jaroslaw Wojcik/iStockphoto, p.62b Andrea Danti/Shutterstock, p.67tl kaarsten/Shutterstock, p.67tr Izabela Habur/iStockphoto, p.67cl Elena Elisseeva/Shutterstock, p.67cr Helder Almeida/Shutterstock, p.67b Peter Nadolski/Shutterstock, p.68t Science Photo Library, p.68c Whytock/Shutterstock, p.68b Jeff Greenberg/Alamy, p.69t Stefan Sollfors/Alamy, p.69u natasha58/Shutterstock, p.69l DigitalHarold/iStockphoto, p.69b Dmitriy Shironosov/Shutterstock, p.70 Vladimir Wrangel/Shutterstock, p.72t sydeen/Shutterstock, p.72b Thomas Deerinck, NCMIR/Science Photo Library, p.73 Science Photo Library, p.74t Sebastian Kaulitzki/Shutterstock, p.74b Laguna Design/Science Photo Library, p.75 Thomas Deerinck, NCMIR/Science Photo Library, p.76t Emilio Ereza/Alamy, p.76b Medical Images, Universal Images Group/Science Photo Library, p.77t Steve Debenport/iStockphoto, p.77bl Bo Valentino/Shutterstock, p.77br Christophe Testi/Shutterstock, p.78 Maslov Dmitry/Shutterstock, p.79 Johann Helgason/Shutterstock, p.80t Alan Crawford/iStockphoto, p.80b HartmutMorgenthal/Shutterstock, p.81t Gregory Dimijian/Science Photo Library, p.81c Dr P.Marazzi/Science Photo Library, p.81b Lena Lir/Shutterstock, p.82 David B. Fankhauser/University of Cincinnati, p.84t Irafael/Shutterstock, p.84b Science Source/USDA/Science Photo Library, p.85t Rklawton/Wikimedia Commons, p.85r worldswildlifewonders/Shutterstock, p.86 Sovereign, ISM/Science Photo Library, p.87t Pasieka/Science Photo Library, p.87b Pascal Goetgheluck/Science Photo Library, p.88t 3D4Medical.com/Science Photo Library, p.88b Zoroyan/Shutterstock, p.89 Paul Lewis and Romilly Hambling/Wikimedia Commons, p.90r Smetek/Science Photo Library, p.90l Justin Kase zsixz/Alamy, p.92t Douglas O'Connor/Alamy, p.92b John Greim/Science Photo Library, p.93 Edd Westmacott./Alamy, p.98t Orca/Shutterstock, p.98u Martyn Chillmaid/Photolibrary, p.98l zmkstudio/Shutterstock, p.98b sciencephotos/Alamy, p.99t Vakhrushev Pavel/Shutterstock, p.99c Charles D. Winters/Science Photo Library, p.99b Vasilyev/Shutterstock, p.100t NYPL/Science Source/Science Photo Library, p.100b Science Photo Library, p.101t Stern/Wikimedia Commons, p.101b Science Photo Library, p.102t Wikimedia Commons, p.102b Cherkas/Shutterstock, p.103t Physics Dept., Imperial College/Science Photo Library, p.103b Källa/Wikimedia Commons, p.104l Andrew Lambert Photography/Science Photo Library, p.104r Andrew Lambert Photography/Science Photo Library, p.106 Mark Garlick/Science Photo Library, p.108 Pieter Kuiper/Wikimedia Commons, p.110 Johann Helgason/Shutterstock, p.111 Andrew Lambert Photography/Science Photo Library, p.112 American Institute Of Physics/Science Photo Library, p.113l Charles D. Winters/Science Photo Library, p.113r Andrew Lambert Photography/Science Photo Library, p.114 Charles D. Winters/Science Photo Library, p.115 Charles D. Winters/Science Photo Library, p.116t David J. Green/Alamy, p.116b Andrew Lambert Photography/Science Photo Library, p.117 Dan Cohen/Alamy, p.118t cstar55/iStockphoto, p.118b Andrew Lambert Photography/Science Photo Library, p.120t Sheila Terry/Science Photo Library, p.120b Andrew Lambert Photography/Science Photo Library, p.121 Andrew Lambert Photography/Science Photo Library, p.122l Andrew Lambert Photography/Science Photo Library, p.122c Andrew Lambert Photography/Science Photo Library, p.122r Alexandar Iotzov/Shutterstock, p.124t NYPL/Science Source/Science Photo Library, p.124c Arnold Fisher/Science Photo Library, p.124r Dirk Wiersma/Science Photo Library, p.124bl Vasilyev/Shutterstock, p.130t Gertan/Shutterstock, p.130u kentoh/Shutterstock, p.130l Andrew Lambert Photography/Science Photo Library, p.130b Claude Nuridsany & Marie Perennou/Science Photo Library, p.131t dani92026/Shutterstock, p.131u Arnold Fisher/Science Photo Library, p.131l Gontar/Shutterstock, p.131b Richard Clark/iStockphoto, p.132 Mariusz S. Jurgielewicz/Shutterstock, p.134t akva/Shutterstock, p.134b Charles D. Winters/Science Photo Library, p.135 mycola/Shutterstock, p.136t gopixgo/Shutterstock, p.136b Dr_Flash/Shutterstock, p.138t Tracy Whiteside/Shutterstock, p.138b Andrew Lambert Photography/Science Photo Library, p.139 Eric Hunt/Wikimedia Commons, p.140t William Henry Fox Talbot/Bettmann/Corbis, p.140b Martyn F. Chillmaid/Science Photo Library, p.141t Charles D. Winters/Science Photo

Library, p.141b Andrew Lambert Photography/Science Photo Library, p.142t Smit/Shutterstock, p.142b jordache/Shutterstock, p.144 broukoid/Shutterstock, p.145 Rob Lavinsky, iRocks.com/ Wikimedia Commons, p.146t Lee Prince/Shutterstock, p.146l Michal Baranski/Shutterstock, p.146c buriy/Shutterstock, p.146r Andre Vieira/MCT/MCT/Getty Images, p.147t Joel Arem/Science Photo Library, p.147b Joel Arem/Science Photo Library, p.148 Andrew Lambert Photography/Science Photo Library, p.150 Zettl Research Group, Lawrence Berkeley National Laboratory and University of California at Berkeley, p.151t Andrew Lambert Photography/Science Photo Library, p.151b Michal Baranski/ Shutterstock, p.152t Denis Selivanov/Shutterstock, p.152b Victor Borisov/iStockphoto, p.154t Foto-Ruhrgebiet/Shutterstock, p.154b chantal de bruijne/Shutterstock, p.155l Graham J. Hills/Science Photo Library, p.155r Science Photo Library, p.156t Błażej Łyjak/ iStockphoto, p.156b Cornelia Togea/iStockphoto, p.157t tunart/ iStockphoto, p.157b Tom Raftery/Wikimedia Commons, p.162t Health Protection Agency/Science Photo Library, p.162c Andrew Lambert Photography/Science Photo Library, p.162b Shebeko/ Shutterstock, p.163t HR Bramaz, ISM/Science Photo Library, p.163c Martyn F. Chillmaid/Science Photo Library, p.163b cosmin4000/ iStockphoto, p.164t Glenn Copus/Associated Newspapers/Rex Features, p.164b sciencephotos/Alamy, p.166t Robert Brook/ Science Photo Library, p.166b Andrew Lambert Photography/ Science Photo Library, p.167t Andrew Lambert Photography/ Science Photo Library, p.167l Sabine Kappel/Shutterstock, p.167r Charles D. Winters/Science Photo Library, p.168tl studiomode/ Alamy, p.168tr Flemming Hansen/iStockphoto, p.168b Martyn F. Chillmaid/Science Photo Library, p.170 OtnaYdur/Shutterstock, p.171 Maximilian Stock Ltd/Science Photo Library, p.172t Maximilian Stock Ltd/Science Photo Library, p.172b Laurence Gough/Shutterstock, p.173 Geoff Tompkinson/Science Photo Library, p.174t The Print Collector/Alamy, p.174b Andrew Lambert Photography/Science Photo Library, p.175 Martyn F. Chillmaid/ Science Photo Library, p.176t Solent News & Photo Agency/Rex Features, p.176l Martyn F. Chillmaid/Science Photo Library, p.176r NASA, p.178t Tek Image/Science Photo Library, p.178b sciencephotos/Alamy, p.180 Omer N Raja/Shutterstock, p.182t ER_09/Shutterstock, p.182b Ivan Cholakov Gostock-dot-net/ Shutterstock, p.183l Andrew Lambert Photography/Science Photo Library, p.183r Andrew Lambert Photography/Science Photo Library, p.184 Martyn F. Chillmaid/Science Photo Library, p.185l Trevor Clifford Photography/Science Photo Library, p.185r sciencephotos/Alamy, p.186 sciencephotos/Alamy, p.188t Phototake Inc./Alamy, p.188b Melissa Carroll/iStockphoto, p.189 Martyn F. Chillmaid/Science Photo Library, p.194t Eugene Suslo/ Alamy, p.194c Matej Michelizza/iStockphoto, p.194b AlamyCelebrity/Alamy, p.195t Foto011/Shutterstock, p.195u Aivolie /Shutterstock, p.195l Hector Chapman/Alamy, p.195b Joggie Botma/Shutterstock, p.196 AlamyCelebrity/Alamy, p.197 Reuters/ Corbis, p.198 Kevpix/Alamy, p.200 Michael Stokes/Shutterstock, p.201t Walter G Arce/Shutterstock, p.201b David Acosta Allely/ Shutterstock, p.202 imagebroker/Alamy, p.203 Rex Features, p.204t Rex Features, p.204r Kumar Sriskandan/Alamy, p.204l NASA/JPL-Caltech/University of Arizona , p.205t Nikada/ iStockphoto, p.205l Andrey Yurlov/Shutterstock, p.205r Bill Bachmann/Alamy, p.206 Phil Searle/Alamy, p.207t Mark Bourdillon/Alamy, p.207b VeryBigAlex/Shutterstock, p.208

SOMATUSCAN/Shutterstock, p.209t TRL Ltd./Science Photo Library, p.209b PJF/Shutterstock, p.210 HABRDA/Shutterstock, p.211 Andy Hooper/Daily Mail/Rex Features, p.212tДмитрий Верещагин/iStockphoto, p.212b Solid Web Designs LTD/ Shutterstock, p.213t Joe Fox/Alamy, p.213b Boris Katsman/ Shutterstock, p.214 Alexey Dudoladov/iStockphoto, p.216t Tomasz Trojanowski/Shutterstock, p.216b Kzenon/Shutterstock, p.217 Tony McConnell/Science Photo Library, p.218t Dusso Janladde/ Wikimedia Commons, p.218b Dusso Janladde/Wikimedia Commons, p.219 Carlos E. Santa Maria/Shutterstock, p.220t Oleg Nekhaev/Shutterstock, p.220b NASA, p.221t Andrey Pavlov/ Shutterstock, p.221b Luciano Mortula/Shutterstock, p.226t yampi / Shutterstock, p.226c Monkey Business Images/Shutterstock, p.226b TebNad/iStockphoto, p.227t kornilov007/Shutterstock, p.227c Heidi Brand/Shutterstock, p.227b GustoImages/Science Photo Library, p.228t Norman Pogson/Shutterstock, p.228b David R. Frazier Photolibrary, Inc./Alamy, p.229 Steshkin Yevgeniy/ Shutterstock, p.230 Marco Hegner/iStockphoto, p.232t Martyn F. Chillmaid/Science Photo Library, p.232c Andrei Nekrassov/ Shutterstock, p.232b kreatorex/Shutterstock, p.233 Zsolt, Biczó/ Shutterstock, p.234t Sheila Terry/Science Photo Library, p.234l Andrei Nekrassov/Shutterstock, p.234r Trevor Clifford Photography/Science Photo Library, p.236 UC Berkeley/Wikimedia Commons, p.238t NASA, p.238cl Andrew Lambert Photography/ Science Photo Library, p.238cr Martyn F. Chillmaid/Science Photo Library, p.238bl Philippe Psaila/Science Photo Library, p.238br Martyn F. Chillmaid/Science Photo Library, p.240 Filipe B. Varela/ Shutterstock, p.242t Maslov Dmitry/Shutterstock, p.242b Awe Inspiring Images/Shutterstock, p.243 Science Photo Library, p.244t Science Photo Library, p.244b AnneMS/Shutterstock, p.246 Prisma Bildagentur AG/Alamy, p.248 Alex Staroseltsev/Shutterstock, p.249 Serg64/Shutterstock, p.250 Colin Cuthbert/Science Photo Library, p.251l Reinhold Foeger/Shutterstock, p.251r Scott Hortop/ iStockphoto, p.256t Friedrich Saurer/Science Photo Library, p.256c Equinox Graphics/Science Photo Library, p.256b Colin Cuthbert/ Science Photo Library, p.257t fzd.it/Shutterstock, p.257c Levent Konuk/Shutterstock, p.257b David Nicholls/Science Photo Library, p.258 DC Comics Inc./Wikimedia Commons, p.260t Viktar Malyshchyts/Shutterstock, p.260b The Print Collector/Alamy, p.261 Hank Morgan/Science Photo Library, p.262 Darkened Studio/Alamy, p.263 Andrew Lambert Photography/Science Photo Library, p.264 Classic Image/Alamy, p.266 Martyn F. Chillmaid/ Science Photo Library, p.268 Emmanuel Laurent/Eurelios/Science Photo Library, p.270 GustoImages/Science Photo Library, p.272t Rasmus Holmboe Dahl/Shutterstock, p.272b Mark Kostich/ iStockphoto, p.273t Cordelia Molloy/Science Photo Library, p.273b Simon Fraser/Royal Victoria Infirmary, Newcastle Upon Tyne/ Science Photo Library, p.275 Martyn F. Chillmaid/Science Photo Library, p.276 FPG/Hulton Archive/Getty Images, p.278 The Print Collector/Alamy, p.279 Steve Allen/Science Photo Library, p.280 EFDA-JET/Science Photo Library, p.281 ORNL/Science Photo Library, p.290t Andrew Lambert Photography/Science Photo Library, p.290c Pedro Salaverría/Shutterstock, p.290b Shawn Hempel/Shutterstock, p.296 Martyn F. Chillmaid/Science Photo Library, p.310–311 Tischenko Irina/Shutterstock, p.310 Kletr/ Shutterstock, p.312–313 Diego Cervo/Shutterstock, p.314–315 Dmitry Naumov/Shutterstock.